Wings To Fly

Bringing Theatre Arts to Students with Special Needs

Sally Dorothy Bailey

WOODBINE HOUSE • 1993

Published by: Woodbine House, 5615 Fishers Lane, Rockville, MD 20852, toll free 800/843–7323.

Cover illustration and design: Elizabeth Wolf

Library of Congress Cataloging-in-Publication Data

Bailey, Sally D.
  Wings to fly : bringing theatre arts to children with special needs / by Sally D. Bailey.
     p.   cm.
  Includes bibliographical references and index.
  ISBN 0–933149–58–1 : $17.95
  1. Handicapped and the performing arts. 2. Bethesda Academy of Performing Arts. 3. Drama—Therapeutic use. 4. Drama in education. I. Title.
PN1590.H36B35 1993
791'.087—dc20   93–19228
                                           CIP

Manufactured in the United States of America

10 9 8 7 6 5 4 3 2 1

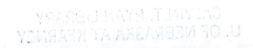

table of contents

acknowledgements

Wings to Fly could not have been written without the support and encouragement of Bonnie Fogel, the Executive Director of the Bethesda Academy of Performing Arts. Bonnie knew of my dream to write a book and was instrumental in making it come true. She researched statistics to back up the need for the book, helped me write a strong proposal letter, solicited letters of support, helped me submit the proposal to publishers, and, when Woodbine House indicated an interest in the proposal, went along with me to the interview. She allowed me to take time during the summer of 1992 in which to write the first draft—and giving credit where credit is due—she came up with the title of the book. She has been throughout the process supportive and encouraging—a true friend and an arts administrator of great vision and fairness.

Much of the information I have to include in this book has not come from other books; it has come from my experiences with over five hundred children with and without special needs who I have taught and observed in drama classes at the Bethesda Academy since the inception of the Special Needs Program. I must thank them for teaching me how to structure a class, how to mediate conflict, how to listen for what is *really* happening and what is really needed in a given situation. In addition, I thank them for sharing their creativity, hard work, and joy. There would have been no book without them.

I am also grateful for the generosity and support which I have received from my students' parents over the years. Without their belief in the power of the arts and their understanding of the value of our work together in classes and performing companies, the Special Needs Program would never have gotten off the ground. I would particularly like to thank Joyce Glenner, who personally rounded up the majority of the actors who joined Pegasus the very first year, and Claudia Segal, who first introduced me to the concept of "seeing the child and not the disability."

Thanks go to all of my colleagues at the Bethesda Academy of Performing Arts who have been open and willing to accept children with disabilities into their classes in the years since the Special Needs Program began. I particularly thank Mandy Hart, Caleen Sinnette Jennings, Elizabeth van den Berg Toperzer, Cindy Bowen, Kathryn Chase Bryer, Tim Reagan, Lisa Agogliati, Gail Gorlitz, Jeanie Hayes Hatch, and Julia Morris, who generously took the time to put their experiences with special needs children on paper and contributed the essays found throughout the book. I feel that their additional perspectives are important and support the premise that the arts can be shared and enjoyed by all.

The photographs in this book were taken by a number of very talented, caring, sensitive individuals who, when they came into rehearsals and performances, were really able to see, feel, and capture the delightful personalities of the actors and the wonderful creative work that they were doing. Thanks to Keith Jenkins, Lea Ann Rosen, Allison Walker, and John Carter!!

I could not have made it through the last year of writing without the help and support of my partner in theatre and life, Jim Marvin, who read drafts of the book, cooked meals, cleaned the house, and provided professional feedback and emotional support.

Thanks also to the other individuals who volunteered time to read various drafts of the book and give me comments to improve it: Mandy Hart, speech pathologist and special needs drama teacher; Cindy Bowen, crisis specialist and special needs drama teacher; Tim McCarty, artistic director of the Model Secondary School for the Deaf; Rud Turnbull, professor of special education at the University of Kansas; and Kathy Porter, special education teacher at Ivymount School in Rockville, Maryland.

I am very grateful for the wise comments and insight of my editor at Woodbine House, Susan Stokes, who from the first outline to the final draft was able to pinpoint potential trouble spots, help with placement of material, and ask all the right questions so that what I put on the page was clear, concise, and accurate. All of her feedback has been "right on." It's great to have an editor whose judgment can be relied on!

Last, but not least, I would like to thank three teachers: Francis Hodge, Jan Goodrich, and Rudolph Bauer. At various points in my life they were there to let me know that I had wings and, if I chose, I could use them.

prologue

A Saturday's Rainbow Adventure

My Saturday's Rainbow drama class went on a trip to Cape May. Early in the morning, we boarded a minibus and headed out to the sea coast. After about two hours, we finally arrived.

We rolled down the dock and up the gangplank of Captain Meriwether's cruiser. "Welcome Aboard!" shouted the Captain and he started up the engine of his boat. In a twinkling we were off for the high seas.

The seagulls called out to each other as they flew around above our heads. The water beneath us was clean and blue. Gentle waves lapped up against the side of the boat. We rounded a bend in the coastline and entered a protected cove. The Captain turned off the motor of his boat and dropped anchor. There in the middle of the cove was what we had come to see—the dolphins of Cape May. Everybody threw on their bathing suits and jumped into the water, splashing and playing and talking to the dolphins. We had a great time!

Around 3:00 in the afternoon the sky started to cloud over and everyone reluctantly swam back to the cruiser. Sam and Phillip didn't want to get back on board. They tied their surfboards to the side of the boat so they could float back with us. The Captain started the cruiser's motor and we left the dolphin cove behind, sadly waving good-bye to our new-found friends.

Suddenly, a horrible squall came up. The rain started softly, but quickly built into a torrential storm with thunder and lightening. Sam and Phillip were knocked off their surfboards!

"Men Overboard!" shouted the Captain.

"Help! Help! We're drowning!" cried the boys as they struggled in the water.

Joey and Amos jumped off the side of the boat and swam to save their friends. Everyone else heaved two huge life preservers into the water and pulled the four boys to safety. Everyone was relieved that Sam and Phillip were saved. We all cheered for Joey and Amos, the heroes of the day.

As suddenly as the storm came up, it dispersed. The sun came out from behind the clouds and the seagulls began to sing again. When we got back to the dock at Cape May, everyone was still excited about the rescue at sea. No one wanted to go home.

"Surf's Up!" shouted Sam and grabbed his surfboard. He started out for the breakers on the beach at a run. Everyone else grabbed their boards and paddled out behind him. Just at the right moment, we all hopped on our boards and caught a big wave to ride back in.

"Wipe out!" screamed Amos and suddenly everyone was rolling around in the surf, laughing and shouting in delight.

After that we had to dry off and begin our journey home. When we arrived back at Saturday's Rainbow, everyone agreed they had had a great day—one they would remember forever!

I shared this incredible adventure one Saturday morning with ten children who were in wheelchairs. We never left the drama room and we never got wet. We went on our journey solely through our imaginations, creating the environment around us with our voices and pantomimed action, yet the whole experience was as real to us at the time as it seems now in my description. When I think back to that day, I know that throughout the trip ten drama students were sitting in wheelchairs in a circle on a brown carpet in an elementary classroom, but in my mind's eye, I see ten smiling, laughing children wearing colorful bathing suits, sporting gorgeous tans, standing on surfboards, and riding a wave in the summer sun. And I know when they think back to this same Saturday morning, they see the same thing, too.

This is the power of the imagination in action. Whatever you want to do, you can do. Whatever you want to be, you can be. No one can limit you. No one can stop you.

introduction

How the Bethesda Academy's Special Needs Drama Program Began

1987 was a year of change for me. I had a Masters of Fine Arts degree in drama and had worked in professional theatre in a variety of technical, administrative, and artistic positions for thirteen years. I loved working in professional theatre, but felt I wasn't using drama to touch people's lives in a real and meaningful way.

I began looking for a way to do this. In February, I ran across the address of an organization called the National Association for Drama Therapy. "This sounds fascinating," I thought, so I wrote for more information. The NADT office forwarded my resume to Jan Goodrich, one of the Registered Drama Therapists in the Washington, D.C., area where I lived. Jan felt that the best way to find out about drama therapy was to jump in and try it, so she offered me an internship with her at Second Genesis, a therapeutic community for recovering alcoholics and drug addicts.

Drama therapy is an experiential type of psychotherapy that uses drama and theatre processes to treat such dysfunctions as emotional disorders, learning difficulties, geriatric problems, and social maladjustments. Drama therapists are trained in theatre arts, psychology, and psychotherapy, and use a wide variety of techniques including improvisation, role-playing, puppetry, mime, masks, theatre games, gestalt and psychodrama techniques, and theatre production as a means of emotional and physical integration.

In drama therapy I discovered an exciting pathway which led through the familiar dramatic landscape that I loved, but approached it from a more meaningful, socially conscious angle. Through the medium of drama I saw people grow, heal, and learn how to connect with themselves and others.

That spring I met Bonnie Fogel, the Executive Director of the Bethesda Academy of Performing Arts in Bethesda, Maryland. The Academy is a not-for-profit arts organization which offers classes in drama, dance, singing, and the visual arts to children and teens in the Washington metropolitan area. Classes and rehearsals are held after school, in the evenings, and on Saturdays. The teachers are professional artists—actors, directors, dancers, musicians, and visual artists—who love children and teach part-time. Students' tuition covers approximately 60 percent of the cost of operation and the rest of the budget is made up through donations from individuals, corporations, foundations, and state and local government.

The Academy (often called by its acronym, BAPA) was founded in 1979 and had recently gone through an amazing growth spurt. The Board of Directors felt it was time to develop a formal mission statement and take on a full-time staff to implement programming. The statement hammered out between Bonnie, Gail Humphries-Breeskin, the Artistic Director at the time, and the Board was that the Academy's mission was to integrate the arts into the lives of children in the community through classes and performance op-portunities.

When Bonnie heard about my internship in drama therapy, her ears perked up. For several years she had been wrestling with a dilemma. The Academy was reaching out to a sizable portion of the metropolitan area's population, attracting students from all over Montgomery County (Maryland), the District of Columbia, and Northern Virginia. However, one segment of the community was not being served—children who had dis-abilities.

Research into public school population statistics at the time revealed a combined total of 39,471 students with special needs enrolled in the public schools of the greater metropolitan area. In addition, there were over thirty private, independent schools in the area specializing in educating students with special needs.

Bonnie had been made aware of the Academy's lack of attention to these students by several close friends who had children with a disability. Their nondisabled children attended classes at the Academy and thoroughly enjoyed their experiences, developing creatively, emotionally, and socially as they had fun learning about the arts. But their disabled children were unable to participate because no adaptations were in place to accommodate them.

Lack of a special needs program did not mean that children with disabilities never took classes at the Academy. From time to time students with mild learning disabilities or attention deficit hyperactivity disorder were mainstreamed into classes. Often there were very positive results. One mother wrote:

Our son, age 13, attends a special school for children with learning disabilities. He has always been active and involved in drama at school, but was always shy about pursuing his interest in a mainstream setting because of his reading disability. We were thrilled that he could be mainstreamed in BAPA's Improvisation class in the Fall. It was the perfect transition for him and improved his self-confidence beyond our greatest expectations. We had never seen him so comfortable and sure of himself on stage.

However, whenever students were mainstreamed, there was rarely communication between parent and teacher about the disability. Sometimes ignorance is bliss, but more often it is a time bomb waiting to go off.

Several teachers, unaware that one of their students had dyslexia, reported bizarre emotional responses when that particular student was asked to read a scene or a monologue out loud in class. Caleen Sinnette Jennings, one of the Academy's finest acting teachers, had one such experience. She had a student who had been a delight the whole semester. Then she handed him a script and suddenly he was bouncing off the walls!

Other drama teachers, uninformed when students had attention deficits or emotional problems, couldn't understand why their normally ordered class suddenly became chaotic. Dance teachers, unaware that a student's confusion between right and left was due to learning disabilities, would leave class totally frustrated at their failure to communicate.

Bonnie heard these stories first-hand after class when the disheartened teachers returned to the cramped little office which everyone on staff shared. Sometimes the teachers blamed themselves. Sometimes they blamed their students. Rarely did it occur to anyone that this was a situation involving a disability that could be addressed and changed.

Physical access was another issue that came up at this time. An embarrassing situation occurred during one of the performances of *The Mikado,* the spring musical. The father of one of the actresses couldn't get his wheelchair through the front doors! The building, an old public school building that was rented out to several non-profit organizations, had been built before accessible architecture was required in the design of public buildings. Traffic in and out of the building was at a standstill for ten minutes while the custodian took out the removable doorjamb between the front double doors to create a wide enough entrance for the wheelchair to pass through. The curtain was held until everyone was safely settled inside the auditorium and no major damage was done, but Bonnie was mortified. First and foremost, she saw the Academy as a service organization and she placed customer satisfaction as the highest priority. Here was a father who had paid tuition for his daughter to be in the Gilbert and Sullivan Performing Company, who had bought tickets for his entire family to come to the show, and he couldn't get in the front door. For the first time Bonnie faced the realization that lack of access for a patron with a disability was a blatant form of discrimination.

Something had to be done.

My training in theatre was primarily in directing and playwriting. I had had a number of experiences working with children and adults with special needs, but no formal training in special education or adaptive drama. In college as a volunteer and afterwards as a teacher's aide, I worked with the drama club at the Texas School for the Deaf in Austin. There I learned sign language and some of the rudiments of theatre of the Deaf.

In graduate school at the Dallas Theater Center, I assisted Mark Medoff when he came in to guest direct *Children of a Lesser God* for the 1980-81 theatre season. Because I knew how to sign, he turned the direction of the minor deaf characters (Orin and Lydia) and all of the deaf and hearing understudies over to me.

Later that year I directed a barrier-free production of *The Butterfly,* an Iranian morality tale, at the Bachman Recreation Center in Dallas. The Bachman Center, which had just opened, was a showcase recreation facility for the disabled. The actors in the production were adults, children, and teens with disabilities mainstreamed with a few non-disabled adults. Teens with disabilities built the costumes and set and served as technicians for the show.

The disabilities of cast and crew members included mental retardation, deafness, learning disabilities, epilepsy, and a wide variety of physical disabilities. This was my first experience with any condition besides deafness. It was a big change and a challenge. There are patterns of communication that work well with deaf actors, but don't work at all with those with mental retardation.

In addition to these experiences, I spent the fall of 1987 as a drama therapy intern at The Art and Drama Therapy Institute in Washington, D.C., which provides services to developmentally disabled adults. All of these experiences were quite challenging and often frustrating. They required a great deal of hard work, determination, and energy, but my overall experience in each case was positive. I was more than willing to tackle something else in the same vein.

I was hired as the Bethesda Academy's Special Needs Director in January 1988. The first six months were primarily to be spent on research, publicity, and curriculum development. However, two pilot creative drama classes were offered after school that spring at Ivymount School, a private school for students with learning disabilities and other special needs located in Rockville, Maryland.

Since I had no formal training in special education or disability, I began researching drama with special populations. I was appalled at the lack of information available. I found a few books, but most of them were vague—long on inspiration and encouragement, short on detailed information and specific interventions.

I fell back on the only resources available—general creative dramatics texts—which offered lots of specific suggestions for activities. In trying out material in my pilot classes, however, I found that many tried-and-true drama exercises did not work well with my learning disabled students.

At this point, I began researching different kinds of disabilities. This avenue of inquiry was not entirely fruitful either; I found only a few books that were written in non-technical terms and had information that could be applied to the drama classroom. However, I started to gain a few insights into why certain activities had succeeded with my students and others had failed miserably.

I also formed a Special Needs Steering Committee made up of parents of children with disabilities, special education teachers and administrators, individuals with disabilities, therapists, and other experts in the disability field. The committee's suggestions and encouragement guided me through the rough times and kept me on track.

In trying to cover all possible experience levels and combinations of students, I devised a program that would provide introductory, intermediate, and advanced experiences for students. I realized that process-based classes were needed for those who were not ready to perform and performance-based classes were needed for those who were. I felt peer classes were as important to offer as mainstreaming opportunities.

The structure of the program that has resulted has four basic components: special needs classes, mainstreaming into regular Academy classes, performing companies and classes that purposely mainstream students with and without disabilities, and outreach classes at other locations.

Special Needs Classes are introductory experiences designed for children and teens with disabilities who have little previous experience in the arts. These classes emphasize developing social interaction skills, expressive communication, and acting or dance skills in an effort to build personal and artistic self-confidence. Classes are small, ranging in size from five to eight students, so that each child can have lots of individual attention and not feel overwhelmed by the size of the group. As in all Academy classes, the atmosphere is kept low-pressure and non-competitive.

Mainstreaming is encouraged whenever students have developed the appropriate social and artistic skills necessary to succeed in a regular Academy class. Many students are mainstreamed from the outset; others can be mainstreamed after one or two semesters in a special needs class. I like to meet with new students and a parent ahead of time to decide if mainstreaming is appropriate and what adaptations need to be made. I supply the teacher of the class with information on the disability and how to make the necessary adaptations in the classroom. I am also available to observe classes when a problem arises that the teacher does not feel confident in solving alone.

Mainstreamed Performing Companies and Classes. From the outset, we felt it was important to create specific opportunities for children and teens with and without disabilities to work together. We wanted them to develop their creative abilities, build friendships, and break down stereotypes about disability. Our most successful endeavor in this area has been the Pegasus Performing Company, an integrated group of teenagers which each year creates an original play through improvisation.

Initially, members of the Steering Committee saw this performing company as a great propaganda device for promoting disability awareness. The actors, however, have had other ideas. While disability is part of their lives, it is by no means all of it. They have many other interests and issues they'd rather focus on. Aaron, who has cerebral palsy and learning disabilities, has been with the troupe since the first year. He says, "It's boring to think about your disability all the time!" For this reason, the plays developed by the troupe reflect general adolescent themes like adventure, independence, growing up, rebellion against authority, experimenting with adult roles, and the ever-popular time travel.

Outreach classes are classes offered off-site. These have ranged from after-school classes which have a recreational bent to classes during the school day which use drama and the other arts as a teaching tool in the special education curriculum. Workshops have been provided for recreation leaders or special educators. Drama components have been provided for special needs summer day camps.

In most cases, outreach classes have been solely for students with special needs. However, we also have provided several mainstreamed classes at other locations with great success.

Over the past four years the Special Needs Program has grown tremendously. The first six months there were two outreach classes and thirteen students. The next full year, six on-site and ten outreach classes were offered, providing an initial drama experience for 99 students. By the fourth year, over twenty different classes were offered to over 250 students. Forty-six additional students were mainstreamed into the regular program. Since its inception, over 500 individuals with disabilities have participated in the program as students, assistants, and teachers.

Many students have enjoyed so much success that they have come back again and again for classes. Records from the 1990-91 academic year indicate 48 students taking their second class, 27 students taking their third class, 22 students taking their fourth class, 10 students taking their fifth class, and 16 students taking their sixth to tenth class.

Mothers have responded enthusiastically to the growth they have seen in their children:

"[As a result of Creative Drama class] Betsy's verbal communication improved (her willingness to express herself). Betsy got an A in Oral Expression on her report card."

"Jacob seems to have improved his ability to approach and work/play with other children. We know he enjoyed the classes and missed them when they were over. He asked several times on Saturdays why we weren't going to drama class."

"Freddie has a really big imagination but didn't really know how to channel it. The drama class helps him have direction. He doesn't have a lot of physical abilities so this gives him an outlet for his creative imagination. He has no other after school activities at all that he enjoys."

"Jane, a non-handicapped child, gained a lot from the experience [being in Pegasus]. Basically, it taught her something about perspective—to be grateful for all she does have—when something in her life doesn't go perfectly smoothly. It was a little anxiety provoking, but she felt she gained from choosing to do this."

During these four years the staff and faculty of the Academy have widened their teaching horizons as students with disabilities have joined their classes. When faced with mainstreaming a child for the first time, most faculty members were fearful and hesitant. Some had no personal or professional experience with disability. They were afraid of not knowing what to do or say, afraid of the reaction the nondisabled children in the class would have to a mainstreamed child, afraid of what their own emotional reaction would be. Their change in attitude and growth in confidence has been astounding.

When I first approached Tim Reagan, one of the Academy's most popular and skillful creative drama teachers, with mainstreaming a boy who has Down syndrome into one of his classes, his reaction was typical. His eyes glazed over and his breathing froze. After a short pause, the first words out of his mouth were "But I don't know how. . . ." Experience has changed this. Last spring when a girl with Down syndrome registered for a place in his class, this now-confident veteran of mainstreaming shrugged his shoulders nonchalantly and said, "Down syndrome? Sure! Why not? Shouldn't be a problem."

Through trial and error I have learned a lot, too. It is no cliche to say that experience is the best teacher. I don't know all the answers, but I'm learning how to ask the right questions. I'm beginning to find my way to problem-solving processes that usually take me where I want to go. I make mistakes, but I'm willing to be open and honest about them and to ask for help.

Above all, I try to listen to what my students are telling me. They are the real experts on what they need—in relation to adaptations, content, and form.

The stories told in this book by myself and my fellow Academy teachers are true. They are examples of real events and real people. In all cases, the names of students have been changed, but the details of the experiences have been reported accurately.

Since drama students and teachers come in both sexes, in the interests of non-sexist language I have alternated the use of the pronouns he and she by chapter to avoid awkwardness or confusion.

Whether you work in the arts, education, recreation, or rehabilitation, this book will help you incorporate drama and the other arts into the lives of individuals who have disabilities. For theatre professionals, general background information on disability has been included on definitions, origins, characteristics, and developmental and educational issues that may affect the teaching of drama. Most of this will already be familiar to special needs professionals. For special needs professionals, basic information on how to teach drama has been included. Most of this will already be familiar to theatre professionals. Specific ideas for adapting basic drama class and play-directing techniques for actors who have disabilities will be useful for both groups.

This book will explain why the arts are important to all people so that you can explain why to others who may not understand.

It will provide you with specific activities and lesson plans that work recreationally and educationally.

It will suggest ways to make your facility, program, and staff attitudes barrier-free.

It will suggest other helpful sources of information.

Most important, it will teach you how to approach adapting activities and programming to specific situations and individuals, so that you can begin to problem-solve on your own.

the need for the arts

Whenever I talk to people about the need for the arts in our lives, I get one of two different reactions. Either the person I am speaking with accepts the integral value of the arts and is tuned in to the wide range of contributions they can make to one's life or he sees the arts as pretty, but useless frills that can easily be done without.

These reactions have nothing to do with the individual's intelligence, cultural background, or educational level. They are based on whether a person has had a positive personal experience with the arts or not.

If you are reading this book, you are undoubtedly in the former category. You understand that the arts are more than just a pleasant way to while away a few free hours once a month. What you may not know is how to explain why the arts are important to those who are not supporters of the arts. Your boss or your coworkers may be in this category. The head of a foundation to which you are applying for a grant may be in this category. If you are attempting to integrate the arts into any kind of program, at some point you will be faced with justifying what you are doing. This chapter and the next will help you do that.

WHAT ARE THE ARTS?

Art is communication.

It is as simple—and as profound—as that.

An artist takes human feelings, thoughts, and ideas and gives them form through symbols that other human beings understand.

An artist is a person who expresses some facet of his or her experience through the medium of art. A few artists are highly trained professionals who earn their living through making art, but they are not the only people

If you have ever sung a song, danced a jig, or drawn a picture, you are an artist. (Photo by Lea Ann Rosen)

who can be called artists. The truth is that we are all artists because at one time or another we have all expressed ourselves through the arts. If you have ever sung a song, danced a jig, drawn a picture, written a rhyme, or acted out your version of an event that happened to you, you are an artist because you have communicated to someone else through art.

The conglomerate term "The Arts" refers to the five major forms that artists have developed as modes of communication: visual art, literature, music, dance, and drama. In each art form the artist's communications are expressed symbolically through the same basic artistic elements: line, shape, color, texture, time, rhythm, movement, space, silence, and sound. Language, another basic symbolic form of communication used between human beings, can be an ingredient in art as well.

THE ARTS AND CULTURE

Since prehistoric times, the arts have been used as a means of sharing complex information between people and as a container to hold culture and pass it on to succeeding generations. Early religious rituals and rites of passage consisted of music, dance, painting, sculpture, and dramatic ceremonial re-enactments of magical events. They taught our ancestors how to behave for survival in a dangerous world. They also eased the anxiety caused by the mysterious forces of nature and death. Pre-historic storytelling preserved religious traditions in the form of myths and historical events in the form of epics and stories, which were passed down orally from generation to generation until the invention of writing.

The same is true of the period of human existence that we call "Historic Time." Much of what we know about all the cultures that have come before our own is preserved in their surviving works of art. In fact, the civilizations, ancient and modern, which we remember as great ones are considered so because of the ideas they captured and passed on to us through their music, statues, paintings, poetry, and plays.

The arts are the most effective media for carrying on a dialogue about current cultural concepts and ideas. This is because art always creates visual, auditory, visceral images which humans respond to sensorially, emotionally, physically, and intellectually.

An excellent example of this is Langston Hughes's poem "Harlem" from *Montage of a Dream Deferred,* which is reproduced below. Take the time to read it through slowly and pay attention to how it affects you.

> *What happens to a dream deferred?*
> *Does it dry up*
> *like a raisin in the sun?*
> *Or fester like a sore—*
> *And then run?*
> *Does it stink like rotten meat?*
> *Or crust and sugar over—*
> *like a syrupy sweet?*
> *Maybe it just sags*
> *like a heavy load.*
> *Or does it explode?**

---

* From *The Panther & the Lash,* by Langston Hughes. Copyright 1951 by Langston Hughes. Reprinted by permission of Alfred A. Knopf, Inc.

Through words Hughes created images that evoke visual pictures in the mind and stir up memories of tastes, smells, textures, temperatures, weights, actions, and emotions, all to effectively capture the essence of an intolerable situation and communicate it to those who might change it.

Lorraine Hansberry read Hughes's poem and wrote a play entitled *A Raisin in the Sun* which attempts an answer to the question asked by the original work of art. Other artists have read the poem or seen the play (or movie) and have responded with their own artistic expressions furthering the dialogue. Community leaders have responded with actions that have changed and will continue to change the original situation that inspired the verse.

The ultimate power in a work of art lies in its symbolic nature. It may originate in one specific instance, but because it is metaphor, it can speak to another situation that involves similar feelings, thoughts, or ideas. The legacy of "Harlem" is not limited to the situation of racism against African Americans about which it was originally written. There are many analogous human situations for which the poem's images can symbolically stand. It speaks to them as well.

The arts continue to serve as excellent cultural teaching tools. They can be used to teach each society's young about the morals, values, and structures of that society. If a society's dramas show the struggle to resolve conflicts fairly and peacefully, the lessons learned in those dramas could be used by members of the audience to resolve their own conflicts in life. If a society's dramas show the resolution of conflict through violence and force, those are the resources that could be passed on to its youth.

The power of the arts as a cultural teaching tool can be used to continue the status quo or to change it. This is why totalitarian governments like to control the arts—and why "subversive" artists like Czech playwright Vaclav Havel get into trouble. Both understand that plays, books, films, graphic images, and poetry can reach the hearts and minds of the people and can be used to carry on a dialogue of values and ideas that can ultimately change the political system!

Because our arts are in forms that exist physically and last over time, they will be used, just as art of ages past was, to pass contemporary ideas, concepts, and history on to future generations. What our descendants will know about us will be what surviving artworks tell them.

THE ARTS AND THE INDIVIDUAL

So far this discussion has placed the arts in the large, formal, overview of World History and Culture, Political Systems and Power. But if we don't come from a family that goes to the theatre or reads great books out loud to each other or hangs famous images on its walls, do the arts really have a personal impact on our lives? The answer is an unequivocal "YES!"

The arts are developmentally among the first learning tools that every human child naturally uses to teach him or herself. In a sense, we are "hard-wired" to become artists, just as we are "hard-wired" to learn language. Infants and young children explore their immediate environment through their senses and through physical manipulation of their bodies and objects outside of themselves. In this sensorimotor stage, they begin to develop the capacity for representational thought, the ability to retain a mental image of objects or events. When they reach the preoperational stage of development, between the ages of two and seven, children are ready to develop the ability to understand, create, and use symbols. This is where language and the arts come in.

Give a young child a pencil, crayon, paint, sand, clay, or any other material that can make a mark or be shaped into a form, and he will begin making lines, shapes, and forms with it. Adults devalue this process by calling it "scribbling" or "making a mess" but it is a very important part of the sensorimotor learning process. The child is manipulating and experimenting with his environment. He continues to scribble because it is enjoyable to effect change, to be in control of a process, *to make something in the world.*

Over time, a child who is allowed to scribble progressively begins to make more and more recognizable shapes. Somewhere along the way, the artistic (symbolic) communication process has started. He is now taking in sensory information, processing it, responding to it emotionally and intellectually, and transforming that image and his response to it into a form outside himself. Eventually, he will notice that his feelings can be given form, too. If he feels angry, he can express it by drawing an angry sky. If he sees a flower on a sunny day and it makes him feel happy, he can paint it in a manner that expresses that happiness. Another important part of the art-making process is the sharing part. Children always share their drawings and creations with their parents. This is not just a bid for attention. This is a way of communicating an experience they had in a more complete way than simple words can express. Our young artist can take what he drew and show his mother his interpretation of what he saw in the backyard and how he felt about it.

Deferred imitation and symbolic play are early uses of drama as a learning tool. In deferred imitation a child observes a behavior performed by another and later tries it out himself in a different situation. Jean Piaget, the famous developmental psychologist, reported a wonderful example of deferred imitation. One day he saw his daughter watching another child in the middle of a temper tantrum. Up until that time his daughter had never thrown a temper tantrum—at least not one of this kind—herself. However, the very next day she decided to try out the kicking, stamping, and crying actions she had observed the day before. Piaget reports that she imitated the actions of the temper tantrum she had seen in a very deliberate manner, as if checking out how each movement felt and what response it would elicit. Deferred imitation involves the symbolic use of memory: seeing an action, remembering its image, and recalling it later on to be tried out.

In symbolic play children recall actions they have seen and explore them through pretending; that is, they use their imaginations to explore their experiences in a new way. Instead of just imitating actions they have seen, they act them out and improvise on them. They begin asking the question, "What if . . .?" Often they use symbolic play to take on adult roles they have seen. Through experimenting with more mature, diverse roles, they extend their role repertoire and learn new behaviors and coping strategies.

I remember setting up a tea party for my dolls at the age of three. I laid my great-grandmother's demitasse china cups out at each place and invited Raggedy Ann, Poppa Bear, and Momma Bear to join me. I can remember being very polite to my guests and carrying on very serious conversations with them as I handed around imaginary cookies and poured water into their cups from my plastic teapot. This was not my first tea party. I had been given a small set of plastic dishes when I was one or two. I'm sure I remember this specific tea party so vividly because it was special. I had begged my mother for days to be able to use the beautiful, delicate, little cups and saucers from my great-grandmother's house. They were antiques and my mother was worried that I would break them, but finally she gave her permission. The teacups didn't get broken. I took great care of them. In fact, I still have them in the china cabinet in my dining room.

My tea parties were not examples of deferred imitation. I had never seen my mother have a tea party. She never drank tea; she only drank coffee at breakfast in the morning. She had never had a formal gathering of friends in for tea—or coffee—which I might have copied. I was imagining something that I had never seen, but had been told about, so I made the situation up as I went along.

Symbolic or dramatic play is at first solitary, like my tea party with my dolls. Then, as children develop their play skills, they become capable of playing with other children. This happens in predictable stages. Between the ages of two and three, children are capable of parallel play, which is essentially solitary play in the general vicinity of another child. The children don't interact with each other; they tolerate each other's activity in proximity. If they get too close, they don't have the skills for give-and-take that are necessary in group play, and conflict can develop.

Between the ages of three and four, children start to acknowledge each other in play, perhaps talking about what they are doing or sharing toys. This is called associative play. They are interacting, they might even be playing the same game, but they aren't playing it together.

Cooperative play, which involves true interrelating, develops around the ages of four or five. It requires a much more sophisticated ability of communication and negotiation as well as a higher degree of patience. Even then, in the beginning, disagreements and fights break out.

I can remember going to my mother at age four in tears because the girl who lived two doors down had come into my basement and interrupted a game of "House" that my best friend, Eileen, and I were playing with Eileen's younger brother and sister. The neighbor stopped the game by inviting everyone (except me) over to her house for Kool Aid and cookies. They all went and left me behind! I was devastated. My mother said it was a lesson in life.

Later on, at seven or eight, I can remember coming home furious, slamming the door to my bedroom, and throwing myself down on my bed in tears on a day when nobody wanted to play the game *I* wanted to play. I hadn't been willing to compromise and neither had they. Another lesson.

Dramatic play as a formal and informal tool for learning is extinguished in children as they go through elementary school. Instead of harnessing and exploiting this natural active, interactive learning method, educators traditionally focus on passive educational methods. Students sit separately at desks and listen to lectures or work on solitary learning assignments like reading and writing out the answers to questions in workbooks. In reading groups students take turns reading out loud—active, but parallel work. Most of the time when the teacher asks a question, it is meant to be answered simply and neatly by one student. Rarely are questions designed to promote messy, noisy, interactive classroom debate.

Dramatic play is relegated to recess or after-school times and deemed appropriate only for recreational purposes. "Play" becomes a word associated with being a "baby." As boys get older, they are channeled away from dramatic play into sports activities, a form of play that teaches the hierarchical structure and behavioral traditions of the American workplace. Girls continue with dramatic play a little longer, but, since it often is dramatic play with dolls, they eventually give it up as "childish." Soon they grow into adults who have forgotten how to play and have lost touch with their innate abilities to express themselves through the arts.

THE ARTS AND PLAY

The word "play" has taken on a frivolous connotation in contemporary American culture. Children are immature and play, while adults are responsible and work. In truth, play is a significant ingredient in many aspects of life, from recreation and interpersonal relationships to education and work. Play serves as the stepping-off place for the creative process. In a sense, all of the arts are forms of play.

Play is not just something people do to waste or fill time. It is a bona fide activity that provides a sense of rest and refreshment for the players. It involves the senses and is often interactive, deepening the relationship between participants.

All play—even informal, improvisational play—is a structured experience guided by spoken or unspoken rules. For a situation of play to come alive, participants must buy into the rules and willingly suspend disbelief.

Playing is fun and enjoyable, but also a means of teaching life skills. It can open up new areas of experience for exploration and examination from infancy to adulthood. Games of peek-a-boo teach object permanence. Making funny faces together introduces babies to nonverbal communication, which in human societies is done primarily through facial expression. Patty-cake develops hand-eye coordination. As children grow older, they begin to learn through imitation, social games, sports, and dramatic play.

Games and imaginary play provide situations for acceptable, appropriate physical contact with other human beings. For example, patty-cake, ring a round the rosie, and tag teach how to touch in a non-threatening, playful manner.

Appropriate social contact is also provided for through play. Team members and opponents get to know each other a little better through playing games and then sharing about the experience afterwards. Many people use the arts, social games, and sports as reasons for making social contact with others. Bridge clubs, bowling leagues, and community theatres are often initiated by friends primarily as an excuse for getting together and socializing.

Play enhances spontaneity and joy. There is a sudden rush of excitement as the pace of a game picks up and all the players focus on the outcome of the roll of the dice, the turn of the card, or the pitch of the ball. Whatever the outcome, the players must be ready to jump in with the next appropriate response to keep the game moving forward. When the right response comes to the fore, the feeling of meeting the challenge of the moment is exhilarating!

Play provides an outlet for many other emotions as well. Children acting out the Grimm's fairy tale "Snow White and the Seven Dwarves" will feel anger at the evil queen, fear of the hunter who is assigned to cut out Snow White's heart in the forest, sorrow at Snow White's apparent death from the poison apple, and delight in her reawakening at the end of the story. To borrow the words of a major television network sports ad, play provides us with "the thrill of victory and the agony of defeat."

Play also involves a paradox of the imagination. Dramatic play happens simultaneously in real time and in imaginary time, in real space and in imaginary space. British psychoanalyst D.W. Winnicott called this real/imaginary time/space overlap the transitional space. The realm of the imagination stretches our minds as we exist in this magical place of make-believe and "in-between."

Understanding the difference between real and not-real is crucial to identity formation and the ability to relate to others. Object relations theorists, beginning with Melanie Klein, hypothesize that the newborn infant does not understand the separation between himself and the rest of the world. He has no sense of boundaries, believing that everything outside of himself is part of himself. As far as he knows, his cries and desires control the universe. But as he has life experiences, some of them enjoyable, some of them disappointing and frustrating, he begins to understand that he is a separate being. Physical boundaries exist between himself, other people, and the objects in his environment.

However, acknowledging physical boundaries is easy compared to recognizing other, more invisible, boundaries that exist between people. Each growing child must learn to make differentiations regarding emotions, thoughts, personal history, and belief systems. Young children often have the mistaken notion that others know what they are thinking. Sometimes they aren't sure which thoughts and feelings are their own and which belong to other people. A little girl begins to cry and her younger brother starts to cry, too. He's not just imitating his older sister's tears. He senses her upset feelings and, not able to separate them from himself, begins to feel upset, too.

One way to resolve this confusion of boundaries is through play where feelings and roles can be tested, explored, and evaluated in a safe, non-threatening imaginary setting. Through interactions and observation in play, the child begins to recognize that others don't always respond the same way that he does. He can't control them and they can't control him, but they can work together and share experiences.

Our technological age has added another aspect to the confusion between the real and the not-real: the differentiation between fact and fiction. Television broadcasts "The News," which is fact; entertainment, which is fiction; and docu-drama, which is a blend of both. Watching television, children and adults sometimes find it hard to tell the difference.

Fact and fiction both hold truths for us, but those truths need to be understood in different ways. Fact actually happened. It makes a statement about What Is or What Was. Fiction didn't actually happen, but could have happened. It asks the question: What If? Facts are to be accepted as true. To accept fiction, one needs to willingly suspend disbelief and enter the zone of play, of make-believe: the transitional space.

Picasso said, "Art is the lie that reveals the truth."

Playing out imaginary stories helps children understand the truth of fiction—how it can be experienced, processed, and believed. In the moment of dramatic play, a child can stand in Cinderella's shoes and experience her emotional situation as if it were really happening. And yet, it is not. Any moment her mother can open the back door to call her into the house for dinner, interrupting the fictional reality. Through these play experiences children begin to learn that the imaginary often seems real, but can be left behind with a simple refocusing of the attention away from the transitional space.

The experience of acting as a fictional character in play also makes the explanation of the fictional roles taken on by TV actors much clearer to a child. Parents can explain that an actor played the part of the scary monster, just as the child played the part of the wicked witch when she and her friends acted out the story of "Hansel and Gretel." The actor wasn't a real monster and the child wasn't a real witch; both pretended to be something they really weren't. The difference between fictional violence and real violence can be explained in the same manner.

The greatest boon of play—particularly dramatic play—is that it allows players to try out new behaviors and ideas in safety—without risk to life, limb, or social prestige. If a player makes a mistake in a game and is put "out," he hasn't died, he's merely lost a turn. If he loses the game, he can play another. If he tries out a new role and doesn't succeed at it, he hasn't failed "for real." He can stop, reevaluate the make-believe situation, and play the role out in a different way. In a sense, because it offers the opportunity to experience real feelings and situations in a safe, imaginary environment, play becomes rehearsal for life.

THE ARTS AND EDUCATION

Until they go to school, children use *all* of their senses to learn in a hands-on, physical manner. They naturally explore the world and express their feelings and ideas through dramatic play, movement, song, drawing, and other untutored forms of the arts. When they enter school at four, five, or six, they are usually thrown into an educational setting which doesn't exploit these powerful tools for learning.

As mentioned previously, the traditional American system of public education focuses primarily on the dissemination of information through teaching methods that are abstract rather than concrete, passive rather than active and participatory, and limited in terms of sensorimotor stimulation. Students listen to the teacher talk in front of the room. They are told *about* information rather than experiencing it themselves.

Teaching through the arts offers students the opportunity to continue learning and communicating through all of their perceptual channels. They can use their senses of sight, hearing, touch, smell, taste, and kinesthesia for receiving and processing information and for expressing themselves.

Learning through the arts becomes active and interactive because the whole person—senses, mind, and body—becomes involved in generating a physical response outside of himself (a painting, a poem, a performance) to information taken in. A student who crams facts and figures at the last minute in order to pass a test soon forgets the answers; but a student who has an experience with the material makes that information part of himself and will remember it for years.

EDUCATION, THE ARTS, AND WORK

One of education's biggest concerns is to prepare students for taking their places in the workforce after they leave school. Every adult must be able to work in some capacity in order to earn enough money to buy food, shelter, clothing, items of personal hygiene, and a few of the luxuries of life.

Businesses are concerned about finding workers who have the appropriate skills to succeed on the job. The workplace has been changing at a tremendous rate over the last century. There are fewer factory jobs and more jobs in the technology and service sectors of the job market. The old jobs required manual skills and the ability to follow directions, while these new jobs stress problem-solving and people skills. This trend in the workplace is projected to continue in the years to come.

The Secretary of Labor's Commission on Achieving Necessary Skills (SCANS) has published two reports on this issue of changing work skills and the responsibility of schools to train students in those skills. "What

Work Requires of Schools" and "Learning A Living: A Blueprint for High Performance" have become a basic reference guide for reforms needed in American schools.

The SCANS reports call for students to be trained in five competencies or thinking skills:

1. The ability to manage resources: setting priorities, managing money and materials, managing people.
2. The ability to work with other people on the job.
3. The ability to acquire and use information.
4. The ability to synthesize knowledge from one situation or system to another.
5. The ability to deal with new technology.

These skills are not covered in current school curriculums nor are they taught through current teaching methods. However, these skills *can* be taught through the arts.

Working in the arts—particularly the performing arts—is a great way to teach time management. Performing artists deal with deadlines constantly. Musical instruments must be practiced every day. Dancers must work out daily to keep their muscles in shape. Actors in a play must learn lines and movement patterns on time. Sets and costumes must be built and in place by opening night. When it's time for the curtain to go up, every facet of the presentation must be ready to go. You can't come out before the show begins and say to the audience, "Sorry, we only know the lines in Act One, so we'll only do part of the play." Or "We didn't finish all the costumes, so just imagine the princess is wearing a beautiful ball gown instead of blue jeans."

Management of resources is another skill artists use every day. Because designers and technicians have to work within a budget to create sets, costumes, and props for the least amount of money, the art of stagecraft has been developed to provide many clever tricks for making the audience believe they are seeing something that really isn't there. The walls of a house on stage might look like solid brick, but in reality it is only muslin fabric stretched across a wooden frame and painted to create the illusion of brick. The pirate's treasure chest might look like it's filled with gold doubloons, but in reality, they are only old poker chips sprayed with gold-colored paint.

The performing arts, in particular, stress interpersonal interaction skills. An actor, musician, and dancer must learn to work *with* others toward the creation of a common goal—the performance. Drama, which often involves the re-creation of real life situations and relationships, is especially useful for developing the ability to work with and understand others. The ability to share and to negotiate solutions to problems is crucial in the workplace and on the stage. In addition, the more clearly a person can communicate with words and actions, the less frequently others will misunderstand him—and the more often he will be able to understand the communications of others.

The process of creating art involves flexibility, spontaneity, and the ability to adapt to change. Each line that an artist puts on a piece of paper requires assessment and adjustment in his overall creative plan. Each moment on stage must be brought to life anew by the performer each time it is performed. Mishaps or mistakes in a performance must be dealt with by the actor, dancer, or musician without stopping the show or letting the audience know anything went awry.

Improvisation in life and in art is important; inflexibility and rigidity will kill the ability to be expressive and creative in any art form, interpersonal relationship, or problem-solving situation. Improvisational styles of different art forms provide hands-on practice in staying in the present moment and thinking on your feet in a situation. For instance, improvisational acting games train students to respond quickly and appropriately to incoming messages from others, a skill which any salesperson, teacher, or personnel manager needs to have. Improvisation also teaches approaching life and work in a flexible, playful manner rather than a stressful, tense one.

Communication is inherent in the arts. And the ability to make connections—between one idea and another, between one person and another—is inherent in communication. Accessing information and synthesizing it are the first steps of the artistic process. The information comes in and is internally evaluated. Connections are made within the artist between the new information and old. A new response is generated and the artist must formulate a way to express that new idea. Here we have practice in information assessment and synthesis, two of the thinking skills mentioned prominently in the SCANS report.

The arts develop self-esteem and teach the importance of seeing a project through from beginning to end. (Photo by Lea Ann Rosen)

In addition to all of this, the arts teach the importance of completion and the rewards of following through with a project. A student who works hard and finishes his art project, whether it is a painting or a performance in a play, has a finished product in the end—something he can be proud of, which he made, and which says something about him! The feeling of accomplishment that comes with completion is one that can't be understood until it is experienced. Once it is experienced, the student learns that the effort and sacrifice involved in working on a project is worth it. Job satisfaction and taking pride in your own work is no longer an abstract idea, but becomes meaningful in personal terms.

The final outcome of an experience in the arts is the development of self-esteem. When a student finishes a project, overcoming all the challenges, obstacles, and frustrations along the way, he starts to feel good about himself. Connections of new knowledge are made inside. Connections of recognition and appreciation are made between himself and others. He sees that he can contribute something which others in the community value. He can feel personal growth and sense his own potential. This creates the motivation to keep going and to keep growing.

chapter two

the arts and disability

The arts can greatly enhance every aspect of our lives: in learning, work, play, relationships, and identity formation. In fact, because they are so basic and so life-affirming, the arts often open up new avenues for stimulation, communication, and growth. If this is true for people who don't have disabilities, it is equally so for people who do have them.

Disabilities—whether physical, cognitive, or emotional—cause a great deal of frustration in the lives of those who have them. Full participation in community life is sometimes blocked by obstacles created by the disability itself, lack of accommodation for it, or prejudicial attitudes by others. Design barriers can limit access to transportation, buildings, and the programs and work opportunities held in those buildings. Traditional educational systems often don't answer the needs of people who must learn in alternative ways. Due to the nature of the disability or the lack of accommodations in the community, the range of choices a person with a disability can make in life, from educational level and career to living situation and lifestyle, can become limited. Faced with a myriad of frustrating and confining situations, a person who has a disability can easily become focused on what she can't do instead of the possibilities and potentials for which she can strive.

The arts break through barriers and limitations. They offer participants many possibilities and options for the successful expression of feelings and ideas. Difficulty on one level of perception or communication does not negate enjoyment or participation on another. In fact, the arts may provide stronger channels for self-expression for a disabled individual than non-artistic media. For example, someone who has difficulty expressing herself in words because of a speech disorder or a learning disability may be able to express herself through pantomime or dance. A student who can't write about something that happened to her might be able to act it out or sing about it and experience the same or even more satisfaction with the successful act of expressive communication.

If an individual can experience success, be valued for her ideas, and have her feelings validated, her self-confidence and self-esteem begin to grow. When attitudes about the self change, obstacles become surmountable. Choices multiply. Life becomes filled with excitement and joy.

Making friends and sharing experiences creates a sense of belonging to the community, of having the right to exist and enjoy life alongside everyone else. To be acknowledged for artistic creations leads to the desire to contribute more—to the self, family, friends, and community.

Government figures vary widely, but statistics indicate that there are between 30 and 50 million people who have disabilities in the United States. This means that between 12 and 20 percent of the U.S. population have some form of disability! These figures indicate a significant number of community members who could benefit from participation in recreational arts programming or through the integration of the arts into their educational curriculum, but who may currently be excluded. Arts and recreation programs are passing up important opportunities to boost attendance figures and income and to generate good will. Educational institutions and rehabilitation services are missing out on powerful tools to build their clients' self-esteem, motivate self-sufficiency, and teach academic, life, and job skills. Even for adults who have been out of the educational mainstream for years, the arts can be a powerful motivational force to unlock unexpected creative potential that has lain dormant for years.

SPECIFIC SKILLS WHICH DRAMA DEVELOPS

Each art form helps student artists develop specific skills. A look at some of the skills that drama enhances will show how participation in theatre arts might benefit a person who has a disability.

LISTENING

Drama builds listening skills. There are lots of opportunities for practicing listening skills in a drama classroom. Directions to games must be listened to in order to play. Stories must be heard before they can be acted out. While acting out a scene, each actor must listen to the other actors in order to know when to say her line and what to say.

In an academic classroom it might be difficult to listen if you aren't interested in the subject being taught or if what is being said is hard to grasp. However, in a drama class listening leads to fun. If the student can listen, she can participate and is rewarded with an enjoyable experience: a fun game, an interesting imaginary experience, lots of positive attention from the teacher and others in the group, the feeling of doing a job well.

In addition to reinforcing the practice of listening, of attending to the human voice, and processing directions being spoken, drama teaches *what* to listen for. There are many tone-of-voice exercises which actors play to teach vocal expressiveness. Listening to the manner in which others are speaking teaches students to recognize emotion and meaning in the human voice apart from the literal content of the words. There are also action/reaction exercises that teach an actor to respond appropriately to what another actor is communicating to him vocally, emotionally, and physically. Even deaf students can participate in these kinds of exercises because emotional meaning and intent put into the voice usually shows up in facial expression and body language.

EYE CONTACT

Many children who have cognitive disabilities or low self-esteem have difficulty making eye contact with others. Eye contact is part of listening and receiving information from others. It is also part of sharing information with others about what you are thinking and feeling. Being able to make eye contact with another person enhances trust as well as communication.

There are many drama games that stress eye contact and therefore develop the ability to use it on stage and in real life. Many trust and non-verbal communication exercises require eye contact, as do action/reaction exercises. Mirroring and other Follow-the-Leader type exercises encourage students to really look at each other. On stage, actors usually look at each other when they are talking unless there is an emotional reason to look

away. Students working on improvisational or scripted scenes can be encouraged to hold eye contact in rehearsal and performance. Once these
habits are introduced through an enjoyable and meaningful experience and
students begin to feel comfortable making eye contact with others, they may
carry over its use into relationships at school and home.

AWARENESS OF THE BODY IN SPACE

Many children with special needs have difficulty understanding how
their physical bodies take up space and can intrude on the other physical
bodies around them. They are often unaware that each person has "personal
space," an invisible area around her body. The boundary for this "personal
space" is different for each person. Some people need a lot of "personal
space" and some need just a little. If someone breaks the boundaries of your
personal space without your permission, you probably will feel threatened.
Sometimes students are aware of their own personal space, but not of the
fact that others have it as well.

Awareness of personal space is a cultural concept that is taught non-verbally. Children normally learn it through observing their parents as they interact within the family and in the world at large. Children who have special
needs sometimes miss out on a lot of information that is taught non-verbally
because their attention is occupied with other emotional, physical, or information-processing concerns.

This lack of awareness of body and personal space boundaries can lead
to personal misunderstandings and fights. One child may innocently stretch
out her arm and unknowingly invade the space of the child next to her. The
child whose space has been invaded gets upset and aggressively hits out at
the invader. Within seconds both are rolling around on the floor throwing
punches at each other.

Drama is a good training ground for developing awareness of space
boundaries. A child can be encouraged to be aware of how she uses her
body and how her body can take up more or less space. Shape-shifting or
transformation exercises stress changing your physical self into other
animals or objects, both large and small, and moving in different ways.
Slow motion/fast motion exercises can create the awareness of how your
body moves through space and at which speeds you have more or less control.

Once a student understands how her body inhabits the space around her, she can begin to learn how her body interacts with other bodies in space. Many movement games teach spatial relationships. Others teach how to touch appropriately and in a non-aggressive manner. (See Chapter Seven for a few examples of these.)

PHYSICAL COORDINATION

Balance, hand-eye coordination, and gross motor skills can be refined through movement and social games as well as through pantomime and acting activities.

Practicing a physical skill for its own sake can get boring. Think of how hard it is to stick to a daily exercise regimen! It's often easier to improve a skill if you are focused on a larger overall objective instead of on the skill itself. Any drama game has a stated dramatic goal, but develops many sub-skills along the way.

A good example of this is the game Elbow-to-Elbow. The teacher calls out different body parts: elbow-to-elbow, head-to-knee, foot-to-back. Each student must connect one of her body parts with the body part of another student. The overall dramatic goal is to get students to work together and contact each other cooperatively. While they are doing this, they are also learning about body parts, making decisions, becoming aware of themselves in space, developing balance, using gross muscles, coordinating body placement, socializing with each other, and much, much more.

PHYSICAL EXPRESSIVENESS

Drama activities stress using the body in a physically expressive manner. A neutral body communicates nothing. A tense body communicates tension, worry, and anxiety. A relaxed, expressive body can communicate any emotion the actor wants to express. Guessing games and transformation games require students to use their bodies in different ways to communicate an idea to others. Pantomime necessitates that students imitate an action as clearly as possible. Creating a character different from oneself encourages expressing emotions in different ways and exploring how other people move and express themselves.

FACIAL EXPRESSIVENESS

The face is an important part of the body. For humans it carries more emotional information than any other part. In fact, communication begins with the face. From the moment of birth, babies are "hard-wired" to make contact with the human face and look into their mothers' eyes. Faces are very elastic. They have thousands of tiny muscles that can create an infinite number of emotional expressions. A facial expression can mask what a person is feeling or express it honestly. Because of this, particular attention is often paid to developing facial expressiveness in drama.

It's very clear what this knight is thinking and feeling as he eats his meal. (Photo by Allison Walker)

Some children with special needs don't know how to express what they are feeling through their faces. Others may have difficulty reading the expressions in others' faces. Working with facial expressiveness in drama class develops ease and appropriateness of expression as well as the ability to interpret the meaning of facial expressions in others.

VERBAL EXPRESSIVENESS

In addition to non-verbal, physical expressiveness, drama deals with expressing ideas and feelings through words. The most obvious way drama can enhance verbal expressiveness is by training students to speak clearly and understandably.

Through improvisation, students can learn to translate thoughts and emotions into words. Everyone needs to learn this skill, but children who have cognitive disabilities sometimes have particular difficulty finding words to express what is going on inside. Spoken improvisational drama can help students practice this skill. Expressing how a character in a fictional context feels can provide a student with enough emotional distance to be able to sort through her own feelings and choose appropriate words. Describing or evaluating what you just saw someone else perform or what you just experienced during an exercise provides an excellent opportunity for the development of critical facilities.

Every verbal communication contains two messages: the text (the actual words spoken) and the subtext (the emotional undertone and intention of the words). Subtext can support and enhance the text, it can give away an underlying message not inherent in the words alone, or it can totally change the meaning of the words being spoken. In everyday living, we use subtext all the time. For example, you could say "She's my best friend" five different ways and each time try to communicate a different emotional meaning. You might mean actually "She's not my friend, she's my enemy," "I can't stand her," or even "She's a cute kid, but she follows me around constantly and I wish she'd leave me alone."

Subtext is another one of those cultural constructs which are taught nonverbally through observation and imitation. Consciously working on the skillful use of subtext helps a student who has missed out on social learning to catch up.

FOCUS AND CONCENTRATION

Focus and concentration are crucial for an actor to develop in order to create an exciting performance on stage. The more an actor can concentrate and focus on her lines, characterization, emotions, movement, stage business, and the other actors in the play, the closer to the dramatic truth of the moment she will come. A low energy performance during which an actor daydreams or wanders aimlessly about the stage without connecting with the other actors is boring for an audience to watch.

Special needs students may lack focus and concentration for various physical, emotional, or cognitive reasons. Focusing on drama games and activities, which are of short duration, but which create intense, enjoyable feelings, a student begins to learn how to focus her attention. The immediate positive feedback from her body, her emotions, the teacher, and her fellow

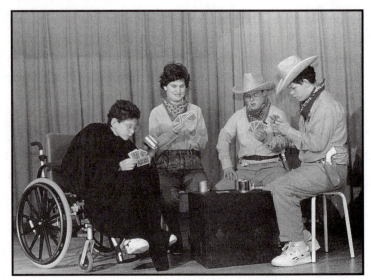

Concentration and focus on stage create an exciting, believable performance. (Photo by Allison Walker)

students reinforces focused behavior and encourages her to pay attention to what is going on in the classroom.

As students move on to more advanced dramatic work, such as improvisation or scene study, they have more opportunities to hone concentration abilities. An improvisational scene stops dead in its tracks if an actor stops paying attention to what is going on. It jumps around and becomes confusing if the actors can't concentrate on the conflict at hand. When rehearsing a scene from a play that has been memorized, an actor must listen for her cue before she can say her line. If she's not paying attention, she will never get to speak her part!

FLEXIBILITY AND PROBLEM-SOLVING SKILLS

The ability to be flexible is crucial in order to get along with others and solve the many different problems that come up in life. Many children with special needs, in trying to cope with physical, relational, or educational situations that seem to be out of their control, can become very tight and rigid in the choices they are willing to make. They stop taking risks and limit themselves to a narrow range of behavior that may or may not be appropriate to the current moment.

For example, a child who has difficulty controlling her body movements because of cerebral palsy could develop an inflexible need to always be in control of every interpersonal interaction. Things have to go her way or no way at all. If she can't call the shots, she might whine, complain, protest, have a temper tantrum, or refuse to participate. Obviously, these are not productive coping strategies. No one can always control other people's behavior and choices. Sometimes you get your way and other times you don't.

Another child might have had a bad experience riding on a bus and refuse to take public transportation ever again. When she becomes an adult, if she is unable to drive a car and is not able to afford to go everywhere by cab, this inflexible choice may limit her ability to get around independently and, perhaps, even to hold down a job.

In drama class, students have the opportunity to try out different roles and behaviors in a safe situation. Different strategies for solving a problem can be acted out and the pros and cons of each evaluated and discussed. Changing points of view on a situation through role reversal often helps students open up their personal perspective on a specific problem or on their general orientation toward themselves and others. Just the experience of standing in another's shoes for a little while teaches flexibility and opens up the possibility that other choices do exist and might be considered.

SOCIAL INTERACTION

Sometimes children who have special needs have poor group interaction skills because they don't have enough opportunities to practice them. They may live isolated existences compared with children who don't have disabilities. They might spend a great deal of time in the hospital or at the doctor's office. They might have to ride the bus for many hours to get to their special school. They might not be accepted by other children in the neighborhood and miss out on social play opportunities there. They might have to spend extra time doing homework each day in order to succeed academically.

Even in regular education classes, school time is rarely devoted to the development of social skills. Each child sits alone at her desk doing her assignment and is permitted to talk with friends only during lunch or recess. A few teachers are beginning to use group learning methods in which a number of students work together to create a project or solve a problem, but interactive learning is not the norm in our educational system.

Drama is a great way to make friends. (Photo by Allison Walker)

Drama classes offer many chances for students to practice working with others constructively and to make friends. The drama teacher is responsible for creating a non-competitive forum where each student is encouraged to do her best and to support others in doing their best. Sharing feelings and ideas, taking turns, being generous and kind to each other should be stressed over perfecting performance skills. Theatre is first and foremost a communal art. Those involved must work together! Contrary to the media stereotype of the prima donna, true artists base their work and interactions on mutual respect.

One positive experience can make a lot of difference in the life of a child. One mother said of her emotionally disturbed son's experience in a creative drama class, "We believe Jacob has made progress this year in his social skills and his ability to express his feelings and that drama class has a lot to do with it."

A wide variety of group experiences are available for students in a drama classroom. The entire class might act out something together in a parallel fashion, expressing different versions of the same idea side by side without interacting. The teacher might lead the group in a transformation game where everyone changes from elephants to monkeys to thorn bushes. The whole group might play an interactive game like Elbow-To-Elbow. Individuals can take turns getting up in front of the group and pantomiming different activities or singing a song. Partners can work together on games and exercises. Small groups can invent an improvisational scene or play a game in which they have to work together to solve a problem. In each type of group experience, students have the opportunity to make positive contact with other students, to give and take ideas, to resolve conflicts, and to make friends.

SELF-ESTEEM

Self-esteem is something that is often in short supply among children who have disabilities. Because they are different from other children in their neighborhood or school and because they may not succeed in academic and social settings—the two main arenas of childhood—they may not feel good about themselves.

Drama is a self-esteem builder. Through dramatic experiences in class and in performances, children can share the creative, vulnerable, and absolutely unique aspects of themselves with others. They can explore who they are, experience success, and begin to feel proud of themselves.

physical disabilities

No two children learn in precisely the same way. One may need to physically walk through the motions to learn a new skill, while another may learn better by watching a demonstration. Obviously, children with disabilities have learning styles that are just as unique as other children's. Particular disabilities do, however, often present similar types of learning challenges to the children who have them. And understanding how a specific disability may affect a child's ability to learn or behave can make it easier for teachers to help him benefit from a drama experience.

For the benefit of readers who do not have a background in special education, this chapter includes basic information on the characteristics of children with the most common physical disabilities. It also discusses some ways of accommodating children with physical disabilities in general within the drama classroom and on stage. More specifics will be included in Chapters Five, Six, and Seven, which describe how to run a structured drama class, how to develop a strong lesson plan, and how to adapt specific activities for students with special needs.

TYPES OF PHYSICAL DISABILITIES

There are many different reasons why a student may have difficulties walking and need to use a wheelchair, walker, or crutches. Orthopedic disabilities—conditions that affect bone, joint, or muscle functioning—can be caused by paralysis due to spinal cord injury or brain trauma, cerebral palsy, osteogenesis imperfecta (also known as "brittle bone disease"), broken bones, arthritis, or a neuromuscular disease such as muscular dystrophy or multiple sclerosis. Whatever the cause, the result is that physical movement is to some degree restricted.

Children with visual or hearing impairments are also considered to have physical disabilities, although their movement abilities are not usually impaired. This is because their disabilities are often caused by a physical difference in the structure of their eyes or ears which interferes with the processing of sight or sound.

Many times a person who has a physical disability has normal cognitive functioning and normal or above normal intelligence. Often he can be mainstreamed into regular drama classes with a few changes in the physical environment to make your space accessible and with a few adjustments in your lesson plans to facilitate his interactions with you and the group.

Sometimes students with physical disabilities also have cognitive disabilities. In these cases, refer also to Chapter Four, which has information about cognitive disabilities and basic classroom adaptations.

There are no hard and fast rules that apply to everyone with any given disability diagnosis. Each individual will be affected in a slightly different way—emotionally, physically, and cognitively. Getting to know your student and his specific needs is more important than any advice this or any other book can give you.

ACCESSIBILITY

The first thing you must do, long before a student with a physical disability signs up for a class, is to evaluate the accessibility of your building and classroom space. If a student can't get in your front door, can't get around inside your building, can't use your restroom facilities, or can't use your classroom equipment, he won't be able to avail himself of your services. Below are some suggestions for making your building, classroom, stage, and activities accessible.

ACCESSIBLE BUILDINGS

In truth, many barriers can be removed at little or no cost. Sometimes it can be as simple as rescheduling a class from the second to the first floor of a building or moving furniture around in order to provide a wider aisle space for a wheelchair to get through a passageway. Sometimes it is as inexpensive as adding a paper cup dispenser next to a water fountain or propping a door open with a doorstop.

Go through your building with the Checklist for Building Accessibility located in Appendix III at the back of the book and evaluate where your facility is barrier-free and where it needs improvement. Ask adults in your community who have different types of physical disabilities to go through your building with you and point out the areas where they would have difficulty. They will find barriers that a person without a disability would not be aware of. Ask them for suggestions on how to make changes cheaply and simply. People who deal with barriers every day have often developed quick and easy common-sense solutions that a nondisabled person would never think of!

"The Arts and 504: A 504 Handbook for Accessible Arts Programming," available from the Government Printing Office in Washington, DC., covers the regulations of Section 504 of the Rehabilitation Act of 1973 which deal with structural requirements for a barrier-free building. This handbook offers many specific ideas on how to make arts programming physically accessible.

If you need professional help in evaluating your facility or in making modifications to it, there are several places you can contact. The Architectural and Transportation Barriers Compliance Board is a U.S. government agency which provides technical assistance on accessibility. The Disability and Business Technical Assistance Center can offer referrals of accessibility experts in your region who have been trained in the accessibility requirements of the Americans with Disabilities Act. (Contact information for these and other national organizations mentioned in this chapter are located in Appendix II at the end of the book.)

You might find an architectural firm in your area which specializes in access issues, but before you hire them make sure their consultant is truly an expert on accessibility and not just a good salesman. Your best bet in locating a reputable architectural consultant on accessibility is to ask an independent living center in your area. Independent living centers are organized and staffed by people who have disabilities. They will know well-qualified, reputable experts in your community. If you are not sure how to find an independent living center, contact the National Council on Independent Living (see Appendix II). They have lists of affiliated and non-affiliated centers for independent living all across the country.

ACCESSIBLE CLASSROOMS

Let us assume that students with physical disabilities will be able to get into your classroom or performing space. How well will they be able to function once they are in that space? Floor surfaces need to be considered. Wheelchairs don't roll well on thick pile carpets. They have an equally difficult time moving over rough or uneven surfaces created by bricked, tiled, or textured linoleum floor treatments.

Very slick surfaces or linoleum floors covered with slippery wax make walking dangerous for students who use walkers or crutches or even for students who have a limp or balance problems. Ask the custodian of your building to switch from regular to slip-resistant floor wax to provide more gripping action under foot. Doing this may cut down on the slips and falls taken by other students as well.

Check your classroom space for barriers that could impede a blind student. Any change in the floor level (created by steps, thresholds, texture of floor surface, or transition from one type of floor surface to another) that is higher than one quarter inch could cause a blind person to trip. Slick floor surfaces are dangerous. Carpet edges that are not tacked down are also potential dangers.

A blind person who uses a cane might have difficulty with a carpeted surface. A cane, tapped against the floor surface, provides aural and tactile information to its user about what is ahead. On a carpet the sound of the cane's taps are muffled and the touch of the cane on the surface is muted.

Canes also provide information about objects that are in the way. However, they don't alert their user to objects that are protruding from the wall, such as fire extinguishers or coat racks. The cane will go along the floor right underneath the object, indicating a clear passageway where none actually exists. Remove protruding objects that don't have to be there. Mark the ones that remain by placing another object such as a planter, chair, or trash can on the floor underneath it or to either side of it.

If you are doing writing, art, or any kind of activity that requires the use of tables or desks, make sure the top surface is high enough for the arms of a wheelchair to fit underneath. For most wheelchairs, this means a clearance of 30 inches from the floor to the bottom of the tabletop. If your tables are not that high, check their legs; some tables have legs that can be extended. If legs can't be adjusted, the table could be temporarily raised by placing four thick objects, such as telephone books or blocks of wood, underneath all of the legs. Make sure that whatever you use will not slip out and pin the person in the wheelchair under the table!

For students who have muscular or motor impairments, adaptive scissors and other art equipment which require the use of less muscle strength or which have firmer or larger hand grips can be purchased through special needs equipment catalogs and supply houses.

Place all equipment and materials to be used by a student in a wheelchair easily within arms' reach. He will not be able to stand up and reach across the table the same way nondisabled students can. Blind students will also need materials placed within arms' reach.

Some individuals who have low vision are very light sensitive. For those who can see better with more light, increase the general lighting level in your classroom. Brighten dark spots or areas where there are potential hazards.

Try to keep the classroom as free from distracting noises and white sound (created by fans, furnaces, or air conditioners) as possible. Blind students need to hear what is going on clearly. Also bear in mind that hearing aids will pick up white noise and sounds that hearing people with normal auditory processing automatically tune out. This can be very distracting and disorienting to a hard of hearing person.

By the same token, be aware of the visual distractions in the room. Lots of competing colors or moving objects could be distracting or confusing for a deaf student. If you stand in front of a moving object, a deaf student, who is visually oriented, will not be able to focus on you!

ACCESSIBLE STAGES

Most theatres have not been designed with wheelchair accessibility in mind. In most theatre designs, stages are raised above the level of the audience and are reached both backstage and in front of the proscenium arch by stairs. Many other backstage areas like dressing rooms, the lighting grid, and the light/sound booth can often be reached only by ladders or stairs.

This, obviously, creates barriers for students who have orthopedic disabilities.

If your organization's stage is inaccessible, some structural modifications are in order. Perhaps a temporary ramp can be borrowed or built to connect the stage or backstage area with floor level. To be safe and usable by most wheelchairs, ramps should be at least 36 inches wide and should not have more than an 8.3 percent slope. In other words, for every 12 feet of horizonal run to a ramp, there should only be a one foot rise. Ramps should also have a railing or raised curb on any open side to prevent wheelchairs from rolling off.

A high stage will necessitate a very long ramp. If space is limited, ramps can be built in an L-shape or with a switch back. Obviously, constructing a ramp of this type can turn into a major carpentry project. An alternative solution might be to rent or buy a mechanical lift to raise students who are in wheelchairs from one level to another.

The Academy had an accessibility problem with its stage which was corrected with a semi-permanent ramp. The Academy rents space in an old elementary school, no longer in use, which belongs to the Montgomery County Public School system. Several years ago permission was granted for the small existing stage to be extended and enlarged with the proviso that whatever changes were made had to be reversible if we were ever to move out of the building. The permanent structure of the backstage area made it impossible to create a ramp without tearing down walls or doing other major physical renovations which would never have met with the school system's approval or with our budget. We did not have a lot of money for the project and knew the accessibility problem needed to be addressed as part of it.

Faced with these requirements and limitations, Steve Holliday, our technical consultant, created a very practical and theatrically useful solution. He added a ramp across the front of the stage extension, parallel to the audience. Actors who cannot climb stairs can enter from the stage right hallway at floor level and cross up the ramp onto the stage. If they need to be on stage at the start of the performance or if they make their first entrance from backstage, they go up the ramp before the show starts to get into place.

Our new ramp was greeted with great enthusiasm by students and faculty alike. Not only did it make the stage accessible to students who have orthopedic disabilities, it made the stage easier to use by all students. Actors

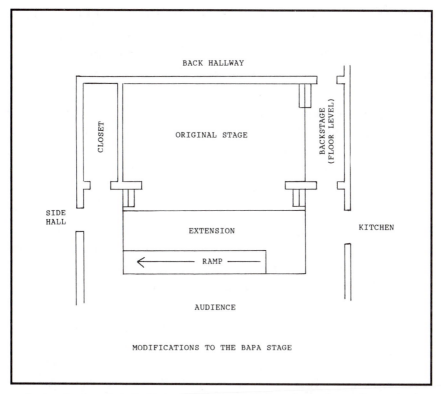

BACK HALLWAY

CLOSET

ORIGINAL STAGE

BACKSTAGE
(FLOOR LEVEL)

SIDE
HALL

EXTENSION

KITCHEN

← — RAMP —

AUDIENCE

MODIFICATIONS TO THE BAPA STAGE

no longer had to worry about making an entrance from the audience in the dark and tripping on dimly lit steps. Dancers could dance up onto the stage. Small children could parade onto the stage, taking whatever size steps their little legs best managed. The new ramp also added new levels to the stage, making it more theatrically dynamic and visually exciting. In various productions, the ramp has been employed as a hillside, a sliding board, a gang plank, and a hiding place from other characters on stage.

For anyone who has the luxury of designing a new stage facility or renovating an old one, I would like to mention a few design choices used to create accessible stages in other theatres where I have worked or performed.

Ramping the backstage entrances to the stage is very helpful. The Bachman Lake Recreation Center in Dallas, Texas, which was designed specifically to be used by disabled persons, solved the issue of stage accessibility by ramping the backstage left area down through an open passage to the stage left hallway. Another variation on this design can be found in the Twinbrook Elementary School in Rockville, Maryland. Stage left is directly connected to a hall next to the theatre by way of an enclosed hallway with a ramp in it which parallels the left side of the stage. An ideal design in this style would offer plenty of backstage space (so actors in wheelchairs could maneuver around whenever they were offstage) and accessible ramped entrances backstage left *and* right.

The Columbia campus of the Maryland School for the Deaf has an auditorium design that is based on the ancient Greek amphitheater. This creates a very exciting and accessible performance space for actors. The stage is on the same level as the first row of the audience. The seating in the house is raked (raised in level row by row) so the audience can see all the action on the stage. This gives audience members an unencumbered, optimum, and very dramatic view of the stage. There is a lobby at the back of the theatre on the same level as the stage, which is connected to it and the house by passageways on either side of the raked auditorium. The light/sound booth is backstage right on the same level as the stage floor. Actors and technicians can get around on stage and backstage easily because everything is on the same level.

If you opt for adding a ramp to the front of an existing stage, as we did at the Academy, consider what types of design treatments will fit architecturally *and* aesthetically into your theatre space. Remember that ramps can be angled in any direction. What direction would create the best movement flow onto the stage? The solution that Steve Holliday created for our theatre fit our unique architectural limitations, and also resulted in enhanced flow for actor movement patterns. Our space configuration coupled with our stage height led to a ramp of a length that fit perfectly when placed parallel to the front of the stage, but your space might fare better with a different design, perhaps a hanimichi-style ramp, like that used in the Kabuki Theatre of Japan, which juts out into the audience at a 45– or 90–degree angle.

Make sure that the architect or consultant who designs your theatre or modifications to it understands accessibility issues *and* the unique needs of theatre architecture. If he doesn't, have an expert in technical theatre design look over his plans *before* you approve them. Theatres which are designed without an understanding of how actors, directors, and designers use theatre space end up with bad acoustics, poor audience sightlines, limited options for actor movement flow, little or no wing space offstage, no fly space above the stage for scenery and lighting, and a myriad of other frustrating architectural problems.

ORTHOPEDIC DISABILITIES

Students who have orthopedic disabilities can participate in most of the typical activities done in the drama classroom. Focus on exercises that develop students' imaginations, verbal abilities, facial expressions, and physical expressiveness in the parts of their bodies which they *can* move.

Adaptive devices like wheelchairs were invented to give the people who use them as much mobility as possible. When acting out stories and scenes, let students who use wheelchairs move around the room just as they normally would at home or on the playground. If a child has cerebral palsy or is paralysed and is unable to move his wheelchair by himself, an assistant can move it for him. There's no reason why Little Red Riding Hood can't go to her grandmother's house in her wheelchair or why the Big Bad Wolf can't follow her in his!

Students in the drama classes I teach for Saturday's Rainbow, a recreation program for children who have orthopedic disabilities, do many of the same activities that students in a regular creative drama class would do. We usually start with a Go-Around or an Imagination Warm-up, then I tell a story, and we act it out together. (See Chapter Six for the structure of a typical creative drama session and Chapter Seven for some drama games that can be successfully incorporated into your lesson plan.)

When guiding the creation of a character, whether it is improvised or scripted, place an emphasis first on the development of the actor's emotional connection with the character and then on his ability to express himself through the dialogue with words and sound. You can include as much movement in scenes and games as your student feels comfortable with.

Every student will be different. Some may feel very comfortable with their bodies and enjoy joining in a spirited aerobic warm-up for the upper body, a relay race, a pantomime game, or a wheelchair dance. Others may feel more inhibited. Gauge your use of movement by the ability and comfort level of the individual.

A wheelchair takes up more space than a body does; therefore, the more wheelchairs in a classroom, the larger your classroom should be in order to

Wheelchairs provide mobility so an actor with an or-thopedic disability can move anywhere he wants on stage and play any kind of role.
(Photo by Allison Walker)

accommodate wheelchair maneuverability. Wheelchair traffic jams can be frustrating and dangerous. When teaching at Saturday's Rainbow where almost everyone uses a wheelchair, I avoid playing games that require a great deal of chair movement because of space limitations in the classroom and because I know students' movement needs will be met in the wheelchair sports session held in the gym during another period. If I had more space, I would feel comfortable including almost any kind of movement game in my lesson plans.

If you are uncertain what type of physical activities are appropriate for your students, National Handicapped Sports can provide you with information on adaptive aerobics, dance, and games for individuals with different kinds of physical disabilities. Contact the Association for Theatre and Disability to find out if there is a dance company in your area that incorporates individuals with physical disabilities in their work. They could advise you on appropriate adaptive movement warm-ups, wheelchair dancing, and games. A recreation therapist who specializes in adaptive physical education could also advise you on ways to appropriately incorporate movement activities into your lesson plan. Other professionals who might offer advice include exercise physiologists, physical therapists, doctors of sports/rehabilitation medicine, or dance/movement therapists who specialize in orthopedic populations.* (See Appendix II for contact information.)

Take a look at your theatre game repertoire to see how you can adapt different activities in order to bypass your students' physical limitations. For instance, a game like "Fruit Salad," in which players sitting in a circle exchange seats whenever their fruit name is called out, could be adapted into one where players change *places*. Places can be delineated on the floor with a taped X and wheelchairs can be moved at the appropriate time to a new location in the circle.

If you can't figure out how to adapt a game or, if in a mainstream situation, the student's movement limitations would put him at a disadvantage to the others in the class, don't play that game. There are hundreds of drama games from which to choose. Choose one that stresses activities and actions that your student *can* do. Let everyone participate from their strengths.

Although it is not necessary to do so, there are many creative ways to incorporate an assistive device into a story, play, or scene. A wheelchair can become the King's throne, the Queen's carriage, a horse, a machine, a boat, or an automobile. A walker can be transformed into a storefront for a merchant, moving camouflage that the hero hides behind, or a cage for a wild animal. Through the use of the imagination, crutches can be turned into a rifle, a battering ram, or the wings of a bird.

A FEW WORDS ABOUT CEREBRAL PALSY

Cerebral palsy is a condition caused by damage to the brain and it affects the brain's ability to control motor functioning in the muscles of the body. There are many causes, including pre-natal trauma, infection of the mother during pregnancy with German measles or another viral disease, lead poisoning, head injuries, and insufficient oxygen to the brain during birth. Affecting both movement and posture, cerebral palsy can range from mild to severe. It can affect the whole body or only part of it (e.g, only the arms or only the legs or only one side). In addition to movement impair-

---

* When looking for a dance or movement therapist as a consultant, make sure their credentials are D.T.R. or A.D.T.R., which means they have been registered by the American Dance Therapy Association. There are many people who call themselves dance or movement therapists who have little or no training.

ment, a person with cerebral palsy may have muscle spasms, involuntary movements, slurred speech, speech delays, and difficulty with sight, hearing, or other sensory perceptions.

Students with cerebral palsy might use a wheelchair, crutches, or a walker, or they might be actively mobile and able to participate in any kind of physical activity. It all depends on the severity of the condition and the parts of the body affected by the disorder. As with other orthopedic disabilities, adjust your class movement activities to the specific abilities and interests of your students.

People who have cerebral palsy fall into the full range of cognitive processing abilities. Some have average intelligence; some have above average intelligence; and about 25 percent have cognitive disabilities. Don't assess your student's cognitive abilities on the basis of physical appearance, speech, or motor coordination. A child who has cerebral palsy can have speech that is so slurred or movements that are so spasmodic, that he "appears" to be mentally retarded. However, the chances are that his mental functioning is completely normal. If you are unsure, ask the child's parents or check with his teachers at school.

Slurred speech can pose a problem in dramatic production where clear diction is important for the audience to understand what the actors are saying. Encourage your actor to take his time and form each word completely before going on to the next. A slower delivery of a line which sounds clearer and more distinct is better than a quickly delivered line which sounds muddy. The key to clear stage diction is to use the consonants in words. Consonants are what creates each word's sound shape. Ending each word clearly with its final consonant (if it has one) will help separate the sound of one word from the next.

Many students who have speech difficulties regularly go to speech therapy. You might suggest the student work on his lines with his therapist. Working on a project that the child is excited and motivated about instead of an abstract speech exercise can often yield positive results.

Understanding the subtext and the intention of the lines and then communicating that to the audience is ultimately more important for an actor than impeccable diction. Even if a student's lines remain slurred, the audience will understand most of what is happening by reading the actor's emotions, tone of voice, intensity, and relationship with the other characters.

A good director can enhance the meaning of a scene by creating clear stage pictures and providing the actors with motivated blocking and stage business that express the dramatic action of the scene.*

One of the issues that has come up in relation to cerebral palsy, at least in mainstreaming situations at the Academy, has been the issue of salivary overflow or, as it is commonly called, drooling. Unfortunately, many people have negative reactions to drooling and this can cause problems when you are trying to help a student seek acceptance in a class in which positive social interaction is important.

The physical reality is that no one has conscious control over his salivary glands. Most people are able to swallow saliva when it builds up in their mouths. Some people (not all) who have cerebral palsy don't have this ability and the saliva stays in their mouths, building up until, with nowhere else to go, it must come out.

I have read a number of articles—some angry, some humorous—by individuals who have cerebral palsy and who involuntarily drool. They don't like drooling any better than anyone else, but they accept it as a fact of their lives. Surgical solutions have been tried for drooling, but they don't offer great success rates. Barrier creams and pump devices have been invented, but aren't really practical.

Speech therapists sometimes recommend chewing gum because the chewing action forces the chewer to swallow periodically. Sometimes a quiet reminder from the teacher to "swallow" works. If you have a sink in your room and are worried about hygiene issues, you could suggest to your student that he wash his hands before class or before a game that involves touching or holding hands. The most practical solution (and the one that puts the individual in control of the situation) seems to be for the student to carry a towel or to wear a terry cloth arm band to wipe away excess drips. If a student who has a drooling problem doesn't use one of these methods, you

---

* *Stage pictures* are the pictures created by the actors' bodies in relationship to each other and to the stage setting. *Blocking* is the theatre term which means movement by an actor on stage. *Stage business* refers to gestures, use of props, and other physical actions (besides blocking) which an actor uses to physically express his character. Stage pictures, blocking, and stage business are three of the tools the director has for expressing the *dramatic action* or what is emotionally happening between the characters in a play.

might suggest one of them. The best thing to do is to model accepting behavior for your nondisabled students. Students always take their cues from the adults in charge. If you are "grossed out" or "turned off" by a student's drooling and show it, the other students in the class will pick up on your attitude and mirror it. If you act as if it is no big deal, they will probably begin to feel this way, too.

You might be able to address the issue indirectly in a creative drama class by acting out a story like "Beauty and the Beast" or "The Ugly Duckling" which deals with outer ugliness and inner beauty.

If you think drooling needs to be addressed more directly (for instance, if fellow students are refusing to hold the student's hand or are making rude comments), sit down and have an open discussion about the situation. (See articles by Caleen Sinette Jennings and Kathryn Chase Bryer in Chapter Eleven for descriptions of how to do this in a sensitive manner.) Ultimately, you and your students must learn to look beyond physical appearance and accept the person inside.

BLINDNESS

In the United States, the term "blindness" is used to refer to someone who has vision of less than 20/200 in the better eye, even with corrective lenses. That is, when 20 feet away from an object, he sees—at best—what someone with normal vision would see at 200 feet. Most blind people are not totally blind, but have varying amounts of visual perception. Some can see light, but not shapes. Others are limited in their fields of vision; for instance, they may not have any peripheral vision or they may not be able to see out of one eye. Different terms for vision impairments include "partially sighted," "low vision," and "legally blind." Blindness can be congenital or caused by diseases such as glaucoma and diabetes, retinal disintegration, muscular disorders, cataracts, infection, or injury to the eye or optic nerve.

Children who are blind need lots of aural, tactile, and kinesthetic stimulation to make up for the information which they miss visually. They need to learn how to structure their environment and remember spatial relationships, so they can function independently. With encouragement to take risks, they can become confident, self-reliant, and independent.

Only five to ten percent of people who are blind learn to read braille, the raised dot system invented in 1824 by Louis Braille. Others access written information through tape recordings or large print material.

When teaching blind students, speak clearly and at a normal pace and volume level. There is no need to shout. Blind people are blind, not hard of hearing.

Remember that many nonverbal communication cues like facial expressions, shaking the head yes and no, shoulder shrugs, and hand gestures are visual communications that cannot be picked up without sight. You will need to verbalize these nonverbal cues.

Many times when we speak to others or ask them to do something, we initiate the interaction with eye contact. You might look at Johnny and say, "Go to the front of the room and perform your monologue now." A blind student will not know you are looking at him or talking to him, unless you address him by name first. "Johnny, go to the front of the room and perform your monologue now."

In a similar vein, a blind person will not know who is around him unless the individuals who are there identify themselves. While he may have a good memory for voices, don't rely on it and don't play "guess who this is" all the time. It is good manners to let a blind student know when someone is entering or leaving the group or the classroom. You might say, "Phil is walking over here. Hi, Phil." If Phil decides to leave after your conversation, he should say goodbye or indicate verbally that he is leaving. If he doesn't, you could say, "Bye, Phil," or "Phil just went over to the other side of the room."

Warn a blind person before you touch him. Tell him if you are reaching out to shake hands.

Often in drama, ideas and instructions are shared through demonstrating an activity, rather than talking about it. Blind students will not be able to see your demonstration. You will need to translate your demonstration into words. If appropriate, you could have your blind students follow your demonstration through touch. For instance, if you were demonstrating how to play The Magic Stick, a pantomime game described in Chapter Seven, and you were pretending the stick was a spyglass, you could say "I am putting one end of the stick up to my right eye and pretending that I am looking through it." Or you could allow the blind student to put his hands on the stick and you to feel the placement of it in relation to your body.

Not all people who are blind read braille. Some need to have scripts read out loud to them or put on audiotape. (Photo by Keith Jenkins)

Many blind people report that their most frustrating and frequently occurring experience is sighted people who jump in and "help" them before finding out if help is actually needed. Always ask before you help. It may be that your student can get around fine on his own and doesn't need any assistance.

If a student has a cane, do not move it from where he has placed it. He has put it where it is easily within reach. He will need to find it later on. If your student has a guide dog, remember that it is not a pet, but a highly trained assistant. Tell your other students from the outset not to feed or play with it. If the children in the class are young and have difficulty understanding this concept, you could talk about other animals that have jobs to do and act them out.

If you do need to guide your student from one place to another, the proper way is to offer your arm and let him hold onto your elbow. He will take his movement cues from the movement of your body. Pick a pace that is easy for him to follow — not too fast and not too slow. Describe obstacles coming up and how to proceed around them: turn right, turn left, step up, step down, etc. If right and left are confusing concepts say, "Turn in my direction" or "Turn in your direction." "This way" or "that way" doesn't mean a thing to someone who can't see where you are pointing. It's a good idea to describe distances in terms of number of feet rather than number of steps as different people have different lengths of stride.

When you lead a blind person to a seat, don't push him down in it. Put his hand on the back or the arm of the chair and he will use that as his reference point. He can take it from there.

Don't feel awkward about using expressions that refer to sight like "See you next week" or "You're looking good today." Your use of language will not be interpreted as insulting or demeaning. People with visual impairments use those words and expressions, too.

Blind students need to feel as much a part of the class as possible. When other students are performing or presenting an exercise in which physical actions happen, assign a sighted student or an assistant to describe what is happening to a student who is blind.

There are many drama games that can be done sitting in a circle. Start with these while your blind students are getting adjusted to the class. Many games highlight and develop tactile and aural sensitivities. I had one blind student whose hearing was so acute that if another student made a noise to indicate his location, she could throw a ball directly to him.

Don't avoid activities which get students up on their feet and moving around. Blind people love to dance, pantomime, play movement games, and use their bodies just like sighted people do. Before you turn your students loose, however, make sure your acting area is open and free of obstacles. If your floor is carpeted, check to see that all the edges lie flat and there are no loose strings to trip on. If your floor is waxed, be sure the surface is not too slick and slippery.

When considering performance opportunities for blind students, many people jump to the conclusion that Readers theatre is the perfect style of performance to use because movement is limited. Readers theatre is a style of performance in which the actors sit on stage and read their lines instead of memorizing them and moving around. Readers theatre is a great way to develop oral interpretation skills because the entire performance is created through the actors' voices. Like radio theatre, Readers theatre relies on the audience's imaginations rather than the physical production to bring the story to life. Since little is performed visually, the entire play must be communicated through dialogue and sound. This type of theatre is an excellent challenge for any student of acting. It trains verbal dexterity and vocal variety. Remember, however, that not all blind people read braille and may, therefore, have a difficult time reading their lines!

Acting involves the voice *and* the body. Don't limit blind students to a style of theatre which limits the development of their acting skills. Blind actors have the ability to move as skillfully on a stage set as they do in their own homes. Spike the furniture on your stage so that each time you set up for rehearsal the spatial relationships are the same.* Then give the blind actors time to explore the space and memorize the distance between the objects.

Use sounds or lines of dialogue for cues in places where sighted actors would follow visual cues.

If your student reads braille, you can type up scripts and assignments for him on a braille typewriter. Computer programs exist which can translate information typed onto a disk into braille. Then the script can be printed out in braille, when the computer is connected to a braille computer printer. To save typing work, there is even a device, similar to the bar-code scanner in supermarkets, which can "read" print from a book and translate it into computer language. Check with local support groups for the blind or schools for the blind to locate brailling equipment or computer programs that can be rented, borrowed, or bought. Some organizations will do braille translating for you for a fee (usually a combination of an hourly rate for the time the project takes plus a charge per braille page).

If your student doesn't read braille or if brailling equipment is too expensive or difficult to find, scenes and monologue assignments can be sent home on tape.

---

* *Spiking* is a theatre term which means marking the placement of furniture or a set piece on stage by placing tape on the floor around its legs or along an upper edge. The item can then be placed in exactly the same position each night. Spiking is also used to make scene changes go faster. The spike marks show the stage crew exactly where each piece should be placed.

DEAFNESS

Estimates place the number of Americans with a hearing loss of some type at 21 million. The vast majority are hard of hearing, while about 2 million are deaf. Very few people are "stone deaf"; that is, they hear nothing. Most deaf and hard of hearing people can hear certain frequencies of sound, but not others. It is all a matter of degree.

Hearing losses may be present from birth or may develop at any time during a person's life. They can range from mild to severe. They can be caused by heredity, birth defects, accident, or illness. Hearing aids amplify sound for certain types of hearing loss, but not for others.

Deafness is not connected to intelligence in any way. The term "deaf and dumb," which meant not being able to hear and speak, went out of vogue long ago because it led hearing people to the mistaken belief that deaf people were stupid. Needless to say, this is not so. There are all ranges of intelligence in deaf people, just as there are in hearing people.

The primary challenge of deafness is language development and communication. The early acquisition of language is essential for the development of thought and cognitive processes. It is also essential for academic, vocational, and social success throughout life. *The Miracle Worker,* a play about deaf-blind Helen Keller, is about the struggle of a child who has no language, and, therefore, no clear method of communication or socialization. In the play, Annie Sullivan, the teacher who finally breaks through the isolation imposed by Helen's physical disabilities, says, "Language is to the mind more than light is to the eye. . . . What is she without words? With them she can think, have ideas, be reached, there's not a thought or fact in the world that can't be hers."

The human brain seems to be "hard-wired" for the bulk of language development to take place in the early years, from infancy to the age of five or six. This is why it is so easy for a young child to learn a second or third language and why it is so difficult for someone who is older. A hearing child passively picks up sound from the moment of birth and receives continuous aural language stimulation throughout his early years. Even when people aren't talking to him directly, he hears what is being said around him, absorbing a great deal of information about how people relate to each other and how the world works. A child who is born deaf or who loses his hearing at an early age, misses that constant aural exposure. The appropriate substitute for deaf children is to receive constant visual language stimulation through signs, gestures, facial expressions, fingerspelling, or cued speech.

Without language, deaf children truly become handicapped. With a language, be it spoken, signed, or cued, deaf children can function as well as hearing children.

There is a lot of controversy in the deaf and hearing communities about the best way to teach language and communication to deaf children. For many years hearing educators insisted on oral communication, teaching deaf children to speak and to speechread. (The term most hearing people are familiar with is "lipread.") Sign language was forbidden in schools for the deaf. Many deaf adults tell stories about how they were punished when they were caught signing at school.

Oral communication has many drawbacks. The major one is speechreading. Only about 30 percent of the sounds of the English language are visible on the lips and 50 percent of *them* look identical. B and P, for instance, are formed with the same lip shape. B is voiced while P is not.

Cued Speech is a recent communication development. It is a system of hand shapes, created in the late 1960s by Dr. R. Orin Cornett, which represent all the different consonant and vowel sounds in the English language. Used as people speak to each other, cued speech signals clarify the visual similarity of lip shapes and solve the difficulty of speechreading. Cued speech is sometimes the preferred communication choice of people who have lost their hearing after they have acquired spoken English.

The communication method preferred by much of the deaf community is sign language. American Sign Language (ASL) is a visual language developed by the deaf for the deaf. It was imported from France in 1817 by Thomas Hopkins Gallaudet, an American, hearing educator, and Laurent Clerc, a French, deaf educator who had taught for many years in schools for the deaf in France.

Many signs in ASL are based on natural gesture; that is, they look like the action or the object they symbolize. ASL syntax and grammar are as different from English as English is from Swahili. In ASL, sentences are structured with the time element first, followed by object, subject, and verb. Negatives and modifiers are placed after the verb. This contrasts with English grammar, which is structured "Subject-Verb-Object." For instance, in English you say, "I'm going to the store now," but in ASL, you sign, "Now store me go" or "Now store go me." ASL also has its own idioms and figures of speech. If someone doesn't get a joke, in English you say, "You missed the boat." In ASL, you sign "Train gone."

ASL is a visual concept language involving the whole body: hands, eyes, facial expression, body tension, and directional inclination. One sign can be expressed in a wide variety of ways and each time takes on the many different shades of meaning that English offers through word choice and tone of voice.

Fingerspelling supplements signs. In fingerspelling, each letter in a word is formed individually using the right or left hand. The word is literally spelled out for the viewer.

Signed English, Seeing Essential English (SEE 1), Signing Exact English (SEE 2), Manually Coded English (MCE), and Pidgin Signed English (PSE) are all sign language systems that involve deaf signs with English sentence structure. They are used most often by hearing people who sign and don't think in ASL, or by teachers at deaf schools who are teaching correct English grammar.

Most deaf people are able to speak. However, even with many years of intensive speech therapy, a deaf person has difficulty creating the same pitches, intonations, and tones that hearing people do. This is because part of the speaking process involves an ongoing self-monitoring of the voice in which the speaker listens to and modulates his voice as he speaks. Deaf people can't hear how they sound and, therefore, can't make those adjustments. Without the ability to self-monitor, their voices can sound flat or high or off-key. Many hearing people jump to the mistaken conclusion that this unusual-sounding speech is a sign of low intelligence and treat the deaf person as if he has mental retardation. Because of this misunderstanding, some deaf people choose not to speak.

People who are deaf have a whole culture of their own of which the hearing world is often unaware. In fact, many deaf people don't see themselves as members of a disability group; they feel deafness puts them instead into a cultural minority. There is a lot of pride in deaf culture. Deaf artists create deaf poetry, drama, and prose. Many communities across the country have their own theatre of the deaf which presents plays in a highly theatrical, visually poetic version of ASL. More and more deaf actors and

Deaf student signing a song. (Photo by Lea Ann Rosen)

performers are becoming known in the hearing world as their talents show up on the professional stage, and in television and film.

Many devices have been invented that make functioning in the modern world easier for deaf people. A Telecommunication Device for the Deaf (TDD), which has a keyboard and video screen, can send visual messages to other TDDs over phone lines, providing deaf people with a communication mechanism in lieu of telephones. Your organization will need one of these if you want to communicate with deaf students and patrons.

When a deaf student signs up for a drama class, the first thing to ascertain is which communication system he uses. A student who uses cued speech will not necessarily understand sign language and vice versa. If the teacher does not know the preferred communication system, it may be necessary to employ an interpreter. Contact an interpreting service organization in your area or call RID, the Registry of Interpreters for the Deaf, for their Interpreting Service Organizations List or their Membership Directory of Certified Interpreters. (See Appendix II for contact information.)

An interpreter will translate the English spoken by everyone in the room to the deaf person and may function as the deaf person's voice. When using an interpreter, always look at and speak directly to the deaf person. Do not talk to the interpreter. He is only there to facilitate communication, not to interact in the situation.

At the Academy we have on occasion successfully mainstreamed deaf and hard of hearing students into dance and visual arts classes without the services of an interpreter. In these instances, the subject matter was so visual and the teacher's verbal explanations so minimal, that interpretation was unnecessary. Drama classes, which tend to be more verbal, need to be interpreted.

If you are teaching deaf or hard of hearing students, there are a number of things to keep in mind. First, use natural gestures and facial expressions as you speak. The more clearly you express yourself in a physical manner, the more you will communicate your message, not only to your deaf students, but to all your students.

Stand where deaf and hard of hearing students can see your lips. Make sure that your face is in the light, not covered by shadows. If there is a window in the room, don't stand with your back to it. The shadow created by the light hitting your back will obscure your facial features. Stand facing the window or in a profile position to it so the natural light can reach your face.

Fluorescent lighting is very hard on the eyes. If possible, use a room with incandescent or natural lighting. If that kind of lighting is not available, open the blinds to allow as much natural light through the windows of the room as possible.

Remember that deaf students can't hear you. I have watched hearing people, who forgot this, yell at the back of a deaf person and then become enraged when the deaf person did not respond. When you speak, face the deaf student and make sure he is looking at you. If he can't see that you are moving your mouth, he may not know you are talking! You can get his attention by waving your hand or by tapping him gently on the shoulder.

When talking to a deaf person, you don't have to shout or exaggerate your speech. Doing so will distort the shape of your lips as you speak and will make speechreading more difficult. Chewing gum or food will also distort your mouth as you talk.

Keep hands and other objects away from your face, so your facial features can be seen as you talk. Large hats will cover your eyes and obscure your facial expressiveness.

When signing to a deaf person, stand between three and six feet away from the student. At this distance you are close enough for him to see your face clearly and far enough away for him to take in your hands and the rest of your body. Standing too close will make it difficult for the student to focus his eyes on you and to take in the top half of your body (the area in which signs are made).

If a student is speechreading you and has difficulty understanding what you are saying, it could be that you are using words that have sounds that are hard to speechread. Try rephrasing your sentence with different words. If the message still doesn't get across and an interpreter is not available, you can always write a note.

If you are signing yourself, be aware of the colors of the clothing you wear to class. Most signs are placed between the waist and the top of the head. In order for your hands to show up clearly as you sign, the colors on the top half of your body need to contrast with your skin color. For example, if you have light-colored skin, black, brown, dark blue, or purple would be good colors to wear. If you have dark skin, white, yellow, orange, or pastels would probably be best. Choose colors that are easy on the eye. For instance, shocking pink or electric green are hard to look at. Also, it is better to wear solid colors rather than plaids, stripes, or patterns.

Try to avoid creating sudden, loud sounds. Noises like a balloon bursting, a loud whine, or a harsh buzzer may be of a frequency that could irritate a hard of hearing person's ears.

When explaining an idea to deaf students, it is often helpful to offer a number of different examples. This will clarify exactly what you are talking about. To a hearing student I might say, "Today we will do age pantomimes. Act out a character at a specific age and we will guess how old you are." To a deaf student I would sign, "Today we will do age pantomimes. Think of a person and pick an age for him. Maybe he is very old, maybe very young, maybe a baby, maybe 16, maybe 32. I don't know. You decide. Act out how that person moves, walks, sits, whatever."

This kind of explanation contrasts with the way you would explain something to a student with a cognitive disability. One or two well-chosen examples are enough for a person who has cognitive processing difficulties to attend to at one time. For a deaf student, many specific examples flesh out your concept and provide dimension to the idea you want to communicate.

This approach mirrors the manner in which ASL expresses ideas. Often a series of signs listing many items in a category will be used instead of inventing a specific sign for that category. For instance, the word "crime," is described through use of the signs for "kill, stab, steal, etc." "Sports" might be expressed by signing "baseball, football, basketball, etc."

Movement games, pantomime exercises, and activities that stress visual, olfactory, kinesthetic, and tactile strengths will all work very well with deaf students. Many deaf people have excellent rhythmic skills and enjoy dancing and making percussion music.

Place greater emphasis on visuality and on physicality in your choice of exercises than on words. For example, if you were doing a sensory awareness exercise with smells or textures, instead of having the student describe the experience in words, have him translate it into movement. Have the student tell a story through pantomime or through a series of frozen tableaux.

This need to place emphasis on the physical is not because deaf people are not good with language, but because deaf theatre stresses the creation of visual images on stage. Deaf actors, therefore, need to develop the skills that they will use in their community and culture.

However, developing physical expressiveness alone is not enough; link all physical characterization work to an emotional base. For example, a successful pantomime of an old man feeding birds in the park should recreate the old man's feelings about the birds and being alone in the park, as well as technically reproducing his movements. An actor who is not emotionally connected to his work, no matter how brilliant his technique, is boring to watch. Audiences need to feel there is a living, breathing, feeling human being beneath each character they see on stage.

If you have a class with hearing and deaf students mainstreamed together, encourage your hearing students to communicate with their bodies as you encourage your deaf students to improvise with words. When doing scripted or improvisational work, keep the action of the scene and all of the characters within the sightlines of the deaf actors. Whether they are speechreaders *or* signers, deaf actors won't be aware a line has been delivered, if they can't see the delivery. (Hearing people, who can hear what is said even if they aren't looking directly at the speaker, take this for granted.)

Incorporate sign language and sign language games into your mainstreamed classes. ASL is an excellent avenue for teaching the expressive use of gesture and how to make emotional-physical connections to hearing and deaf acting students alike.

Some deaf people do speak and there might be an occasion when a deaf actor is cast in a speaking role. If so, he may need some diction coaching in order to be intelligible to audience members. See the section earlier in this chapter on working with students whose speech is slurred due to cerebral palsy. Focusing on consonant action should help. Practice in diaphragmatic breathing will help with projection and breathiness.* If the student takes speech therapy, he could work on his lines with his therapist.

Above all, don't fall into the stereotyped belief that because deaf students talk with their hands they will necessarily be experts at pantomime or movement activities and poor at verbal ones. I have met deaf people who could use their hands and bodies expressively and others who were physically unexpressive and inhibited. I have met deaf people who are extremely loquacious; I know others who are not. Deaf people are as individual and unique as hearing people. See the person and not the disability.

---

* An indepth discussion of vocal production is beyond the scope of this text. For more information, see *Freeing the Natural Voice* by Kristin Linklater or *The Use and Training of the Human Voice* by Arthur Lessac, two standard texts on the subject.

chapter four

cognitive disabilities

Cognition is the process of knowing. It is one of the major functions of the brain and involves perception, memory, judgment, concept formation, and decision-making among many other brain processes. Cognitive disabilities interfere with the brain's ability to process, organize, understand, store, recall, and use information.

The brain is a very complex human organ. There are millions of neurons (brain cells) and millions of neurological pathways and connections in each individual brain. While brain chemistry may be very similar, no two individuals who have normal cognitive functioning process information in exactly the same way. Because of the intricacy of the brain, cognitive disabilities disrupt brain functioning along a very large continuum. Different categories of disabilities (i.e., learning disabilities, mental retardation, attention deficits, etc.) indicate similarities in processing disturbances, but the ability to function within each category of disturbance varies greatly from one individual to another. As with physical disabilities, people who have cognitive disabilities need to be looked at as unique individuals.

The area of cognitive disabilities is perhaps the one approached with the most trepidation by novices. This may be due to lack of contact. Our educational system tends to shunt those who learn differently off to places where they are not seen frequently and where they don't often interact with the rest of the student population. While this may be done with the best intentions, this kind of structure creates a free-floating suspicion in the minds of the regular education students, as they grow up, that these special education students are too different, too strange, maybe even too dangerous, to participate socially with everyone else. They carry this prejudice with them into adult life and usually have no opportunity to test its validity.

Once you get to know someone who has a cognitive disability, you will begin to throw away those old stereotypes and fears and realize that she is just a person who processes information differently. She might need more time to understand or to respond; she might rely more on different sensory channels than you do (i.e., she might be a visual learner or a kinesthetic learner instead of an auditory learner); she might have difficulty with abstract reasoning and need concrete examples. Whatever her cognitive difficulties, she is still a person who needs and wants to express herself and to connect with other people—and with your help, she can do this better.

This chapter reviews the characteristics of the most common cognitive disabilities and suggests some general ways of involving children with these disabilities in the theatre arts. Later chapters include information on adapting specific drama activities for children with cognitive disabilities.

TYPES OF COGNITIVE DISABILITIES

LEARNING DISABILITIES

Learning Disabilities (LD) is a catch-all phrase which lumps together many different kinds of information-processing difficulties that interfere with an individual's ability to take in information from the world around her or to put a response back out. If you have a learning disability, your ability to learn, to communicate through spoken or written language, and to understand the world around you is affected. Sometimes there is a processing delay and it takes longer to put the message in or to get a response back out. Sometimes the message gets totally scrambled and can't be understood or isn't understood very well. In any case, information-processing is the key.

In our modern age of computers and telecommunications, we usually think of information-processing in reference to machines, not human beings. Actually, the mechanical model is a good reference point, because computers are based in a very simplistic manner on the organic processing system of the human brain. In machines, which are much less complex creations than we are, the input and output of information is channeled through switches that code data as it is entered into the unit to tell the machine what to do. For example, a computer takes in information through its keyboard and processes the information inside its central processing unit through various electronic circuits. When a response is called for by the operator of the computer, the machine retrieves the processed information on the video display screen or through the printer.

In human beings, data enters through the sense organs and travels to the brain, the information-processing center, via the nerves through electrical impulses. The brain sifts through, evaluates, and comprehends the data. Then the nerves send electrical impulses back to the speech center, the fingers, the face, the legs, or whatever part of the body needs to respond to the processed information.

A person with a learning disability might have a deficit somewhere in her visual, auditory, tactile, olfactory, taste, vestibular, or kinesthetic channels. The problem is not with her eyes, ears, skin, nose, taste buds, or balance sensors, per se. In fact, when tested, the sense organs of a child with LD might show no organic dysfunction at all. The problem is somewhere in one of the millions of pathways into the brain from these organs or out of the brain to the muscles which regulate the body.

No one has a perfect brain. In any given human body a number of connections are bound to be blocked or poorly developed. This means that the cognitive functioning of each individual will fall somewhere on a wide continuum of information-processing abilities. Viewed from this perspective, it's quite possible that almost everyone could be said to have some kind of learning disability. Individuals who are diagnosed as LD just happen to have blockages that impede their learning and, therefore, the blockages in their information-processing systems become obvious. Medical scientists don't know for sure what causes learning disabilities. Research indicates a wide range of possible origins including genetic inheritance, lack of enough oxygen during birth, fetal alcohol syndrome, drugs ingested by the mother during pregnancy, lead poisoning, poor diet, allergies or high sensitivities to environmental chemicals, a tumor or lesion in the brain or neural pathway, damage from sudden vascular change, or injury due to brain trauma.

Some learning disabilities have specific names. Dyslexia is the inability to process words and letters well. It affects the ability to read and spell. Dyslexia primarily involves a visual deficit, but there are auditory, kinesthetic, and tactile deficits involved as well. Students who have dyslexia will often reverse letters, seeing "d" instead of "b," or "g" instead of "p." They also reverse the placement of letters within words, reading "saw" instead of "was."

Dysgraphia is difficulty with creating written language or encoding sound into a visual, kinesthetically produced symbol. Dyscalculia is poor math ability. There are many other learning disabilities and combinations of LDs that don't have fancy Greek names. Individuals who have auditory processing problems can physically hear speech, but have difficulty sorting through sounds to make sense of what they hear. For example, a student might be able to hear the teacher talking, but not be able to sort out her words from all the other sounds in the room. Normal auditory functioning allows us to focus on the speaker and block out background noise. Without that ability the world becomes a confusing and chaotic place!

Sometimes special education experts break learning disabilities down into four categories which focus on the different academic areas affected: difficulties with spoken language (speech or language delays), difficulties with written language (dyslexia and dysgraphia), difficulties with math (dyscalculia), and reasoning impairments (organizing and integrating thoughts, making decisions and judgments).

Whatever the source and whatever the category or name, learning disabilities cause many similar behavior symptoms in students. The following list highlights the most common. Some children exhibit a few of these symptoms; some exhibit many:

- poor listening skills
- poor eye contact
- low frustration tolerance
- restlessness
- active or hyperactive
- easily distractible
- coordination problems
- poor gross motor skills
- poor fine motor skills
- poor hand-eye coordination
- poor spatial awareness
- difficulty expressing themselves in words

- difficulty forming words and sounds correctly
- difficulty with directional concepts such as up and down
- difficulty with time concepts
- difficulty with sequencing (putting actions or items in order)
- difficulty dealing with more than one item at a time
- poor memory skills
- poor abstract reasoning skills
- poor problem-solving skills
- poor decision-making skills
- difficulty making transitions
- rigidity and inflexibility
- very emotionally labile, shifting between moods quickly and (to the "normal" adult observer) for no apparent reason
- little impulse control
- unsophisticated
- emotionally immature
- poor social skills
- low self-esteem

The good news is that these processing difficulties don't have anything to do with the child's intelligence. By definition, students with learning disabilities are of normal to above normal intelligence. Moreover, LD students can be gifted and talented in many areas.

While LDs can lead to failure in the academic classroom without appropriate support and teaching, they don't necessarily lead to failure in the arts. Many students with LD can express themselves through movement, sound, and facial expression more clearly than they can through words. Suddenly, with an appropriate outlet for all the feelings and impressions they have been wanting to express, they change from inarticulate balls of frustration into graceful, funny, angry, focused, eloquent actors and actresses.

Faye was twelve years old and had so many emotions bottled up inside her that sometimes she seemed ready to explode. She was not allowed to express these feelings in school or at home and with no outlet, they became all the more intense. (Well, I shouldn't say she never expressed them. Some-

times she *did* and then she got into trouble because she expressed them inappropriately!)

When she signed up for my creative drama class, everyone from her teachers to the principal of the school told me, "You'll love Faye—she's *quite* dramatic." Their tone of voice seemed to add "And you're going to have your hands

Drama allows kids with special needs an appropriate, creative outlet for their feelings and ideas. (Photo by Keith Jenkins)

full!" As it turned out, Faye was not a handful—she was delightful. As herself, Faye had trouble saying what was on her mind, but give her a character to act out and she could play every shade of emotion that person was experiencing. In one session we acted out "Cinderella" three different times. She went from playing the most long-suffering, mournful Cinderella I'll ever see (complete with real tears when she couldn't go to the ball) to the meanest, nastiest, most spiteful Evil Stepmother who ever walked the face of the earth, to a Fairy Godmother so loving and kind you wished she were your own.

Success is hard to come by in the academic classroom. There is only one correct way to spell most words. There is only one right answer to "What is the capital of Outer Mongolia?" 2 + 2 only equals 4. In drama, however, there are many right answers and few wrong ones. In fact, for many improvisations and theatre games, the more answers you can generate to a question, the better. How does the color red make you feel? Angry, happy, excited, energized, on fire, and hungry are all correct answers. There are many different ways to act out an old man, a butterfly, a boy flying a kite, because those creatures behave differently in different situations.

In a drama class, students who have LDs have the opportunity to use an alternate, stronger method of expressing their ideas. If they're not so good with words, they can use sound and movement. If they're not very coordinated, but they're great with facial expressions, they can say what they need to say that way. If they can't read, but they can make up dialogue on the spot, they can become experts at improvisation. As long as they are expressing an idea the best way they can, they've succeeded. And they deserve applause.

When teaching LD students, you may need to proceed at a slower pace than you normally would so students have more time for processing what you are saying. If your normal speaking rhythm is fast, slow down a little. Take a pause now and then. Too much information given all at once can be confusing. Allow students processing time so they can keep up with you.

By the same token, directions to an exercise or game given all at once can be overwhelming. Students may not be sure which action needs to be done first, second, third, etc. and because of this sequencing confusion, they might forget one or more of the steps in the process. Break instructions down into small steps and present them one at a time. For instance, instead of saying, "Everyone find a partner and line up by the window back to back." You might say, "Everyone find a partner." When everyone has a partner, then you would say, "Bring your partner over here by the window." When everyone is on the correct side of the room, you can say, "Line up with your partner." After they are lined up, you can tell them to stand back to back.

Clarity in explanation is important. Rather than offering three or four different examples, choose one good one to get your point across succinctly. If you were assigning a pantomime and said, "I want you to pantomime flying a kite. Think of all the different problems you might encounter: there might be no wind, there might be too much wind, your string might get tangled, your dog might come by and run away with the kite, the kite might get blown up into the branches of a tree . . ." you may be providing students with too many images to simultaneously hold in their short-term memory. By the time they have visualized the first image, they may have forgotten the later ones or vice versa.

One clearly presented example can serve to get your point across just fine. "I want you to pantomime flying a kite. Let's imagine one problem you might have while trying to fly a kite. Suppose there was no wind and you couldn't get the kite up into the air. What might happen?" Have someone act out that situation. Then ask for students to think of other situations to act out.

In a similar vein, learning how to make choices is important, but offering too many options to students can be confusing and frustrating. Present two choices instead of three or four. Instead of asking, "Which would you rather do first—listen to a story, draw a picture, sing a song, or play a game?" ask "Would you rather listen to a story or play a game?"

Exercises, examples, and activities should be as concrete as possible. Some beginning drama games that involve pantomime of "invisible" objects or manipulation of an imaginary concept are difficult for many LD students. For example, Space Balls is a pantomime game in which an imaginary ball is created from the shape of your hands and the space between them. The Space Ball is passed around the circle. Each person makes the Space Ball bigger or smaller or heavier or lighter before passing it on to the next person. LD beginners, having nothing concrete or real to focus on, often have difficulty manipulating the imaginary ball, keeping its shape, and following its progress around the circle. A more concrete pantomime game like The Magic Stick, which puts an actual object into the student's hand, will often be more successful. (See Chapter Seven for more examples of how to make abstract games concrete.)

Teachers in the academic classroom often carefully structure the physical environment for their LD students to help them create order for sensory input which can seem overwhelming and chaotic to them. A child's desk may be divided into specific areas for specific supplies or types of work. Places in the classroom might be color coded or labeled to delineate where books, supplies, and materials are to be kept. Work areas in the classroom are laid out in configurations that aid in concentration and give students a feeling of safety and containment. Schedules are often consistent from day to day or carefully laid out for students at the beginning of each day so they know what to expect.

A drama classroom is usually an open space without many of the physical structures that help LD students define their boundaries and focus their attentions in the academic classroom. Usually there are no desks and often there are no chairs. Structure must be added for children who cannot create structure on their own. If students have difficulty sitting in a circle or staying in their own place while sitting, create a circle on the floor with colored tape and, if necessary, tape X's at intervals on the circle to indicate where each student should sit. Small carpet squares are also useful for delineating clear seating areas and have the added flexibility of being able to be moved to any part of the room and placed in any configuration. Chapter Five will go into more detail about how to structure the physical space, your lesson plan, and your teaching style.

Certain types of learning disabilities create specific challenges for the drama teacher. A student who has dyslexia or another reading disorder should not be put on the spot to read a script out loud in class. If you must do script work, you could give her the script a week in advance to work on at home with her parents or you could provide an advance copy of the script on tape so she can listen to it and familiarize herself with it at home. If these strategies prove to be unsuccessful, you might want to forget about script work and focus instead on creating characters and scenes through improvisation.

Students who have auditory processing problems may have difficulty understanding verbal directions or listening to stories. If a student with an auditory processing problem doesn't seem to be getting your message, it will be useless to raise your voice. The issue is not one of volume. Provide her with visual images that support your verbal instructions. Write your directions on the blackboard or explain your idea through a chart or diagram. Use gestures and physical demonstrations to clarify your meaning. Write out homework assignments or class rules on a separate sheet of paper to be taken home. When telling stories, show pictures of the characters. If your students read well, you could use a picture book with large print and let them help you read the story out loud. They will then be able to focus on the visual words and imagery and allow that to supplement the auditory information.

After a run-through of a play, directors typically give their actors "notes" or comments on things to change or improve. Most directors give notes verbally and the actors write them down to review later. An actor who has an auditory processing problem or one who has dysgraphia will have difficulty with this task. One option is to ask an assistant or another actor who is able to help to write down your comments for her. Another possibility is to type up your notes for this actor after rehearsal and give them to her at the next rehearsal.

SPEECH AND LANGUAGE DISORDERS

Speech disorders involve difficulties in producing speech sounds or problems with vocal quality. People who have speech disorders may have problems with articulation, pitch, volume, and/or quality of the voice. They may be unable to form certain consonant sounds, such as "l," "r," or "th." Stuttering, a speech disorder that affects more than a million people in the U.S., interrupts the rhythmic flow of words.

A language disorder involves inability or delay in understanding and/or using words in context. A person with a receptive language disorder might see or hear a word, but not be able to understand its meaning. A person with an expressive language disorder may understand a word's meaning, but not be able to use the word herself. She may have difficulty with semantics (the proper use of words and their meanings) and generalize one word to mean many others. For instance, a student may use the word "chair" when referring to any kind of furniture. She may use inappropriate grammatical patterns: she might say, "Me go store" instead of "I'm going to the store." She may have a limited vocabulary or may develop language at a slower pace than children of a comparable age. As a result of these language impairments, she may have difficulty understanding others, following directions, or expressing her own ideas.

Speech and language disorders can be the only disability a person has or they can be coupled with learning disabilities, mental retardation, autism, or cerebral palsy. It has been estimated that one quarter of the students in special education programs in this country's public schools in 1988-89 had some kind of speech or language disorder.

Give students with speech and language delays the opportunity to express themselves through pantomime and movement as much as possible.

These are skills that they can use to supplement their vocal communication and they need to develop them. However, don't limit their opportunities to use words whenever they can or whenever they want to; they need practice in this mode of communication, too!

If a student has difficulty expressing herself in words, give her time to process and/or formulate what she wants to say. She will never learn how to express herself verbally if she is not given a chance to practice. Waiting for a response can be hard if other students do not have language delays or if they have short attention spans. If other students show impatience, remind them that each person in the class has the right to express her ideas and opinions and this particular student just needs a little more time to get her ideas out. If the class is involved in a Go-Around type of exercise where each person says or does something in turn, you might be able to give the student who has the delay more time to formulate her response by passing over her turn and coming back to her when she is ready.

If you have a student who stutters or who has difficulty forming certain sounds, you can reword the difficult words in a script to make them easier to say. For instance, one of the characters in a play was named Penelope Pittstop. Two of the actors who had to say her name had trouble with the "p" sound. So we changed "Yes, Ms. Pittstop," to "Yes, Ma'am."

Sometimes people who stutter find that they don't stutter when they are singing. Country singer Mel Tillis is a prime example of this. If your student enjoys singing, you could showcase her talents through a song, rather than through a monologue or scene. Songs are actually highly emotional monologues put to music. A well-structured song, particularly one from a musical play, will have the same emotional and thought progression as any well-written dramatic speech. Through the song, the character evaluates how she is feeling and what she is going to do about it, sometimes going through a character change or making an important decision by the end of the song. Good singers are emotionally connected to their material and act a song as well as sing it.

ATTENTION DEFICITS

Attention Deficit Disorder (ADD) and Attention Deficit Hyperactivity Disorder (ADHD) are cognitive processing disabilities involving the sensory processing systems of the brain. Both disorders involve distractibility and an inability to focus attention on one thing for an extended period of time. Frequently poor muscular coordination and poor spatial awareness are symptoms as well.

ADHD has the additional components of hyperactivity and extreme impulsivity. Some experts think that the hyperactive behavior displayed by ADHD children is due to their attempts to stimulate their under-aroused nervous systems, which are missing vital neurotransmitters—chemicals which carry sensory messages to and from the brain.

Because of their impulsivity, many children with ADHD have difficulty inhibiting aggressive behaviors. In times of stress, they find it hard to stop and think things through; they just react. Often this gets them into conflicts with peers, siblings, parents, and teachers. Attention deficit disorders affect every aspect of a child's life from sleep to work to play.

Experts estimate that between 5 and 10 percent of school-aged children in the United States have ADD or ADHD. About half of these children with ADD/ADHD have a learning disability in addition to their attention deficit and about half do not. Like people who have learning disabilities, people who have ADD or ADHD are often of normal or above normal intelligence.

The neurological causes of these two disorders are hotly debated in the scientific community. Different camps defend different causes: genetic inheritance, damage from brain trauma, obstetrical complications, allergies or hypersensitivities to certain foods and chemicals in the environment, thyroid dysfunction, sensory integration dysfunction of the subcortex of the brain, or chemical imbalances in the brain.

It's not that a child with ADD or ADHD has a short attention span; it's that she has difficulty choosing which stimulus out of the thousands of stimuli in her immediate environment to pay attention to. In one particular moment the senses of a girl with ADHD could be processing the sound of the traffic outside, the teacher's voice, the scratching of chalk on the blackboard, two girls whispering and passing notes behind her, the hum of the air conditioner, a fly buzzing by, the fragrance of the roses on the teacher's desk, the smell of lunch cooking in the cafeteria, the odor of automobile exhaust, an itch from a mosquito bite, an ache from a skinned knee, the pinch from shoes that are brand new and not quite broken in, a scratchy tag on the back of her shirt, the bright blue bookbag sitting on the floor next to her, the writing on the blackboard, the writing on her paper, all the different colors of the books in the bookshelf to her left. . . . Everyone else in the class is processing the same sensory information, but everyone else isn't being confused or distracted by it.

Doctors, parents, and educators deal with ADD and ADHD in a number of different ways, depending on their assessment of the causes. Behavior modification therapy is the most common method used to treat the behavioral symptoms of ADHD. The first step is to identify certain target behaviors which the parent or teacher wants to change. Then an appropriate, alternative behavior is chosen to be substituted for the inappropriate one. For instance, the inappropriate behavior might be "wandering around the room" and the appropriate substitute might be "sitting at your desk." A program is set up to provide positive reinforcements or rewards for the performance of the appropriate behavior. In the case of a student who tends to wander around the classroom, the teacher might put a sticker on her behavior chart for every fifteen-minute interval she stays in her seat during the school day. Other frequently used positive reinforcers include food, tokens, points, money, privileges, or other kinds of treats. Choice of reward depends on the age, interests, and motivation of the child. In more elaborate reward systems, which enhance impulse control, tokens or points are accumulated to be traded in at a later time for food, privileges, or toys.

Negative reinforcement for inappropriate behavior is accomplished through the removal of the positive reinforcers, removal of attention, and/or administering an aversive or unpleasant experience immediately after the inappropriate behavior. Stickers could be removed from a chart, privileges could be lost, tokens that had been previously earned could be taken away.

Teachers and therapists also teach students with ADD/ADHD specific problem-solving strategies for handling stressful situations, set clear behavior limits, and structure physical environments to help them focus and concentrate. For instance, if a child has a need to move around the classroom in order to learn, the teacher might set up two desks on opposite sides of the room which she can travel between during the day. This provides for her movement needs within clear physical and psychological boundaries.

When a child loses control, she is often encouraged to take a "time out" away from the group. This serves several purposes. It allows for a cooling down period. It removes the child from incoming stimuli that may have been overwhelming. From a behavior modification standpoint, a time out also removes the child from being the center of attention as the result of an inappropriate act (thus not reinforcing inappropriate behavior with attention). It provides the child with opportunities to think through and remedy the situation she has created. She gets the distance she needs to see and make positive choices. If she is unable to see these choices on her own, she may need to be guided through her options by the teacher. Chapter Five goes into more detail about how to use behavior modification techniques in the drama classroom.

Some children are prescribed stimulants, most commonly Ritalin™, to control their ADD/ADHD symptoms. If the dosage of stimulant is correct, the child will show no side effects and will probably behave in a normal, focused manner. However, finding the correct dosage for medication of this kind is not an exact science and the appropriate dosage can change over time as the child grows. If the dosage is not correct, side effects include drowsiness, irritability, dizziness, dry mouth, nausea, loss of appetite, insomnia, skin rash, headaches, or stomachaches. These will, of course, affect the student's behavior while in your class.

Children who take stimulants to control hyperactive behavior usually take a dose in the morning before coming to school and a dose at lunchtime. The peak of effectiveness for medication is usually a four-hour period. If the medication wears off before the next dose is given, ADD/ADHD symptoms will return quickly. This means that if your drama class is scheduled in the late morning before lunch or in the late afternoon, you might notice a return of hyperactive behavior.

If you know a child is on medication, alert parents if you notice side effects or if the medication seems to be wearing off before it should. You may be providing them with useful information of which they were unaware. In the case of over- or under-dosage, they may ask their doctor for an adjustment in the dosage. If the child is in the process of a change in medication or dosage, parents may need feedback on: 1) how the child is responding to the change, and 2) when the medication is wearing off.

If your class is at a time when parents do not want their child to be medicated (some parents want to limit the amount of time their child takes medication to school hours), you will have to deal with negative behavior symptoms through behavior modification techniques.

In the early 1970s, Benjamin Feingold, M.D., a pediatrician and allergist, discovered a biochemical link between hyperactive behavior and the chemicals in certain foods and food additives. He postulated that this was due to sensitivities these children have to a particular class of low molecular weight, unstable phenol-based compounds. He espoused a diet that eliminates synthetic food coloring and flavoring, certain preservatives, foods with natural salicylates, and aspirin and medications containing aspirin.

Check with parents to see if any of your students are on the Feingold Diet before you offer snacks to them! Even something as seemingly innocent as an apple (which contains natural salicylates) can send a food-sensitive child bouncing off the walls within minutes.

Other experts feel that the root cause of much of the hyperactive symptoms observed in school children today is related directly to the myriad of chemicals we are exposed to daily in our homes and schools. The use of chemicals as ingredients in synthetic fabrics, building materials, art supplies, paint, pesticides, cosmetics, perfumes, and cleaning compounds has exploded in the last 50 years. Only 8 million tons of chemicals were produced in 1945; currently over 108 million tons are being manufactured each year.

If you wear perfume, aftershave, or some other kind of scent, and you have a child who has ADHD in your class, you might try an experiment. Wear the scent and notice if the student's hyperactivity increases when you stand close to her. Does the same behavior occur when you are not wearing the scent? Watch for heightened hyperactivity during art projects. If you are using paint, clay, or another art material to which a student is highly reactive, you might want to find an alternative material.

John Ott, a photobiologist, has done numerous studies on how light affects behavior. He hypothesizes that standard fluorescent lighting, the kind used in institutional classrooms across the country, causes hyperactive behavior symptoms due to the emission of stressful x-rays and lack of exposure to a full natural light spectrum. If pure, natural sunlight rates 100 on a scale of 0 to 100, cool-white fluorescent lights rate 68 and warm-white fluorescents rate only 56. His videotaped studies of hyperactive school children show a marked behavior difference between children in classrooms with standard fluorescent lights and those in classrooms with full-spectrum, radiation-shielded fluorescent tubes.

Chances are that the building you teach drama in is lit by standard fluorescent lights and there is probably very little you, in your position as teacher, can do to change it. However, you can supplement the light by opening the blinds and curtains to let in as much natural light as possible. If you feel children in your class are particularly light sensitive, you could also bring in additional lighting sources, full spectrum or otherwise, to enhance the quality of light in your classroom and cut down on the irritating flickering quality of the fluorescent lighting.

I feel that ADD and ADHD are two of the most difficult disabilities to deal with in a drama classroom. This is because a drama class is primarily a focused group experience. Everyone needs to work together on the same activity. If one or two or *all* of the students are wandering aimlessly around the room paying attention to twenty different things simultaneously, the class can't move forward. It stops!

I taught a creative drama class in which attention deficits were present in some form in every one of the five children. Instead of seeming like a class of five, it seemed like a class of fourteen! Andrew wanted to make sounds with every object he touched. Michael wanted to explore every corner of the room over and over again. Peter couldn't sit still for more than ten seconds. Angela alternated between drawing and traveling around the room in circles talking to herself. Georgia had questions about everything *except* whatever we were doing. My assistant teacher and I spent so much time trying to capture everyone's attention and keep it focused on the lesson that we didn't accomplish very much each session. Every week we evaluated what had worked and what hadn't worked and revised our teaching strategy. We had many small successes, but we never fully succeeded for more than a fifteen-minute stretch, let alone a whole class period, in leading the group to work together.

The key to working with children who have ADD/ADHD in a drama classroom is to provide as much structure as you can in the physical space and in your lesson plan. Rules must be clear, written down, and visibly posted somewhere. Activities must be concrete, active, and exciting enough to hold the attention. The opening or warm-up activity is crucial for capturing attentions and starting class off on the right foot.

Transitions between activities must be smooth, clear, and swift or your student with ADD/ADHD may become anxious in the unstructured time.

You might lose her to something more interesting in the room or she might act on her anxiety and get into a conflict with another student. Chapter Six describes a number of ways to make strong transitions within a lesson plan.

When planning transitions, consider the time before class officially begins and the time after class officially ends as transitional times as well. A student with ADD/ADHD who arrives early may feel lost and unfocused. Involve her in a fun, productive activity to focus her attention. Drawing, modeling in clay, playing with blocks or Legos, or playing with puppets are all excellent pre-class activities. Endings also have the potential for creating anxiety in your students with ADD/ADHD. A pleasant, calming closure activity at the end of class is crucial for setting up the transition from drama class to whatever is next. See Chapter Seven for suggestions for closure activities.

Don't despair if it seems like your student is not paying any attention to you. Sometimes it only appears that way. One summer I taught at the Ivymount Day Camp in Rockville, Maryland, which is for children who have learning and other cognitive disabilities. None of the children in the class of four- and five-year-olds seemed capable of focusing their attentions on anything or anybody. During Native American Week we had an "Indian campfire" in drama class and I told them three different short Sioux legends about how the animals were created by the Great Spirit. I thought they got a little bit of what I said, but their counselors were sure the storytelling session had been a complete waste of time. The next day a Native American guest speaker came to share Native American crafts and costumes with the whole camp. The group's counselors were astounded when their campers very confidently started telling her one of the legends I had told them the day before!

TOURETTE SYNDROME

Tourette syndrome (TS) is a neurological disorder, probably caused by a defective gene which interferes with the body's manufacture of the neurotransmitter dopamine. Unlike individuals with ADD/ADHD, who may not have enough dopamine in their systems, individuals with Tourette syndrome may have too much of it, or, they may have an extreme sensitivity to it. The end result is that their internal neurological processing connections are sped up.

On the down side, this causes uncontrollable muscular tics and twitches, extremely impulsive behavior, compulsive repetitions of words or actions, quick emotional changes, and unusual vocal noises such as grunting, barking, repetitive throat clearing, or recognizable words that erupt spontaneously and erratically. Thirty percent of individuals with TS have coprolalia, an uncontrollable urge to say obscene or socially inappropriate words. On the up side, people who have TS tend to be extremely quick-thinking, creative, intelligent, and fun-loving individuals.

Motor and vocal tics can sometimes be slowed or eliminated by neuroleptic drugs such as Haldol™ or by clonidine, which retard the release of dopamine in the system. These drugs often have negative side effects, however, making the person who takes them feel sluggish, dull, and unable to concentrate.

About 50 percent of people who have Tourette syndrome also have symptoms of ADHD. Ritalin™ and other stimulants that work well with others who have ADHD usually make tics and other TS symptoms worse. Doctors sometimes prescribe tricyclic antidepressants instead. However, these medications can create side effects such as lightheadedness upon standing, mild memory impairment, dry mouth, blurred vision, and sedation.

At least 50 percent of people with TS also exhibit symptoms of obsessive-compulsive disorder (OCD), a neurological condition that compels a person to think a certain thought or to repeat a particular action over and over again. The compulsive action is a coping strategy to stop the obsessive thoughts, reduce anxiety, or prevent a feared event from happening. Examples of compulsive activities you might observe are repeated hand washing, turning the lights in the room on and off, or continually smelling, touching, or rearranging an object. If students with OCD try to ignore or stop their obsessions or compulsions, they become very anxious and fearful. Since OCD symptoms are caused by a chemical imbalance, they can often be controlled through medication. Like other medications, these drugs can have side effects, including nausea, diarrhea, heartburn, headaches, and insomnia, but they make it possible for students with OCD to concentrate on the activities of daily life.

Forty percent of children with TS have a learning disability that may affect their ability to read, write, spell, or compute. Be sensitive to this possibility when you are introducing written scripts to a class for the first time.

Individuals with TS can have poor fine or gross motor coordination, poor balance, difficulty with the difference between right and left, and clumsiness due to perceptual-motor problems. Because of this, students may need extra help or extra time for practice when learning dance routines or playing movement games. They may also need assistance when participating in art activities that require highly developed fine motor skills.

Sensory integration problems—difficulty with organizing and using sensations from the different sense organs—may be present in some students with Tourette syndrome as well. On one side of the sensory processing spectrum, persons with TS may be hyper-reactive, or over-sensitive, to sensations of touch. This can cause them to have a lower threshold to pain, to have an intense dislike for the texture of certain fabrics, art materials, or foods, or to react negatively to a sudden, unexpected touch. On the other side of the spectrum, they may be hypo-reactive, or under-sensitive, to sensations of touch. Hypo-reactive individuals may have a higher threshold to pain than normal. They may also have difficulty discriminating differences in texture, and this, in addition to tics and poor muscular coordination, may cause them to be clumsy when manipulating small objects or doing projects that involve fine motor skills. They also may be unaware of how strongly they are touching or bumping up against students who have normal sensory integration.

Some children with TS are hypersensitive to certain odors. If a student in your class complains about a smell, it could be because it is highly offensive to her. If the odor is caused by something in the room like a new rug, remove it, or open the windows to air out the smell. If it is caused by a room deodorizer or cleaning compound that is regularly used, ask if the custodian of your building can switch to a fragrance-free product. If the smell is from your perfume or aftershave, avoid wearing that fragrance on the days you teach.

TS symptoms are often exacerbated by stressful situations. Taking a test under a strict time limit, trying to suppress tics in order to fit in or not disturb others, being teased or put on the spot will often increase tics or impulsive outbursts of aggressive behavior. Give your students as much time as they need to complete in-class assignments. Break down a large assignment into small, manageable segments. For example, if you are assigning lines to be learned in a play, ask for the lines from Scene 1 to be learned for one re-

Mainstreaming a Child with Tourette Syndrome
by Elizabeth van den Berg Toperzer

As the spring semester started, I was feeling confident about mainstreaming. I had had a number of positive experiences with students who had learning disabilities and developmental delays. As always, the special needs director had given me a list of the students with special needs who she knew would be in my classes and suggestions for how to adapt my teaching approach to them. What we didn't know was that a crucial line had been left off the class registration form. This line asked if students had "any special or medical needs of which we should be aware."

I had a large group in one particular acting class—fifteen students—but felt I could handle them. In the first class we were standing in a circle doing some beginning warm-up exercises when I heard a popping sound, like someone snapping gum. This is a "no-no" in my classes. I identified the culprit and informed him that gum was not allowed during class time.

Very abruptly he asked, "Can I talk to you?"

I was quite taken aback by his manner, but answered, "Sure." He crossed the circle towards me, stopped right in front of me, and said, "You see, I have Tourette syndrome and sometimes I make strange sounds and noises. Pop. Pop. Pop."

"Oh," I answered. I was completely thrown. I had no idea what Tourette syndrome was. Here was a student, taller than I, behaving oddly, and making strange sounds. Fourteen other students were

hearsal and the lines for Scene 2 at the next one, rather than requiring the whole play to be memorized on one day. A number of small assignments that are due one at a time will seem less overwhelming than one large project due all at once.

Stress reduction strategies are not, as a rule, taught in academic classrooms, although they probably should be. Drama classes, however, are excellent arenas for learning and practicing them. Physical warm-ups, sensory awareness sessions, concentration games, progressive relaxation, and guided watching me, waiting for my response. "OK," I said, "Thanks for letting me know. Let's continue."

So I continued the class with Gerald occasionally bursting out with a "Whee" or pop popping along. As soon as class was over, I cornered the special needs director. She was as surprised as I was because this student was new to the Academy, but she immediately reassured me, explaining what Tourette syndrome is and providing me with literature on it. I couldn't believe we had not been forewarned—that even with the special needs line left off the registration form, Gerald's mom had not felt it necessary to inform us of his condition.

Gerald was an excellent artist. Exploring his characters by drawing them first helped him to feel comfortable with his acting and the scenes he worked on.

He was very upfront about his disability, but hardly made any sounds after that first class. He explained that they seemed to be more prominent when he was nervous, as he had been that first day.

As we got closer to our final presentation, he expressed concern about being nervous and making sounds during the performance. I explained we would help him be as prepared as possible so that he would be less nervous. And if he popped—so what?

Indeed, he did pop, but only once, and his character work was very strong. Despite what for me was a rocky start because I was not prepared, things worked out quite well.

imagery exercises (see Chapter Seven) are tried-and-true tools which professional actors use to release stress and help them deal with nervousness. You may find that any of these techniques done at the beginning of class or before a run-through or performance serves to relax *all* your students and allows them to perform with more ease and enjoyment. In addition, these coping strategies can be used when students find themselves in other stressful life situations.

Motor and vocal tics come and go in severity depending on the overall stresses a student is dealing with in her life and depending on her current neurological state. She will have good days and she will have bad days. A student with TS who is going through a severe period of tics may feel more comfortable if she knows she can go somewhere to release the tics in private. It may be helpful to arrange with her in advance that, if she feels the need, she can go out into the hall or to the bathroom or, if it is a nice day, outside in order to discharge her tics.

Often tics and other symptoms are reduced when the body is in motion. Including some form of physical activity—either a warm-up or a movement game—in your lesson plan, may provide a positive outlet for this. If the need to move around comes over a student during a part of the class which does not involve movement, you could give her permission to leave the classroom for a short time in order to engage in some kind of releasing physical activity that works to reduce her stress level.

Students with TS may find making transitions between activities difficult. They get involved in one activity and find it hard to stop and move on to another. You can help by ending each game or exercise in class decisively. If there is not an obvious end to the game (some games like Duck, Duck, Goose or Indian Chief can continue for as many rounds as the players want to play), warn students that the final round of the game is coming up. You might say, "We will play three more rounds. [play that round] We have two more rounds to go. [play that round] We're on our last round. [play that round] That's the end of the game."

Move quickly from one activity to another. In other words, don't leave a lot of "down time" between activities. As soon as one activity is over, move students into the configuration for the next one, and begin explaining what they will do. For example, after the last actor has her turn with the Magic Stick, say, "Now I would like everyone to move over to this side of the room and sit down. We will be sharing some scenes next. Who would like to present their scene to the class first?" See Chapter Six for more suggestions on how to make good transitions within a lesson plan.

Motor and vocal tics can be disconcerting to the teacher and other students. It is important to explain to a class from the outset what Tourette syndrome is—particularly that it is not a mental illness or a communicable disease, but a chemical imbalance in the brain. The other students need to understand that the TS symptoms are involuntary and are not being done on purpose; that, in fact, the student with TS has little voluntary control over them and that teasing, staring, or nasty comments will only make them worse. This may be more difficult for the other students to accept if the tics seem malicious rather than innocuous in nature. For instance, it will be harder for a class to accept a student whose tics involve kicking, spitting, or swearing than it will be to accept a student who blinks her eyes or jerks her head to the side.

Punishing a student for tics that are disruptive or violent will not make the tics go away. In fact, it could make them worse. If you feel behavior management of any kind is necessary, focus on pro-active strategies rather than reactive ones. Instead of responding with a consequence after something goes wrong, be on the lookout for potentially difficult or hazardous situations and intervene *before* the problem happens. For example, instead of playing a game like Elbow-to-Elbow that involves a lot of physical contact and could cause a tactilely sensitive child with TS to hit out aggressively when touched unexpectedly, you could play a game like Pass the Sound/Pass the Movement in which students invent and "pass" sounds and body movements around the circle, but don't make any physical contact.

The best thing that the teacher and other students can do is to ignore tics and other symptoms. Concentrate instead on the positive aspects of the TS student's personality and her creative contributions to the class. As in any classroom situation, the teacher has the key role in modeling for the other students how to treat the student who has a disability. Ignoring TS symptoms and making positive comments about the student's class work will go a long way to help her appreciate her strengths and to point them out for others to focus on.

Students with TS are usually highly verbal and intuitive. This, coupled with their impulsive tendencies, makes for drama students who are very adept at improvisation and games that require on-the-spot, impulsive decision-making. You will probably find a student with TS to be the most uninhibited and imaginative student in the class.

While this impulsive quality can be her best asset as a drama student, it can also be her worst. Expect impulsive comments and behavior and don't be offended by them. You and everyone else in the class probably have the same impulses, but because of the chemical composition of your brain, you have the ability to censor them and *not* act on them. Your student with TS can't, so sometimes inappropriate comments and actions pop out along with all her appropriate creative ideas.

Verbal tics sometimes create stuttering, which can interrupt line delivery in a scene. Students with TS may talk very quickly or they may pause, struggling to find a way to say a difficult word. They may also use loud or pressured speech that sounds unnatural. The best way to deal with these kinds of speaking difficulties is not to put additional pressure on the student. The more tense she feels, the worse her stuttering or hesitations will become. Tell her she has all the time in the world to get the line out. Make the vocal rhythm an integral part of her character's speech rhythm. Give her a prop to manipulate or some kind of stage business for her character to do in times of vocal stress to take her focus and the audience's focus off of the problem.

For more ideas of how to work with a student who has Tourette syndrome in a mainstream situation, see the sidebar in this chapter by Elizabeth van den Berg Toperzer and the section in Chapter Eleven by Caleen Sinnette Jennings.

MENTAL RETARDATION

Mental retardation (MR) is a condition that impairs intellectual functioning. Generally, people are considered to have MR if they score 70 or below on an I.Q. test. There are over 200 known causes of mental retardation, including genetic abnormalities, birth trauma, hormone deficiencies, brain damage through accident, lead poisoning, and disease.

Children who have mental retardation can learn; they just learn at slower rates than other people. When she was in elementary school, Amy Turnbull, a regular education student, described her mentally retarded brother's learning ability this way:

> *I was five years old when my parents explained to me that my brother has mental retardation. They said that his brain works slower than other people, and it takes him a longer time to learn. They also said he could always learn things. I asked how Kate's and my brain worked, and they said our brains work fast. I then asked if brains were like record players with the slow and fast*

speeds. They said that Jay's brain works on the slow speed and our brain [sic] works on the fast speed. Jay might be slow and Katie, my sister, and I might be fast but all of us can learn.

In addition to taking information in at a slower pace, people who have mental retardation are generally very literal. They may need concrete, physical examples in order to understand. Looking at a demonstration of how to peel a potato and actually doing it while being guided by a teacher may make more sense than listening to a description or reading about how to do it.

People with MR may have difficulty generalizing information from one situation to another. For instance, they may learn how to peel a potato with a potato peeler, but may not make the connection that the same tool could be used to peel a carrot or an apple.

People who have mental retardation tend to be rigid and inflexible in their approach to solving problems. If new information is suddenly added to a process that they have learned or if a social interaction takes an unexpected turn, they may have a hard time thinking of an alternative strategy to solve the problem or complete the task. Even if another solution is offered to them, they may find it hard to try a new or different way.

Often students who have mental retardation need to proceed at a slower pace than other students. They may need to have instructions broken down into small, individual steps. Each step needs to be presented one at a time. If you present too many steps simultaneously, even if they are simple ones, your student will have difficulty retaining them in memory and in sequence. This is especially true for a brand-new task.

When you are explaining an idea, you don't need to explain your point two or three different ways or provide many examples. Over-explaining will be as confusing to a student with MR as providing her with too many steps at once. One good example will suffice. Choose examples and explanations for simplicity and clarity. Show it while you tell it.

For example, when presenting the game The Magic Box to a group of students, I would put the Magic Box in the center of the circle and say "Inside this box is any present you can imagine. I'll show you how it works. First, I'll decide what I would like to be inside the box." I would think for a second. "Then, I open the box . . ." I would take the lid off the box. ". . . and take my present out . . ." I would pantomime lifting my object out. ". . . and show you what it is." I might pantomime placing a ring on my finger. Then I would ask, "What do you think I got out of the box?" They would say, "A ring!" I would say, "That's right! Now show us what *you* would like to get out of the box." Each person would take a turn to show us what she imagines is in the box for her.

Many students with MR have difficulty speaking clearly. Certain sounds may be hard for them to form, they may hesitate as they search for words, or they may have trouble speaking fluently. Let students use as much or as little language as they feel comfortable with. If there are words in a play that are difficult to say, change the words to ones that are easier. For example, if it is too hard for an actor to say, "Come here immediately," maybe it would be easier for her to say "Come here right away" or "Come here now."

Some students with MR excel with verbal activities. If your students don't, there are plenty of drama activities that emphasize sound and movement. Try rhythm and movement games and activities that incorporate music, pantomime, and dance. Focus your lesson plans on drama activities that they can do and that they enjoy. See Chapter Seven for examples of drama games that work.

Don't assume that a student who has difficulty expressing herself through spoken language doesn't understand what is being said to her. Receptive and expressive language are two separate brain processes. She

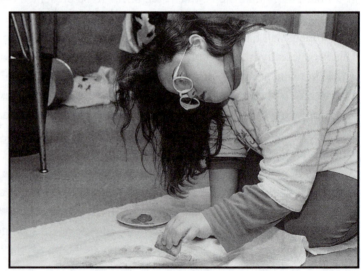

Building and painting the scenery, props, and costumes is how some students like to contribute to a production. (Photo by Lea Ann Rosen)

Drama class provides many opportunities to hone social skills. (Photo by Lea Ann Rosen)

could understand everything you say, but not have the ability to translate that understanding into words or to actually speak words back to you.

If you ask a question and don't receive a reply or if you request a response and don't get one, it could be that your student knows the answer, but is not sure how to say it. She may need a little extra time to figure out how to express an idea that she wants to share. You may have to invest a little time to find out what she understands, how she really feels about a situation, or what she wants to do. She may need you to rephrase your question or request so that it is more structured or not as open-ended. For instance, if a student looks upset and I ask her "What's wrong?" she may not be able to tell me. But if I ask "Are you feeling sick?" She can respond with a yes or no. If her answer is no, I might try asking if she is angry, confused, upset, tired, sad, unhappy, or any other specific emotion that seemed appropriate to the situation. If she says she is angry, I might ask who she is angry at or what made her angry. Slowly, but surely, I would get to the root of what was bothering her.

Some people with MR who have speech difficulties have been taught sign language as an expressive language alternative. A student may be able to say through signs or gestures what she cannot say in spoken language. If you are having difficulty getting through to a student or getting a response, try communicating through sign language or natural gesture.

One common type of mental retardation is Down syndrome. It is caused by a chromosomal mutation which results in 47 instead of 46 chromosomes in the cells of the child's body. People with Down syndrome tend to have very similar physical characteristics. They have a distinctive broad round face with high cheek bones; close-set, almond-shaped eyes; small, low-set ears; and a flat bridge to their nose. Of note for anyone who does physical activity with a student who has Down syndrome: some individuals have a condition known as atlantoaxial instability, which is a misalignment of the top two vertebrae of the neck. If overextended or flexed, the vertebrae can shift position and squeeze or sever the spinal cord, causing paralysis or death. Just to be safe, ask parents if their child has this condition before doing any kind of physical activity that puts stress on the neck!

I have noticed that students with Down syndrome usually have very warm and loving personalities. They love hugs and dote on praise. However, upon occasion, they can also be *very* stubborn and inflexible! Once they get into a bad mood, it's almost impossible to get them back out. If a conflict develops between two students at these times, a compromise can be almost impossible to arrange. My best suggestion for dealing with Down syndrome stubbornness is patience and gentle humor. Don't try to force the situation; you can't. Be loving and understanding and, if that doesn't work, give your sulker some time by herself to cool off and brood for awhile. She'll either get it out of her system—or not. If you can't jolly her back into a good mood that session, don't shame or embarrass her. By the next class, she'll be back to her old lovable self again.

There is no need to have lower standards of behavior for students who have mental retardation. They can understand what is appropriate and acceptable behavior. Explain your classroom rules clearly in the first session. Make them positively worded, simple, clear statements of the behavior you expect. Explain what the consequences will be if a student breaks a rule. Follow through with those consequences if a rule is broken. See the section on Behavior Management at the end of Chapter Five for more information on this subject.

AUTISM

Autism is not as clearly understood as most other cognitive disabilities. It seems to be primarily a disorder of sensory integration abilities. CAT, PET, and MRI scans of individuals who have autism have indicated that some areas in the brain are under-active while other areas are over-active. Intellectual functioning in people with autism can range from very low to very high levels.

The causes of autism are not known. For many years researchers and social scientists mistakenly blamed poor maternal nurturing. Today the consensus seems to be that environmental and psychological factors play a role, but that autism is primarily biological in origin, caused by either poor fetal brain development, birth trauma, or genetic abnormalities. Current interventions include behavior modification therapies, special diets and nutritional supplements, experimental drug treatments, facilitated communication, and social skills training.

Children who have autism are often over-sensitive to sights, sounds, smells, and especially to touch. Loud or sudden sounds are painful to their ears and certain smells are perceived as very offensive. It is very difficult for them to pay attention simultaneously to more than one sensory component of an experience, object, or person. Often they have to block out one type of sensory input in order to attend to another. For instance, in order to listen to an announcement on the PA system in a busy bus terminal, a person with autism might have to shut her eyes.

At times people with autism totally isolate themselves—literally retreating into a world of their own. This may be because the incoming sensory stimulation is so overwhelming. They can't filter out parts of it and they can't pay attention to all of it, so they block out everything. Self-stimulating behavior, such as spinning in circles or focusing on spinning objects, seems to calm and refocus them.

Sometimes people with autism prefer relating to mechanical objects over people. A child who is autistic may choose day after day to play exclusively with a vacuum cleaner or the venetian blinds on a window instead of interacting with the other children in her play group. This tendency may, in part, be due to her strong visual system and her need to stay in control of her environment. Mechanical objects are guaranteed to do the same thing again and again while people change all the time.

Individuals who have autism tend toward perseverative (repetitious) behavior and become fixated on thoughts and ideas that are either pleasing or painful to them. They become upset if there is any kind of change in their daily routine or physical environment. All of this makes sense—with a nervous system that becomes overstimulated easily, as little variety as possible in surroundings and social interactions would make the processing of incoming sensory messages easier.

People with autism find it very difficult to handle two motor tasks at the same time. For instance, it would be hard to sing and clap at the same time or to walk and talk. This kind of synchronization problem can make it difficult for students with autism to create, use, and understand rhythms.

People with autism seem to be "right brain thinkers." They tend to score high in fluid intelligence and in nonverbal thinking skills (i.e., the visual, spatial, metaphorical, and pattern-making processes of the brain). They don't do as well with verbal intelligence, sound inference, logic, and understanding the sequential steps in problem-solving. Often they are visual and/or kinesthetic learners and may be very adept at creating with their hands. Approaching a student through these learning channels in a classroom situation may be more successful than using auditory or lecture methods.

Children with autism usually have language delays and difficulty expressing themselves in words. To release tension and frustration when they are unable to communicate that they are bored or have been over-stimulated, they sometimes respond with violence aimed at themselves, others, or objects in their immediate vicinity.

While some children with autism withdraw into silence, others may display incessant talking, repetitive questioning, and seemingly uncontrollable laughter. Their attempts at communication in these instances may have more of a quality of "talking at" the people around them, rather than "talking to" them. They can become obsessed with subjects that have deep, personal meaning for them. Instead of being ignored, these obsessive interests can be guided into constructive pathways to help the child make a solid connection with the world. For instance, Temple Grandin, who considers herself a "recovered autistic," became obsessed with cattle chutes and squeeze boxes as an adolescent. She pursued her obsession with the encouragement of several teachers and mentors and is now one of the world's foremost designers of livestock handling facilities. Because individuals with autism don't communicate and interact well with others, are easily over-stimulated, and prefer routine over variety, participating in a drama class can be difficult for them and for the teacher. While the social interaction opportunities offered in a drama class can be therapeutic and educational, a basic level of social skills is necessary in order to participate. Some children who have autism don't have this basic level of social ability. The amount and constant variety of sensory stimulation can be too much to handle. The bodies of all the other students moving around in space, gesturing, talking, laughing, and making noise can become so overwhelming that some children who have autism shut down. Drama classes are filled with variety. Even if a teacher sets up a basic structure for her lesson play that stays the same (for example, always beginning with a Go-Around, followed by a physical warm-up, a drama game, a story, and the enactment of the story), the elements of that structure will be different every week. Some students can't handle the variety.

I had a student who had autistic tendencies in a creative drama class. Angela could handle solitary and parallel play, but had trouble participating in any activity that involved associative or cooperative play. She didn't like to sit in a circle with the others and listen to a story (associative play), but she could sit at the table with the others and draw a picture on her own (parallel play). She had difficulty acting out the story with the other students (cooperative play), but she could go off by herself and act out the characters alone in another part of the room (solitary play).

Our greatest artistic breakthrough with her was, perhaps, a social regression for Angela. She drew cats. Only cats. In fact, she drew the same cat over and over again. She wouldn't draw anything else. When asked to do so, she would put the crayon into another person's hand and say, "You draw it." She kept repeating, "You draw it. You draw it. You draw it," until the other person did. If the other person didn't, she became very upset. Because she didn't like to sit with the rest of the class while I told the story, I allowed her to go to the table on the other side of the room and draw. During these times, there was nobody else to draw for her, so she drew cats. Even though it didn't look like she was paying attention to the story, she heard every word.

One week Angela came in talking animatedly about "Goldilocks and the Three Bears," which we had acted out the week before. Before class she tried to get me to draw Goldilocks sitting on the three chairs. I decided to be stubborn and see if I could entice her to draw it herself. She wouldn't, so I started class before a conflict could develop over the drawing situation. When the story started, as usual, she went over to the table and began to draw. She was unusually involved with her work. I wasn't telling the story that week, so at one point, I meandered over to take a look at what she was doing. Lo and behold, she was drawing a very complex and detailed rendition of Goldilocks and the three Bears' chairs.

I was very impressed, but not as impressed as her mother, who informed me after class that this was the first time Angela had ever drawn anything herself other than a cat. From that class on, Angela stopped asking others to draw for her. A predictable pattern developed. Each week she would come in talking excitedly about the story we had acted out the week before. While I told the story for the current week, she would draw a picture of the characters from the previous week. I'm not knowledgeable enough about autism and art therapy to know what that means, but I hope that by opening up her ability to make her own visual images, one of her few avenues for interacting with other people wasn't shut down.

If a child who has autism takes your drama class, you can make several adaptations to help her succeed. First, be aware of how much sensory stimulation there is in your classroom. If there are lots of toys, props, or odds and ends lying around, clean them up. Simplify the visual design of the room so it is not as distracting. Limit distracting sounds inside and outside the classroom, if you can. Avoid drama games that incorporate sudden, loud noises or busy physical gestures which would over-stimulate. Make sure you have enough assistants in the class. Students with autism sometimes need one-on-one help in order to participate in group activities. Guide your assistant to stay with the student and redirect her attention to the group when necessary with gestures and physical orientation in addition to short, simply worded positive statements.

A student who has autism needs to know where stimulation is coming from. Being surprised from behind with a friendly hand on her shoulder will make her feel threatened rather than secure. If you or your assistant touch her, a heavy, downward or inward pressure (called "deep touch") would probably be more easily tolerated by her than a light, gentle touch.

The student needs to feel in control of the amount and type of stimulation she is getting. Provide a quiet, safe place in the classroom where she can go to get away from the group when she feels it is necessary. This place should have very few visual and auditory distractions. Warmth and deep pressure tend to lessen arousal. You could provide a blanket in the space that the child could wrap herself in or some pillows she could burrow under. If she needs to spin, allow her to spin in her safe place.

When you speak to your student, look her right in the eye and continue to do so, even if she tries to avoid eye contact. Don't let her lack of eye contact with you discourage you. Your student may want to make eye contact, but be unable to. Eye contact is an important communication skill that she needs to learn. You can only help her to make it if you persevere despite her apparent rejection of your eyes.

Use lots of vocal variety and facial expression when talking to your student, even if she speaks in a flat voice and shows little expression. Just as with eye contact, the only way she can learn clear, expressive communication skills is if she has a good role model.

Play drama games that will enhance eye contact, vocal expressiveness, and use of the face, body, and gesture to communicate emotions and ideas. These are all skills that your student with autism needs to practice.

As much as possible, follow a similar routine in your lesson plan from week to week. You could start class with a beginning ritual and/or end class with a closure ritual that is always the same. (See Chapter Seven for opening and closing activities.) If there is a game that the students in the class love to play, you could play it for a short time every week. If you are teaching creative drama and always tell a story, have students sit in the same place in the room each time. Always place the audience area and the performing area in the same place. Keep the arrangement of the room the same from week to week.

Let the student use her sense of touch and kinesthesia (the body's sense of itself in space) as primary learning tools. If she has a strong visual sense, focus on that learning channel as well. Have her draw a picture of a character before she acts it out or ask her to create a statue with her body that expresses how she or the character she is playing feels. (Chapter Ten talks more about ways to teach through different sensory learning channels.)

If she is having difficulty participating with exercises, you might want to involve her with some technical aspect of the class. For instance, if you are using a tape recorder in a number of exercises, you might ask her to run the tape recorder. If your story needs sound effects, bring in rhythm instruments and other objects that can make sounds and let her be the sound effects person while the other children act out the story.

Students with autism might also like to become involved in the technical aspects of theatre production: building sets, props, or costumes, running the sound board or lighting console during shows, working the fog machine, or doing some other aspect of backstage technical assistance.

If drama is not an appropriate outlet for a student with autism, suggest that her parents try a dance, music, or visual art class where there is less social interaction and more individualized, hands-on motor activity. Visual art, in particular, might offer some avenues for self-expression and communication within easily self-determined, self-controlled confines.

chapter five

getting off to a good start
basic adaptions for the drama classroom

Many different types of drama classes can be offered, depending on the age of your students and the skills you are interested in developing. The most common classes are creative drama, improvisational acting, and scene study. Specialty classes include puppetry, radio drama, mask drama, mime, voice and diction, acting for the camera, Readers theatre, Shakespearean acting, and auditioning skills. All can be taught successfully to children who have special needs and all have something to offer them.

This chapter focuses on general adaptations and issues which should be considered before embarking on any kind of drama class. Chapter Six and Seven discuss specific issues related to creative drama and improvisational acting classes, Chapter Eight discusses specifics about puppetry, and Chapter Nine goes into detail about how to develop and rehearse original plays.

CLASSROOM SPACE

The physical space in which a drama class is held will greatly influence the kind of work that is done in it.

Your drama space should have as few physical barriers and visual distractions as possible. It should not be too large or too small. Gymnasiums and school cafeterias are usually too large. In these types of spaces students have difficulty settling down to work. They run around, shout, and generally behave as if they have suddenly been transformed into NBA Basketball stars. They are not intentionally misbehaving. They are, in fact, engaging in the appropriate behavior for a large, open space. They will have difficulty understanding that you want to use the space in a different way and you will have a great deal of difficulty trying to persuade them to do so.

A drama space should be a quiet place without a lot of auditory distractions. If your space is not soundproof, ask neighboring classrooms if they will agree to do a quiet project at the same time you are doing drama. It's very hard to tell a story or create a character when you are competing with someone else's distracting noise.

Good acoustics are important in a drama room as well. Students can't focus on what is being said by the teacher or by others if they can't hear well. Students with and without auditory processing problems will become distracted in a room full of live sound. Instead of moving out in one direction and being absorbed by the walls, floor, and ceiling, as it does when the acoustics are good, the sound continues to bounce off the surfaces in the room, creating a hollow echo effect. The source of the sound becomes hard to determine and students are not sure where to focus. Poor acoustics are another reason why gymnasiums and cafeterias are not good choices as drama spaces.

A school stage would seem to be the first and best choice as a space for a drama class. This is not always so. Stages can be very distracting places. Young children or students who have low impulse control and are easily distracted can't focus on the lesson because the space is too exciting to be in. Instead, they want to hang on the curtains or run backstage to hide.

A stage is a formal performance space. Its best use is for rehearsals for formal presentations or for performance skill training. Holding a creative drama or an improvisational acting class on stage can change the tone of your work from informal/ experiential to formal/presentational. Working on a stage, students tend to start performing *for* their classmates instead of improvising naturally *with* them.

An open, medium-sized classroom is often the best place for a drama class. This kind of room provides an informal space in which students can explore expressing their ideas and engage in process-oriented work. If you are in a classroom filled with desks, push the desks out of the way to make an open space in the middle of the room.

A large carpet creates a warm and welcoming area on which everyone can sit together. If students have trouble staying in the same place or understanding their physical boundaries, have them sit in chairs or on small carpet squares.

Bright, even lighting is important so everyone can see the teacher and each other clearly. Some environmental specialists believe fluorescent lighting, which is in all of our educational and recreational institutions, is a major source of health and behavior problems. They believe students are adversely affected by the flickering quality of the light, low level radiation emitted from the cathode tubes (the older the tube, the more radiation), and the fact that fluorescent light is composed of only 56-68 percent of the spectrum of natural sunlight (missing the blue and ultraviolet frequencies).

Regular fluorescent tubes can be replaced with full-spectrum, radiation-shielded tubes, which imitate natural light. However, these are more expensive than regular tubes and their purchase is usually not within the drama teacher's authority. The next best solution is to supplement fluorescent lighting with natural light from a window. If you can add extra incandescent or full-spectrum fluorescent lighting fixtures to the room, the quality of light will improve markedly.

Beware of activity rooms with lots of paraphernalia in them. A room full of toys or sports equipment is too distracting! If your room is filled with many interesting objects, put them away before class. Tape butcher paper over tempting shelves. Cover table displays with paper or fabric. It may take you ten or fifteen extra minutes to prepare for class each week and to restore the room to its original state afterwards, but, believe me, it is *worth* it!

I taught an after-school drama class at a learning center for special education students. Initially we were assigned to the physical/occupational therapy room. It was filled with see-saws, bikes, balls, swinging ropes, and climbing apparatus of every kind. I was able to hide or camouflage everything except the large wooden jungle gym in the corner. My students had a lot of impulse control problems and for them the jungle gym was like a giant child magnet. They couldn't stay off it! I started out with a class rule that no one could climb it during class. That didn't work. I set up a contract with them that stated they could play on it before class and at snack time, but not at other times. That didn't work. I tried working the jungle gym into the story. That didn't work. They wanted to climb on it from the time they entered the room until the time they left. Finally, I had to switch the class to the library. While not without its distractions, nothing in the library came close to being as enticing as the jungle gym!

TEACHING PERSONNEL

A drama class for special needs students needs to be run by at least two teachers. The lead teacher takes responsibility for planning the lesson and leading the class in most of the activities. In a creative drama class, he is usually the one who tells the stories and provides narration for the enactment of the story. In a performance-based class, he usually directs the scenes or the play. In all cases, he is the one who keeps the class moving forward.

The lead teacher needs to be strong and firm. He must communicate clearly and be able to pace his explanations at the speed his students process information best. He must remain aware of the current interest and attention level of individuals and the group as a whole so he knows when it is time to end one activity and begin a new one. Patience, flexibility, and a sense of humor are perhaps the most valuable qualities a lead teacher can have.

Assistant warms up with student.
(Photo by Lea Ann Rosen)

The assistant teacher has an equally important role in the classroom. He provides the support that allows the lead teacher to keep the class moving forward. He models appropriate behavior for the students, providing an example for them to copy. He refocuses the attention of wandering individuals onto the activity at hand. He assists students who need extra help or extra attention during class. One student may need help finding the bathroom. Another may have difficulty cutting with scissors. Another may fall and need help getting up. He provides disciplinary intervention. Two students might get into a fight and need to be

The Role of the Assistant
by Cindy Bowen

The goal of the assistant in a drama class is to help the teacher carry out the lesson plan and objectives for the class. A large part of this involves providing individual children with the attention they need in order to be creative and use their imaginations freely. In order to achieve this goal, the assistant may need to take on many different roles during the course of a lesson.

Communication. An assistant will be able to carry out these roles if the teacher has given him specific guidelines. Clear communication between the teacher and assistant is very important. Before each semester begins the teacher and assistant should meet to discuss the goals and expectations for themselves and the group. Before each class, they should briefly go over the lesson plan and specific goals for the session. After class they might need to check in with each other on how class went and what needs to be done, if anything, before the next class meeting.

Set-up/Clean-up. Some of the custodial tasks that need to be done include helping to get materials ready before class, removing distracting objects from the classroom space, sitting with early arrivals, escorting kids to the bathroom, and helping to clean up after class. All of these tasks help the teacher begin class on time and help the class run smoothly.

In classes with children with special needs, the assistant may need to help students make the transition into the classroom. Often children coming into the class have news they want to share. It is important that they be able to do this. The assistant can be there to meet this need and help settle the class before the lesson begins.

Behavior Management. When the teacher is telling a story to the group or giving directions for an exercise, the assistant takes responsibility for discipline. Often children with attention problems and hyperactivity need re-direction. It is important that the teacher be able to continue with the lesson so the whole group does not become distracted by one student's behaviors. In addition, letting the lesson continue without disruption helps motivate those who are having trouble paying attention join back in. If the class goes on, the disruptive child is not given positive attention for the disruptive behavior and there is less motivation for him to continue it. The on-going class activity is present for him to re-join at any time he chooses.

Behavior management also includes providing positive reinforcement. It is important to praise and support each student. Let them know what they are doing right! This encourages them to be more open and develops their self-esteem. The assistant can play a big part in helping to create a positive atmosphere and encourage success through positive reinforcement.

Player/Participant. Perhaps the most important role the assistant takes on is as a player/participant in the class. When the teacher is explaining a new activity or reading a story, the assistant should participate with the students with interest and energy. This provides children with a model to follow. Often when children see an adult being focused and spontaneous in play, they feel more able to let themselves become involved. When children see adults experimenting and taking risks, they feel as if they have been given permission to do the same. If they are new at drama and feel unsure about what to do, having a model to watch gives them ideas to take and expand on.

An assistant who is playing with the students views what is happening from within the group and has a much better sense of how the

separated. Someone might lose control and need to take a "time-out." The assistant deals with most emergencies as they arise so the lead teacher doesn't have to stop the class.

A good assistant is crucial. Without someone to handle the inevitable problems that arise on the periphery, the lead teacher, who is holding the center together, must stop to handle each and every problem. As soon as the class loses its guide and focal point, students' attentions begin to wander. Soon their bodies have followed their minds and they are all over the room, involved in some other activity than the one everyone had previously been students are feeling and what kind of assistance they need. He can also help the teacher pace the group. A "player" often has more control than an "observer" because he is coming from within the drama rather than from without and can intervene in the action "in character" or "in role."

When a child is hesitant or shy, sometimes just an arm around his shoulder or a little verbal encouragement ("Come on, this is fun!") is enough to motivate him to join in. If necessary, the assistant can provide one-on-one guidance. For example, if a child is shy or has language delays, the assistant could stand with him as he acts out his part. If he seems at a loss for words, the assistant could suggest some words that the character might say. The assistant can provide praise as the child enacts the part, thereby encouraging him to take more chances and become more expressive as he continues in his role.

The qualities a good assistant needs include flexibility, the courage to take risks, interest in the group and the group process, respect for the students and their ideas, lots of energy, and the ability to pick up on verbal and visual signals for help from the teacher *and* the students.

Open communication and a relationship based on respect and trust between the teacher and the assistant, as well as between the assistant and the group, will enhance each activity and lesson plan and will promote creativity and imagination in the classroom.

engaged in together. Once you lose a group's attention, it is not easy to get it back.

An assistant is also a handy dramatic resource in the classroom. He can take on a role in a story that no one wants to play. If the group is working in pairs or in teams, he can fill in when there is an uneven number. When the class has been divided in two, he can become the leader for one group while the lead teacher works with the other. If there are more than two groups working, he can circulate among the groups along with the lead teacher. When a group is rehearsing a play, the assistant can act as the stage manager, help students who are not on stage learn their lines, or rehearse a separate scene simultaneously.

A good assistant stays focused on what is happening in class at all times. He participates in activities whenever he is not off on the side solving a problem or assisting someone who needs extra help. He needs to be friendly, but firm, and retain his patience and sense of humor under fire.

Some teachers like to team teach together and share the roles of lead and assistant teacher. This is fine as long as each knows which role he is playing when. Trouble arises when the lead teacher stops to deal with a behavior problem and the assistant tries to take over the class or if both stop to deal with the problem and leave the class rudderless.

I watched this happening during rehearsals for a show at a camp for emotionally disturbed children. The counselors were so used to jumping in immediately to head off behavior disturbances that whenever one camper acted out, all three counselors would stop and focus on him. The rest of the campers had to wait until the counselors got back to them. Since they had difficulty dealing with unstructured time, they ended up getting into trouble, too. A lot of time was wasted and not much work got accomplished. The campers started to hate rehearsal—not because they didn't like drama—they insisted that they did —they didn't like being set adrift by their group leaders.

Because of their physical or emotional disabilities, some students need one-on-one help all the time. In this case, a class may need to have a second assistant who is specifically assigned to that student. Sometimes the one-on-one assistant can be a slightly older student who is hired as a "companion" to take the class with the child who has the disability. In either case, this one-on-one assistant needs to stay with the child at all times.

Some classes need two or more assistants to help out generally. Assistants must work as a team. Rather than assigning each assistant specific students to be responsible for, every assistant should work with every student. That way all the students get to know all the teachers and vice versa. Besides, there's no guarantee that two different students assigned to one assistant won't need his attention at exactly the same time. What are the other assistants going to do? Twiddle their thumbs and watch while he tries to be in two different places at once? That's not team work.

There are several qualities key to being a successful drama teacher or assistant in any drama classroom. To begin with, a good drama teacher must know how to play and be spontaneous with his students. As mentioned in Chapter One, drama is a form of play and spontaneity is one of its major ingredients. Inflexibility and rigidity on the part of the teacher will kill the sense of play and creativity in students.

However, having a playful approach does not mean the teacher should be childish or become one of the kids in the class. The teacher is the guide to the dramatic experience and the referee for games and conflicts. Students need to know that the teacher is in charge; that he will create structure and set limits fairly.

Another key is creating a safe, supportive atmosphere in which children can express their ideas and feelings without feeling judged, categorized, or caustically criticized. A good drama teacher focuses on the potential in students. He starts with

Being an Assistant Teacher for a Special Needs Child
by Julia Morris

I served as the assistant teacher in a Dramatic Play class in which a young boy who had sensory processing difficulties was mainstreamed. The experience I had is difficult to put into words, but I will try.

During every Dramatic Play class I spent working with Randy, a feeling of love would hit me and linger on long after class was over. The feeling sprang from my interactions with him and from his mother's response to our work. Randy's mother, a relatively young woman, waited outside the classroom with her younger son. She waited expectantly, ready to hear anything positive, anything good. Her reaction was something to see. The simplest achievement would set her face aglow—and I mean it really glowed!

As Randy had *such* a desire to be part of the class, I always had something to offer, even if it was as simple as telling her that Randy only needed to use his "special spinning square" twice during the class. Whenever she ran into me outside of class or during the next semester (when I was no longer working with Randy), she would again light up. Behind a simple "Hello," she seemed to be saying, "Thank you for caring. Thank you for taking the time to include my child."

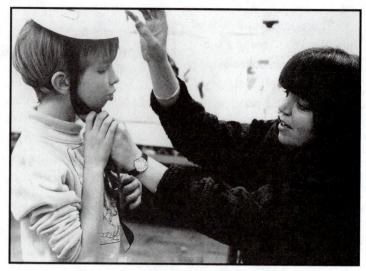

A good drama teacher must be able to play and be spontaneous. (Photo by Lea Ann Rosen)

where the student is, accepts that, and works on developing what could be. He doesn't try to destroy what is there and replace it with something else, but uses current skills and abilities as a starting point on which to build.

A third key quality to good drama teaching is the ability to recognize and respond to "Magic" when it happens. What I call "Magic" is that spark which lights up the hearts and minds of everyone in the room at the same time. "Magic" happens every time something truly creative and spontaneous and truthful clicks in a group. Suddenly everyone in the room is on the same wavelength—totally focused, imaginatively involved, and completely immersed in the work going on. The drama space is not just a room anymore; it becomes transformed into a highly charged transitional space in which anything can happen. Time seems to stand still. Students become "potential beings," capable of intense bursts of creativity, cooperation, and appreciation.

You can't force "Magic" to happen, but you can prepare a favorable climate for it through the way you treat your students and through your expectations of how they should treat each other. "Magic" can only happen when individuals feel respected, feel they can take risks without undue fear of criticism or attack, and know that even their silly or crazy ideas will be appreciated and accepted.

To successfully teach drama to a student who has a disability, there is one additional key. Avoid the trap of your own or society's prejudices, preconceptions, and stereotypes about people with disabilities. Throw them away so that they don't blind you to the unique individual who is your student. Learn instead to SEE THE PERSON AND NOT THE DISABILITY.

This does not mean to ignore the disability or to forget that the disability is there. SEE THE PERSON AND NOT THE DISABILITY means don't let the disability get in the way of your relationship with the person. Look past the outer differentness to see the inner sameness underneath that connects us all. We all experience the whole spectrum of human emotions and they need to be appropriately expressed, shared with others, and validated. We all want to be acknowledged, accepted, and appreciated. We all want to be loved. We all have creative ideas no matter what our level of cognitive functioning is.

If you can connect with an individual's feelings, dreams, and creativity, you will connect with that person's inner self. If you can value the unique contribution that each person makes to a group, the individual will feel valued as well. If you can begin to see your student in terms of his potential instead of his limitations, in terms of his strengths instead of his weaknesses, you will begin to bypass the trap of confining your vision only to his disability. Believe that each person in your class possesses imaginary wings and can be taught to fly!

PREREQUISITES TO TAKING A DRAMA CLASS

The first prerequisite for a successful experience in drama is that the student wants to take the class. He must be willing to participate in the activities, to play and have fun, to express his feelings and explore those of other people. A good teacher can motivate someone who is shy or confused, jolly a student out of a bad mood, negotiate a solution to an interpersonal conflict, but is powerless against a closed mind.

The few children who have dropped out of special needs drama classes that I have taught have done so because they never really wanted to be in the class in the first place. Their parents thought it would be a good idea for them to take a drama class, but never asked their children if they wanted to take it. Forced into a situation not of their own choosing, these students became stubborn and belligerent, refused to participate, to follow the rules, or to get along with anyone in the class. They felt bad, I felt bad, and their parents felt bad. We all chalked up another slash mark on the negative side of the life experience blackboard.

The second prerequisite to begin in drama is that a student needs to have achieved a basic ability to connect with and interact appropriately with others. Drama is rarely taught as an isolated, individual activity. A drama class almost always happens in a highly interactive group situation. There must be a minimal willingness on the part of the student to cooperate and work with the teacher and the other students.

Students who have major emotional disabilities—either hostile, anti-social behavior or severe withdrawal from others—have difficulty succeeding in drama. They might do better starting out in the arts with music or visual art, both of which involve expressing feelings and developing artistic, physical, and cognitive skills in a setting where the work is more independent and less interactive. After their self-confidence has grown and they start liking themselves better, they can begin working on their ability to get along with and respect others.

Another alternative for them might be to participate in a group which plays social games and/or non-competitive sports. Competition between individuals or teams reinforce the negative social values the child already has. Caught in a situation which focuses on winning or losing, the child begins to worry about being deprived of approval. Win-win experiences in which cooperation is stressed will let him off the hook. He won't have to constantly measure himself against others to see if he is better or worse. He can focus on participating with others and learning to enjoy himself. Eventually he will develop the ability to work and play in a group.

ASSIGNING STUDENTS TO THE APPROPRIATE DRAMA CLASS

Activities and assignments in drama, as in any other subject, need to be appropriate to the maturity level, attention spans, interests, and abilities of the students in the class. If the range in any of these areas is too wide, the class will have difficulty working together. For this reason, placement in the appropriate drama class is essential.

PLACEMENT BY AGE

Students in the primary grades are usually enrolled in a creative drama or puppetry class. Students in middle and high school take improvisational acting or scene study classes. Depending on their maturity level and interests, students in grades 4-6 can opt for whichever type of class most appeals to them. Classes for adults usually begin at age eighteen and no further separation according to age needs to be made.

Since students who have special needs are not always in graded academic classes or may be mainstreamed in school with younger students, I organize special needs classes around the three analogous age brackets: ages five through nine, ages nine through twelve, and ages twelve and older. Anyone eighteen or older who has finished high school is an adult.

I have successfully taught creative drama classes for special needs students which had a wider age spread. In one, the ages ranged from five to fourteen! However, there are several obvious drawbacks to an arrangement of this kind. One is the difference between the attention spans of a five-year-old and a fourteen-year-old. There are also big differences in emotional maturity and interests. Older students can usually handle more complex dramatic material than younger ones can. They want to spend time exploring projects and exercises in more depth. For a class with a wide age span to succeed, students must love drama, like each other, have similar interests, and be willing to put aside age differences to work together harmoniously.

PLACEMENT BY DISABILITY

When I first started the special needs program at the Bethesda Academy, I was strongly advised by several special needs educators NEVER to mix children who have learning disabilities and children who have mental retardation. They said that these two groups would be like mixing oil and water—they would not get along together. The different cognitive needs of each group required a different kind of presentation of information. To add insult to injury, the children who had learning disabilities would feel stigmatized. This may be true in a traditional academic setting, but it is not necessarily true in the drama classroom. However, I was just starting out and the advice I received had been so strongly worded that I followed it to the letter. I offered Creative Drama (LD) and Creative Drama (MR) in my Special Needs Program class schedule.

I was also advised—in equally strong terms—not to mix students who have physical disabilities with students who have cognitive disabilities. This advice created no changes in my plan, as I had anticipated mainstreaming anyone with a physical disability. We did offer a special acting class for the purpose of mainstreaming deaf and hearing teens together, but didn't have enough students that year to make it happen.

When I came to structuring Pegasus, the mainstreamed performing company, I found myself in a quandary. I needed to mix teens with and without disabilities, but I wasn't supposed to be mixing disabilities with each other. After much deliberation, I decided to accept everyone who was interested and capable of participating and to let the chips fall where they may. The individuals who joined had a wide variety of disabilities: Down syndrome, cerebral palsy, blindness, William syndrome, severe learning disabilities, and mild learning disabilities. Over the course of our first year together, I discovered that everyone was perfectly capable of understanding what was going on and felt fine about working together. A great time was had by all and no one felt stigmatized.

Since that time I have stopped offering different special needs drama classes for different types of disabilities. For students who are not yet ready to mainstream, I offer one class in each age category. I have mixed students who had physical disabilities, learning disabilities, mental retardation, and multiple disabilities. We don't worry about the distinctions and differences between us, we just learn about drama and have fun together. Students who function at higher cognitive levels serve as leaders in the group and help out the others.

As far as adapting teaching techniques to the different kinds of needs in the classroom, I have found that each child in *any* drama class has different needs and different styles of processing information. To effectively teach each student, I must adapt my techniques and approach to each one, disabled or not.

Having said that, I will add that if you can arrange for children of similar cognitive and/or emotional functioning levels to be grouped together, don't hesitate to do so. Any teacher's job is easier if the number of issues being addressed are within a certain limit. More work can usually be accomplished together.

The two greatest determinants of a child's ability to function successfully in a drama classroom are his emotional maturity and his group interaction skill level. Specifically, a child must have enough impulse control, focus, and flexibility to work out the conflicts which inevitably occur when two or more people are involved in a project together.

PLACEMENT BY EXPERIENCE LEVEL

It can be helpful to offer a beginning or introductory level class and an intermediate or advanced level class. Beginners often need more structure and more time to learn the rules and develop social interaction skills. Students with a year or so of drama under their belts will start the first class ready to go and may become impatient waiting for the new-comers to get up to speed.

On the other hand, students who have some experience can be role models for beginning students and can help them learn appropriate behavior and new skills more quickly. They already know what to expect and how much fun drama can be. A strong recommendation from a peer will often sell an idea or concept better than any song and dance from the teacher.

HOW MANY STUDENTS TO INCLUDE IN A CLASS

Overcrowding a drama class causes frustrations for teachers and students alike. Drama teachers like to give each student quality individual attention. Drama students need to have enough opportunities for participation in each class to learn and grow. Students who sit around too much get bored and lose interest. They stop paying attention to the work in class and begin to misbehave in order to get attention from the teacher.

Several years ago the Academy decided to limit class size to fifteen. Our teachers generally feel that between ten and twelve students is the optimum number for a regular acting class. Eight to ten students works well for a rambunctious group of young creative drama students.

Special needs drama classes work best with five to eight students in them. In a smaller group situation, everyone can receive a lot of extra individual attention and encouragement. Students who have perceptual difficulties or attention deficits are not overwhelmed by too much sensory stimulation. Students who have impulse control problems don't have to wait too long before taking a turn. Very shy children feel less pressured with fewer people to relate to.

All Academy classes for very young children (ages three to five) have an assistant. All special needs classes have at least one assistant. Large classes and classes in which one or more students with disabilities are mainstreamed can be assigned an assistant if necessary and practical.

Experience has taught us not to push the number of students in classes too far over the optimum number. It's not worth it in terms of student, teacher, and parent satisfaction. Whenever we have registrations over the limit, we close the class, start a waiting list, and try to open up a second class.

Mainstreaming affects the optimum number of students in a class. A student who has a disability usually needs a little more attention in order to succeed. The teacher must often make adaptations in the classroom and in his teaching style to accommodate the student's learning style or physical requirements. This can affect his division of time, attention, and energy among all of the students in the class. One way to deal with this is to add an assistant to the class.

Since each student deserves an appropriate share of class time and teacher attention, we needed to find a new method of figuring optimum class size in order to accommodate all individuals who might sign up for any given class while not overloading the teacher. A good guideline was suggested by one of our Special Needs Steering Committee members who had been the principal of a special needs public school. In his experience, each special needs student required the same amount of teacher attention as two regular education students. He suggested that when figuring appropriate class size, a student who has special needs be counted as two students.

Following this formula, a creative drama class of eight students, two of whom had special needs, would be counted as a full class of ten. If we chose to add more students to the class, we would need to add an assistant to keep a good teacher-student ratio in the classroom.

BEHAVIOR MANAGEMENT

If everyone could get along all the time, follow directions, and respect themselves and others, teaching would be a breeze. However, every student and teacher has bad days just as they have good ones. Disagreements happen. Personality conflicts sometimes develop between individuals. It's easy to bring emotional baggage from earlier in the day along with you to drama class.

Students who have disabilities have to contend with extra complications in their lives which can create disturbances in a classroom. Without a doubt disabilities create frustrations in the lives of those who have to contend with them. It can be extremely upsetting when your body or your mind isn't within your conscious control and won't do what you want it to do. Some emotional reactions you see may stem directly from frustration over a task that is too difficult or may start if a student is rushed to solve a problem that, for him, is very complicated and challenging.

The emotional fall-out from years of frustrating experiences can become more handicapping than the initial disabling condition and color a person's whole attitude and approach to life. Some individuals stop trying and withdraw. Others become timid and helpless. While the response of some might be anger, others might become morose and depressed. Rigidity and inflexibility, being unwilling to consider and choose different options in a given situation, can result from fear of failure.

CREATING A SUPPORTIVE ENVIRONMENT

Some students may enter your classroom expecting to fail because they have failed in academic or social situations so many times before. It is the teacher's responsibility to create an environment which is geared toward success rather than failure. This can be done by putting your focus on students' efforts and attitudes and on their progress as artists, rather than putting it on the end product.

In a supportive classroom no student is labeled "good" or "bad." To label a child will place a value judgement on his character and assign him a negative or positive role to play out in the classroom. What should be evaluated is work and behavior, not character. Appropriate class work and behavior is rewarded with praise and attention. Inappropriate work and behavior is pointed out and dealt with in an appropriate, nonjudgmental manner.

When students feel accepted for who they are and feel safe from attack or judgement, they are freed from acting out old emotional scripts of failure.

They can allow their most creative, most social, and most fun-loving selves out to play and interact with others without fear that they will be put on the spot or negatively criticized.

COOPERATION VS. COMPETITION

Competition often creates conflict in a group situation. Keep competition to a minimum. Too much of our contemporary American society is based on cut-throat competition. This creates an atmosphere of hostility and aggression: the only way I can succeed is to make you lose.

Play games which stress cooperation rather than competition. Focus on the fun of playing the game, on working together with friends, and on coming up with creative solutions to problems. Point out creative, expressive work done by each individual or team as it happens, so students learn to appreciate the work itself, rather than what that work means in terms of winning or losing. If a game does involve a winning and losing team, stress good sportsmanship. I always insist that the winners of the game congratulate the losers of the game on a good game played.

SETTING UP THE RULES

Be sure the rules of the classroom are set up clearly at the beginning of the first class and reviewed at the beginning of the next few sessions until everyone is aware of them. Talk about the reasons behind having rules. The purpose of rules is not to impose rigid discipline on students from the outside, but to create a structure so they can appropriately control themselves and you can run an orderly class in which they will be safe.

Try to have no more than five important rules of behavior. If you have a long list, students won't be able to remember them all. Present the rules in the form of positive statements which express what students are expected to do, rather than what they are not supposed to do. Post your rules somewhere in the classroom.

My rules usually are:

1. Listen to and look at whoever is talking.
2. Keep your hands and feet to yourself.
3. Respect the ideas of others.
4. Follow directions.
5. Do your best.

If I am teaching in a very distracting space, I sometimes need to add:

6. Leave the things in the room we are not using alone.

Don't expect a student to follow a rule that has not been explained to him. Don't assume that students understand how to behave politely, how to respect other people's property, how to pay attention, or how to follow directions. Remember that having poor social skills does not mean that a student is "bad." It just means he has poor social skills. Use drama class as a forum in which he can learn better ones.

Contracts. If you find that your rules are not working and you are having behavior problems with the class as a whole, you might have a discussion in which the students set the rules for themselves and come up with a contract. Write out the contract and have everyone, including the teacher, sign it to signify that they will abide by the rules and the agreed-upon consequences, if the rules are not followed.

If one student is having difficulty behaving in class, an individual contract can be drawn up between student and teacher delineating the issues and how the student is going to try to control himself. The teacher can agree to modify class structures or permit the student self-regulatory measures in time of stress. For instance, a student who has ADHD might need to leave the group and take a short break in a quiet, non-distracting part of the room whenever he feels he is being over-stimulated by the group activity. Taking a "time-out," in this instance, becomes a method the student can use to control his own behavior rather than a disciplinary action taken by the teacher. Consequences for inappropriate behavior, such as losing a turn or having to sit out for the rest of a game, can also be spelled out in an individual contract.

MODELING

Children are natural imitators. They can learn what is appropriate by observing others who are behaving appropriately. Before they can imitate, however, they need to know *what* to imitate. Demonstrate positive behavior by modeling it yourself and having your assistant model it. Call attention to students who are modeling positive behavior and praise them: Susie is working so well with Johnny!

NON-VERBAL CUES

You naturally use non-verbal cues all the time: eye contact, gestures, looks, facial expressions, sounds of pleasure and displeasure. Become conscious of how you are using your nonverbal communications and enhance them to positively reinforce behavior you want and discourage behavior you don't want. Smile, nod "yes," and make pleasant sounds when a student is doing good work. Frown, shake your head "no," wrinkle your brows, hold up your hand in a stop gesture as warnings that you want certain behaviors to stop.

TOUCH

Most children enjoy a gentle pat on the shoulder or arm when they have done a good job. However, be aware of where and how you touch children. Link your touch with a word of praise to clarify why you are touching them.

Children who have Down syndrome tend to be very warm and demonstrative about their feelings. They often like to hug or kiss teachers or other students. This can become distracting or inappropriate. Explain to them that other people have personal space and do not always want to be touched. You can say, "We are all friends here, but hugs (or kisses) are inappropriate (or "not OK") during drama class." If this doesn't work, you could limit the time when hugs can be given to times of greeting and leave taking.

Some children, especially those who have been physically or emotionally abused, do not like to be touched. Respect their sensitivities and personal space.

Children who have ADD/ADHD, TS, autism, or other types of sensorimotor disabilities are often tactilely defensive. They will pull away from a light, gentle touch. This does not mean they don't like to be touched; they may respond positively to a firm touch. Standing behind them, touch their shoulders with a firm, downward pressure. This kind of pressure seems to center them and can be used as a technique to calm them or help them focus when they are about ready to spin out of control.

A child who has a sensorimotor disability can sometimes get himself back under control by pressing down on his head with both hands, by pressing up against a wall with both hands, or by doing other isometric exercises which create a similar straight, downward or inward pressure.

CONTRACT FOR DRAMA CLASS

We, the Thursday afternoon Drama Class, agree to behave by the following rules while we are in drama class:

1. We will LISTEN TO AND FOLLOW DIRECTIONS.
2. We will RESPECT OTHERS IN THE CLASS. This means keeping our hands and feet to ourselves: no hitting, pushing, or fighting of any kind. This also means we will say only nice, friendly things to each other.
3. We will STAY ON THE RIGHT SIDE OF THE ROOM.
4. We will ONLY PLAY ON THE JUNGLE GYM DURING SNACK TIME.
5. We will ASK PERMISSION TO GO TO THE BATHROOM OR TO GET A DRINK OF WATER DURING CLASS. This means that *after* Sally or Angela say we can go, we will *walk* out of the room.

If we are going to the bathroom, we will walk directly to the bathroom. If we are boys, we will only go into the boys' bathroom. If we are girls, we will only go into the girls' bathroom. After we are done, we will walk directly back to the OT/PT Room and rejoin the group.

If we are going to the water fountain, we will walk directly to the water fountain, get a drink, and walk directly back to the OT/PT Room. We will not run into or look into any other rooms on the way.
6. We promise to DO OUR BEST. This means concentrating on the story, working hard, obeying all the rules, and staying with the rest of the group during all activities. We will not wander around the room or do something else.
7. We understand that IF WE BREAK ANY OF THE RULES, we will be asked to take a TIME OUT until we are ready to rejoin the group and follow all the rules.

Sincerely,

Always be careful to avoid touching a student in a private, inappropriate place which would violate his personal space or which could be misinterpreted as being physically or sexually abusive.

VERBAL REMINDERS AND POSITIVE REINFORCEMENT

Side-coach all the time. Praise good behavior. "Susie, you are doing a wonderful job!" "Sam and Eric, you are both working together so well today! I'm really proud of the job you are doing."

Make statements about behavior that you approve of or skills you see developing. "John is following the rules of the game." "Bill is paying attention very well today." "Mary is becoming an excellent mime."

Head off problems you see brewing by reminding students about rules or directions. "Remember, keep your hands to yourself." "Stay away from the costume rack."

REWARDS

Rewards can come in many guises. Praise, positive feedback, and encouragement will make any student thrive.

If you have a number of students in class who have difficulty getting along, you can set up special reinforcing activities they will be able to do, if they cooperate. One creative drama class for LD students taught by one of my colleagues, loved to play Duck, Duck, Goose. If everything went well in class, she would let them play it for the last five or ten minutes. Duck, Duck, Goose became their ritual closure activity.

You could provide a special snack midway through or at the end of class if students work well together. Check with parents and your administration before you do this, however. Some people don't like using food as a reinforcing tool. Others may not want to have meals spoiled. Some children are on special diets like the Feingold Diet or have allergies or sensitivities to certain foods like sugar, caffeine, or chocolate. It will not do to have one or two students unable to participate in the reward of the whole group.

Colorful stickers can also be used as rewards. Many special education classrooms use sticker charts to keep track of the success a student has in class. You can do this, too. Even nondisabled students love getting stickers. They are a visual proof of a job well done and can be shared with parents and friends.

If you are rewarding just one behavior, you could make a chart which has a space for one sticker for each class period. If you are rewarding more than one behavior or if you are rewarding a behavior each time it is performed, you may want to make a chart which has a number of spaces for each class period.

The time chosen for giving stickers out is up to the discretion of the teacher. Stickers could be given every time the appropriate behavior is performed or at the end of each class. Rewards are more reinforcing if they are given immediately after the appropriate behavior is done, but you might not want to interrupt your class frequently.

FREEDOM TO ASK QUESTIONS

Tell students that it is always OK for them to ask for help or for more information. Questions might be about anything from how to do an exercise to where to find the bathroom. Students might need assistance in doing an art project or in dealing with another student who is being insulting or offensive. If your students feel they have permission to ask questions, they can clarify confusions and misunderstandings before interpersonal problems or frustrations arise and turn into major conflicts.

GROUP DISCUSSIONS

Never underestimate the value of a group discussion when interpersonal problems occur in a group. Whenever students have the opportunity to contribute to solving a problem, they will own the solution and try to make it work. They may be able to give you insight into their difficulties which you had never thought of. They may be able to tell you how they deal with this problem successfully in school or at home.

When students talk with each other about how they feel, they form new bonds of friendship and understanding as they recognize how we are all more alike than different. Group discussions can be very helpful in mainstreamed groups. Go around the circle and let each student share what bugs him the most or what he feels most insecure about. Everyone has a special need of some kind and everyone needs the support of others to deal with it.

Pegasus, a performing group for teens with and without disabilities which I direct, had a lot of growing pains in its first few seasons as we worked through interpersonal conflicts. A number of the actors had known each other for years and were entrenched in dealing with their frustration, disagreements, and miscommunications with each other in very inflexible, impatient, and bull-headed ways.

Our first year we had a least one argument per rehearsal. Every time a conflict arose, we stopped and talked about it. I insisted that everyone's ideas were valuable and that we needed to give everyone a chance to share. If a number of good ideas were in competition, we tried to work out a compromise in which the best aspects of all the ideas were put to use.

By the second year the Pegasus actors were respecting each other more. We only had major disagreements in the early part of the year. Our third year we had only one argument the whole season and the minute it erupted, both combatants immediately realized they had overstepped their bounds. They separated, cooled off, and then apologized. I was impressed at their growth and maturity.

In a sense, learning to be an artist is the process of learning how to make choices about how to express yourself most eloquently, clearly, and truthfully. Teaching your students how to make choices is part of their artistic training as well as part of their socialization, so don't feel that time spent in discussion is a waste of class time!

Sometimes a group discussion goes well, but sometimes it degenerates into a blaming session. I had this happen during the third session of my very first creative drama class for learning disabled students. Everyone in the class came in wired from a wild, unusual week at school. The day was rainy which also seemed to affect their behavior. A number of exercises we did were successful, but everything broke down when everyone, holding hands in a circle, was acting out a large hot air balloon. They started pulling on each others' arms, bumping into each other, shoving, and pinching.

I stopped the class and tried to get them to talk about why they were having such a tough time working together. They were so overwrought that they were unable to verbalize any feelings or reasons. They just started accusing each other of ruining the class. I explained that no one person was at fault and the best thing would be for everyone to forgive everyone else and start over. That seemed like an excellent solution at first, and everyone started hugging each other and saying, "I'm sorry."

However, Ginger was still very upset. Drama class was extremely important to her and she felt the whole day had been ruined. Instead of hugging Roberto, she went up to him and angrily said, "It's your fault! I hate you, Roberto." Taking her lead, all the other students suddenly started hitting each other, yelling, "I hate you! I hate you! I hate you!"

Marilyn, my assistant, was a musician. For some serendipitous, intuitive reason, we both looked at each other and started singing "If You're Happy And You Know It" at the same time. Immediately, everyone else joined in. We had to sing eleven verses of the song before the mood in the room turned upbeat and forgiveness was truly in the air. The twelfth verse we made up was "If you're happy and you know it, hug your friend." They did and the emotional storm was finally over.

The moral of this story is "Sometimes none of the reasonable solutions work and you have to punt."

IGNORING NEGATIVE BEHAVIORS

Usually when negative behavior is disrupting class in a major way or creating a safety hazard, it must be dealt with the minute it occurs. Sometimes, however, negative behavior can be extinguished by *not* paying attention to it. Whether you pay attention to a behavior or not will be a judgement call you will have to make in the context of the situation. Remember that if you allow negative behavior to go on, you are allowing that student to model behaviors you don't want to be copied.

WARNINGS

Some teachers like to use an "early warning system" before imposing consequences. Code words or phrases can be used to remind a student that his behavior is on the verge of getting out of hand. "911!" (the phone number commonly used for emergencies in many communities) is a phrase that Tim Reagan, one of the Academy's drama teachers, has found useful because through humor it indicates that a serious line is about to be crossed. It's also a short phrase that doesn't interrupt the flow of class. Other teachers at the Academy have used "911" with great success. They have found that after a while their students start reminding each other to behave by saying "911!"

The words "appropriate" and "inappropriate" can be good buzz words to use in describing behavior. They are often used in the special education classroom to provide a non-judgmental alternative to the words "good" and "bad." Students who are familiar with these words will respond to them because they know what they mean. "OK" and "Not OK" are also good non-judgmental words to use in describing behavior.

Some teachers like to provide students with a series of warnings. Maybe the first warning is verbal. At the second infraction, the teacher writes the student's name on the board. The third time the teacher puts a check mark by the student's name and the fourth time the student must face consequences. This allows a student who has problems with self-control several chances to readjust his behavior.

CONSEQUENCES

Sometimes a rule is broken because of poor communication, a mistake, projected/misplaced emotions, or lack of awareness of the rule. When this happens it is best to deal with the situation through a short, rational discussion with the parties involved in order to clarify the confusion.

Sometimes a conflict will arise, not because something upsetting has happened in class, but because something upsetting has happened *before* class. Gail Gorlitz, one of the Academy's visual art teachers, tells a story about a child who entered her classroom so wound up that he jumped through the door, leapt across the table, and knocked over another boy who was innocently standing in the middle of the room. In talking to his mother later, she discovered that he had recently come to this country from China. The first major cold snap of the winter had hit that day, so when he went to school in the morning, he wore his winter coat, a pink down jacket he had brought from his homeland. In China, it is culturally acceptable for a boy to wear pink, but not in America! From the moment he arrived at school he was unmercifully teased by all the boys for wearing a "sissy" jacket. His response was to ball up the jacket, throw it into a heap on the floor of the closet, and refuse to wear it. Needless to say, he got in trouble with his teacher and his mother. By the time he entered Gail's classroom, he was ready to explode! And he did!

Other times a rule is broken deliberately as a means of getting negative attention or hurting a perceived "enemy" in the class. When this happens, consequences must be imposed by the teacher or discipline will break down. Consequences usually involve removing the student from the group activity until he can work cooperatively with other students.

When warnings are not heeded, a "Time-Out Chair" in another part of the classroom can be an excellent behavior management tool. "Time-Out Chairs" provide students with a place and time to cool off and evaluate their actions.

Before each class begins, set up your "Time-Out Chair" some distance away from where the majority of class activity usually happens. Make it clear that anyone who cannot participate appropriately will be asked to take a "time-out" there.

If a student begins misbehaving or showing off during an activity, stop the activity. Give the student a choice to either participate appropriately or take a time-out. He may take this last chance and turn his behavior around. If he doesn't, tell him, "If you can't choose to behave appropriately, then you must take a time-out." If necessary, have your assistant accompany the student to the "Time-Out Chair," but try not to provide him with any additional attention to reinforce his inappropriate behavior. Replace the student in the activity, if needed, and continue working with the group.

If the offense was not major, sitting in the chair from one to three minutes in order to regain personal control may be enough. You can say, "You may rejoin the group after three minutes, if you feel you can participate appropriately." Younger students usually need to be given a time limited "time-out" so they don't feel as if they are being abandoned.

If the offense needs to be discussed with the student before he rejoins the class, allow him to cool off for a few minutes. If two children have been involved in a fight, you might need to send them to separate "time-out" spaces and let them get a little distance on their conflict before working out the problem between them.

When talking out inappropriate behavior, ask the student why he thought he was unable to participate in the activity appropriately. Then ask what he will change about his behavior so that he can participate again or what he can do differently if a similar situation should arise in the future. When processing a conflict between two students, ask each to report only on what *he* did in the situation, so he can admit to and own his own behavior. If you allow each to tell what the other did, your discussion will degenerate into a blaming session and nothing will be resolved.

The teacher or assistant should always remain calm when talking with a student about his behavior. Getting angry will change the confrontation into a power struggle between teacher and student. Word your discussion of the situation in terms that are non-judgmental. The student is not bad, he just made an inappropriate choice. You do not dislike him or think anything less of him because of it. Everyone makes mistakes.

Use simple language. Keep his options open. Focus on the choices he has made and the choices he can make in the future. This puts him in control of himself. He takes responsibility for his past and future behavior and the teacher or assistant is not turned into a lecturer, a bully, or a nag who is forcing a behavior change on him.

EXTREME SITUATIONS

Drama is fun and students want to be part of the group. They are usually motivated to modify their behavior so they can continue to have a good time. However, on rare occasions it is necessary to remove a student from the room or to continue the time-out for the rest of the session.

Therapeutic Holds. On very rare occasions, a student may lose control and become physically violent. If this happens, it may become necessary to restrain him with a therapeutic hold. Therapeutic holds are not common behavior management techniques in the drama classroom. I have only had to use a therapeutic hold once in five years.

Stand behind the student and firmly hold his arms wrapped around his body as if he were in a strait-jacket. In this position, he cannot hurt you or another student, he cannot destroy property, and he will not hurt himself. Remain calm vocally and physically. Talk to the student in a quiet, calm voice. Remind him of his choices. Tell him you are holding him so he won't hurt himself and you will release him when he regains his self-control. When he calms down, gently release him. Ask him to sit down and talk about the problem quietly.

COMMUNICATION WITH PARENTS

Parents can be a great resource in helping you manage a student's behavior and in providing you with good ways to deal with unpleasant situations.

When you have had a problem in class, check in with the parent who comes to pick up the child after class or at the end of the day. You are not doing this to "tattle" on the student, embarrass him, or create problems for him at home. If you have dealt with the behavior in class, there should be no need for additional consequences to be imposed. However, parents need to be made aware that their child is having a problem.

Approach parents in a calm, reasonable, non-judgmental manner. You can say, "Johnny had a problem in class today." Or say, "If you have a minute to talk, I would like to tell you about a situation that came up today." State the facts of the case simply and briefly: what the student did or said and what you did or said.

If enlisted as a member of the same team (a team which is on the side of the child), parents can be your best ally in heading off future problems. They can remind the child on the way to drama class of the behavior that is appropriate. They can provide you with insights as to why this behavior occurred and what you might do to prevent its occurring again.

If the behavior continues and the child must be removed from the class, the removal will not come as a complete surprise to the parents. They will have been involved with the situation from the beginning and they will have worked with you on solving it. They won't feel that you are making an irrational decision or scapegoating their child.

It is usually best to check in with the parents immediately after class because this is immediately after the behavior occurred. However, there are times when you or they don't have time to talk or when it would be inappropriate to discuss the situation in front of the child. If this happens, call the parent at home sometime before the next class meeting at a time when it is convenient for them to talk with you. Use your common sense. Mealtimes and bedtimes are obviously *not* good times.

Children with special needs tend to bring home more negative reports than positive ones. Be sure to give parents feedback when their child has done a good job, too! Letters home which provide updates on what the class has been doing and on upcoming events keep parents involved. A quick note or a few comments after class to share a success that their child has had is greatly appreciated. When parents know that you are seeing and appreciating the positive aspects of their child as well as dealing appropriately with the negatives ones, they will become your loyal supporters.

chapter six

creative drama and improvisational acting classes:
further adaptations for the drama classroom

CREATIVE DRAMA

THE CREATIVE DRAMA SESSION

Creative drama is an informal, improvised, extemporaneous dramatic event which may involve the acting out of a story or scene, usually a fairy tale or contemporary children's story. Through the creative dramatic process, feelings, attitudes, and ideas of oneself and others are explored and expressed.

Creative drama can be done with students of all ages. However, preschool and elementary aged children usually take creative drama classes. Middle and high school students usually take acting classes that focus on improvisational acting or scene study. An age overlap falls in the upper elementary years (Grades 4-6). Placement in a creative drama or an acting class depends on the student's sophistication and drama skill level. In my experience, students who have special needs typically retain an interest in fantasy and fairy tales longer than their nondisabled age peers. Because of this, they are often happier in a creative drama situation. Their interests don't usually begin to shift to "older" material until they reach adolescence. Even then, fantasy often continues to have a firm hold on their imaginations.

Presentation of creative dramatic scenes is informal. It is work done "in process" or "in progress" *by* the group *for* the group. Training students in theatrical skills for the stage or creating a play to be formally performed for an audience is not necessary or even desirable. The content of the dramatic work, the informal process of learning together through activity, and the development of the imagination are the important aspects of creative drama.

Of course, a scene developed through creative dramatics can be performed for an audience. However, when this is done, the focus of the work changes from one of learning and process to one of performance and product. After a certain point, the class must stop exploring and start rehearsing. As the performance deadline draws near, energy must be focused onto refining and perfecting the work already created.

THE DRAMATIC ELEMENTS

The elements involved in a dramatic story or scene are similar to those in literature. Plot, characters, and dialogue create an idea or theme. However, there are two major differences.

First, in drama, all the elements are brought to life by actors, instead of by words on a page. The story unfolds in real space and time rather than being an imaginary event which happens purely within the mind of the reader.

Second, the descriptive narrative that is found in books is rarely found in drama. Information is largely expressed through the characters' dialogue and actions. It is true that some plays have narrators and that creative drama teachers often serve as the narrator for the story as it is being enacted; however, in both these cases, narration is only the glue that holds the dramatic action together and facilitates progression from one scene to the next. It is never the primary focus of the enactment. From an artistic standpoint, the less narration is involved in a play, the stronger its dramatic structure.

The plot of the scene or play is structured with a beginning, middle, and end. Most of the time the plot in creative drama is based on a fairy tale. It is also possible to create an original story with a group or to change the plot of a familiar story to create a new ending. I had one class that decided they wanted *The Wizard of Oz* to end with Dorothy staying in Oz and marrying the Tin Woodman. Another class wanted to explore what might have happened if Goldilocks had apologized for her actions and become friends with the Three Bears.

The plot is fueled by characters who have goals they want to accomplish and problems they need to solve. Improvisation comes into play as the actors create the dialogue or words that the characters say. Dialogue in a creative drama class is created on the spot by the actors, not memorized beforehand. This gives students a lot of freedom for problem-solving and role-playing as well as for developing their verbalization abilities and group interaction skills.

WARM-UPS

Depending on the age and attention spans of the students, a creative drama session usually lasts between 45 minutes and an hour. Class begins with a warm-up activity to focus students on the class and prepare them to work together. Warm-ups could be physical exercise, a social game, a movement activity, a sensory exploration, an imagination game, or an art project. Often these serve as skill builders for the work that is going to be done in class that day or an introduction to the story and characters. See Chapter Seven for descriptions of warm-ups.

THE STORY

Warm-ups are followed by a story that is read or told by the teacher and then acted out by the class. Stories can be traditional fairy tales, myths, legends, fables, or contemporary children's stories. Often I ask my classes what stories they would like to act out. Invariably they want to work on stories that deal with issues they are working on in their own lives. Bruno Bettelheim's book *The Uses of Enchantment* is an excellent exploration of how the conflicts and themes in fairy tales developmentally parallel those in the lives of children. One of the reasons why "Cinderella" is such a popular story is that it deals with the need to be recognized for all your inner beauty and exceptional qualities. It also provides a healthy outlet for children to evaluate their parent/child conflicts (the Evil Stepmother represents the "Bad Mother" who punishes them and doesn't let them do what they want, while the Fairy Godmother represents the "Good Mother" who is nurturing and warm).

SETTING UP FOR THE STORY

Before you can jump into acting out a story, a few decisions must be made. First, roles must be assigned to students. Methods of doing this will be discussed later in this chapter.

Then the space must be set up for acting out the story. Desks, chairs, or other objects can be arranged to create the "set" or locations needed for the story. Masking tape on the floor can be used to delineate rooms or, if you are setting up all locations simultaneously, to distinguish one locale from another. Setting up all locations at once is usually a good idea for smooth scene transitions, especially in a story that moves back and forth between places. Scene changes in the middle of a story take time and you can lose the attention of your audience and actors if you stop to move "scenery" around.

REHEARSAL

To ensure safety, rehearse any unusual physical actions, such as physical combat between hero and villain or acrobatics, ahead of time. One good technique for safely handling battle scenes is to pantomime all weapons so no one gets hit and to move in slow motion so each actor remains physically in control. In this way, a rehearsed, slow-motion battle can become a beautiful ballet. The actors don't forget they are acting and turn their staged fight into a real one. You could even help your actors retain the dance-like quality of their battle by adding music to it or by having the audience or other characters provide a rhythmic beat.

Some teachers like to let their actors practice character movements, voices, or important lines before jumping into the story. If a group is very new to drama, I often have everyone act out all characters together before I allow them to make character choices. If the story was "The Three Billy Goats Gruff," I would have the students stand up and practice walking and talking like THE BIG BILLY GOAT, The Middle Billy Goat, and the little billy goat. Then I would have them all practice being Trolls. Having an experience with all of the characters beforehand can encourage a wider range of choices and warm the students up to the idea of using their bodies and voices to create a character.

ACTING OUT THE STORY

Once all the preliminaries are in order, the story can be acted out. Have the students who are in the first scene take their places in the acting area. Those not in the first scene can sit to the side where they will make their entrance or they can sit in the audience until it is time to join the scene. Either way, everyone who is not in the story at any given moment should be paying attention to what is going on.

Acting as the narrator, the teacher can structure the story and help it to unfold. "Once upon a time, long, long ago, in a country far away, was a girl named Cinderella. Her mother was dead and she lived with her wicked Step-mother and two ugly Stepsisters. Every day her Stepsisters would make her do all the household chores. . . ." Notice that the narrator quickly moved the story into an action the actors could perform.

Beginning creative dramatic students need more narration to help them through a story than experienced ones do. The narrator can cue actions, entrances, and exits, "Suddenly, there was a knock on the door. It was the messenger from the King with an invitation to the ball." If the actors aren't sure what to do next, the narrator can remind them, "Cinderella was so upset, she started to cry." She can also cue lines, "So Cinderella said . . . And the Prince replied . . ."

Creative drama class acting out "The Four Chinese Brothers." (Photo by Lea Ann Rosen)

If students are non-verbal, they can pantomime the story to narration. In this situation, the narration must be kept mainly to actable actions, so the actors aren't standing around with nothing to do while the narrator talks.

In any case, if you are narrating a story, don't bulldoze your way through. Leave enough space for your students, verbal and non-verbal, to add lines if they want to. I have been surprised by students who never spoke a word for weeks and suddenly came out with all the right lines (and more!) when acting out a familiar and beloved story like "Goldilocks and the Three Bears."

Children love using colorful costumes and props when acting out stories. With students who have cognitive disabilities, costumes and props can be instrumental in helping their imaginations come alive and giving form and substance to the story for them.

However, don't feel that you have to go overboard about providing physical accoutrements. You can leave some things to the imagination. Actors who have everything given to them aren't as challenged to use their bodies and voices expressively or to stretch their imaginations to the fullest.

REPLAYING THE STORY

If time permits and interest is high, students may want to act out the story again. Replaying the story with students taking different roles allows them to experience the action through more than one point of view. A child who is playing the little billy goat gruff may have a very different experience from a child who is playing THE BIG BILLY GOAT GRUFF. The little billy goat is afraid of the Troll and escapes by using her wits. THE BIG BILLY GOAT GRUFF is physically capable of standing up to the Troll and knocking him off the bridge. An actor who plays only the little billy goat might remain afraid of the Troll. If she has a chance to play THE BIG BILLY GOAT as well, she may no longer fear the Troll because her character has competently handled the situation and saved her brothers. After this experience, she may even be brave enough to try to act out the Troll herself!

If they are satisfied with one time through the story, move on to another dramatic activity. It's always better to over-plan activities for your lesson plan than to under-plan.

CLOSURE

Class can end with a discussion of the story, a related art activity, or a drama game that provides closure for the session. (See the next chapter for ideas for closure activities.) Sometimes it's nice just to take two minutes to go around and let each person say what her favorite activity was that day. Class ends on an upbeat note, the work of the day is reviewed, and the teacher has an idea of what activities made the biggest impression on individuals and the class as a whole.

STRUCTURING A CREATIVE DRAMA SESSION

LESSON PLANS

When putting a lesson plan together, alternate between active and passive activities. This allows your students to work off excess energy by using their bodies actively, then resting from their exertions. They will be able to concentrate better because of the variety. If you structure your activities appropriately, you won't need to take a break in the middle of class. The order of the activities will provide all the rest time necessary.

If your class begins with a quiet opening warm-up, move on to an active game before having your students settle down to listen to the story. After a ten-minute story, they will be ready to get up again and act it out.

In the same way, if you are doing a session of theatre games, move from an active game to a passive one and back to an active one. You might start out with a physical warm-up, sit down for a pass-around pantomime or imagination game, play a rousing movement game, lie down for a guided fantasy relaxation, and end with a series of pantomimes.

Too many active games in a row will run one kind of group ragged and spin another kind out of control. Going directly from one quiet activity to another is a sure fire way to turn your students into wiggleworms. The next chapter has suggestions of good drama games to play.

PRE-CLASS ACTIVITIES

If you have a group that tends to straggle in for class at different times, it is a good idea to keep the early-comers constructively occupied. If students like to draw, this can be a very useful pre-class activity. You could let them draw anything they want or you could ask them to draw a character in the story you will be acting out that day. This will begin to focus them on the work that will be done in class.

Pre-class activities need to be interesting enough to hold attention, but not so interesting that students don't want to leave them to begin class. Everyone rarely finishes a project at the same time. Try to find a stopping point that everyone can agree upon. Projects not quite finished before class can be finished at the end of class or taken home for the final touches.

BEGINNING CLASS

Open class in a clear, sure way. Gather everyone together. Sitting in a circle, everyone is grounded and can see everyone else. If students have trouble staying in their own spot in the circle, use colorful carpet squares to help them define their sitting space.

Some groups enjoy a rundown of exactly what is going to happen in class that day. You might want to list all the activities planned for class in order on the blackboard or on a large sheet of paper. This will keep your students (and you!) organized. Many special education teachers go over the day's schedule with their students the first thing every morning. They leave the schedule up all day so that if students get confused, they can look at it and reorient themselves. This technique will work just as well for you as it does for academic special education teachers. In addition, many of your students may be familiar with the routine already.

Other groups like to begin class with the same activity each week: a physical warm-up to music, a circle game, a check-in on how everyone is feeling. The opening becomes a comforting ritual they can count on.

One of my creative drama classes insisted that I start with the same welcoming ritual each week. Everyone sat in a row of chairs and I would walk down the row, throw open my arms, and say, "Welcome, Tanya! Welcome, Jason! Welcome, Jeremy!" As I said each person's name, he or she would stand up, take a bow, and say, "Thank you!" "That's me!" "Hurray!" or something else appropriate to being welcomed to the group. A number of opening activities can be found in Chapter Seven.

TRANSITIONS

Make sure the transitions between activities are clear and smooth. Students become anxious and distracted if transitions are confusing or it takes too long between activities. As much as possible, set up your equipment and supplies before class or have things organized and easily within reach. This way you will be ready to start the next activity as soon as you are finished with the one before it.

Don't allow students to wander aimlessly around the room. Direct them in a strong, firm voice to the place they need to be in order to begin the next activity. Move there and take up the position they should be in, so they can see what you want them to do as well as hear your directions. "Everyone stand in a circle in the middle of the room." "Everyone come over here and sit in one of these chairs."

GIVING DIRECTIONS

Whenever you are explaining how to do something, whether it be playing a game or making an art project, present each step in the sequence separately. Don't run through all the directions from start to finish and expect your students to have any concept of what you are talking about. Most adults who have normal cognitive functioning can't follow a whole sequence of verbal directions that are thrown at them all at once.

A way to break down a sequence of directions might be as follows: "I'm dividing you into Group One and Group Two. [Do this.] Group One stand in a line over here. [Do this.] Now I want all of you to face the blackboard. [Do this.] Group Two stand in a line right here. [Do this.] Everyone face Group One. [Do this.]"

As you present each step, illustrate it through as many different sensory channels as you can. Say, "Sit with your legs crossed." Have your assistant actually sit with her legs crossed to provide a visual image of what "Sit with your legs crossed" means. When they sit down and cross their legs, they will understand kinesthetically what sitting with crossed legs means. If they can't figure out the position by looking at how your assistant is sitting, move their legs into the correct position so they can feel it in their own bodies.

Give clear directions. Use simple, plain words.

State what you want from students rather than what you don't want. It takes the brain more time to process negative statements than positive ones. When the negative comes in, the brain takes it and removes the negative to find out what the positive action would be. Then it adds the negative back in to cancel the positive action out. I am not learning disabled, but my brain freezes every time I see a traffic sign with a slash through it. I have to stop and consciously reason out if I am supposed to do what the picture shows or if I'm not supposed to do it.

Students who have information-processing problems can get lost and confused as they do this. A student can pick up the negative message (Don't hit Billy) as a positive one (Hit Billy) and act on it.

Processing negative commands into their positive components can leave children at a loss as to what behavior the teacher wants instead. Many times we give a command that has two parts: the spoken message and the unspoken one. The unspoken message is culturally understood as the natural outcome of the spoken one. For instance, the unspoken message of "Don't talk" is "Listen." But a student who has missed picking up cultural constructs because of cultural isolation or a disability, will only know what he *shouldn't* be doing. You need to fill in the missing message.

Learn to phrase requests in a positive manner. Tell students what you *want* them to do. Instead of saying, "Don't talk while others are talking," say, "Listen when others are talking." Instead of saying, "Don't hit other students," say, "Keep your hands and feet to yourself."

Rephrasing your communications from negative to positive is easier said than done. Communication style is habitual. If you tend to phrase your directions in a negative manner, you will need to consciously think through directions as you give them for a time. After awhile your communication habits will change and you won't have to stop and think about it as often.

STORIES FOR CREATIVE DRAMA

CHOOSING A STORY

Some stories are easier to act out than others. A lot depends on the structure of the plot and whether the characters have clear, actable goals. When working with beginners and with students who have cognitive disabilities, it is crucial to choose a story with a strong, clear dramatic plot structure and easily actable characters.

Some stories have very succinct and clear plots. They are based on a "one, two, three" rhythm pattern. The characters in these stories are usually one-dimensional; that is, they have one main action to play and no major decisions to make. "The Three Little Pigs" is one example of this kind of story. There are three Pigs. Two of them are lazy and one works very hard. One by one, they meet the Salesman and buy their building materials. One by one they build their houses of straw, sticks, and bricks. The Wolf, who is very hungry, decides he wants to eat the little Pigs, so he blows down the first and second house, but can't blow down the third house. Hard work wins the day. End of story.

"Goldilocks and the Three Bears" also follows this pattern. Goldilocks is a little girl whose major character trait is curiosity. After she breaks into the Bears' house, Goldilocks tries out their chairs (Big-Middle-Small), their porridge (Too Hot-Too Cold-Just Right), and their beds (Too Hard-Too Soft-Just Right). When the Bears return home, they check out their belongings in the same order: chairs, porridge, beds. They find Goldilocks in the bed where she fell asleep. She wakes up and runs away. End of story. Other stories that use this pattern include "The Three Billy Goats Gruff," "Little Red Riding Hood," and "The Little Red Hen."

Series in threes are very comforting to children. And adults. Enough tension can be generated from "one, two, three" that the relief from the resolution is satisfying—but there's not *too* much tension and it doesn't take *too* long to get to the end. Children who have cognitive disabilities often have trouble with sequencing and with mentally holding onto more than one idea simultaneously. They can follow the sequencing in these "one-two-three" patterned stories without getting confused or feeling anxious. These stories fit the shorter attention spans associated with many cognitive disabilities as well.

The next step up in plot structure complexity are stories that begin with a "one-two-three" pattern, but add some complications that postpone the resolution of the plot. "Rumpelstiltskin" is an example of this type of story. The Miller's Daughter is locked in three different rooms to spin straw into gold. A funny little man appears each time and offers to help her, but before he will, she must give him something of value. In the third room she has no jewelry left and must promise to give him her first baby. Time passes and the baby is born. She has three chances to guess the little man's name or he'll take the baby. She must send her Messenger throughout the land to collect names for her to guess. "Rumpelstiltskin" takes a little longer to act out because the plot is more involved. In addition, the characters are more complex—they have important decisions to make.

Another kind of story offers a dramatic plot structure in which the hero must pass through a number of trials, each more difficult than the one before. Sometimes a number of different characters try to solve a problem, but can't. Finally the hero comes along and succeeds. In "The Fisherman and His Wife," the Wife keeps sending her Husband back to the Magic Fish to get better and better houses to live in. In "The Stone in the Road," the King blocks the only road into town with a gigantic stone and hides to see if anyone in his kingdom is thoughtful enough to move it. He watches while many different characters walk by and ignore it—until finally the Miller's Son pushes it out of the way.

There is more to remember in these stories. More characters are involved. More events happen. Sometimes the events are causally connected, but sometimes they aren't. (Strong causal connection means that the first event causes the second event which causes the third which causes the fourth, etc.) The less strong the causal connection in a plot, the more difficulty students with cognitive disabilities will have following it. To remedy this, the teacher as narrator needs to focus on the through-line, or main action, and keep the story moving from scene to scene.

The more complex the plot of a story, the more difficult it will be for beginning creative drama students to act out. "Peter Pan" and "The Firebird" are examples of stories that have lots of characters, lots of locations, and many twists and turns in the plot. They are great for advanced students, but confusing for beginners.

Look for stories with lots of actable actions in the plots. Many paragraphs of flowery description by the narrator does not qualify as actable action. Beware of stories that say "Many years passed and the princess grew in beauty and wisdom." It is very hard to act "growing in beauty and wisdom." "Falling in love at first sight" is also hard to act.

Beware of stories that say, "And many suitors came and each one tried to make the princess laugh, but no matter what he did, each one failed." "Many suitors trying" is too vague to be acted. If you want to do a story of this kind, the storyteller must invent different specific actions for each suitor. Without more specifics, when the actors arrive at the suitor scene, all the suitors will walk into the room and just stand there.

Another plot device that can be problematic when dramatized is repetition. Be careful of choosing stories that repeat identical plot or character actions more than two or three times. "The Elves and the Shoemaker" is a good example of this. In most versions, the shoemaker leaves leather out for the elves to make shoes on four or five different nights. The first night he doesn't know anything will happen. The second night he leaves the leather out to see if it will happen again. The third night he and his wife stay up and watch. "And every night the elves would make shoes and he became rich and prosperous." Each time the elves are doing exactly the same thing— making shoes. This will hold the attention of very young children and children who are into repetition, but it will not hold the attention of inter- mediate or advanced groups.

Another warning: beware of casting actors as characters who don't have a dramatic purpose in the story. Lords- and Ladies-In-Waiting usually don't do anything dramatically important. They are not involved in moving the plot forward. Confidants of the hero or heroine usually don't do much ex- cept listen. Passive heroes, like the Young Master in "Puss In Boots," also pose an acting problem. Student actors who have parts that don't give them anything to do, get bored and either wander off or get into trouble.

Stories with strong plot structure that I have used successfully with beginning creative drama students who have special needs include "The Three Little Pigs," "Little Red Riding Hood," "The Three Billy Goats Gruff," "Goldilocks and the Three Bears," "The Peddlar and His Caps," "The Stone in the Road," "The Tortoise and the Hare," "The Lion and the Mouse," "The Magic Toy Shop," "The Little Fir Tree," "Why the Evergreen Trees Keep Their Leaves," "The Frog Prince," "The Giant Peanut Butter and Jam Sandwich," and "The Gingerbread Boy."

Intermediate groups enjoy acting out "Hansel and Gretel," "Cinderella," "Snow White and the Seven Dwarves," "Rapunzel," "Rumpelstiltskin," "Jack and the Beanstalk," "The Golden Goose," "The Dragon and His Grandmother," "The Fisherman and His Wife," "The Man and the Tiger," "King Midas and the Golden Touch," "The Brementown Musicians," "Sleeping Beauty," "The Princess Who Couldn't Cry," and "The Wizard of Oz."

Advanced groups can handle more complex stories like "Aladdin and His Magic Lamp," "The Firebird," "The Maids in the Mirror," "Snow White and Rose Red," "Mufaro's Beautiful Daughters," "East of the Sun and West of the Moon," "Persephone and Demeter," "The Labors of Hercules," and "The Six Servants."

A good source for stories is Winifred Ward's *Stories to Dramatize,* published by The Children's Theatre Press in Anchorage, Kentucky.

TELLING A STORY VS. READING IT

Telling a story to a class is much more effective than reading it from a book. Storytelling is more active. A good storyteller makes eye contact with her audience, invests herself emotionally as she describes the plot and vocally acts out the characters. All of this captures the attentions of the listeners and hooks them into using their imaginations as they follow along. Students become primed for their own enactment of the story, for they start to feel that the story is not a past event, but is happening now.

Telling a story gets the drama teacher more involved. When you read a book, you are processing information that is outside of yourself, that was formulated by another person. When you tell a story, you make it your own. You become intimately familiar with the plot and characters, you develop an emotional relationship with the material, and you communicate that familiarity and those emotional connections with your listeners.

A lot of teachers are afraid to tell a story. The first fear I always hear is "What if I forget a part?" You won't forget anything if you prepare yourself properly. "But what if I prepare myself and I forget something anyway?" Even if you do forget, if you know the story well, you will be equipped to mend your mistake with ease. Story listeners who are enjoying themselves are very forgiving of a storyteller who is also relaxed and having a good time.

To prepare to tell a story for the first time, read it over a number of times. The first time, just read for enjoyment, and when you are done, remember the emotional reactions you had. Were there any funny parts? Any exciting parts? Any romantic parts? Where did you feel tension begin to build? (Story-telling pace usually picks up as tension builds.) Where was the climax, the place where the tension was relieved? What are the strongest images that remain in your memory once the story is over?

As you read through it again, make a list of the characters and how they are related to each other. Outline what happens in the story. Try to see how

A good storyteller uses emotion, facial expressions, gestures, and character voices as she tells her tale. (Photo by Keith Jenkins)

one event causes the next event. If you can find the causal connections in the story, you'll have found its plot.

Sometimes you need to adapt a story. It may be too long or the plot may meander around too much. Find a way to cut out the extraneous scenes and make it tighter. Some of the events in the story may not be causally connected. Invent a way to change what happens to make events connect. There may be some violence that you would rather not have students act out or some action that is indirect and not clearly actable. Maybe a character's motives are a little muddy. Feel free to make a story stronger for your dramatic purposes. Since prehistoric times storytellers have changed and adapted stories to their own purposes. You'll be joining a long and respected tradition.

When you feel you know the story well and can hold the order of events in your mind, practice telling it. As you speak, keep an image of the characters in your mind's eye—what they look like, where they are, what they are doing, how they feel about it. This image may be private to you, but it com-

How I Became a Storyteller
by Mandy Hart, MA, CCC-SLP

I have always loved reading stories to children, but I have discovered that telling them is much more rewarding.

When I first started leading drama classes, I was extremely nervous. I didn't want to tell the stories because I was afraid that I would forget parts or leave out important characters or confuse the sequence of the story. Instead of telling them, I would read the stories, paraphrasing the difficult vocabulary to insure that the children understood all the words. The children enjoyed the stories, but there was no spontaneous participation and no "magic."

At the time, because my reading was so animated and because I was able to make a great deal of eye contact in between sentences, I felt that it wouldn't make much of a difference if I read or told the story. Now that I tell stories all the time, I realize that it does make an incredible difference!

Gradually, as my confidence grew and I became more familiar with the stories, I became less and less dependent on reading the written text. This provided me with more freedom and allowed me to be "in the moment" as I shared the story. It's great not having to stick to the exact lines written in a book! I felt more free to move around and I really started having fun acting out the different parts. "Magic" began to happen. The children became more involved in the story and began participating spontaneously—bursting out with what was going to happen next. Heads would turn when I pointed down the road to the giant's castle as I told "Jack and the Beanstalk." I began asking the children questions about the story as I told it. In response, they would act out their answers.

Depending on the children's levels and auditory processing skills, I often begin with stories that are very familiar to them or I use a story that has a significant amount of repetition.

My assistant teacher, Cindy Bowen, often tells the story together with me. I narrate and Cindy and I take on different parts, acting out the story as we go along. We agree upon which roles we will do before class, but we don't rehearse what we are going to do or say. We let it happen spontaneously. The children love this. It excites them. They can't wait for their turn to act out the story.

Many stories have repetitive lines that have rhyme and rhythm. I preserve these. If I need to, I memorize them beforehand to pass them on to the children. Usually, by the end of a session, the children have incidentally learned all the lines and are having fun with them. Making up dialogue once we start acting out the story becomes easier because they have a good start on what each character needs to say. The continuous eye contact I am able to make as a storyteller engages the children and helps them to focus on the story throughout its presentation.

I still usually tell stories with the book open in my hand with the pictures facing the children. Apart from being a good visual aid, especially for children who have attention difficulties or auditory processing problems, the book remains my security blanket. But sometimes, when the children are able to focus without a visual aid, I tell a story on the spur of the moment and keep the book on the bookshelf!

I know that it will be scary for you to move from reading the text to making it up, but take it gradually. Practice with friends and children you feel comfortable with. Be confident that you know your stories. I'm sure you do—you've probably known most of them since you were about five years old!

Telling stories has made teaching creative drama more enjoyable for me and for the children in my classes.

Telling stories is wonderful.

RELAX AND HAVE FUN WITH IT!

municates itself to your listeners and they begin creating their own images. Their images won't be identical to the one you have in your head, but they will be there—and they might even be better than yours!

You can start practicing by telling the story to a tape recorder and playing it back to hear how you've done. Or you can tell the story to a friend. As you share different parts, note your listener's reactions. You will know when you are being clear and when vague, when dramatic and when boring, by watching the reaction in your listener's eyes, face, and body. After you're done, ask which parts of the story were clear and which were not. Find out which moments your listener remembers most vividly. Those are the moments when you were most connected to the material. Your ultimate goal is to be connected to the story the entire time.

When you feel you can get through the whole story without leaving out parts and when you can retain your emotional connection with what is happening, you are ready to tell it to a class. If you want, write a skeletal outline of the plot and key phrases of dialogue on notecards to keep with you the first few times you tell it.

Each time you tell a story, you will make discoveries about it. Each time it will get better. New ideas about ways to improve the structure of the story or enhance a line of dialogue will occur to you. Sometimes you can put those new ideas into practice on the spot. Other times you can file them away for the next time.

Storytelling is truly a magical experience. When a group of children are captured by a story, all movement in the room stops. All their attention and energy becomes focused on the storyteller. Their eyes open wide and their imaginations start churning. This energizes the storyteller and feeds her creative process. It creates an atmosphere of magic which continues over into the enactment phase of the creative drama class.

ASSIGNING CHARACTER ROLES

When assigning character roles for a story, I ask each student who she would like to play. Sometimes it falls out evenly and everyone wants to play a different character. More often, however, a number of people want to be the same character. When this happens the teacher has several options. The story could be acted out more than once, each time rotating the roles to different children.

Another way to handle this is to have two or more students share a role. One student can be Rumpelstiltskin #1 and another can be Rumpelstiltskin #2. They can work together as a team or take turns jumping in the window each time the Miller's Daughter is locked in a different room. You can make sure each has an equal number of interactions by designating who is speaking or acting through your narration. "Rumpelstiltskin #1 grabbed the ring from the Miller's Daughter's as Rumpelstiltskin #2 began spinning the straw into gold. Both laughed gleefully!"

Sometimes there is a role that nobody wants to play. It might be because the students don't identify with it or because they don't understand what the character is doing in the story or because it's a very minor part and everyone wants a major part. On occasion students won't volunteer to play evil characters. (However, many find that playing the bad guy can be the most fun!) When I can't get a volunteer for a role, my assistant or I usually play that role.

One of my most memorable moments in creative drama happened while acting out a version of "Cinderella" with five Cinderellas (three girls and two boys who all had Down syndrome) sharing the role. We had two Prince Charmings. My assistant and I played all the other parts. As the Evil Stepsisters we were mean! We ordered the Cinderellas around. They had to scrub the floors and wash the windows and beat the rugs and do the washing and iron the clothes and manicure our nails and brush our teeth and wash and dry our hair and mend our clothes. Then we made them get us ready to go to the ball. And we laughed at them because they couldn't go!

For the next scene my assistant became the Fairy Godmother while I became the Narrator. Stepping outside the story I was struck by the beauty of the dramatic moment in progress. I saw five Cinderellas, all in ballgowns, sitting in a circle around a big orange pom-pom (which served as our pumpkin). They were listening intently and seriously to their Fairy Godmother tell them they had to leave the ball by midnight. There was so much belief in their eyes, so much trust, so much Magic in the room, that I almost started to cry. It didn't matter that there were five actors playing the same role. It didn't matter that their names were all Cinderella. It didn't even matter that two of the Cinderellas were boys and they were wearing dresses! They were all having the time of their lives.

Sometimes there are more students than roles and they don't want to double up. Sometimes there are students who would rather watch than participate that day. When this happens, the students without roles can become audience members during the acting out of the story. Being an audience member is very important work!

A FEW ACTOR GUIDELINES TO KEEP IN MIND

UNDERSTANDING THE DIFFERENCE BETWEEN PRETEND AND REAL

First and foremost, student actors need to understand that they do not become the fictional characters in the story or in drama games. They are only pretending to be them for a short period of time. Some children understand the difference between real and pretend, but some do not. It may seem like a simple concept to explain, but it's not.

You can say, "When we act, we are pretending to be somebody else [Cinderella, Prince Charming, the Evil Stepmother]. We act *as if* the situation were real. But it isn't. You are still yourself. I am still myself. We can pretend this room is a palace, but we know that it is really our classroom."

Often it's better to teach the concept through action rather than through words.

I got into trouble the first time my very first class of students with learning disabilities acted out a story. They did such a good job of pantomiming and playing imagination games during our initial class period that I made the mistake of assuming they understood the difference between real and pretend. For the second class period I decided we'd act out "Caps for Sale" (also known as "The Peddlar and His Caps"). I brought a big sack full of colorful hats for the Peddlar to use. The minute he saw them, Roberto decided he wanted to be the Peddlar. In the first scene he grudgingly let the townspeople try on his hats in the marketplace. They didn't like them and gave them back. So far so good. But when he got to the forest and fell asleep under the tree, he lay down on top of his hats and wouldn't let any of the monkeys steal them. As far as Roberto was concerned, he *was* the Peddlar. I had given the hats to him personally and he was not going to let anybody else take them away from him.

If the monkeys couldn't steal the hats, the story couldn't continue. I tried to explain to Roberto that the monkeys needed to steal the hats because that's what happened in the story, but he grabbed the hats and held them closer to him sobbing the whole time, "But, they're mine! They're mine!"

I had to stop the story. We all sat down and talked about the difference between pretend and real. I didn't get much of a response from Roberto. He still had the hats clutched tightly to his chest. At this point, it was time for class to be over. (Truly a case of being saved by the bell!) I don't remember how I got him to leave the hats behind. I think maybe his mother helped me separate him from them.

After thinking about it, I decided the class needed to go back to Square One. The next few sessions we played lots of drama games in which they pretended to be something or someone else. We did a guided imagery exercise each session. We worked out a lot of interpersonal problems between group members. After everyone firmly understood the concept of pretend and real, we tried acting out stories again. Ever since that experience, I have tried to introduce the concepts of pretend and real to new students slowly, starting them off with several sessions of games and pantomimes before moving on to stories.

STAYING IN CHARACTER

Actors must learn to "stay in character." This means that while acting, they must behave consistently like that character. They move like the character would move. They say things the character would say. They can invent new things to say and do, but whatever is invented must be consistent with who they are portraying. The actors must also stick to the plot of the story unless everyone has agreed ahead of time that the story is going to be changed.

Throughout the enactment, actors must stay focused on the pretend situation of the scene or story. In the middle of a scene, it is not OK to turn around and push Billy because you were mad at him before class started. It is not OK to switch from one character to another. It is not OK to decide to quit halfway through and do something else.

LISTENING TO EACH OTHER

Actors need to listen to each other. Each character in a story must respond appropriately to what the other characters say to him or her. The only way to do this is to listen to what is being said by them. If no one is listening to anyone else, the whole scene will break down into total confusion!

RESPECTING EACH OTHER'S WORK

Actors must respect each others' contributions to a story. Each actor can decide how she will interpret her character. If someone else has other ideas about how that character should be interpreted, she can share those ideas when she has her chance to act that character. It will not do for actors to step out of character to argue or criticize each other during the enactment of a story. One of the great things about drama is that each person can have his or her own interpretation for each role.

AUDIENCE GUIDELINES FOR THE CREATIVE DRAMA CLASSROOM

Set up your audience area clearly with chairs or mats for audience members to sit on. Place them on a side of the room where light from the windows won't glare into their eyes or throw the actors' faces into shadow. If your audience members have difficulty staying out of the acting area or your actors tend to wander into your audience space, use masking tape to create a line on the floor between the performance space and the audience space.

Appropriate audience behavior is very important. Audience members are there to share in the work of the actors, so they need to pay attention to what is going on. You might want to review the following guidelines the first few times your students are audience members for each other:

AUDIENCE GUIDELINES

1. Sit quietly in your seat.
2. Watch and listen to the actors.
3. Respect your fellow audience members' personal space. (In other words, keep your hands and feet to yourself.)
4. If you have a comment or idea, remember it for later on.
   — Speaking out during the story will distract the actors.

Being a good audience for fellow students and sharing in their work is very important. (Photo by John Carter)

— After the story is over, everyone can talk about how the story went and what they liked or didn't like about it.

5. Respond appropriately to the actors' work.
   — Laugh *with* the characters and not *at* the actors.
   — Show your appreciation by applauding.
   — Booing or saying mean things will hurt the actors' feelings.

If a student in the audience becomes impatient as she is waiting for her turn to act, tell her that as an audience member she is playing an important part, too. Her reaction during the story will help keep the actors on track and her comments at the end will help them to become better actors. Remind her that she will get her turn as soon as this version of the story is done. If this doesn't work, ask her to remember the last time she acted out a part in class. She probably wants the audience to watch her and enjoy her work. When she acts, she probably does not like it if audience members pay no attention to her or laugh at her or tease her or make nasty comments. Others will respect her only when she respects them. If she is still being disruptive, have her take a time-out where she cannot disturb the actors and other audience members.

IMPROVISATIONAL ACTING

Improvisational acting involves the creation of characters and dramatic situations that are not based on a written script. In many ways improvisational acting is an outgrowth of creative drama because actors are engaged in a very similar informal process in which original scenes are created by the actors on the spot. In addition to creating scenes, students in improvisational acting classes work on developing their acting skills through drama games and exercises.

The appropriate age for students studying improvisational acting can range from pre-teen to adult. The development of spontaneity, flexibility, and problem-solving skills are highlighted in improvisation. These skills are all highly valued tools for living in our modern age. Students with special needs may have even more reason to develop them in order to survive creatively in a complex and difficult world.

LENGTH OF SESSION

The length of a session can range from an hour to two hours, depending on the students and the project. Obviously, students with strong group skills and long attention spans can handle a longer class. Individuals who process information slowly might need a class of medium length so they can enjoy their work without feeling rushed. Students who really love the improvisational process will want to stay in class for as long as they can!

If the class is basically devoted to skill building and the improvisational process, the class can be short or long, but if the creation of an original play is part of the purpose, a longer class may be necessary in order to provide the time necessary for improvisational exploration and rehearsal of the finished piece.

BASIC CLASS STRUCTURE

The basic structure for an improvisational acting class follows that of creative drama. Class typically begins with a warm-up activity of some kind, followed by acting games that teach specific acting skills. The focal point of the session is the creation of scenes or stories through improvisation. Early sessions in a series of classes might consist solely of games to assist students in developing the appropriate improvisational skills in order to create scenes successfully. As sessions continue, more time will be spent on scene work. An improvisational acting session usually ends with some kind of closure activity. See Chapter Seven for examples of drama games and other activities.

Many activities used in an improvisational acting class are similar to those used in creative drama. More complexity is added, as older students have usually achieved a higher level of skills and can handle more complications. More time is usually allotted to each activity since students' concentration abilities are also stronger and longer. There is usually more independent group work and team activities than in creative drama, encouraging students to work together on their own.

SETTING UP AN IMPROVISATIONAL SCENE

Every scene has a beginning, a middle, and an end. The beginning establishes the characters and introduces the conflict. The middle develops the conflict. In the end the conflict is resolved.

A good approach for creating scenes is to start with specific choices about the important structural dramatic details: Who, Why, What, Where, When, and How.

Who. The *Who* are the characters. A scene can have any number of characters. With beginning improvisation students, keep scenes small and simple. Many beginning actors don't know how to keep a conflict clear and listen to what the other actors are saying. It is less distracting for them to work on improvisational listening and response skills if fewer students are involved. In the beginning, work on many short scenes that each have two or three actors in them rather than one long scene involving everyone.

When setting up a scene, only include characters who are absolutely essential to the conflict you have chosen. Each character in a scene needs to have a reason for being there. The characters might be directly involved in one side or other of the conflict; they might also be involved in complicating the conflict or helping to resolve it.

Don't overpopulate a scene with lots of extras who aren't directly involved in the dramatic action. An overpopulated scene tends to lose its forward momentum and can degenerate into confusion as the minor characters or extras try to keep busy. The main conflict becomes blurred or lost and may never be resolved.

Why. Each character must have certain goals or objectives which she will try to accomplish during the course of the scene. To give each character a sense of urgency to accomplish those goals, each must also have strong reasons to justify her goals. These reasons are called the character's motivation or her Why.

If an actor is unsure of her purpose in a scene, her goal or objective can be clarified by asking, "What do you want?" or "What does your character want?" If an actor is unclear on her motivation, she can be asked, "Why are you doing this?"

What. The *What* of a scene is the conflict or problem created for the characters by the situation they are in or by their crossed purposes.

As previously mentioned, each character has a different objective to accomplish during the course of a scene. Sometimes those objectives lead the characters to work together for the solution of a problem. For example, two characters lost in the woods have the same conflict and the same overall objective: they both want to find a way out. However, they might have different motivations. One might need to get to the nearest hospital because she has a broken leg. The other might be homesick for his family. They could both work together to solve their problem.

More often than not, characters' objectives are at cross purposes and therein lies the conflict of the scene. Taking the example of the two characters lost in the woods, despite their common goal, they might *not* be able to work together and end up fighting instead of helping each other solve their mutual problem.

Usually a character faces some kind of conflict inside at the same time she is facing a conflict outside. Before she can solve her outer conflict, she must choose between two different inner goals. The inter-character conflict of a scene might be between a drug dealer who wants to hook a teen on cocaine and the teen who wants to stay clean and sober. The inner character conflict is within the teen who must make a choice. She wants to stay clean and sober, but at the same time she wants to look "cool" to her friends. Once she solves her internal or inner character conflict, she can solve the outer or inter-character conflict of the scene. If actors skip over an internal conflict inherent in a scene, stop them and side-coach them through it. Clarifying what each character wants can help the actors understand what the conflict is.

Where. The place or location in which the scene takes place is the *Where*. Sometimes this is also called the setting.

When choosing a place for a scene, be as specific as possible: John's living room, the playground outside of school, the loading platform at the train station. If the Where of a scene is clear and specific, many ideas for solving the conflict can come out of the setting.

Before beginning a scene, decide how the Where will be physically set up. Use desks, chairs, and other physical objects in your classroom to help create the space. If your scene is set in an interior, you could use the backs of chairs to outline your walls, turning chairs sideways to indicate entrances and exits. If you have a number of rugs, they could delineate the boundaries of rooms or locations within them. You could tape out the walls on the floor with masking tape. Students need the extra physical structure to help them create the location in their imaginations. If everything is invisible, they will forget where the boundaries and important objects are. A specific setting helps them make specific acting choices and stay in the Where of the scene.

When. The *When* is the time, day, season, and year in which a scene happens. Again, be as specific as possible. Does the scene happen this year or last year or one hundred years ago? Is it 4:00 after school on a Wednesday in May or is it 9:00 on a Saturday night after a football game in October?

The When can be used to create a sense of urgency to force the characters to resolve the conflict. If the scene is about cheating in school and the big test is going to begin in five minutes, Bobby will be trying harder to convince Julie to help him cheat and Julie will feel under more pressure to say yes or no, than if the When of the scene is two weeks ago when the teacher first announced the test date.

How. The *How* is the plot of the scene—how the dramatic action unfolds. The plot for an improvisational scene can be developed in two different ways. It can be pre-planned step by step, creating a basic scenario for the actors to follow. This pre-planning can be done by the teacher or by the actors who will be in the scene or by the whole class working together. The actors will follow the scenario as they improvise the dialogue and act out the scene. This is a good method for beginners to use because they can focus on the creation of their dialogue and character within the given plot structure.

The other method is to set up the characters, the conflict, the time, and the place and let the plot develop extemporaneously as the scene is played out. The actors use ideas for solving their problems as they occur to them during the improvisation and until the scene ends, no one knows what exactly will happen. Actors using this method must make sure all action is motivated and makes sense. Everyone must remain flexible and listen for all the unexpected twists and turns that might happen.

TROUBLE-SHOOTING DURING IMPROVISATIONS

SIDE-COACHING

If actors get lost, stuck, or confused during a scene, you don't have to leave them dangling. The teacher has several options for side-coaching to get them back on track.

Freezing. If all that is needed is a word or two, you can tell the actors to momentarily freeze in character. When you say, "Freeze," they stop all talking and movement, as if you had touched the pause button on a videotape player. While they are frozen, you can give them your suggestions. When you say "Unfreeze" or "Continue," they continue with the scene.

Take a Time-Out. Step in like a referee at a sporting event and take a time-out. Stop the scene and discuss the situation or the characters' objectives with the actors. Once the problem seems to be clarified, have them con-

Actors freeze while the teacher side-coaches during an improvisation. (Photo by John Carter)

tinue the scene from where they left off. Some students feel that the only way they can "erase their mistakes" is to start over. This is not necessary, but if starting over from the beginning would help clear up the confusion, let them begin the scene again.

Simultaneous Side-Coaching. You may want to make minor adjustments to the action or offer an actor encouragement without stopping the scene. Offer comments and suggestions while the students continue to act. Just as when "freezing," actors should stay in character as they listen to your coaching.

This type of scene adjustment requires good concentration skills on the parts of the actors. Students who have cognitive disabilities may have difficulty concentrating on two things at once. They may be unable to process what is happening in the scene and what you are saying simultaneously. If this is the case, it is best to side-coach during a Time-Out or Freeze.

FINDING AN END TO A SCENE

Sometimes actors get so involved in their scene that it goes on and on and on. If the scene is interesting and is holding the attention of the class audience, let it go on. But if the conflict of the scene gets sidetracked and the audience begins to get restless, the teacher may have to step in and help them find an end to the scene. This can be done by side-coaching comments like "You need to focus on the problem in the scene," or "You need to solve the original problem, which was _____." If you need to be more direct, you can say "Now you need to find an end to the scene." If the actors are enjoying being in the limelight and are postponing ending their scene, give them a time limit. "You need to find an end to this scene in two minutes."

ENCOURAGEMENT

Give your students lots of positive encouragement as they begin acting out scenes. They need to know what is working almost more than they need to know what is not working.

Students Who Won't Participate. If you have students who are shy or hesitant to work at first, don't force them to participate. Sometimes new students need to observe for awhile before they feel confident enough to risk participation. It may take two or three classes before someone who is shy feels safe enough to join in. Don't worry as long as the shy students are attentive to the work that the other students are doing. Keep offering them the opportunity to join in and eventually they will. You may even be surprised by the sensitivity of the work they contribute, once they feel comfortable enough to become active in the group.

One of my students would not join in improvisations until the end of the second semester. He stayed on the sidelines and watched. He said he did not want to act, he only wanted to do the sound effects for our play. I said that this was OK because stage technicians are important, too.

Our last class period we decided to act out a very exciting situation: a few other students and I were stuck in a burning building and everyone else was going to be on the fire fighting team. Being a fireman sounded like a lot of fun to him, so, out of the blue, he volunteered to take a part. I said, "Great!" but didn't make a big deal out of it.

It was a very dramatic scene. People were shouting for help and jumping from the building into the arms of the waiting firefighters below. Before I could jump, I was "overcome by the smoke" and "passed out." He ran into the building, pulled me out and "revived me." From the things he said to the other actors around him, I think he really believed I was hurt. He was very relieved when he found out I was OK. Because of this experience, everything changed for him and suddenly he wanted to act. The next semester he volunteered for scenes all the time and each year his part in the play has gotten bigger and bigger.

As I think back on it, I believe part of his hesitation to join in was because of his shyness and part of it was because of his confusion about what was pretend and what was real. I think he feared that if he acted out another character, he would turn into that person and wouldn't be himself anymore. As he participated in the scene, he realized that although he was "fighting a fire," there really were no flames in the room and that even though I was pretending to be unconscious, I really wasn't.

MAKING UP DIALOGUE

If a student has trouble making up dialogue, ask her to think about how her character feels in this situation. Or ask her to think about what she might say if *she* were in a similar situation. If words won't come, maybe she could express how her character feels or what her character would like to do about the situation through movement.

Once again, patience and positive stroking will evoke more in the long run than trying to force the issue.

WORKING TOGETHER

At first, plan scenes with the whole class working together under your aegis. This will help them understand how to plan a scene.

Advanced students can be divided into smaller groups to work on their own. This encourages their independence and creativity. You or your assistant can check in with them to keep them on track and make sure they understand the assignment. Each group could be assigned the same situation to work on or they could be assigned different ones. After they come up with their scene and practice it, they can share it with the whole class. Let them know that you are there if they have any questions.

A good size for an improvisation group is two, three, or four students. Groups larger than four tend to have trouble coming to consensus. Allow each group ten to twenty minutes to plan and rehearse their scene. Be flexible. The time needed will depend on the complexity of the scene and how well the group is working together.

Circulate from group to group as they work to check on their progress. Give them lots of encouragement when they are working harmoniously and coming up with creative ideas. Offer constructive suggestions when they seem to be stuck or when they are having difficulty coming to an agreement. Try not to solve their problems for them, but offer them alternatives from which they can choose.

When assigning students to work groups, it helps to know what kind of relationships they have with each other outside of class. Sometimes friends work together well because they already have a natural trust and ability to communicate with each other. Other times putting friends together creates friction.

Be aware of the cognitive levels and abilities of the members in a group. If your class is mainstreamed, don't segregate students with and students without disabilities into separate groups. Divide them up so they have opportunities to discover each others' creative strengths and support each others' weaknesses. In a class that is not mainstreamed, if possible, assign one member who has a high cognitive functioning level to each group.

Also be aware of students' leadership styles. Make sure each group has at least one strong leader. If everyone in a group is passive, nothing will get accomplished. On the other hand, if you have two strong leaders in a group, make sure they are capable of flexibility. Two strong, rigid leaders will have difficulty compromising with each other.

Working together on group scenes can be very satisfying in the end, but learning to compromise, accept group decisions, and share creative ideas can be a struggle in the beginning. Whenever conflicts flare up between group members, remind them that they are on the same team and everyone's ideas are valid and important. Everyone deserves a chance to be heard. Everyone's opinion counts.

DISCUSSION

After a scene is acted out for the class, it is often helpful to take some time to discuss it with the actors and the audience.

Keep the actors in the acting area. A good question to ask them is "How did you think the scene went? What did you feel worked?" Then ask them to evaluate where they had problems. Good questions to ask are "What was difficult for you?" or "What did you feel didn't work?"

Then ask for input from the audience. Always focus first on the positive aspects of the scene: what the actors did that "worked" or was effective. Only after you have covered what the actors did well, should you ask for comments on what did not work or what could have been done better. There is a distinction between something that did *not* work and something that could have been done differently and had a better outcome. More often than not, an actor's choice is not *wrong,* but a different choice might have worked better in the scene.

Criticism should be aimed at the choices in the scene rather than at the individual who made them. Everyone is learning and everyone can improve their skills through practice and feedback. No one is perfect. Not even professional actors who win awards for their work are perfect. It is good to remember that even famous actors are always in training, always evaluating their performances and trying to make them better. Constant improvement and study is the mark of a true professional and a true artist.

Train your students to think positively rather than negatively. Constructive criticism gives an actor food for thought and can be used to improve her skills and performance. Destructive criticism and personal attacks only hurt people's feelings and shut them down so they won't try again. Your best tool in guiding your students to learn how to criticize constructively is through your example: how you criticize and how you phrase your questions. Don't be afraid to stop a critical comment that is couched in negative, non-helpful terms and criticize it! (Again, criticize the criticism and not the student making it. For instance, instead of saying, "John, you are being really insensitive," you might say, "John, that comment was a little insensitive. Could you think of something Susie could have done to make the scene better?")

EVALUATING CONTENT CHOICES

Acting choices can "work" on two different levels. They work on a content level and they work on a technical level.

Content choices deal with the choices that the characters made, not the choices that the actors made. There is a distinction. An actor might allow her character to make an unwise choice because that is something her character might legitimately do! For instance, a girl in a scene might be so angry at the mean man down the street for running over her dog with his car that she throws stones at his house and breaks a window. In this case, you can criticize the character, but you must congratulate the actor. She's done a good job of creating a believable character.

To evaluate content choices, ask questions like:

- What happened in the scene?
- What did the characters say? Did it make sense?
- What did the characters do to find a creative solution to their problems? Did that make sense?
- How else could the characters have solved their conflict?

EVALUATING TECHNICAL CHOICES

The other level on which a scene can be evaluated is its technical level. How did the actors use their dramatic skills and techniques to structure the scene? Questions that relate to this level might include:

- Did the actors stay in character?
- Did the actors listen to each other?
- Did the actors stick to the scenario (the plan they made before they started acting out the scene)? If not, why? Did their new choices improve the scenario or weaken it?
- Did the actors solve the conflict (problem) or not?
- Did the actors make their characters' objectives and motivations (their "why" or their reasons for doing things) clear?
- Did one action in the scene logically lead to the next action? (Did what was happening make sense?)
- Did the scene keep moving forward or did it get stuck in one place and never end? If it did get stuck, why do you think that happened?
- What are some different choices the actors could have made?

REALITY VS. FANTASY

In discussions of improvisational scenes, it may be important to take time in the beginning to separate what is real from what is pretend. Adolescent students may not have worked out the distinction between reality and fantasy and they may need some extra help. Stress that the actor is not the same person as the character she portrays in a scene. The actor is real. The character is fictional. The character may act as if she is real, but she is not real. When an actor plays a role, she does not change inside. She is still the same person she always was. She puts on the character the same way she would put on a Halloween costume. She can take the character off when she is done with the scene, just like she would take off a disguise.

You can ask an actor how she felt about what her character did or how she (the actor) felt during parts of the scene when she seemed to be very involved. Did her character feel the same way she did or did her character feel different? An actor can feel similar to how her character feels if she shares a similar personality or belief system. Or she can feel very different.

While a character is doing something "bad" (lying to the principal, cheating on a test, getting into a fight, robbing a bank), the actor might feel a rush of excitement. This can be confusing because the rush of excitement feels good, but the character has just done something that the actor knows is "bad." Some students may need help sorting through this.

Relationships between characters in a scene can also cause confusion. Two good friends might refuse to act out a scene in which their characters have an argument. A boy and a girl might refuse to portray characters who are romantically involved or married because they are afraid others will think the feelings in the scene are real. Sometimes a boy and girl improvising a romantic scene will become so involved in the imaginary situation that they confuse the characters' attraction for each other with an attraction that may or may not exist between them in real life. The same confusion between actor and character feelings can arise in scenes of disagreement and dislike as well. In all of these situations it is important to clarify that the actors are playing a role, that they are different from the characters they are temporarily portraying, and that the other people in the classroom or in the audience also understand that the characters and situation of the scene are not real.

LENGTH OF DISCUSSION

Some scenes will generate long, involved discussions; others won't. If a scene creates a lot of strong feeling and food for thought, it is important to allow students the time to process it before moving on to the next scene or activity. Students holding on to a strong feeling or a confusion from a previous scene, will tend to behave inappropriately to get rid of the feeling if it is not resolved in a timely fashion.

If a scene does not generate a lot of discussion, just move on to the next one. Discussions don't *have* to cover all the points mentioned above. The teacher will usually want to focus on a few main issues that worked or didn't work, or on particular acting skills she is currently helping her students develop.

■ chapter seven

lesson plans and activities that work

As mentioned in Chapter Six, many warm-ups, drama games, and acting exercises are used with all age groups. At different developmental levels, different skills are addressed. The older the student, the more complexity can be added to the exercise. The longer the student's attention span, the longer each exercise can be sustained with interest. Older, more mature groups can handle activities which include more independence and group interactions.

CHOOSING GAMES FOR BEGINNERS

USE CONCRETE GAMES

With beginners and with students who have cognitive disabilities, focus on concrete, rather than abstract activities. The difference between concrete and abstract can be illustrated by comparing two different versions of the same basic pantomime game.

The Magic Tube (Concrete)

Material needed: Empty cardboard paper towel roll.

Group configuration: Everyone sits in a circle.

Purpose: To stimulate the imagination and develop pantomime skills.

Action: Imagine an object that is the same shape as the tube (it could be the same size or bigger or smaller). Using the tube as the imaginary object would be used, show the group what you have in your hand. The group guesses what it is. After each student finishes his turn, he passes the tube to the person next to him in the circle. Go around the circle once or continue around the circle as long as the group shows interest in the game.

Variations: Use a plastic cup, a frisbee, an embroidery hoop, a Nerf ball, a large, colorful scarf—any object that is a different shape.

Suggestions: Use an object that is unbreakable because students will bang it around. Also, use a soft object so no one gets hurt if hit with it.

Space Objects (Abstract)

Material needed: None.

Group configuration: Everyone sits in a circle.

Purpose: To stimulate the imagination and develop pantomime skills.

Action: Using the shape of your hands, create an invisible object through pantomime. Show the group what you have by using it as you would use the object if it were really there. The group guesses what is in your hands. Each student takes a turn. Continue the game as long as the group shows interest.

Variation: *Space Balls*—create different kinds of balls.

Differentiate size, shape, and weight. The student who creates the ball throws it to the student next to him in the circle. This student catches it and changes it to a different kind of ball before passing it on.

Using the Magic Tube, students have a concrete object to focus on and manipulate. This provides enough visual and kinesthetic structure to serve as a mental anchor. The object-in-hand holds the shape in space and serves as a spatial reminder for the student while he searches back through visual and kinesthetic memory to match it with a similarly shaped object.

I have used this exercise with individuals who had very low cognitive functioning abilities and they were as capable as intellectually gifted students in making amazing, creative connections. Whenever I tried the game in the abstract with them—without the object in hand—they had much more difficulty visualizing the pantomimed object in their mind's eye and imagining a new one.

If you have a source book of acting exercises, go through it to separate the concrete exercises from the abstract ones. Then go back through the abstract ones and think of ways to invent a concrete variation of it. See the Bibliography for some recommended source books.

USE SIMPLE GAMES

Beginners and students who have cognitive disabilities do best with simple games. If you try a game and it doesn't work, remove a level or a complication.

Here are several different variations of an Animal Pantomime Guessing Game that will work for different levels of groups:

Bird, Beast, and Fish (most complex)

Material needed: None.

Group Configuration: Two or three teams of four to eight actors in different corners of the room; group leader in center.

Purpose: To develop pantomime skills, physical expressiveness, problem solving, and cooperative abilities.

Action: Team members number off so each actor has a rotation order. Then each team sends Actor One to the group leader in the center. The leader whispers the name of the same living creature to all the actors. They run back to their group and act out the animal with no sound in front of their group. They can act it out in any way. They can use part or all of their bodies. They can show what the animal looks like or what it does. They can show another creature's reaction to it. As the actors act, their team members yell out guesses. When an actor hears the correct animal, he motions everyone to sit down. The leader asks for the person with the correct answer to raise her hand and share the answer. If it is correct, that team wins a point. For the next round, each team sends Actor Two to the group leader and the game continues until one team has reached the agreed upon score for winning the game.

Comments: It is helpful to check on the correct answer instead of trusting that the first team to sit down has guessed correctly. In the heat of the game, an over-enthusiastic team can misinterpret an actor's animal gesture to mean "Sit down" or the actor can mishear a team member's guess.

If an actor makes a sound, his team is disqualified from competition in that round. If the other team has heard the sound, no one gets a point.

This version of animal pantomimes takes a great deal of impulse control to play. It can overstimulate children who have ADHD, Tourette syndrome, emotional difficulties, or sensory integration problems. The number of rules and sequences involved may make it too complex for students who have severe cognitive disabilities.

Animal Herds I (medium complexity/abstract)

Material needed: None.

Group configuration: Two teams on opposite sides of the room.

Purpose: To develop pantomime skills, physical expressiveness, problem solving, and cooperative abilities.

Action: Each team collectively agrees on an animal to jointly act out for the other team. Team One goes first and pantomimes their animal for the other team. Team Two gets three guesses. If they don't guess correctly after three tries, Team One adds the animal's sound. Then the teams switch and Team Two acts out their animal for Team One.

Scoring: Usually I don't present this game as a competition. The idea is not to fool the other team; each team should be trying to act out their animal so that the other team *will* guess correctly. A correct guess means good acting as well as good guessing. However, some classes insist on keep track of points. In this case, I usually make correct guesses without sound worth two points and correct guesses with sound worth one point.

Animal Herds II (medium complexity/concrete)

Material needed: Pictures of different animals.

Group configuration: Two teams on opposite sides of the room.

Purpose: To develop pantomime skills, physical expressiveness, problem solving, and cooperative abilities.

Action: The teacher shows Team One the picture of an animal. Together, the team acts out the animal on the picture without sound for Team Two. Team Two gets three guesses. If they don't guess correctly after the third try, Team One adds the animal's sound. Then the teams switch and Team Two acts out a different animal for Team One.

Scoring: Correct guesses without sound are worth two points. Correct guesses with sound are worth one point.

Comments: Pictures of animals work better for clarity, secrecy, and large-scale recognition than whispering the name of an animal to a large group.

They also present a visual image to young children who may remember the animal upon seeing it, but may not remember if only given a name.

This version does not require the group consensus skills of Animal Herds I.

If the acting team begins invading the space of the watching team, divide the acting area in two by making a line with masking tape in the middle of the floor.

If children have difficulty controlling the impulse to say the animal's name out loud when they see the picture, ask them to cover their mouths with their hands and say the animal's name to themselves in their heads or whisper the name behind their hands so the other team can't see it or hear it.

Simplification: If students don't have the impulse control to act out the animal without sound, let them use sound from the beginning. But be aware that often students using sounds will start to rely solely on the noise the animal makes and stop being physically expressive. If this happens, remind students to "act with your bodies as well as your voices."

Animals, Animals, Animals (simpler)

Material needed: Pictures of animals.

Group configuration: Everyone in a group together.

Purpose: To develop pantomime skills, physical expressiveness, and group cooperation.

Action: Show the entire group a picture of an animal. Act it out together with or without sound.

Comments: Here we have moved from a team game into an exercise involving the whole group in parallel play. Students must remain aware of others' personal space and not attack other "animals."

Animal Go-Around I (simpler)

Material needed: None.

Group Configuration: Everyone sits in a circle.

Purpose: To develop pantomime skills, physical expressiveness, decision making, and ability to share and appreciate the work of others.

Action: Each student acts out his favorite animal.

Variation: Each student acts out the animal he would most like to have for a pet, the animal he thinks is the scariest or softest or fastest or slowest, etc.

Animal Go-Around II (most structured)

Material needed: Pictures of animals.

Group configuration: Everyone sitting in a circle on the floor or in chairs.

Purpose: To develop pantomime skills, physical expressiveness, ability to share and appreciate the work of others.

Action: Each student takes a turn looking at the picture of an animal and acting it out for the group.

If you misjudge the complexity level at which a group can play a game, you will know immediately. They will not understand the rules and the class will quickly start disintegrating into chaos. To make sure the problem has not been *your* directions, stop once and clarify the rules. If this doesn't work, don't make the situation worse by insisting that they play it your way. Stop and simplify the game. Or stop and switch to another activity. You can always try a simplified version of the game in another session.

WHEN AN ACTIVITY BOMBS

Sometimes a game will work wonderfully with one group and totally fail with a similar group. You may have misjudged the abilities of the students in one of the groups. You may not have explained the game clearly enough. The failure may have been due to factors outside your control, like the weather or the emotional states of the class members on the day you try the exercise.

If an activity doesn't work, drop it and go on to the next one on your lesson plan. Don't waste time feeling bad about it and don't become upset with your students. Take an attitude of "What will be, will be." There are hundreds of drama games. If the game teaches a crucial acting skill, you will be able to find another game to teach the same thing.

WARM-UPS

Warm-ups release physical and emotional tensions that have built up during the day prior to drama class. Once these tensions are released, students will be able to concentrate on your class better.

Warm-ups energize students who are weary by getting their blood moving and by carrying revitalizing oxygen to their muscles.

Warm-ups focus students' attentions on the work at hand by bringing them mentally and physically into the present moment.

Warm-ups also serve as a relaxation tool because they are activities that rely primarily on right-brain functioning. This gives students a break from the cognitive left-brain activities that they have been engaged in almost exclusively during the school day.

For very shy or inhibited groups, warm-ups can help to break the ice and loosen up creative thinking. Since they are done with everyone simultaneously, no one is singled out or put on the spot. Everyone can feel part of the group.

A warm-up usually lasts from five to fifteen minutes, depending on the tension and concentration levels of the class members. When the class seems relaxed and engaged, you will sense it. At that point, bring your warm-up to a swift, but satisfying conclusion and move on to your games, storytelling, or scene work.

Warm-up activities can include group check-ins, physical exercise, physical or mental relaxation exercises, pantomimes, social games, drama games, imagination games, sensory explorations, singing, or an art activity.

GROUP CHECK-INS

Have everyone sit in a circle. Go around and let each person "check in." Ask each student to share how he is feeling or something exciting that has happened in the past week or something exciting that he is planning to do in the near future. It is important in group check-ins that everyone listen to everyone else and not "check-out" after having his turn. The purpose of an activity of this kind is to bring a class together and help everyone get to know each other better.

Keep each student's "check-in" brief and to the point. If someone begins to monopolize the conversation and it is not interesting to the others, they will get bored and stop paying attention. In a situation like this, you can say, "Thank you for sharing this story with us, but I think it's time to give someone else a turn to speak." If this happens on a regular basis, you can create a time limit for each person or you could put some other kind of limit on the response. For instance, you could ask everyone to say how he feels using only one word or to share one place he went on his vacation.

NAME GAMES

Name games are helpful for learning names in the first session and for reviewing them in succeeding sessions. Usually name learning is an aural/visual process. Name games make it a visual/kinesthetic process as well.

Go around the circle and have each person say his name and make a movement or rhythm to go with it. Robert might clap his hands twice. Cindy might hop up and down. Frank might stamp his foot once. Have the group repeat the name and movement or rhythm after each person introduces himself. Then see if anyone can remember another's name and movement. Robert might say, "Frank" and stamp his foot once. Frank would repeat his name and movement and then might do Cindy's name and movement, passing the game on to her.

Variation: If that game is too abstract for your group, each person can say his name and act out something he likes to do. After everyone introduces himself, ask students if they can remember another student's name and action. Or just review names.

In subsequent groups, names can be reviewed by saying the name of another person in the circle and tossing him a nerf ball or beanbag.

There are many welcoming songs into which students' names can be inserted. If your group likes to sing, this can be a fun way to review names at the beginning of class.

Many social games also involve naming others in the group.

GO-AROUND PANTOMIMES

If you are in a check-in circle, it is easy to segue into a go-around pantomime activity. Students can take turns pantomiming something they like to do, their favorite sport, their favorite animal, their favorite food, something they do at school each day, something they do when they go home, something they do on vacation, something they do in the fall, winter, summer, or spring, etc.

It is best to keep a go-around moving. If students are shy or need some more time to think of something to act out, they can skip their turn. Later, when they feel more confident or get an idea, you can come back around to them.

Groups love go-around pantomimes. It's a great way for students to share something about themselves and get to know each other. It's a quick way to get everyone involved.

Go-around pantomimes are also an easy, pain-free method of introducing solo performance work to shy students. They feel safer taking a turn while sitting in an informal circle than when getting up on a stage or standing alone in front of a classroom.

Go-around pantomimes can be done while students are catching their breath after a physical warm-up or between active games.

PHYSICAL EXERCISE

Release muscular tension through any combination of the following physical exercises. As students do each movement, ask them to imagine that the tension (or the "tight" or "sore" or "hurting" parts) in their bodies is loosening up and falling out of them. The purpose of physical exercise in a drama class is not to build up muscles, but to relax them. Place emphasis on tension release and muscle warm-up, doing the activity gently and carefully.

Some groups love to do physical warm-ups to jazzy, upbeat music. Find out who their favorite recording artists are and bring in tapes of their music. After a few weeks, students will start bringing in their own favorite tapes for you to use during warm-ups. Students take great pride in contributing to class in this way.

The teacher or assistant can lead the physical warm-up. Students can also take turns being the warm-up leader. Give everyone who wants a turn a few minutes to lead the group.

If you stretch one side of the body, you should stretch the other. If you rotate in one direction, you should always reverse and go in the other direction. This balances the work the muscles experience and assures that you have addressed the tension in all body parts. If you have students with physical disabilities who cannot move part of their bodies, warm up the parts of their bodies that they can move.

Shaking. Gently shake each part of your body: your hands, your elbows, your arms, your head, your shoulders, your hips, your knees, your left foot, your left leg, your right foot, your right leg, your whole body.

Stretching. Stretch each part of your body. Stretching increases the supply of blood to body parts. Stretch: toward the ceiling, toward the floor, toward your right, toward your left, backwards (with your knees bent a little bit), toward the person on the opposite side of the circle.

Stretch out your legs one at a time as you lean against a wall.

Sit on the floor with your legs in front of you and stretch forward reaching for your toes.

Open up your legs into a V. Grab your ankle with the hand on that side of your body and reach over your head for that foot with the arm of the opposite side.

Try some yoga stretches like the Cobra, the Bow, or the Cat Stretch which release the muscles of the back and give the spine a chance to arch in different directions.

Swinging. Loosen your body a little more by swinging it gently from side to side. Bend over and swing your arms in front of you like the clapper in a bell. Stand up and swing your arms from above your head to the floor as you bend at the waist. Swing your legs one at a time. Let your breath go with you as you swing. You can even make a gentle "Ahhh" noise or a sigh as you let the air out. Allow the momentum from one swing to carry you into the next.

Swimming. Move your arms as if you were doing the Backstroke, the Crawl, the Breast Stroke, the Butterfly Stroke, the Side Stroke, or the Doggie Paddle. As you swim, imagine that you are in a cool, blue pool enjoying a perfect summer day.

Rotating. Circle each joint of the body in small and large, fast and slow circles. Rotate in each direction. Rotate your wrists, arms, head (always do this one slowly), shoulders, waist (upper body), hips, legs, ankles (do this last one sitting down).

Bouncing. Bounce or bob gently up and down as if you were a ball. Try to imagine that you are as light as air.

Floating. Imagine that you are filled with helium and like a hot-air balloon, you can float slowly and gently away.

GUIDED IMAGERY RELAXATIONS

There are groups who will not sit still long enough to do a guided imagery relaxation and there are groups who thrive on them. Test out your class with a short one and see how they respond.

Begin by having your students lie on the floor on their backs. It helps if they take their shoes off and loosen tight belts, but if this seems weird to them, forgo it. (If students are in wheelchairs, they can stay in them.) Relax the whole body progressively from toes to head or from head to toes. Ask students to tense and release each body part: toes, feet, calves, thighs, buttocks, stomach, back, chest, hands, lower arms, upper arms, shoulders, neck, and face. As they tense each part, have them be aware of the muscles in that body part. As they release each part, tell them to imagine that all the tension is melting out of them or evaporating out of them or draining out of them.

Another relaxation method is to have students imagine as they breathe in that they are breathing warmth and sunlight into their bodies, warming up their muscles and relaxing them. They can start with their toes and fill their entire body up with sunlight or helium or energy. Use whichever image seems to work best for them.

Once they are relaxed, if you want, you can take them on a guided trip in their imaginations. You can structure the imaginary journey so that they have choices to make along the way. They could take a walk in the woods, they could go to the bottom of the sea, they could take a space flight to Mars.

Often progressive relaxation and guided imagery trips are enhanced by tapes of environmental sounds or instrumental music. I like to find interesting music and make up a fantasy trip to go along with it. Journeys can be based on a favorite fairy tale or an adventure you know your students would like to have. Time machines, hot air balloons, magic carpets, and mystical ships are excellent guided imagery devices for spiriting your students away to a far away time and place.

Good sources of guided imagery scripts are Maureen Murdock's *Spinning Inward: Using Guided Imagery with Children for Learning, Creativity, and Relaxation,* and Gay Hendricks's two books on Centering.

When students come back from their journeys they can share what happened to them or draw what they saw in their mind's eye. If they are not in the sharing mood or they need to move on to something more active, you can continue with the next activity in your lesson plan.

Guided imagery sessions are useful motivational tools for improvisation projects, especially when you want students to visualize a set of characters or a specific location. They also serve as good rest breaks in the middle of a long class period, giving students a chance to refocus when they get wound up or tired.

DRAMA GAMES

The following collection of drama games is by no means exhaustive. There are many thousands of games and game variations. I have included as examples a few games which have worked well for me with different special needs groups.

Please don't limit yourself to the games included here. Look through creative drama and improvisational acting books for ideas. Invent your own games and variations. A list of recommended game and drama books is located in the bibliography at the end of this book.

SENSORY OBSERVATION GAMES

Sensory observation games teach basic awareness skills. They are excellent exercises for students who have cognitive or physical disabilities because they develop sensory and information processing channels which can be used to enhance many areas of their lives.

Blindfold Walks. Blindfold walks can be done in pairs or by a whole group together.

In pairs: One student is blindfolded and the other leads him around the classroom space or outside. The leader can guide by touch or by voice or both. Do this exercise slowly. The leader must pay close attention and take care of the blindfolded partner so he does not hurt himself. The leader guides him to experience the textures, sounds, smells, and spatial arrangement of the environment in a new way. After five or ten minutes, partners can switch roles.

In a group: A whole group in a long line can be blindfolded. Each person holds on to the shoulders of the person in front of him. The first person in line, usually the teacher or assistant, is not blindfolded and leads the line around. It is helpful to have one person free to reconnect students who have lost their handhold on the shoulders in front of them.

Blindfold exercises are good tools for developing trust with other members of a group. It is extremely important that seeing partners do not play tricks on their blindfolded charges. These are good group building exercises, but if your students cannot handle being responsible for the safety of another, wait to do these types of exercises until they can.

Some students fear being blindfolded. Blindfolds can throw off balance and disorient the wearer. Be sensitive to this. When a student expresses fear, you will need to make a judgement call whether you are seeing real panic or just nervousness about trying something new. Encourage the nervous to try the exercise, but give the truly fearful an easy out: quietly turn them into an obstacle remover or a door-opener so they can participate in the activity in a way that feels safe for them.

Blindfold exercises are also excellent disability awareness exercises. If you have a blind student in your class, a blindfold exercise will give your sighted students a chance to experience the world from his perspective.

Airport. A variation of the blindfold walk, this exercise provides practice in listening to and following directions and in giving clear verbal commands.

Set up an obstacle course in your classroom using objects and students. One student is the "Airplane," which is coming in for a landing at the airport. Another student is the "Air Traffic Controller," who must guide him through the obstacle course with verbal directions. Speed is not at issue here; accuracy is. The "Airplane" is supposed to make it all the way through the obstacle course without crashing or "denting a wing." Count the number of times the "Airplane" touches or bumps into an object or person. Was this because he was not listening to or following directions or because the "Air Traffic Controller" was not giving clear enough directions?

This game requires strong concentration skills. It is best used with a small group so that most students have a chance to participate as either the "Airplane" or the "Air Traffic Controller" within a 15- or 20-minute time period. However, I have had a few groups who were happy to play this game for an hour and retained interest and concentration!

Change Three. Change Three is a visual observation game. It may be done in pairs or with one student standing in front of the whole group. Have the partner or group take a close look at the "Changer" to see exactly what he has on and how he is wearing his clothes, hair, etc. When they are sure they know what he looks like, the group hides their eyes while the "Changer" changes three things about his appearance. He might untie one shoe, pull his shirt out of his pants, and roll up his sleeves. If you can't trust your group to keep their eyes closed, the "Changer" can go behind a curtain or partition to change. When he is done, the group or partner looks him over and tries to see what is different.

Variation: If three changes are too many for a group to remember, change one or two items instead. If a group is very sharp, you can have the "Changer" change up to five or six things!

Which One Is Missing? This is another visual observation game. Collect a number of small objects and lay them out on the table. Let students look at them until they think they remember all the different objects. Cover the objects with a scarf and remove one, two, or three of them. Lift off the scarf and see who can remember what is missing.

Copy the Shape. One student takes a body position for 10 to 30 seconds and the rest of the class observes and tries to remember the body shape. Then that student relaxes and a volunteer from the group tries to reproduce the position.

Variation: Have the student hold the position while everyone tries to copy it as faithfully as possible.

This exercise develops visual memory and visual/kinesthetic links in the central nervous system.

Back Writing. Back Writing is a variation of the ever-popular "Telephone" or "Gossip," focusing on tactile awareness and memory instead of listening skills. Have students sit in a line, one in front of the other. Draw a letter or number slowly and carefully on the back of the last person in line. He draws what he felt on the back of the person in front of him, and so on down the line. The person in front draws what he thinks the letter or number is. If it is not the same as the one you drew, figure out where it changed and if it changed only once or several times.

This game can be done as a race between two or more teams.

Indian Chief. Indian Chief is a very advanced visual observation game, but even children who have difficulty with it love playing it.

Everyone sits in a circle. One person goes out of the room. The teacher picks a leader or "Indian Chief" by pointing to him. (It is important not to say the "Indian Chief's" name out loud because you don't want the person outside the room to hear it.) The "Indian Chief" begins doing a physical action, such as clapping his hands, snapping his fingers, or nodding his head. Everyone in the circle must copy him exactly. Every time he changes his action, the group changes with him.

The person in the hallway returns to the room and observes the group to figure out who is "Indian Chief." The trick is to look for whoever is changing the action first. The observer has three chances to guess who the "Indian Chief" is. If he guesses correctly, he rejoins the circle and the "Indian Chief" goes out into the hall to be the observer for the next round. If the observer guesses incorrectly three times, he must return to the hall and try again the next round.

Group members should not look directly at the "Indian Chief" all the time or it will be obvious to the observer who the leader is. Yet they must try to remain aware of what the "Chief" is doing at all times so they know when he changes his action. This in itself can be a real challenge!

Students love being picked to be the "Indian Chief" and they love going out into the hall, but they can become very frustrated if they don't understand how to find the "Indian Chief." They may have difficulty if they have poor visual observation skills or attention deficits. Your assistant can help by staying with the observer and pointing out things to look for.

If students become upset about having to go back out into the hall because they guessed wrong (after all, most of us *do* feel badly when we fail), change the rules of the game so that the observer can rejoin the circle whether he gets the answer right or not. The point of playing this game is not to punish a poor observer, it is to have a good time practicing observation and concentration skills.

Dog and Bone. This is a listening, observation, and body awareness exercise rolled into one. One student is the "Dog." He is blindfolded and lies down on the floor on his stomach, pretending to be asleep. An object representing his "Bone" is placed in front of his "Paws" (but he may not touch it). The rest of the class stands at an agreed-upon distance. Tape out a starting line on the floor to delineate boundaries. One by one students try to sneak up on the "Dog" and steal his "Bone."

If your "Sneakers" are in wheelchairs, you could set the "Bone" up on a table in front of the "Dog" instead of down on the floor so it is within easy reach.

If the "Dog" hears any noise or senses any movement, he is supposed to bark and point in the direction of the noise. If caught, a "Bone Stealer" must go back to the starting line. If a student steals the "Dog's Bone," he becomes the "Dog" for the next round and the old "Dog" rejoins the group.

Variation: The Queen (or King) Has a Headache. One student, playing the ruling monarch, sits blindfolded in a chair at one end of the room. The idea is that everyone must be completely quiet because the "Ruler" has a headache. One by one students try to sneak past the "Ruler" without making a sound. If the "Ruler" hears anything, he moans dramatically and the "Sneaker" must go back to the starting line.

Children love these games. They enjoy the challenge and excitement of sneaking up on each other. For some children this game is a real challenge because they have difficulty controlling their body movements and the sounds they make. Being "Sneakers" gives them good practice in becoming more aware of how they move and when they make sounds. It develops their concentration abilities. "Dogs" and "Rulers" get to practice concentration and listening skills as well as their ability to detect sound directionality.

Listening to Sounds. Most students enjoy listening to sound effects on cassette tape and identifying what is creating the sound. Some groups can do this for five minutes and some groups stay enthralled with this activity for an hour! You can record live sounds yourself or buy a sound effects tape to play. I have edited together sounds from a number of different tapes to give variety between animal, nature, and man-made sounds.

Making Sound Effects. Bring a number of noise-making implements to class and experiment with making different kinds of sounds. Make your own class sound effect tape.

Sound Symphonies. Divide the class into two teams. Have one team make one kind of sound, for instance, honking car horns. Have the other team make another kind of sound, for instance, beeping taxi horns. Signal one group to begin making their sound, then the other. Regulate the volume at which each team is making its noise with the level of your hands, high being loud and low being soft with all variations in between.

Sound Environments. Create an environment through sound. Each student chooses a different sound for that place. You could create a farm, a forest, a city street, or any place imaginable. The teacher or a student serves as conductor and regulates when each sound comes in and goes out and what the volume level is.

Sound Stories. A sound story is a story that can be enhanced with sound effects made by the class as you or your assistant tells the story. Many creative drama books have examples of sound stories in them or you can write your own. The Saturday's Rainbow Adventure in the Prologue of this book started out as a sound story exercise, but became an imagination/pantomime experience as we did it. Sound stories are most fun when they are tape recorded and played back so students can hear themselves on tape.

Sound stories are excellent beginning exercises to use with beginning, young, and nonverbal students. Success is built in. Almost everyone can make sounds. If they can't make vocal sounds, they can usually make sounds with objects. Everyone works together. Everyone listens very hard when the tape is played back to hear his voice or sound effects. There is great excitement and pride when a student hears the noises he made or those made by a friend. I'm not sure why, but the sound effects recorded for sound stories *always* sound good when they're played back.

MOVEMENT AND PANTOMIME GAMES

Movement and pantomime games teach body awareness and control.

Freezing. Students move around the room until the teacher says "Freeze!" Then they must stop and freeze in position. They can move again when the teacher says, "Unfreeze" or "Go." This is a good game for teaching listening skills and body control. Freezing is a good technique to use as a group control device when students get a little wild and need to be calmed down. You can also use it when you need to stop the action to sidecoach a story or improvisation. If you like, have students move to music and freeze when the music stops.

Emotion Freezes. Students move around the room and when the teacher names an emotion, they freeze into a statue expressing that emotion.

Variation: The teacher names an emotion and students walk around the room in a manner that expresses that emotion. When he says, "Freeze," they freeze into a statue of that emotion. This variation allows students to explore the emotion before committing to a physicalization of it.

The Magic Box. Place a large, colorful box with a top on it in the center of the circle. The Magic Box can hold any object of any size from any place in the world. Each student must first imagine what is in the box for him. The first student opens the box and "takes out" what he has imagined. He shows the others what it is by pantomiming how to use it. Then he closes the box and the next person has a turn.

Variation/Complication: Before you can take something out of the box for yourself, you must put a gift in it for someone else.

Interestingly enough, even though this is an abstract pantomime exercise, it works because students have the concrete box out of which the imaginary objects come.

Pass the Sound/Pass the Movement. Everyone stands in a circle. One person invents a sound and a movement to go with it, which he passes to the person standing next to him. That person mirrors the sound and movement back to the first person. Then the second person invents a new sound and movement to pass on to the next person in the circle. Sound and movements are passed on, mirrored, and then a new set invented all the way around the circle.

Don't allow a student to think too long about what sound and movement to do next. This is a spontaneity exercise! If a student can't think of something immediately, rather than stop and lose momentum, have him repeat the sound and movement he received until something new comes to mind.

Simplification: The same sound and movement can be copied and passed around the circle. After each go-around, a new student originates the next sound and movement.

Simplification: Pass only a sound or pass only a movement.

Pass the Sound/Pass the Movement is an excellent, quick-moving warm-up. It develops flexibility, spontaneity, and concentration.

Environmental Walks. Students walk around the room and the teacher suggests different environments or situations that would cause them to change the way they are walking. Examples of environments to walk through might be: mud, sharp rocks, ice, a rainstorm, a desert, the bottom of the sea, a jungle, a mountain, fly paper, quicksand.

Variation: Shoe Walks Students imagine they are wearing different kinds of shoes which the teacher suggests as they walk around. They could wear cowboy boots, ballet slippers, ice skates, high heels, flip flops, shoes that are too tight. How does each different kind of shoe change the way they walk?

Variation: Speed Walks Move at different speeds: fast motion, regular motion, slow motion, very slow motion. Try different activities at different speeds. Try talking at different speeds.

Variation: Space Walks Walk around the room without bumping into anyone else. Start at slow speeds and over the course of several weeks work up to very fast speeds. This is a great game for teaching body control and the concept of personal space.

Transformations. As the teacher suggests different plants, animals, and objects, students change their body shapes to transform themselves into something else. Give students a slow count (three or five) in which to make their transformation so they have time to think about what shape they are about to become and can grow into it.

Variation: After students become good at playing this game, have them work together to create the shapes of plants, animals, and objects.

Variation: Teach the concepts of big and small by alternating between big animals and small animals or big objects (that the students must create together) and small objects (which they create alone).

Variation: Use this game as a visual art introduction to teach different kinds of lines and geometric shapes. For instance, to create a triangle, one student could bend over and put his hands on the floor or he could join hands with two other students or three students could arrange themselves on the floor in a triangular configuration.

Variation: Use this game to teach the shapes of numbers or letters.

Making an Entrance. When an actor enters the stage, the audience needs to know how he is feeling before he says a word. This is a good exercise for teaching non-verbal expression of emotions. The teacher and one student go out of the room and decide on an emotion he will act out. Then the teacher comes back in and everyone in class says together, "Make your entrance!" The student enters the room acting out what a person would do and how a person would move if he were feeling that emotion. The class guesses what emotion the student is acting out.

Age Walks. People move in different ways at different ages. A baby crawls awkwardly. A happy six-year-old skips. A pregnant woman waddles. An old man hobbles. The teacher and one student decide on an age he will portray through movement. The class guesses what age he is.

Variation: Portray an age and emotion at the same time.

Variation: Portray a profession through movement.

Scarf Dancing. Bring long, colorful scarves made from light, diaphanous material to class. Let each student choose a scarf he likes. Play soft, flowing music like "The Blue Danube Waltz" and let students make their scarves dance in the air as they move to the music.

This exercise easily segues into a **Scarf Toss, Scarf Juggling,** or a **Magic Scarf** game (students try out different ways to wear the scarf). For Magic Scarf, motivate their imaginations by asking "What could this be?" or "How else could you wear this?" Students will turn the scarves into belts, wedding veils, aprons, dresses, blindfolds, ties, capes, and more!

The "Ghost" Game. Divide students up into two teams. One team goes out of the room or behind a curtain. They have a large sheet and choose one member to cover himself with it from head to foot. The "Ghost" must change the way he moves and the shape of his body to fool the other team. He can try to move like another member of the team or he can try to totally transform his shape and movement. The other team must guess which member of the first team is underneath the sheet. They have only one guess, so they must come to consensus. A correct guess is worth one point. After each guess, teams switch places.

Tips for Using Movement/Pantomime Games with Students Who Have Orthopedic Disabilities. Start with games that focus on the parts of their body they can move with ease and that engage them on an imaginative level. If they can move their upper bodies, games like The Magic Box, The Magic

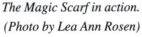

The Magic Scarf in action.
(Photo by Lea Ann Rosen)

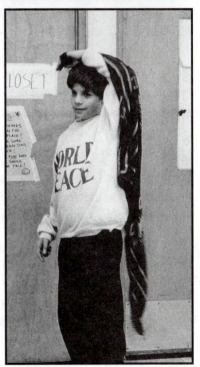

Stick, The Magic Scarf, or Transformations would guarantee more success than Environmental or Shoe Walks. Once their confidence is built up and their imaginations are warmed up, you can move on to games that use more movement, such as Making an Entrance or Pass the Sound/Pass the Movement.

IMPROVISATIONAL GAMES

Improvisational games add the dimensions of plot, dialogue, and character to basic movement games. Often students are paired or divided into groups to work together to solve the improvisational assignment.

Statues. Statues can be done in pairs or by a whole group.

In pairs: One student is the sculptor and one is the lump of clay. The sculptor creates a statue from the "lump of clay" expressing a concept suggested by the teacher—perhaps an emotion or an occupation or an animal or a character from a story. The statue must remain frozen in the shape that the sculptor places it in.

In groups: One student is the sculptor and several students are "lumps of clay" that are turned into a group statue expressing an emotional situation between characters. Have the other class members guess who the characters are and what is happening in the "scene."

Statues can remain inanimate or they can be brought to life. This is a good technique for introducing the concept of improvising dialogue. Say, "If this statue came to life, what would it say?" The signal to come to life could be a touch on the statue's shoulder or some magic words.

Danisha Crosby, one of the Academy's acting teachers, found Statues to be a very good game for providing structure for Phil, a student with ADHD. Before acting out each story, she asked each student to create a statue of his character using his own body. This helped everyone, but particularly Phil, have a kinesthetic experience with their own character and discover an appropriate physicalization. They explored statues of their characters at different moments in the story. Whenever Phil started to become distracted during the story, she would ask him to get back into character by freezing as a statue of his character at that moment in the story.

Occupations. Divide students into pairs. Each pair must decide on a job that two people do together or that one person does for another. They act out the job for the class (with or without dialogue) and the class guesses what it is.

The Hat Game. Collect a number of hats worn by different kinds of people. You might have a cowboy hat, a nurse's hat, a chef's hat, and a graduation mortar. Give each student a turn to put on the hat and act out the character who would wear it. Students can use pantomime only or make up something that character might say. Limit each session of this game to about four hats. If a group loves this game it can be played again and again with different kinds of hats each session it is used.

Variation: Lay out a variety of hats. Let each student pick a different hat. Improvise a scene in which these characters are thrown together. For example, maybe they all get stuck in an elevator together or maybe they are shipwrecked on an island. How does each character walk and talk? How do they get along with each other?

Environments. Environments is an excellent exercise for introducing the elements of an improvisational scene.

Divide the class into two groups. Each group decides on an environment or place with characters that they will create for the other team. The environment might be a movie theatre, a post office, or a school room. The first group sets up the room as that environment and begins to play their parts in it. Characters talk to each other, but try not to say the name of the place. The second group watches until they think they know where they are. They attempt to enter the environment and become a character in it. If they are correct, the other characters will respond to them. If they are not correct, the other characters will ignore them. When everyone has been integrated into the environment, the round can come to a close and the other group can take a turn.

If an interesting scene conflict develops while playing Environments, keep the scene going and try to find a plausible resolution.

Interview. Interview is a character development game, a drama version of "Twenty Questions." It requires students to behave and think as a character who is different from themselves. It forces them to make character decisions. It can be used as an acting class exercise or it can be used to enhance character development when rehearsing a play.

One student decides on a character that he will impersonate. It could be a fictional character or a historical character, but it must be someone everyone in the class could know. He must walk, talk, and move like that character during the interview. The character sits in the "Hot Seat" and the class asks him questions. They cannot ask his name, but they can ask anything else about him. After they have interviewed him for awhile, they can guess who the character is. Then another person has a chance to play.

This game can also be played as a TV talk show with one student being the TV host and others coming on as guests.

Group Storytelling. Group storytelling is a good way to teach story structure, plot development, and listening skills.

Sit in a circle. One person begins a story. After setting up the scene with a few sentences, he passes the story on to the next person. That person continues the story for awhile and passes it on until the story has gone all the way around the circle. Ideally, the story begins with the first person and ends with the last person in the circle, but it doesn't always work out that way.

For a story to make sense and have continuity, everyone must listen to the story as it goes around. Each new storyteller must continue with the same characters and solve or develop the conflict that has been set up so far. To start telling another story before the first story has ended doesn't fulfill the assignment.

Students must be flexible enough to let the story change. Once the story passes beyond them, they lose their control over what is going to happen. If someone further on in the circle takes the story in an unforseen direction, that's OK.

Beginning storytellers, like beginning improvisers, usually try to solve everything with violence. However, they soon discover that killing the hero off might be exciting for a moment, but it ends the story rather abruptly. Guide students to find more creative solutions to conflicts between characters, ones that keep the story going.

If students get confused about whose turn it is, use a prop to officially designate who is the storyteller. Students not holding the prop should be listening and not speaking. A "microphone" or a "Magic Feather" or "Magic Flower" works well because it can easily be passed from hand to hand.

If students have difficulty passing the story on, limits can be placed on the amount of time allotted to each storyteller. Each student could talk for 30 seconds or for one minute. Another method is to allow each student to tell one portion of the story: one sentence or three sentences or one whole scene.

Record the story as it goes around. Then the class can play it back and everyone can listen to how it developed.

If the story is recorded, it can later be transcribed onto paper to be revised, used as a scenario for further development, or just copied to take home.

One class that enjoyed making up stories decided to illustrate them and make a book as their end-of-the-semester project.

ART ACTIVITIES

Visual art activities can be used to motivate and enhance the physical, emotional, and verbal work you are doing in drama class. Don't feel because you are teaching "drama," that you can't include other forms of art in your lesson plan. The arts work best when they are interconnected and integrated with each other.

There are many kinds of visual arts. If you have blind students, choose an art activity that involves three dimensions like weaving, sculpting, or mask making rather than a two-dimensional activity like drawing or painting.

Drawing. Have each student draw his favorite character or the character he has been assigned to play. This will help him visualize his character more clearly.

Map Making. Many stories involve a journey which the main character takes from one place to another, having many adventures along the way. Before or after acting out a story like this, students can draw or sculpt maps of the journey. This will help them visualize the events and places the characters experience in the story.

Props and Costumes. If there are important props or costume pieces, students can make them to use before they act out the story. Maybe the king needs a scepter or a crown. Maybe the unicorn needs a horn, the rabbits need ears, or the birds need wings.

Think through the props you will be making and come prepared with materials that are easy for your students to manipulate. Know the level of your students' fine motor skills before you attempt a major art project or students will get bored waiting for help with the parts they can't do themselves. It's OK to pre-cut and pre-organize materials as long as you leave your students room for their own personal creative touches to the project. For instance, if you know you will need crowns for twelve dancing princesses, arrive with them already cut out—ready to be decorated and assembled.

An art project can be an outgrowth of the story. After acting out "Beauty and the Beast," students might enjoy learning how to make tissue paper roses to take home. After "The Five Hundred Hats of Bartholomew Cubbins," students might like to decorate their own hats. After "Hansel and Gretel," your class might like to learn how to make gingerbread houses!

Murals. Work together to make a group mural of the story. Choose a specific scene from the story or have everyone paint in the character he played in a pose that most expresses his personality. This takes planning beforehand so no one oversteps anyone else's personal space boundaries. Flexibility and the ability to compromise are also vital issues in mural-making, as students must be willing to let others' visual ideas about the story be in the scene along with their own.

Puppets. Simple puppets can be made out of paper plates, wooden spoons, paper towel rolls, or paper bags. A puppet show version of the story can be done in class, or puppets can be made after acting out a story so students can take them home and continue exploring the story dramatically.

Puppets can be helpful tools for enticing participation from a very shy student or one who is having difficulty improvising dialogue. A puppet can serve as a safe, distancing mechanism when acting with his own body and voice seems to be too threatening or overwhelming. The puppet is "not me," so he can project a funny voice and personality onto it without feeling judged or put on the spot. See Chapter Eight for more detailed information about puppetry.

Makeup. A session with makeup can be fun. The easiest, fastest type of makeup to use is a water-base makeup which can be painted on like water-colors. Kryolan makes Aquacolor palettes in natural skin tones and bright primary colors. Create clown or animal makeups. Design a fantasy makeup for monsters or fairies.

If you have young children with short attention spans or poor fine motor skills, the best idea is to paint the makeup designs on them yourself. Older children can paint on each other or look in a mirror and paint themselves.

One way to design a makeup is to start with a blank face chart on a piece of paper. The chart can indicate the basic outline of the head, ears, nose, mouth, and eyes, but leave all details blank. Create the makeup design by filling in the face chart with magic marker or colored pencil. Then go from the page to the face.

Harriet Lesser, an art teacher, has invented another way to design makeup that takes the individual child's face into the design in a more imme-diate way. It is also a great way to explore makeup with students who have allergies or who don't want to put anything on their faces. Tape a sheet of clear acetate to a mirror. The child sits directly in front of it and looks through it into the mirror. He draws the makeup design directly onto his own facial image (on the acetate) with magic marker. Rolls of acetate can be bought at most art supply stores. Make sure you purchase acetate which will hold the marker. Otherwise, the marker color will bead up and rub off.

Mask-Making. Mask-making is another way to explore characters and add an interesting art activity to your class. Simple masks can be made from paper plates and attached to the head with elastic or string ties. You might want to cut out the eyes and attach the ties before class. Have students draw on the face or glue on objects (buttons, yarn, ribbon, colorful plastic lids, etc.) for three-dimensional features.

Simple masks can also be made from medium- to large-sized paper bags. Cut out eyes and half-moons on the shoulders (this makes them fit better). Then have students draw on the face. Both of these types of masks can be made in ten to twenty minutes.

Some art supply stores sell neutral masks made out of white or clear plastic. These can serve as a simple form to build or paint on. More elaborate masks can be made from papier mache molded around a head form or from foam rubber. Build up the features by painting or gluing on more foam shapes, feathers, yarn, and other decorative three-dimensional shapes.

If your students are older, have patience, and aren't tactilely defensive, you can build masks directly onto their faces using plaster of Paris bandages. The advantage of this type of mask is that it fits the individual's face perfectly.

Rolls of gauze covered with plaster of Paris can be bought at many drug stores or medical supply stores as well as at some art supply stores. Before class, cut the rolls into small gauze squares.

Cover the student's hair completely with a shower cap or bandanna so it doesn't get caught in the plaster. Cover his face, particularly eyebrows and any areas which have facial hair, with a thin layer of petroleum jelly. The ideal position for mask-making is lying on the back with eyes closed; however, I have made masks on students who were in a sitting position.

The teacher and assistant can make the masks on the students or students can take turns making masks on each other. Wet the strips of bandage

Mask-making: Student waits while plaster of Paris gauze dries. (Photo by Keith Jenkins)

with warm water and work the plaster around a bit to fill in the holes in the gauze. Place on the face in overlapping layers. Blend the plaster as you go. The student cannot talk while the bandages are placed on his face. At least three or four layers of gauze squares are needed to make the mask thick enough. You can make a full face mask or a half mask. You can cover the entire face including the eyes and cut out eye holes later or you can leave holes for the eyes as you work. Be sure to leave holes around the nostrils so the student can breathe!

The plaster will dry in ten to fifteen minutes. During that time the student must remain lying quietly on his back. Then the mask can be loosened if the student wiggles his face a little. Lift the mask off.

The mask will need to dry for several days and may need several more layers of plaster gauze—added to the top—to make it strong enough. Character features can be built up with more layers of plaster gauze or with foam rubber or styrofoam shapes glued on. Then the masks can be painted. When you are using plaster gauze and want to build large facial features, such as a long, pointy beak, create the shape you want with cardboard or buckram and then layer on top of that form with gauze. If you build up a large feature using only gauze, the mask will become too heavy and will press down on the actor's face.

Punch holes in the sides of the mask by the ears with an awl. Measure how much elastic you need to hold a mask on the actor's head. Then thread the elastic through the holes and tie it off.

This kind of mask project involves several class periods. It might be fun for an advanced creative drama class or a movement/mime class that is preparing a special presentation.

CLOSURE ACTIVITIES

Ending a class on an organized, upbeat note is as important as starting it off well. Good endings are a matter of finding the proper emotional and physical balance as one activity concludes and another begins. Students need a chance to calm down from the intensity and excitement of drama class and refocus themselves for whatever is coming next. Closure activities help the teacher and students put their experience into perspective before moving on. Many closure activities can be done with any age group.

Running Out of Time. At first, you may find that you over-plan for a class and run out of time. This is not so difficult to deal with if you are playing a game. Warn students that you are running out of time and stop the game at the end of the next round.

Ending is more difficult if your students are in the middle of an exciting improvisational scene or creative drama story. Telling them that they can finish next week usually doesn't offer much consolation. Keep track of time as you move from one activity to another in your lesson plan. Don't start a scene or story unless you know you can move it to a quick ending if you begin to run out of time. After awhile you will be able to gauge about how many activities a particular group of students can get through on a typical day.

If you are halfway through a creative drama story and you suddenly realize that there are only five minutes of class left, try using your role as narrator to facilitate "jump-cutting" from the climax of one scene to the next. Say, "We're running out of time and we want to finish the story, so I'm going to speed things up a little." Cut the development of each remaining scene to a minimum and let students fill in the important pantomime action and important moments of climactic dialogue. Finish with the whole class together in an ending tableau as their favorite characters in the story.

For an improvisational scene, warn the actors. "We have five minutes left. You need to find an ending for this scene." If they keep going, warn them again, "OK, you now have two minutes left. This scene needs an ending." Some scenes won't end and you must step in and freeze the actors. "Freeze. I'm sorry. We're out of time. This week at home, see if you can think of a good way to end this scene."

Check-out. In Creative Drama, acting out the story is usually the penultimate activity. Afterwards, the class can spend a few minutes discussing what they enjoyed most about the story. They might want to share their favorite moments or which character was their favorite to play.

In Improvisational Acting classes, students can sit down and review the games they played, what they learned that day, and what they enjoyed doing the most.

Songs. Singing always brings people together in a very positive way. You might find an "ending" or a "goodbye" song that can serve as an ending ritual each week. You might sing a favorite song suggested by a member of the class. The end of class is not the best time to teach a new song, but it is a good time to review a song that was learned earlier.

Art Activities. Art is a good way to tie together dramatic activities that have been done that period. Have students draw their favorite scene from the story acted out that day. See the section on "Art Activities" earlier in this chapter for more ideas.

Guided Fantasy. A short guided fantasy might serve as a good closing activity. It can calm students down and provide a safe transition from the end of class to going home or moving on to the next class in the day.

A Favorite Game. Some groups have favorite games that they like to play again and again. The end of class is a good time to re-play a game. It provides a feeling of safety and familiarity to students before going out to face something new.

Passing Games. Gather students into a circle and have each person pass a compliment around the circle to the person next to him. Another passing game is Pass the Expression. Pass sad faces or happy faces or funny faces around the circle. Hold hands and pass a squeeze around the circle.

Making a Wish. Pass a "magic object" like a crystal or a feather around the circle. Each student makes a wish on the object while it is in his hands.

BUILDING LESSON PLANS FOR A CREATIVE DRAMA CLASS

A strong creative drama lesson plan uses warm-ups and games as motivational devices and skill-builders for the acting skills that will be needed in that day's story. The following pages offer suggestions for how to lead up to a story through games and acting exercises.

"THE TORTOISE AND THE HARE"

"The Tortoise and the Hare" is a fable that has characters who live life at two very different speeds. Each of the speeds has an emotional effect on the personality of the characters. The Tortoise is very slow and deliberate. The Hare is very quick, impatient, and boastful. Prepare your students for this story by focusing your warm-up activities on practice in acting at different speeds.

A detailed lesson plan for this story might look like this:

1. Pantomime Go-Around (fast animals/slow animals).
2. Fast/regular/slow actions and voices.
3. Fast/regular/slow freezes.
4. Regular race.
5. Slow motion race.
6. Tell "The Tortoise and the Hare."
7. Set up the race course in the room.
8. Practice character walks and voices.
9. Choose characters for the story.
10. Act out the story.

Start class with students sitting in a circle. Go around the circle and ask each one to act out a slow animal. Then go around again and act out a fast animal. Talk about different speeds. Together pantomime a series of actions like clapping hands, nodding yes and no, waving, etc. in regular motion, fast motion, and slow motion. Then try talking in a regular speed, in fast speed, and in slow speed. Get up and practice moving in slow motion, regular motion, and fast motion, freezing the students between each speed change.

Organize a short sprint across the classroom. Delineate your starting line and finish line with masking tape on the floor. Then organize a Slow Motion Race. The difference between a slow motion race and a regular race is that in a slow motion race the *last* person to cross the finish line wins! It may be hard at first to get across the idea that in order to win a slow motion race, the racers must do what would lose a regular race, but once your students catch on, you won't believe how slowly they'll move! If the slow motion race is frustrating for them, run one more fast sprint across the room to release their tension.

Tell the story. Take a few moments at the end to talk about what the moral means. "Slow and steady wins the race" doesn't always make sense to young children. The Hare doesn't win because he doesn't keep at it. He stops to eat, he visits friends, and eventually he takes a nap. The Tortoise just keeps moving. The moral means, "If you quit or fool around, you'll never finish the job you started, but no matter how slowly you work, if you keep plugging away, you'll succeed."

Take some time to lay the race course out in a very clear way in the room. If you have a carpet, the race could follow its edge all the way around the room. You could tape the race course out on the floor. Signs or "landmarks" in the room could show where to go first, second, third, and so on. However it is set up, students need a visual path to follow. If your race course is vague—"Just run around the room" or "Run over there and then over here and then . . .," your students will lose their way and the story will fall apart. Decide ahead of time where the Hare will stop to eat, to chat, to fall asleep.

Practice running the race course with everyone as the Hare and then practice with everyone as the Tortoise. Choose characters and act out the story.

NATIONALITY/CULTURE THEMES

Focus on a particular culture or nationality for one or a series of classes. Bring in pictures, maps, and examples of folk art, clothing, or other items indigenous to that culture to show students. Learn a song or folk dance from that country. Talk about names in that culture and how they are different from ours. For instance, in China family names are put first instead of last, as in most Western cultures. Native Americans place a great value on names, which are often based on nature or on deeds that an individual has done. Depending on the tribe, the individual earns, dreams, or chooses his name, unlike children in Western societies who are given their names at birth, often to carry on a family tradition. Make food, clothing, or art in the style of that culture. For example, if you are focusing on Mexico or the Southwestern U.S., you could teach students how to make God's Eyes (folk art that brings good luck) or how to roll their own flour tortillas. Tell and act out stories from that culture.

TOY STORIES

There are lots of stories about famous dolls like Raggedy Ann, Winnie the Pooh, or Paddington Bear. Begin class with a Go-Around in which each student thinks of his favorite toy. As a group, act out several different toys that will be characters in the story. If you can find music which suggests the toys, students will enjoy acting out the toys with the music. Then tell the story. Act it out. End by drawing a picture of favorite characters or favorite toys.

ANIMAL STORIES

There are many stories that revolve around animal characters, from "The Frog Prince," to "The Musicians of Bremen." Try different kinds of animal pantomime games as lead-in activities to the story.

Practice making the animal's sound in different ways, to express the different emotions the animal character feels in the story. A frog could "Rib-bit" sadly, happily, angrily, or hungrily. Create a character voice for an animal based on the qualities of its real animal sound.

If the story involves differences in size, as in "The Lion and the Mouse," "The Three Billy Goats Gruff," or "The Three Bears," practice acting out creatures who are large and small. Practice talking in a big voice and a little voice. Practice making big movements and small ones.

Learn a song about one of the animals in the story.

Make a mask to wear while acting out the story.

*Student pan-tomiming a moose.
(Photo by Lea Ann Rosen)*

BUILDING LESSON PLANS FOR IMPROVISATIONAL ACTING CLASSES

Start the semester off with lots of games and activities in which students can get to know each other. Group games in which everyone participates and works together are crucial to developing trust and problem-solving skills that will be needed for creating improvisational scenes later. Give students enough individual opportunities to begin developing verbal and physical expressiveness, but be careful about putting individuals on the spot to perform for the group before they are ready. A nice mixture of group games and individual skill-building activities for a beginning group might look like this:

SESSION ONE

1. Name Game—say your name and pantomime your favorite animal
2. Elbow-to-Elbow
3. Transformations—change your body into different shapes
4. The Magic Stick
5. The "Ghost" Game
6. Go-Around—pass the sheet around and each person wear it a different way.

Slowly introduce your actors to solo and partner work:

SESSION TWO
1. Name Review—bean bag game
2. Emotion walks—walk around expressing different emotions
3. Making an Entrance
4. Season Pantomimes—in pairs act out something you might do in the summer, winter, fall, or spring
5. Imagine your favorite food's smell and taste
6. Pass a facial expression around the circle.

A later session in the semester might look like this:

SESSION FOUR
1. The Magic Box
2. The Hat Game—with 2 or 3 hats
3. Environments—2 rounds
4. Group story telling

By the end of the semester, you may be warming-up with a game or two and then opening up the floor for suggestions of scenes which could be created:

SESSION ELEVEN
1. Pass the Sound/Pass the Movement
2. Scene work
3. Discussion of scenes
4. Group hand squeeze

SHARING WITH PARENTS AND FRIENDS AT THE END OF THE SEMESTER

FORMAL PRESENTATIONS

Many schools and organizations like their performing arts classes to make a presentation at the end of each semester or year for parents and friends. In different places presentations are called by different names: recital, showcase, highlights, sharing, the class play.

There is often a lot of pressure to show parents that they have used their money wisely in enrolling their child in this class. Some of the pressure comes from the administration and some from the parents. Teachers put pressure on themselves because they want to show their students' artistic growth. Students put pressure on themselves because they want to shine in their parents' eyes.

Presentation of work from a class that is geared around skill development is problematic at best. Creative drama and improvisational acting classes are process- rather than product-oriented. Whenever formal presentations must be made, rehearsals begin. Whenever rehearsals begin, informal class exploration and skill building stops.

There is also the dilemma of the rehearsal schedule. If a presentation needs to be put together, at what point in the semester should rehearsals for it begin? Three class periods before the presentation? Five class periods before? Eight? The appropriate amount of time for rehearsing a project depends on the students and the complexity of the project being undertaken.

When classes turn into rehearsals, a different dynamic takes over. Class is now about reproducing a result that once was improvised: enhancing it and improving it so that it is clear and can be shared with others. Stage technique comes into play because the audience needs to see and hear the actors.

Suddenly the class is in the middle of the creation of a one-act play which takes on more production values and greater importance the closer performance time comes. Parents start making costumes, teachers start building sets, students start getting nervous and upset.

The truth of the matter is that sometimes it is not in the best interests of students to perform at the end of a semester. The pressure of preparing for a presentation is often too much for beginning students to handle. If they will not feel comfortable presenting themselves in front of an audience, it is far better to devote class time to the development of expression, self-confidence, and improvisation skills. There will be plenty of opportunities to perform in the future. When children are pushed on stage too soon and have a bad experience, they may not want to try again. I have heard too many horror stories from adults who had traumatic experiences in performance situations as children to believe that everyone should always perform.

When formal presentations are appropriate, keep them simple and keep them short. Provide lots of structure and lots of rehearsal time so that students are sure what they are doing. To achieve a polished performance in the professional theatre with trained actors, directors generally like to schedule at least an hour of rehearsal for every minute on stage. Obviously, that degree of rehearsal and precision is not required or necessary for a student presentation; however, the guideline is worth bearing in mind when undertaking a project.

Build in fail-safe techniques to keep students on track during performance:

- Keep dialogue improvised so that it doesn't have to be exactly the same each time.
- Keep the play moving through a narrator (yourself or your assistant) who can remind students of what comes next and can improvise if something goes wrong.
- Use an assistant as a character in the play who can remind student actors (in character) of what comes next.
- Use music cues to remind students of exits and entrances. Different characters can have "character themes" which play each time they come on stage.
- If you need to, record the dialogue on tape and have the actors pantomime to it. Then they can concentrate on remembering movement instead of trying to remember movement *and* lines.

Above all, remind your students, tell your parents, and remember yourself that this is a work in progress, not a finished product. If something goes wrong, it is not the end of the world. It's just a taste test, not a full-course meal.

IN-CLASS SHARINGS

There are alternatives to formal presentations. One is an in-class sharing in which parents and friends are invited into the last class to participate in a typical class. Favorite games and exercises can be taught to the guests by the now experienced students. Parents can be teamed up against students for games or families can work together against other families.

In Creative Drama classes, parents can be invited to take on characters in the story and act alongside their children. In Improvisational Acting classes, parents can be included in role playing and the creation of scenes.

A great time is had by all in this kind of sharing situation. Students forget to be nervous. Parents have the opportunity to see their children in a relaxed, absorbed state. They can see them interact with others. As students work and play alongside their parents, they can see a new side of the adults in their lives—the playful, creative side.

A cautionary note: let parents know ahead of time that they will be expected to participate in the class with their child. If parents sit and watch, the class will turn into a formal presentation situation—one which hasn't been rehearsed! Students will feel self-conscious and unprepared and will begin to act out negatively. The whole situation will fall apart.

VIDEO PRESENTATIONS

A good way to present a story that the group has been working on, without the pressure of performance, is to videotape work as it is going on in class. A number of different sessions can be videotaped and edited together for a final class presentation, or a special story, scene, or character development exercise could be staged for the camera. Students and parents can watch the presentation and enjoy it together without the nerves and worry that accompany a formal presentation. You will be sharing your process as a product.

SPECIAL CLASS PROJECTS

If students have done a number of art projects over the course of the semester, have the class spend some time mounting their work and set up an art gallery in the room for the final class. Students can serve as tour guides through the gallery.

If students have developed a series of stories, they could be presented in a reading for parents. Similarly, if students have developed a sound tape of which they are particularly proud, the tape or a section of it can be shared.

If you must give a final presentation of some sort, look at your options with an eye to ways you can show your students off to their best advantage and keep the situation as relaxed and informal as possible. Success should always be the operative word.

chapter eight

puppetry

Puppetry is a form of drama that can be very popular and successful with students with special needs of all ages. The process of creating a puppet play is enjoyed by the puppeteers and the experience of performing for an appreciative audience enhances feelings of self-esteem.

There is a lot of prejudice against puppetry as an art form in our contemporary American culture. Puppet Theatre is generally considered appropriate entertainment fare only for young children. While puppetry is enjoyed by children and can be done by children, it is no more a "childish" art than acting, singing, or dancing. Far Eastern countries like Burma, Thailand, and Japan have classical puppet traditions reaching back hundreds of years. Their puppet theatres present plays about important cultural and moral struggles and are attended by the whole community. Europe also has greatly respected puppet theatres which perform to large audiences of all ages. Great American puppeteers like Peter Schumann, founder of the Bread and Puppet Theater, and the late Jim Henson, inventor of the Muppets, are adult artists who have created puppets and plays for adults as well as for children.

THE ADVANTAGES OF PUPPETRY

There are many advantages to working with puppets. Students expect a performance experience at the end of the semester. Most of what they do during class is focused toward that final goal of performing the puppet play. This helps prepare them for being in a performance situation. The process becomes the product in a step-by-step, logical, visual, auditory, kinesthetic progression which uses right-brain as well as left-brain intelligences and abilities.

Because a puppet play is a highly structured situation in rehearsal and performance, students can be introduced to performing in a situation in which they will feel safe. Puppeteers are hidden away behind the puppet stage so the audience doesn't see them. They have an assigned space back-stage and usually don't have to do much moving around. They have very specific movements to make, which can be carefully choreographed and familiarized through repetition. This doesn't mean they won't be nervous before performing, but it does mean that they can be prepared and feel com-fortable with what they are doing.

Puppetry is a particularly good performance vehicle for shy students. They are shielded from the eyes of the audience by the puppet stage, yet their characters are out in full view. Nobody out front knows for sure who is playing each character, so the pressure of being seen and judged is off. Many times very quiet children become incredible "hams" when put behind a puppet stage for the first time. They blossom as performers in a way they never could if physically put on a stage themselves. In a sense, they are freed to express themselves dramatically for the first time.

Another advantage to puppetry is that students begin working on a pup-pet play knowing that they will have a finished product to take home, some-thing concrete they have made and can be proud of. The puppet becomes a treasured memento they can keep to remember the class and performance.

An actor uses her own body, but she is inside her own body and can't see it from the outside. A puppeteer uses her own body, but can see her char-acter from the outside as she manipulates it. As a puppeteer, a performer can have the best of both worlds—being performer and audience at the same time.

Because a puppeteer can see her character as an entity separate from her-self while she performs, puppets help an actor understand that the character she is portraying is separate or different from the actor herself. Some begin-ning actors are afraid that if they pretend to be someone else, they will be-come that other person. With a puppet, a student can project whatever emotions and words she wants onto the character on her hand without worry-ing that someone in the audience might confuse that character with her . . . and without becoming confused herself.

Through puppetry, students can become involved in an in-depth creation of their characters and the play. They make the decisions that affect what their characters look like and, in some cases, how their characters move. Having a physical creation outside of themselves that they can see and touch, makes inventing dialogue and character reactions easier for some children.

ISSUES TO THINK ABOUT BEFORE CHOOSING PUPPETRY FOR A CLASS

While puppetry has many advantages, there are some issues to take into consideration in regard to your drama students.

First, do your students have the concentration ability and interest level to stay with one project over an extended period of time? Young children and children who have very short attention spans or impulse control problems do better with projects that can be accomplished within one class period or, in some cases, within ten minutes! They have difficulty putting off gratification from the present to a future moment. If you try to involve them in a long-term project, they may become bored or frustrated.

Second, do your students have the hand-eye coordination and the fine motor skills to construct puppets and manipulate them? If your students have very good fine motor skills, you are free to build any kind of puppet. If your students have physical limitations, pick a type of puppet that is easy for them to make and maneuver. Rod puppets can be manipulated by anyone who can grasp a stick. Hand puppets require more manual dexterity. Marionettes are the most difficult of all to use.

Because puppeteers' vision of onstage action is limited by their physical placement behind the curtains of most puppet stages, puppeteers must rely primarily on sound cues rather than visual cues during performance. This makes participation in puppet plays difficult for deaf students. However, there are some types of puppet stages, particularly those used for marionettes in which the puppeteers look down on the stage from above, which would allow deaf students a wide range of vision and, therefore, the ability to participate successfully in the puppet show.

Another alternative for deaf students, if you have access to the right equipment through your school, might be to provide the puppeteers with a backstage video monitor of the onstage action. This method was developed by Jim Henson so he and the other Muppeteers could keep track of how the Muppets looked to the TV camera during taping. Normally, the Muppeteers manipulate their Muppets above their heads and watch what is happening on monitors placed below them. A videocamera could be set up in the audience with a feed cable going backstage to a TV monitor positioned somewhere deaf puppeteers could see it.

Good assistants are crucial in puppetry classes. The more complicated the building process and the art materials, and the more fine motor difficulties your students have, the more help they will need. It is better to arrange for a few extra assistants during the building process, than to let your students flounder. A student who becomes overly frustrated while trying to construct her puppet may give up on the whole project in despair.

Choosing the right person as an assistant for a puppetry class is as important as having enough of them. The assistant needs to be able to understand what the student envisions and help her create the effects *she* wants. The assistant does this by providing the missing manipulative skills or the extra hand needed for holding something in place. The effective assistant shares her expertise and knowledge of the art materials with the student. She shows how to create the effect the student had in mind with the materials at hand without taking over and doing the project herself.

Taking over a project or changing a student's ideas are not acceptable. The teacher and the assistant are there to serve as guides—to facilitate the child's creative vision, not their own. If you take over the artistic function from your students, they will know that you don't value their ideas. They will lose their enthusiasm for the project and stop contributing creatively to class.

The last thing to take into consideration is to determine if puppetry is an acceptable undertaking to your students. While puppetry *is* appropriate for students of any age, the students in question have to believe it is appropriate for them. If a class of adolescents or upper elementary school students have bought into the narrow American belief that "puppetry is only for young children," you could be fighting an uphill battle. You might get through to them, but chances are they won't allow themselves to experience the creative challenge and joy of puppetry.

CREATING AND DEVELOPING A PUPPET SHOW

CHOOSING THE STORY

Students need to be committed to a puppet project from the outset. The best way to get them to commit is to involve them in the decision making. Let them choose the story that will be turned into the puppet play. Ask for suggestions of their favorite stories. Write down all suggestions and talk about the pros and cons of each. Which stories have the most interesting characters? The most exciting plots? The fairest division of roles? Will the dialogue be easy to make up? Will any parts be difficult to stage? Some stories might not have enough characters for everyone to have a part. Some might have too many characters. If there are more characters than students, are a few puppeteers willing to make and manipulate more than one puppet?

Avoid dramatizing favorite television shows or current movies. The characters are familiar to everyone, but the situations usually won't develop into interesting plays. Be wary of stories with a weak plot structure. They will be as hard to dramatize as a puppet play as they are in a creative drama class.

While younger students will suggest fairy tales and children's stories, older students may want to dramatize a classic poem like "'Twas The Night Before Christmas" or "Hiawatha's Childhood." They could base a puppet play on a well-known novel like *Oliver Twist* or contemporary youth fiction like *Charlie and the Chocolate Factory*. They could also create an original play about a social situation that they face or a fantasy situation of their own devising. Any material that can be dramatized can be dramatized through puppetry.

After the class has talked about all the ideas and eliminated the ones that everyone agrees won't work well, take a vote on the remaining ideas on the list. There may be a clear favorite, in which case, you are on your way.

If the group is split, you need to guide them to a choice that is acceptable to everyone. One way to get a sense of where a general consensus might lie is for each student to vote for every story she would like to do, instead of limiting herself to one vote for her favorite story on the list. Then you will see where the interests actually fall among all the possibilities. In a class of ten students, if nine would be willing to do "Cinderella," seven would be willing to do "Sleeping Beauty," and five would be willing to do

"The Valiant Little Tailor," you know you'll have the most interest and commitment if you dramatize "Cinderella."

In the case of an emotional deadlock between two highly contested stories, you could split the class into two different casts and create two puppet plays. Make sure if you do this that you have enough assistants to handle two rehearsals going on at the same time in different rooms. Making one cast wait while another rehearses becomes boring for those waiting—and is not a good use of class time.

CASTING THE CHARACTERS

Deciding who will play which role can be difficult, especially if the leading character is an extremely popular one like Cinderella or Oliver Twist. It is rare to find a group who can divide up the roles without getting into a conflict.

If a class has very mixed abilities, sometimes the teacher needs to step in as the director to cast the roles herself. The larger, more verbal roles go to the students who can handle them better while the smaller or less verbal roles go to the less verbal students. In this way, success can be ensured for every member in the class.

Another option is to cast by lottery. Have each student write her name on a slip of paper and put it into a hat. The teacher starts with the first character on the cast list and pulls a name out of the hat. Whoever's name is on the paper gets the part. The lottery continues until all roles have been cast.

Another method is a bit more complicated, but takes each student's choices more carefully into consideration. Each student writes down her first and second choice of role (or first, second, and third choice) on a piece of paper. The choice papers go into a hat and the teacher casts each part in the story, pulling out slips of paper from the hat. If Cinderella is the character up for casting, the first slip of paper that the teacher pulls out that has the name "Cinderella" on it as a first choice, plays that part. If the first choice on the slip of paper has already been cast, the paper goes back into the hat. When all the first choices have been used up for each role, the remaining roles are cast from second choices pulled at random from the hat. This method takes longer, but usually ensures that students get their first or second choice for a role.

With the lottery method, each student might not get her favorite role and each role might not go to the actor most suited for it, but students feel that their desires have been taken into consideration. They have had an equal chance to get the part they wanted and the teacher has not played favorites.

CONSTRUCTING THE PUPPETS

Once the roles in the play have been cast, the construction of the puppets can begin. Making the puppets is a very important component of a puppetry class. To be sure, buying them at the store would be easier, but students would miss the opportunity to make essential character choices and create every aspect of the play.

Working in three dimensions frees many right-brained students who normally fail in our language-oriented, left-brained educational system. Creating their ideas in space, rather than in words or in two dimensions, they often demonstrate amazing problem-solving abilities and invent incredibly imaginative designs.

I was working with a special education class on a project that put poetry and puppetry together. They were dramatizing several poems by A. A. Milne, including "The Four Friends," which features Ernest the Elephant, Leonard the Lion, George the Goat, and James the Snail. Ramona came to me for advice on how to make Ernest's elephant tusks. I looked over the art materials I had brought and couldn't see a good solution. "Maybe two straws?" I suggested weakly.

She screwed up her face and shook her head, "No."

I had to agree. "It's not the best idea," I said. "Maybe we can think of something better."

Suddenly Delia was standing next to us with a pair of scissors and an empty masking tape roll in her hand. Delia was about ten and rarely spoke. She couldn't read more than a few words. She was in the process of making George the Goat, who in E. H. Shepard's illustration has very prominent horns. She had looked at the empty masking tape roll and realized that if it were cut into two halves, it would become the shape of goat horns . . . or elephant tusks! I was so excited, I wanted to jump up and down! She had solved the problem brilliantly—much better than I had—using her spatial intelligence and her right-brain mode of thinking.

Before building your puppets, it is best to explore them a bit so students can imagine them visually and kinesthetically. You might want to lead a short improvisation in which each student pantomimes a day in the life of her character. You could take turns saying something each student's character might say, or think of words to describe her personality.

Have each student draw and color a picture of her character. Through this process she can make some initial choices about color and details about her puppet character. This drawing can be the visual plan she works from as she makes the actual puppet.

TYPES OF PUPPETS

There are many sizes and shapes of puppets, but based on manner of manipulation they fall into five main categories: finger puppets, hand puppets, rod puppets, marionettes, and ventriloquist dummies.

Finger Puppets. Finger puppets fit onto the fingertips. They can be made out of plastic, foam, cardboard tubes, or stiff fabric like felt, leather, or netting. In order to make finger puppets, students need excellent fine motor skills because the basic construction and decoration involves small, intricate detail work. Since they are so tiny, finger puppets are fine for a puppet show that is going to be videotaped up close, but they are too small to be seen well on a stage in front of an audience. Because of the motor skills needed for construction and their limitations in live performance, I don't recommend finger puppets for most students with special needs.

Hand Puppets. Hand puppets fit over the hand. They can be made out of fabric, old socks, paper towel rolls, old mittens, paper bags, paper plates, papier mache, styrofoam balls, ceramic clay, or foam rubber.

The simplest form of hand puppet is one with a puppet body and head which the puppeteer moves up and down as it talks. Another type can be made with movable arms. The middle fingers hold up the head while the thumb and pinky are inserted into the arms of the puppet's body. Hand puppets can also be made with moveable mouths created by placing the thumb in the lower jaw and the rest of the fingers in the upper jaw of the puppet.

Rod Puppets. A rod puppet is, simply, a puppet on a stick. Some rod puppets have additional rods attached to the puppet's hands so they can be moved independently of the body.

Shadow puppets are a variety of rod puppet. They are cut out of a flat surface (cardboard, heavy paper, or metal) with an eye to their outline. Details can be cut out of the puppet to create the illusion of clothes, hair, or objects in hand. Sometimes shadow puppets have moveable arms and legs that are jointed and manipulated by additional rods. Usually the shadow puppet is placed behind a translucent screen and light is cast from behind to create a shadow on the screen.

Combination Hand-and-Rod Puppets. A puppet in which the mouth *and* hands move is a combination hand-and-rod puppet. In order to create a puppet of this kind, rods or sticks are connected to the hands of the puppet on the outside. These are manipulated from below by one hand of the puppeteer while the other hand, which is inside the puppet, moves the mouth.

The Muppets are hand-and-rod puppets made from foam rubber. We are not aware of the rods because they are made invisible through the skill of the Muppeteers and the magic of television.

Hand-and-rod puppets require highly developed fine motor skills and good hand-eye coordination. Only attempt them with a very advanced, physically adept group.

Marionettes. Marionettes are puppets with complete bodies that move by means of strings attached to all their major body joints. The strings are manipulated by the puppeteers from a platform above the puppet stage instead of from below, as with most other types of puppets.

Marionettes are difficult to make and operate. Strings can easily be tangled and if they bump into each other in performance, a major marionette traffic jam can result. Only attempt marionettes with an advanced, experienced group of student puppeteers.

Ventriloquist Dummies. Ventriloquist dummies also have complete bodies. The puppeteer or ventriloquist sits in full view of the audience with the dummy sitting on her lap. She places one hand into the dummy's head from behind and manipulates the head and mouth. The ventriloquist, as a character or as herself, holds a two-way conversation with the dummy. She speaks for herself and she "throws his voice" (speaks without moving her lips) whenever the dummy says something.

Again, ventriloquist dummies are difficult to construct, but if students want to try, there are ways of working full-sized puppets and human actors creatively into a show together.

SIMPLE PUPPETS AND HOW TO CONSTRUCT THEM

Tools and Materials. Scissors, crayons, felt tip markers, paint, sequins, glitter, construction paper of different colors, buttons, yarn, beads, pipe cleaners, ribbon, seashells, feathers, and scraps of fabric are very useful materials for puppet making. Save all sizes of colorful plastic bottle tops from shampoo, spices, nut cans, and other household containers to be used as three-dimensional eyes, noses, ears, and mouths. Old pieces of jewelry and small, lightweight, odd-shaped items can also be recycled into faces and accessories. Google eyes can be bought at art supply stores. Ping pong balls and other small round objects make wonderful eyes, too.

Rubber cement is best used for gluing paper. White glue works well with glitter and three-dimensional objects, but takes a long time to dry. This can be frustrating if objects that have been glued keep moving around as the student continues to work on the puppet. Often objects glued on with white glue will come off later as the puppet is being used in rehearsal or performance.

The best glue to use for three-dimensional objects is hot melt glue. Hot melt glue will attach most items onto a puppet quickly and strongly without the mess and drying time necessary for white glues. The only problem is hot melt glue BURNS if it is touched before it cools. If your students are young or have fine motor problems, the assistant or the teacher should always be in charge of handling the glue gun.

Avoid sewing whenever possible. Sewing by hand or machine takes time and involves fine motor skills and patience that most puppetry students don't have.

Paper Bag Puppets. Paper bag puppets are simple and inexpensive to make. Collect small brown or white paper bags. Color media will show up better on white bags because there is more contrast. The bottom of the folded bag is used as the face. The section under the bottom fold is the inside of the mouth.

Create the puppet's face, clothes, and hair with felt tip marker, crayon, or paint. Lightweight media, such as small buttons, sequins, yarn, fabric, and colored paper, can be added as well. Avoid using heavy objects; the paper of the bag can't sustain their weight.

To manipulate a paper bag puppet, place one hand inside the bag with the fingers in the bottom section. Move the fingers up and down slightly to make the mouth move.

Some students have difficulty working paper bag puppets. They can't "see" the way the mouth works and they have difficulty coordinating the small muscles in their fingers and hands. Instead of slipping their fingers into the folded bag, they open it up and hang it on their hands or they ball the whole "face" up in their fists.

Demonstrate an already finished puppet to your students before they begin making their own. Don't assume they will understand how the puppet works just by watching you work with it. Talk with them about *how* the mouth moves and let them try it on the demonstration model and on a plain paper bag before they start making their own puppets. If they can't understand the concept of the mouth, make a different kind of puppet with them.

Paper bag puppets are easy to store, but unfortunately, they are easily wrinkled or destroyed. If your students are hard on puppets, choose a sturdier kind of puppet to make.

Cardboard Tube Puppets. Another very simple and inexpensive hand puppet can be made from cardboard tubes. Collect the rolls left over from kitchen towels, wrapping paper, mailing tubes, and toilet paper to give students a variety of heights and widths. Heights of tubes can also be adjusted by cutting them down with a matt knife. Cover the tubes with white butcher paper (rubber cement works well for this) so they have a surface that can be easily colored with crayon, marker, or paint. The tube becomes the base of the person, which is drawn or painted all the way around to become the puppet character. Fabric, sequins, buttons, feathers, yarn, colored paper, and other media can be glued onto the puppet as well to make hair, hats, clothing, and other character details. White glue or rubber cement works fine for attaching lightweight media, while hot melt glue is best for heavier, three-dimensional objects.

The interesting design challenge with tube puppets is created by the circular nature of the tube. Students aren't working with a separate flat front and back side of a piece of paper. They must figure out how to continue the character's body and costume all the way around the tube.

Tube puppets can be manipulated by placing them over two or three fingers. Students sometimes find this hand position awkward and the tube may fall off during an action sequence. A more secure method is to hot melt glue a popsicle stick, tongue depressor, or dowel rod inside the tube. The puppeteer holds onto the stick.

Paper Plate Puppets. Paper plate puppets are also simple, inexpensive puppets. The paper plate is the puppet's face, which can be decorated with crayons, marker, paint, or lightweight media such as buttons, yarn, and sequins. A popsicle stick or tongue depressor is glued to the back of the plate at the "neck" for the puppeteer to grip. Fabric can be glued to the front of the plate from the "neck" down to serve as the puppet's clothing and hide the puppeteer's hand.

A more complicated variation of paper plate puppets creates a moveable mouth and head. This works particularly well for animal characters. Fold one paper plate in half so the back of the plate is folded against itself. Cut a second plate in half. Staple or glue the front of each half of the cut plate, rim to rim, against the front of each half of the folded plate. The cut edges of the second plate will end up by the fold of the first plate.

The inside of the folded paper plate becomes the inside of the mouth. The outside becomes the snout and face. The puppeteer's fingers fit inside the top fold and her thumb slips inside the bottom fold to make the mouth move. Fabric can be added to the plate to create the neck of the animal and hide the puppeteer's arm. Ears, eyes, nose, and mouth can be drawn or glued on.

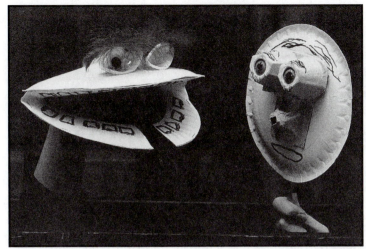

Paper plate puppets. (Photo by Lea Ann Rosen)

Paper plate puppets can be made into full-length people-sized puppets as well. Whole bodies made of fabric, cardboard, or paper plates attached together can be added to the paper plate head. The puppet is controlled by a stick connected to the head from behind. If arms are fabric, they can be made moveable by attaching rods to them. Arms made from paper plates or cardboard can be made moveable if jointed at shoulders, elbows, and/or wrists with paper fasteners and attached to rods.

Full-length, moveable puppets usually require more than one puppeteer. This can be a good challenge for students to coordinate their movements and bring one character to life together.

Sock Puppets. Anything made out of paper is going to have a short shelf life. Sooner or later, paper puppets rip or wrinkle. If they get wet, the paper will disintegrate and the color will run. The most durable of simple hand puppets is the sock puppet.

Buy colorful socks at a thrift store or bring in unmatched socks from home. The socks can be partially stuffed with polyester pillow stuffing to shape heads or snouts. The sock can be held in a number of different positions, each giving the puppet a different look. The toe of the sock can be used as the nose of the puppet with the heel as the forehead. The sock can be held upright making the toe the top of the head with the heel in the front as a chin. The sock toe also can be straight up with the heel in the back to create a long, straight, upright shape.

Fabric, trim, buttons, beads, yarn, colorful jar lids, and other three-dimensional media can be used to create character features and clothes. Bring in a lot of colorful, unusually shaped objects and art materials and let students use their imaginations.

Wooden Spoon Puppets. A very quick and simple stick puppet can be made from a wooden cooking spoon. Either side of the bowl of the spoon can become the face. Paint or glue on facial features. Add yarn, netting, or fabric hair. Either paint the stick or cover with fabric to create clothing.

Foam Rubber Puppets. Foam rubber puppets are excellent for puppet show performances because their large size and facial features carry a long distance to the audience. They are fun to make. Look for flat sheets of foam rubber between one-half and three-quarters inch thick. Foam rubber of this kind can be purchased from stores that sell foam for mattress and sofa cushions. Foam rubber carpet padding can also be used.

Cut a rectangle of foam rubber about 12" x 18." Hot melt glue the 12" ends together and hold until the glue sets. This will create an 18" high foam rubber cylinder. The seam where the two ends come together will be the back of the puppet's head.

Measure up about four inches from the bottom of the cylinder in the front (approximately one quarter of the way up). This is where the mouth will be cut. Make a horizontal cut about one third of the way around the cylinder.

Wooden spoon puppets. (Photo by Lea Ann Rosen)

Using a straight ruler, measure the distance from one edge of the cut to the other through the middle of the cylinder. This will give you the diameter of the circle you will need to make for the inside of the puppet's mouth. Halve the diameter to find the radius of the mouth. Use a compass, opened to the width of the radius measurement, to make a circle on a piece of corrugated cardboard. Cut the circle out and paint it red. When the paint has dried, fold the circle in half (with the red on the inside of the fold). Hot melt glue the edges of the circle onto the cut foam edge of the mouth. The fold of the cardboard circle will be on the inside, middle of the cylinder.

If you are working with very young students or students who have fine motor problems, you may want to pre-cut and pre-glue the cylinders together and pre-glue the mouths. Both beginning steps require holding the foam in place while the hot melt glue sets. This requires patience, stamina, and enough manual dexterity to avoid being burned by the hot glue.

Create eyes with ping pong balls or other round objects. "Eyeballs" will stay glued to the cylindrical surface better if first glued into small paper party favor cups or onto empty plastic scotch tape rolls. This provides the "eyeballs" with a flat base. Irises can be painted onto the eyeballs or "google eyes" can be glued onto them.

Create noses, ears, eyebrows, and other facial features with pieces of foam, colorful jar lids, seashells, feathers, buttons, pipe cleaners, poker chips, or other interesting objects. Foam rubber lips can be added to cover up the corrugated cardboard at the mouth. Add hair, hats, and jewelry. Fabric glued around the bottom of the cylinder will hide the puppeteer's arm and create the illusion that the body of the puppet continues below the head.

The puppeteer inserts her hand up through the bottom of the puppet and holds onto the cardboard mouth. To help establish a firmer grip and prevent damage to the cardboard from sweating fingers, hot melt glue a mitten or a glove onto the mouth. Fingers of the glove or mitten go on the top of the mouth and the thumb goes on the bottom so the mouth opens and closes easily. Find out if the puppeteer is right handed or left handed (or which hand she intends to hold the puppet in) before gluing in the mitten or glove.

Foam rubber head puppets can be taller or shorter, thinner or fatter, but 12" x 18" creates a good mid-sized puppet that is easy for any age puppeteer to handle.

Flat Rod Cardboard Puppets. Students draw their characters on a heavy piece of poster board, color it with felt tip marker or paint, and cut out the shape. The shape is hot melt glued on a dowel rod and the dowel is painted black. In the tradition of the propman in Asian theatre, students dress in black and perform in front of a black curtain, so only the puppet shape is visible in performance.

It is not necessary to make the face of the puppeteer disappear; dressing in black is a stage convention.* The audience "agrees" not to see the puppeteer, just as they "agree" to believe the puppet is a living character during the course of the puppet show. However, if creating a complete illusion is important and you want to make the puppeteers totally disappear, you can cover their hands with black gloves, their heads with black hoods, and their faces with black mesh fabric (hot glue or sew the black mesh inside of the hoods to hold it in place). Covering faces is not a good idea if your puppeteers have balance or vision difficulties.

Rod Head Puppets. Puppet heads can be sculpted out of papier mache or carved from thick chunks of foam rubber or styrofoam. Heads can also be soft sculptured from stuffed sections of nylon stockings.

Glue a sturdy plastic or wooden dowel rod firmly into the head. Make it thick enough so it will hold up to a lot of waving around, but not so thick as to be hard to hold by the puppeteer.

Paint the head or cover with fabric. (If you use foam rubber or styrofoam, you may need to cover it with fabric or papier mache before painting it because many kinds of foam will disintegrate if painted or glued.) Paint or glue on facial features. Create hair with yarn, fabric strips, feathers, or pieces of fake fur.

One way to create fabric clothes for the puppets is to cut out two identical bodies from heavy cloth. Holes can be punched with a single-hole paper puncher along the edges which need to be sewn together, and students can thread heavy yarn or cord through the holes. Then hot melt glue the neck of clothes around the base of the puppet's neck.

---

* A *stage convention* is an unspoken agreement by all members of an audience to accept or believe in a stage fiction. For instance, every time a play begins, the audience agrees to "suspend their disbelief" and believe that the actors who are performing on stage are real people in a real place living out an important moment of their lives.

An easier way is to buy old baby clothes from a thrift store and hot melt glue them to the puppet's neck. Using actual clothing adds a finishing touch that really makes a puppet come alive. Hands can be made from stuffed nylon stockings, gloves, or mittens.

Additional dowel rods can be attached to one or both hands at the wrists to give the puppeteer the ability to make arm movements.

Shadow Puppets. Shadow puppets rely on their shape alone to give definition and detail to the puppet character. Have students work out their ideas on paper first. This way they can cut their design out with scissors first and test the shadow it makes. When they have found a pattern that communicates the character through its shape, they can use their paper design as a pattern and trace it onto heavy matt board or foam core. If students can't handle a matt knife, assistants will need to cut the puppets out for them.

Moveable arms and legs, mouths that open and close, or body halves that swivel can be created by punching a hole in overlapping joints and joining the sections with a paper fastener or small nut and bolt.

Fabric, feathers, and other shapes that cast a shadow can also be added to the puppet. For the character of The Fisherman in a shadow puppet version of "The Fisherman and His Wife," one student attached a piece of plastic netting to the Fisherman's hand. On screen it looked like his fishing net. It was large enough for the Magic Fish to "swim into it" in the first scene of the show.

Glue the shadow puppets to long dowel rods and the puppets are ready to go.

Making shadow puppets require a lot of manual dexterity (particularly cutting ability) and patience during the construction phase. Only attempt this kind of puppet if your students can do the work or if you have a lot of assistants to help with the cutting.

SCENERY

Scenery is often unnecessary for a puppet play. Changing a lot of things around between each scene can be distracting and difficult during a performance. It is better to leave the scenery up to the imagination of the audience than to slow down the pace of a show with a lot of scene changes.

However, if you choose to include scenery, backdrops can be painted on large sheets of butcher paper, poster board, or unbleached muslin. Backdrops can also be made from large sheets of felt with felt shapes glued on to create the scene. Three-dimensional objects on stage (like castles or houses) can be constructed from cardboard boxes and tubes, decorated with paint, construction paper, and interesting shapes. You could also use cardboard or poster board cut-outs reinforced with a triangular brace from behind. (Note: cut-outs tend to fall over during the performance as the puppets move around behind them. Boxes are sturdier and more stable.)

CREATING THE SCRIPT FOR A PUPPET PLAY

Puppet plays present a number of performance challenges. Puppeteers have a lot of different responsibilities to juggle simultaneously. Like regular actors, they need to remember their lines and movements. They need to say their lines loudly and clearly enough to project them from behind the stage out to the audience. They also need to manipulate their puppets from what is usually a cramped, unnatural position underneath the visible plane of the stage. Sometimes more action is happening behind the scenes of a puppet play with actors jockeying for position as their puppets cross the stage to make their entrances and exits, than is happening in full view of the audience. Add the barrier of a wooden or metal stage between the mouths of the puppeteers and the ears of the viewers and it is a wonder the dialogue of a puppet play can be heard at all!

Professional puppeteers handle this situation by wearing body mikes that pick up and amplify their voices as they speak their characters' lines. Student puppeteers rarely have access to this kind of sophisticated equipment.

I have found that taping the dialogue of the puppet play ahead of time is the best way to cut down on the amount of technical responsibilities for each puppeteer *and*, at the same time, ensure that the audience can hear the play clearly. Puppeteers don't have to remember what to say or what comes next. They listen to their own voices on the tape and synchronize their puppet's actions to what they hear. This, and not bumping into the other puppeteers, is often more than enough for them to contend with during a performance.*

The script for a puppet play can come from many sources. Puppet plays do exist in play collections and can be used for performance in the same way regular play scripts are used.

You might choose to narrate a play directly from a book if you are dramatizing a poem or a short story where it is important to keep the rhythm and rhyme of the author's original words intact. Dr. Seuss, Shel Silverstein, and A.A. Milne are children's poets who come to mind in this instance. The sense of fun and the build up and release of tension in their work rely a great deal on their word choices, rhymes, and unique rhythm patterns.

However, for the most part, my recommendation is to guide your class into creating scripts of their own. This provides them with the opportunity to learn the process of playwriting. The script can be tailored around the strengths and abilities of the student puppeteers. The dialogue will be expressed in their own words and manner of speaking instead of that of a professional playwright and will, therefore, sound natural and free coming out of their mouths. Instead of the puppet characters conforming to someone else's vision of the story, the students can create their own characterizations through dialogue and action. As they add their own creative touches to the story, their version of the play will come to life.

Never underestimate what a group of students can learn from the process of creating an original play. Over the course of one year I saw tremendous growth in a group of students who took three trimesters of puppetry at the Center School, an independent school for children who have learning disabilities. All were between the ages of seven and ten and were quite artistically talented.

---

* Pantomiming puppet actions to a tape will obviously not work for deaf puppeteers who aren't able to hear the tape. In addition, most deaf people have poor articulation and projection skills. This makes the option of having the puppeteers perform the dialogue of the play live difficult as well. While I have never done puppetry with deaf students, it seems to me that the best solution would be to create a very visual, physical puppet play which is carefully choreographed and timed out for the puppeteers and have several live, hearing narrators voice the dialogue for the audience during the performance. Another option might be to create a puppet ballet that is choreographed to music and tells the story with no dialogue.

The puppetry class was held once a week. The first trimester my students had no belief in their creative abilities and took little initiative in suggesting ideas for a play. They had faced so much failure in their lives that they were afraid to take a chance on anything. Trying to interest them in a project was like pulling teeth. Finally, I read them Shel Silverstein's "The Missing Piece," and they were agreeable, if not particularly enthusiastic, about adapting it into a play. I wanted puppets that would provide quick, positive feedback, so we made simple flat rod cardboard puppets. They couldn't read and they wouldn't improvise dialogue, so I narrated the play. Only a few students were excited about the idea of performing, but once they got in front of the audience, their attitudes completely changed. Suddenly, the story and the style of the performance came alive for them. One boy, who a week before had steadfastly refused to participate in rehearsal, turned into the most expressive, excited, focused puppeteer on stage. At curtain call, he wouldn't stop bowing or smiling. He was lit up like a neon sign! Needless to say, the show was very well received and most of the class elected to take puppetry again.

The second trimester we tackled two plays: the girls insisted on "Cinderella," while the boys were attracted to the adventure and bravado of "The Valiant Little Tailor." This time their puppets, made from different-sized paper tubes, became much more elaborate. They threw themselves into making scenery and props: castles and ballrooms, pumpkins and carriages, fly swatters and jam sandwiches. A number of students volunteered to work on art projects at home. We worked through many serious differences of opinion as we improvised the dialogue for "Cinderella." Everyone had *strong* ideas about how Cinderella should be portrayed. The performances at the end of the trimester were smashing successes and almost everyone signed on for puppetry again.

By our last trimester, things were really cooking. I felt they were ready for a more challenging artistic project, so we built foam rubber cylinder puppets. The girls, by now a fully functioning team, decided to make up an original fairy tale entitled "The Magic Kangaroo." I was a little hesitant to give my approval for this after the rather tense recording sessions we'd had with "Cinderella," but I was gratified by the way they handled themselves as they developed their play. They listened to each other and respected each others' ideas. When two people had good ideas, they found ways to incorporate both into the story. The boys opted to modernize "Goldilocks and the Three Bears" and adapt it into "Spike and the Three Bears," the story of a young punk who breaks into houses in the forest.

I couldn't have been prouder of the work these students did and the distance they traveled over the course of nine short months.

The first step in creating an original puppet play is to divide the story you have chosen into scenes. Then make a list of the events that happen within each scene. This scene breakdown is the scenario for the play. It will serve as a guidepost to keep the class on track as the play is fleshed out with dialogue, sound effects, and action.

It is often helpful to have students act out the story on their feet once before trying to write it down or record it. This makes the characters and the action more real, more concrete for them. They can visualize what the characters are doing and how they are feeling better after they have actually done it themselves.

If your group does not read well, the best way to devise the script is to improvise the play directly on tape. Review the scenario for each scene and briefly practice what each character needs to say and do. Improvise the scene once on its feet and then sit down to improvise it in front of the tape recorder. If the improvisation goes well, you can move on to the next scene. If someone makes a mistake, just stop and try again. Don't get frustrated. Stay loose and have fun with it.

If you think your students would have difficulty going back and forth between improvising on their feet and sitting in front of the tape recorder scene by scene, improvise the whole story from beginning to end during one session, so that they have had the kinesthetic experience of the story one time.

If your group can read and write, students can work together to imagine what each character will say and do in the play and then put their ideas into writing. Follow the scenario scene by scene as students share their ideas about how to tell the story. Often there will be many good suggestions for one given moment in the play. Choices must be made and some ideas will need to be adapted or changed. Building a script in this way develops problem-solving skills and the ability to compromise. A student, an assistant, or the teacher can serve as the scribe to write down the dialogue as it is made up. The process of creating and writing down the play may take several sessions. When it is completed, the script can be typed up and copied so each puppeteer has her own.

Groups that can read, but don't have the patience to sit down and write out their script word for word, can improvise their dialogue directly onto the tape like non-readers. Then their improvised tape can be transcribed onto paper to create a typed script which they can rehearse and refine.

If you are working with a written script, rehearse it a number of times before you record it. Work on timing, pacing, cuing, character voices, vocal variety, sound effects, and use of pauses. When the cast is ready, record the script. Record scene by scene and take short breaks between each one to keep the puppeteers' voices fresh and their energy at a high level. Recording a script can be great fun, but students tend to put themselves under great pressure to make it sound good and to avoid mistakes. Remind them that if they goof up, it's OK. The scene can be recorded again.

As the director, you will have more than enough to concentrate on, working the tape recorder and keeping the cast motivated and working cooperatively together. Don't waste time and energy trying to make this recorded version perfect. If you want, record several different versions of each scene. You can edit your show tape from the in-class tape. When some-body makes a mistake and you need to re-record a scene, don't bother rewinding the tape to the last good spot. Chances are you'll go back too far and record over something you wanted to keep. Continue recording on the tape and edit out the "out-takes" later. After rehearsal when you are in a quiet place and you aren't under time pressure, you will be able to make editing decisions methodically and calmly. You can also add special effects like music or sounds from a sound effect tape when you edit.

Editing is easier if students leave a moment of silence before and after each "take." That leaves the editor space on the tape to cue up without picking up sound from another "take."

Complete quiet in a room is very important during a recording session. Tape recorders don't filter out unwanted sounds. Every noise in the room will go into the microphone and onto the tape. Remind students before each take to only talk when it is time for their character to speak.

You might want to test various rooms or areas in your room to find a place that has good acoustics for recording. Some spaces are too echo-y. Voices recorded in those spots will have a tinny, distant quality. Other spaces seem to focus the sound and create a very realistic, strong quality to the sounds on the tape.

It is very easy to edit a tape using the dubbing system on a two-deck cassette recorder. Listen to your original tape all the way through and make notes of which "takes" are the good ones and where you need to start and stop. If certain sections of a scene need to be cut out, time how long the cut should be and what sounds will begin and end the cut. Then go back to the beginning of the tape. Place the original tape in the playback deck and place a blank cassette in the recording deck. Set the machine up for normal speed dubbing. Dub the sections of the tape that are good "takes" and pause the recording deck whenever you want to edit out a section.

Now that you have your show tape, you are ready to begin staging the puppet show.

PUPPET STAGES

The first thing to consider when staging a puppet play is the puppet stage itself. Sometimes a make-shift stage can be fashioned from furniture in the classroom. Two long tables placed end to end can be turned into an acceptable, if cramped, puppet stage. Drape a solid-colored cloth over both tables or tape butcher paper to the front sides to hide the puppeteers from the audience and create a unified, finished look. Students sit or lie on the floor behind the tables and hold their puppets up over the edge. Scenery can be taped onto the wall behind the table. If any three-dimensional props are used in the show, the tabletop serves as a place to set them.

A short bookcase (between four and five feet high) that has been pulled out from the wall can become a useful puppet stage. Students stand behind the bookcase and have more room to maneuver than if they were sitting on the floor. If the back of the bookcase is facing the audience, the puppeteers can use the bookshelves facing them to store props or puppets when they are off stage. If the bookshelves are facing the audience, cover them with a large solid-colored cloth to hide the books or objects in the shelves and throw the focus of attention to the puppets on top. The top of the bookcase is a handy place to set props on during the show.

Puppet stages can be designed and built from wood or draped metal frames. If you are making the effort to build a stage, be sure there is plenty of room for puppeteers to stand or sit comfortably and move around back-

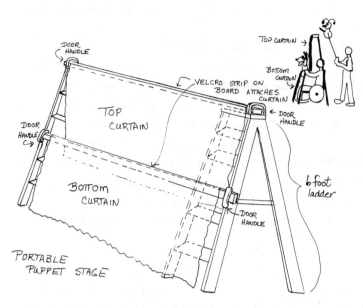

PORTABLE PUPPET STAGE

(Labels in illustration: DOOR HANDLE; TOP CURTAIN; VELCRO STRIP ON BOARD ATTACHES CURTAIN; TOP CURTAIN; DOOR HANDLE; BOTTOM CURTAIN; DOOR HANDLE; TOP CURTAIN; BOTTOM CURTAIN; DOOR HANDLE; 6 foot ladder; DOOR HANDLE)

stage. Consider the type of puppets students will be using. Where is the puppeteer's hand in relation to the puppet? Where is the puppeteer's body in relation to the stage? Hand puppets require puppeteers to be closer to the edge of the stage than rod puppets do. Is there a way to position the puppeteer so her hand does not have to be stretched way up in the air every time her puppet comes on stage? Will your puppet stage need to be moved around to a number of different places or can it be kept permanently in one spot? If you have students sitting in wheelchairs, can they sit comfortably, make their puppets visible, and still not be seen from the audience?

In trying to devise a puppet stage that addressed some of these problems (specifically portability, adaptability to wheelchairs, and providing a comfortable hand position for both hand and rod puppeteers), I came up with an easy-to-assemble design from items that can be purchased at any hardware store.

I started with a base made from two six-foot wooden step ladders. Because they form a triangle when opened, step ladders are more balanced and secure than a single upright pole would be.

A large screen-door handle turned sideways on the top step of each ladder holds a wooden board in place between them. (When purchasing materials, check the handle against the width of the board you are buying to make sure it fits through.) A piece of black fabric is velcroed to the wooden board to mask the top half of the puppeteers sitting behind the stage. This top board also creates an upper stage that can be used for puppets on long rods. Two more door handles about 30 inches up from the ground (not 30 inches from the bottom of the ladder, which is on a diagonal from the floor), holds a second wooden board in place across the front. A second piece of black fabric is velcroed to this board to hide the legs of sitting puppeteers. This board creates a lower stage which can be used for hand puppets.

Because the lower board is farther forward than the top board (due to the diagonal line of the ladders), a space is created for wheelchairs or legs of sitting puppeteers. If there are no wheelchairs to contend with backstage, the entire sitting area can be filled with benches end to end, creating maximum sitting space.

Sitting puppeteers' faces are directly in front of the top curtain. They hold their puppets up in front of it at their approximate eye level. This simultaneously places the puppets above the lower curtain or puppet stage. This arm position is less stressful than holding the puppets up over their heads.

If you build your own stage, paint the entire structure black, so it does not visually distract from the puppets and is the same color as the curtains. Black tends to be the least distracting color to an audience and will usually throw the puppets into the highest contrast. However, if you would rather have blue or red or green curtains, paint your puppet stage to match. If your puppets are colors that blend into the color of your stage curtains, you might want to make a curtain of contrasting color to use for this particular show.

Puppeteers should wear black, if possible. Black is the color of invisibility on stage. Dressed in black, they will blend into the background. If an arm is stuck a little too far out, it will be less distracting if clothed in the same color as the curtain.

STAGING AND REHEARSING THE PUPPET SHOW

If possible, position puppeteers backstage in places where they can remain for the majority of the play. Characters who have a number of conversations with each other will probably need to be placed next to each other. Help each puppeteer find a relatively comfortable position to be in when her puppet is on stage and when her puppet is off.

Practice making entrances and exits neatly and efficiently without bumping other puppets or puppeteers. If one or two characters have to move from one side of the stage to the other, try to arrange everyone else in a manner

Portable puppet stage in action with foam cylinder puppets. (Photo by Keith Jenkins)

that can make this possible. Puppeteers who have to climb over each other backstage are in an awkward and potentially dangerous situation.

Listen to the tape and have each puppeteer practice synchronizing the lip, arm, or body movements of her puppet with the words her character says and the actions her character takes. Then put it all together with the puppeteers in place behind the stage.

Remind your puppeteers to respect each others' personal space even though they are crowded closely together. They need to put aside personal conflicts for the moment and cooperate with each other for the good of the show.

If accidents happen and someone gets elbowed by mistake, counsel puppeteers to apologize and to forgive graciously. Rehearsals and performances are not the times for grudges and hard feelings.

Validate how hard your students are working and, if they are in an uncomfortable position, acknowledge how uncomfortable they feel. Unfortunately, uncomfortable positions are the lot of all puppeteers.

Give lots of encouragement and tell them what a good job they are doing. Praise them when they work hard at getting along.

SAMPLE PUPPETRY LESSON PLANS

Here are two sample puppetry lesson plans. The first shows the development of a single puppet show worked on by all members of the class over the course of ten weeks.

BAMBI

WEEK ONE

- Talk about puppets: what kind of puppets are there, what kind have you made, what do you like about puppets?
- Introduction Go-Around: Pass Fred the Frog around to each student, who invents a funny voice for him and lets Fred introduce him to the other students.
- Decide on a story for a puppet show ("Bambi" was chosen).
- Listen to part of the story of "Bambi."
- Decide which character you would like to play.
- Draw a picture of your character.

WEEK TWO

- Read the story of "Bambi" (a shortened Walt Disney version).
- Act out favorite parts of the story.

WEEK THREE

- Start making sock puppets.

WEEK FOUR

- Improvise and record dialogue for three-quarters of the story.

WEEK FIVE

- Paint the puppet stage.
- Listen to the edited version of the work done last week.

WEEK SIX

- Make scenery.

WEEK SEVEN

- Finish improvising and recording dialogue.
- Continue working on puppets.

WEEK EIGHT
- Finish working on puppets and scenery.

WEEK NINE
- Rehearse puppet show.

WEEK TEN
- Rehearse puppet show.
- Perform puppet show.

This second lesson plan shows how class time can be scheduled if two puppet plays are being worked on simultaneously. My assistant worked with "The Three Bears" while I worked with "The Magic Kangaroo."

THE MAGIC KANGAROO and SPIKE AND THE THREE BEARS

WEEK ONE
- Divide class into two groups.
- Decide on stories ("The Magic Kangaroo" and "Spike and The Three Bears").
- Decide which character each student will be.
- Draw a picture of your character.

WEEK TWO
- Read "Goldilocks and The Three Bears" out loud.
- Begin making foam rubber puppets for both shows.

WEEK THREE
- Continue working on puppets.

WEEK FOUR
- Continue working on puppets.

WEEK FIVE
- Continue working on puppets.
- "Three Bears" begin working on scenery.

WEEK SIX
- "Magic Kangaroo" work on puppets.
- "Three Bears" work on scenery.

WEEK SEVEN
- "Magic Kangaroo" work on puppets.

- "Three Bears" improvise dialogue on tape.

WEEK EIGHT
- "Magic Kangaroo" improvise show tape, finish last two puppets.
- "Three Bears" practice with show tape and finish scenery.

WEEK NINE
- Run through both shows with tapes.
- Puppet Performances.

PERFORMING THE SHOW

Keep your puppeteers calm before the show begins. The best way to do this is for the adults in charge to remain calm themselves. Children will model whatever behavior they believe is appropriate to the situation and will match their emotional state to yours.

Check all puppets to make sure no last-minute repairs need to be done before the show.

Double-check the position of all puppeteers, puppets, and props before the show begins.

Do a sound check to make sure puppeteers can hear the tape clearly backstage and audience members can hear it clearly out front.

It may be helpful for the teacher or an assistant to remain backstage during the performance to troubleshoot and solve unforseen physical problems. Eyeballs and hats fall off at the most inopportune moments. Puppets get stuck to clothing or other puppets. Props fall off the stage just when they're needed in the scene. Moving puppeteers trip and get tangled in others' arms and legs.

After the show have the puppeteers come out from behind the curtain with their puppets in hand to take a bow. They have earned their recognition and they should have the chance to be acknowledged by their audience publicly.

Students feel a great sense of accomplishment and pride after performing a puppet show. Part of it comes from knowing they have taken a project from start to finish themselves. Part comes from the acknowledgement and appreciation they receive from their audience, which tells them they have contributed something valuable to their community.

I worked with a special education class at Meadow Hall Elementary School in Rockville, Maryland, on a puppetry project aimed at motivating reading skills and teaching students how to approach and accomplish a project step by step. Their teacher wanted to involve her students in a project that engaged every learning channel and that exploited her students' visual and kinesthetic strengths. They made beautiful sock puppets and wrote and recorded their own puppet plays. She shared about her students' reaction to performing their original puppet plays for parents, friends, and schoolmates:

> *We were a hit! The classroom was packed to overflowing with parents and relatives of all ages. We did "The Lion and the Mouse" and "Spike and the Three Rad Bears" for the Education Fair Tuesday night. They [the students] set up everything. . . . The next day we performed in the A.M. and P.M. for two classes at a time. We also did the show every other day until the entire school had viewed it (including the HeadStart and Special Education teachers).*
>
> *The kids are so proud of their accomplishments and are working the puppets with more ease and excitement. Classes are impressed, asking many questions as to how they got their ideas and how things were made. We have videotaped each play twice and will make copies for those who want them. The principal enjoyed the show and said it was the "Best" he had seen, and one teacher suggested we send it to a children's T.V. station.*

I saw the videotape of the performances that she mentions. The students *do* grow in confidence and ability with each succeeding performance. Best of all, after the first performance a large computer-generated thank-you note appeared above the puppet stage. It was sent to the puppeteers from one of the regular education classrooms who had seen their plays. It read, "WHAT AN INCREDIBLE PLAY! THANK YOU! WE LOVED IT!" How could you get any better validation than that?!

■ chapter nine

developing original scripts for performance

I t is essential for novice performers to experience success. Quite obviously, a successful early experience will encourage them to continue developing their artistic skills, while an embarrassing failure will discourage them
from ever getting up on a stage again. A teacher or director can enhance success by carefully choosing dramatic material which is appropriate to the
performers' skill levels, limiting material to an appropriate length for the
skills and attention spans of the performers, and providing enough rehearsal
time for the performers to feel prepared when they step in front of the
audience.

Performers who have special needs may need additional support or adaptations in dramatic material in order to achieve success. Most scripts focus
on verbal abilities and this may create obstacles for actors who have certain
kinds of disabilities. They may be unable to memorize large sections of
dialogue from a conventional play. They may not be able to communicate
well through words, but can express themselves exceptionally well through
movement. They may have short attention spans or difficulty with sequencing or any manner of other physical or cognitive processing problems which
make a previously scripted traditional play difficult to prepare and perform
successfully.

One way to ensure performance success is to develop original material
which is geared to the specific abilities and strengths of your performers.
This approach is student-centered, the theatre version of "teaching to a

student's strengths." Let your performers do what they do best and help them learn to do it even better.

An approach of this kind will not lead to stagnation and repetition of more of the same. The more skilled and confident actors become, the more challenges they want to take on the next time. The very first play that my Pegasus performing company created, *Dreams, Nightmares, and Fantasies,* was extremely simple. Much of the dialogue was recorded so that they wouldn't have to memorize lines. Remembering the blocking, pantomiming to the music and voice-over tapes, and remembering to get the correct props for the next scene was more than enough for the actors to contend with that first year. They performed their play seven times, always to wildly enthusiastic applause, and in the course of performing found their artistic voices and uncovered a desire to use drama to communicate.

The next year they clamored for a much more complicated script and took on the challenge of memorizing their own lines. Audience members (people not related to the actors) who saw both seasons' shows were astounded at the major leap the troupe made from artistic and technical standpoints.

Improvisationally developed work is a positive choice to make for beginning or disabled performers for other reasons as well. It is much easier to understand and to learn something that you create yourself. The ideas are yours, the thought processes are yours, the primary mode of expression (be it words, music, or movement) is yours, the dialogue is expressed in your sentence structure and vocabulary.

Most importantly, improvisationally developed plays put the students in charge of the idea-generating. They are given an outlet to explore and express the issues that are in their hearts and minds. This is particularly important for adolescents. Teenagers don't think adults ever listen to them—and sometimes, they are right about this. Much of teenage rebellion originates when teens' ideas are not heard, acknowledged, respected, and validated by the adults in their lives. If adolescents start feeling that their ideas, contributions, and abilities are not wanted or appreciated, their behavior towards the adult world changes from cooperative to passive withdrawal or aggressive hostility.

Individuals of all ages who have disabilities face a similar situation. The community ignores them, discriminates against them, or excludes them.

Their voices are not heard or, if heard, not valued. Nondisabled playwrights typically create disabled characters who have little basis in reality and often perpetuate negative or untruthful stereotypes of disabled people. One of the most blatant examples of this are movies in which the deaf character speechreads perfectly and then talks to the hearing characters in a perfectly modulated voice using impeccable English sentence construction.

Creating your own play gives voice to the feelings and ideas inside in a constructive way. It provides a forum for evaluating and solving problems. It offers an avenue for appropriately sharing hopes, dreams, and concerns with others, building bridges of communication instead of blowing them up. Nothing enhances self-esteem more than sharing an important part of yourself with others and having them not only accept it, but applaud it.

Teachers and directors often don't consider the option of creating original work with their student actors because they are operating under a number of assumptions:

1. Creating an original play is "cheating."
2. An original play is not a "real" play.
3. Creating an original play is too hard.

Let's take a look at the first assumption. Creating an original play is not cheating. There is no more reason that a group of actors should *have* to perform *The Crucible, Guys and Dolls,* or any other well-known play or musical than a square peg should *have* to be forced into a round hole. If your actors' abilities do not "fit" the needs of a previously written script, it is not cheating to create a play that "fits" them.

In fact, molding a play to fit a specific group of actors, as opposed to molding a group of actors to fit a play, is a time-honored theatre tradition! Many playwrights originally wrote their plays to enhance the talents of a specific group of actors. All of William Shakespeare's plays were written to be performed by Richard Burbage, Will Kempe, Augustine Philips, and other members of the Lord Chamberlain's Men, the acting company to which he belonged. He created roles and dialogue which exploited the unique talents of the actors in the company, showing them off in a good light.

Commedia dell'arte troupes which traveled the European continent during the Renaissance created plays which showcased the improvisational comedic talents of their members. Each commedia actor specialized in playing one specific type of stock comic character. He or she (commedia troupes were the first theatrical groups to hire women to play female characters on stage) would perfect the *lazzi* or comic business for which that character was well known.* Each troupe developed a number of scenarios using the stock characters that their actors specialized in. At each performance, the company would choose a scenario and improvise a play on the spot for the audience. If a troupe had a leading actor who specialized in playing Harlequin, the tricky servant, their scenarios would revolve around Harlequin. If they had a leading actor whose specialty was Pantalone, most of their plays would focus on the foolish acts of an old miser.

The French actor/playwright Moliere, who provided entertainment for the court of Louis XIV, wrote comic roles for himself and the actors who were in his troupe. *The School for Wives*, a play about an older man who is in love with a young girl, was written as an acting vehicle for an aging Moliere and his pretty, young wife. Even today many contemporary playwrights like David Mamet and Mark Medoff create their plays with specific actors in mind for certain parts.

On to the second false assumption: An original play is not a "real play." This is absolutely untrue. I get very angry when a well-meaning adult walks up to me after the performance of an original script developed by one of my performing companies and says, "That was cute, but why don't you let your students do a *real* play like *Oliver!* or *The Pajama Game?*"

In essence, the message they are giving me is threefold:

- Young people are incapable of having their own ideas and expressing them in dramatic form.
- Only a professional playwright can write a "real" play.
- Only a play which has been produced on Broadway can be considered "real."

I cannot disagree with this idea of plays and playwriting too strenuously.

---

* A modern equivalent of *lazzi* would be the Marx Brothers' classic handshake in which Harpo gives the other person his knee instead of his hand, Abbott and Costello's famous "Who's On First" riff, or the Three Stooges physical bits which show up repeatedly in their movies.

Every play that ever existed started out as an original play. In order for that original play to be a "real" play, it doesn't need to be published, it doesn't need to be written by a professional playwright, and it doesn't need to be produced in New York City. It just needs to be performed somewhere for an audience.

False assumption number three: Creating an original play is too hard. It is true that creating an original play can take more time than choosing appropriate material that has been written by someone else. It is true that more time must be spent developing the piece and shaping it before it can actually be staged and rehearsed. It is also true that creating an original play can be difficult. The actors must be involved in the process of developing the play. This necessitates cooperation and negotiation skills on everyone's parts. It also requires flexibility, fairness, and a good sense of dramatic structure. But however time-consuming and difficult it may be, creating an original play is not *too* hard to do.

There are many ways to use improvisation to create original plays. Each theatre artist develops his or her own style and approach to solving the dramatic question "What if?" What will be presented in this chapter is the process I have used with my improvisational performing troupes. I do not suggest the methods I use are for everyone. They may work for you or another improvisational method might be more compatible with your teaching/directing style. Several excellent references on improvisational acting methods have been included in the Bibliography at the end of the book for those who would like to learn different approaches. However, I hope that a description of what I have done with my groups will spark ideas which you can use in developing plays through improvisation with your own acting troupes.

INITIATING THE PROJECT

At the Bethesda Academy I direct two performing troupes. Pegasus is a mainstreamed group for teens with and without disabilities. The ages of the actors range from 12 to 21. Pegasus meets one afternoon each week for a two-hour rehearsal which includes a snack break halfway through. The first year the group had eight members. Since then its size has fluctuated between 14 and 17. We usually lose members only when they graduate from

Icarus actors rehearse a dance number.
(Photo by Lea Ann Rosen)

high school and move on to college or jobs which conflict with rehearsal times or when they "fly up" into Icarus.

Icarus is a group for young adults with special needs. Icarus members can be as young as eighteen, but most are in their mid-twenties and a few are in their mid-thirties. The group is not yet mainstreamed; I am currently working on changing that. Icarus meets once a week in the evening for an hour and a half. The company started out with six members and has grown to eighteen over the course of three seasons.

Each group spends about six months creating and rehearsing an original one-act play. Each play grows at its own unique rate, but the basic process in each case has been very similar. To date Pegasus has created *Dreams, Nightmares, and Fantasies* (1989), a revue of seven different dreams; *Just In Time* (1990), a time travel adventure; *Guns Ablazing* (1991), a Western melodrama; *Double Crossed Bones* (1992), a pirate adventure; and *Death By Grammar* (1993), a murder mystery. Icarus has created *If. . .* (1991), a musical revue; *Some Enchanted Evening* (1992), a musical about falling in love; and *The WBAP Love Hour* (1993), a live radio show revue of music from the 50s to the 90s. Each play has been between 20 and 45 minutes in length.

CONTRACTS

Before an actor joins the troupe, I ask him to sign a contract which clearly states his responsibilities to the group and to himself during the course of our work together. This outlines up front what my expectations are in terms of actor behavior and commitment. This way no one can say, "But I didn't *know* I would need to go to so many rehearsals!" Everyone understands that once he decides to join the group, he has made a promise to see the project through from the beginning to the end. There's no "I have too much homework today, so I'll stay home from rehearsal," or "I'm bored with the show, so I'm going to quit." Disaster would strike if several of the actors decided to quit after a script had been created around them and the play was in rehearsal! Working as an ensemble—supporting each other and sticking together over the long haul—is one of the most important aspects of any theatre company.

Parents are very appreciative of the use of contracts because it helps them teach the concept of commitment to their children. It serves as a good backup tool for getting reluctant actors to rehearsals on days when they'd rather stay at home.

One first-time Pegasus performer started suffering from stage fright a week before the first performance. He told his mother he wanted to quit the show because he was too nervous to go on. She was able to say, "Every actor must learn to deal with nerves. You signed a contract that promised you would be at every rehearsal and performance. I can't let you quit." (She called me before rehearsal that day and let me know the emotional situation. We were able to address the issue of being nervous that afternoon with a group discussion about how to get over stage fright and how the actors could jump in and help each other out if one person forgot his lines.)

JOINING THE TROUPE

The Academy's calendar year follows the regular academic calendar. We begin in September. Each year there are returning actors who have been with the troupe before and new actors who are joining for the first time. Some of the new members have been in acting classes at the Academy or elsewhere. A few have never done any acting before, but have the group skills, enthusiasm, and confidence to join the troupe and succeed.

I don't hold auditions for either group because I find that auditions create an unnatural situation in which to first meet another person. The auditioner feels tense, nervous, and strained. He doesn't behave like himself because he's worried about what kind of impression he's making. He always assumes that the auditor is thinking the worst about him and becomes inhibited and tongue-tied. Even if an auditor bends over backwards to put an auditioner at ease, the situation remains that of one person sitting in judgement on another.

PEGASUS PERFORMING COMPANY CONTRACT

Agreement has been made _____ for _____
                              (Date)   (Student/Actor)

to become a member of the Bethesda Academy of Performing Arts'
PEGASUS Performing Company.

    I have talked with the Directors and my Parents about my commitment
in becoming a member of PEGASUS and I understand my responsibilities.

    I understand the importance of each of the guidelines listed below
and I agree to follow them.

1.   I agree to **attend every rehearsal and performance**. If I am
sick or if there is an emergency, I will notify the BAPA office at (301) 320-
2550 of my absence as soon as possible.

2.   I agree to **arrive on time** for every rehearsal and performance.

3.   I agree to **behave in an appropriate and professional manner** at every rehearsal and performance.

4.   I agree to **learn my lines and do any work assigned**.

5.   I agree to **keep my parents and/or guardian informed** of all
rehearsal dates and times, all performance dates and times, and any changes that happen in the PEGASUS schedule.

6.   I agree to **respect others and their ideas**.

7.   I agree to **respect and care for all equipment**, supplies, scripts,
books, costumes, props, make-up, scenery and lighting equipment which
belong to BAPA and PEGASUS.

8.   I agree to **follow instructions** given to me by my directors.

9.   I won't use PEGASUS as an excuse not to complete my school work.

10. I will always **do my best**.

_____

Student Signature   Date

_____

Parent/Guardian Signature

_____

Sally Bailey, Director   Carol Gulley, Director

At the same time, there needs to be some kind of sifting process in order to make sure new individuals who sign up for the performing company are ready for an intermediate dramatic experience, capable of becoming a member of an ensemble, and appropriate for the group. There is also the added necessity of making sure they understand they must make a year's commitment to the work of the group.

My sifting process has become an orientation interview. I ask all interested potential members to come to a group session in which I can explain the process we are going to go through during the year and the type of commitment they need to be willing to make. I usually ask parents or transportation providers to stay so that they understand the time commitment and the process, too. Their support will be invaluable if the commitment is to be carried out.

I show a video of some of the work that has been done by the group in the past so they can see the other people who are in the group and the type of work we do. I let them ask me any questions they may have. I explain the contract and give them a copy to take home. I ask them questions about the types of dramatic experiences they have had in the past. If I don't know the individuals at the interview or if I can't get a good sense of them from their comments and questions, I have the group play a few drama games just to see where their imaginations and group interaction skill levels are.

Before they leave, I ask them to take a week to decide whether becoming a member of the performing company sounds like something they would like to do. They don't have to make their decision right away. If they want, they can wait until the first rehearsal (which is usually the next week), to sign up.

I have rarely had to turn anyone away. Both Pegasus and Icarus are composed of a wide variety of individuals who have different levels of cognitive and physical functioning. They are all able to work well together because they have learned to respect each other's creativity and they enjoy each other's contributions to the group.

Sometimes, however, joining the troupe is not appropriate for an individual. One year I knew the Pegasus Company was going to be composed of a very large and rowdy returning bunch. A shy, non-assertive beginning actor might have become lost in the group. I feared this would happen to one of the potential members who was non-verbal, inexperienced, and had a low level of cognitive functioning. I recommended that he take a year of improvisational acting to develop his confidence and skills. He did so. The following year he joined the troupe and had a very successful experience.

THE OVERALL PROCESS

The first three or four sessions are spent building an acting ensemble, developing basic improvisational acting skills, and deciding what the play will be about. Once we have chosen our topic, we develop it through improvising characters and situations which relate to it. The improvisation process usually takes between five and seven sessions. Then I take the material which the actors have generated in class and structure a written script from it, taking into consideration as many of their ideas and suggestions as possible.

The actual rehearsal period once the script is complete takes a minimum of ten sessions. We read through the written script, block it, and rehearse it until everything flows smoothly. The script serves as a basic guideline or structure for the actors. Lines need to be memorized, but they can be changed and improvised on. Things stay very loose even after we open the show. Although the same dramatic events happen each time, no two performances have ever had identical dialogue.

GETTING STARTED

For a group to work well together, they need to develop trust, a spirit of camaraderie and acceptance, and the ability to work together as a team. This can be accomplished through introduction games in which actors share information about themselves and through basic drama games in which they learn about each other through relating physically, verbally, and socially to each other. Basic acting skills that need to be developed by all members of an acting ensemble include the ability to make eye contact, listening skills, observation skills, imagination skills, projection and diction skills, and basic skills for improvising dialogue and creating characters. Often I will focus our beginning sessions on skills that the group had particular difficulty with the previous year.

CHOOSING AN IDEA

Actor input and choice in the subject matter of the play is crucial. It is important to put the actors at the center of the creative process so that they can own it. We spend from ten to thirty minutes each of the first few sessions brainstorming ideas to use for the play. Typically, I ask them to think about situations, characters, and ideas which would be exciting to work on and I write down every suggestion that is made, no matter how outlandish. If only a few ideas are suggested the first session, I ask them to think about more ideas over the course of the next week and we add to our list the next class period.

One year Pegasus developed the following list of ideas:

Halloween
The Night of the Living Dead
Maniac Mansion (making fun of horror movies)
Little Shop of Horrors
Ghostbusters or something where ghosts are haunting a house
School— a student is in trouble
Head of the Class
At the beach
Karate—spoof Ninja turtles
Cops/Detectives/Police Officers/Spies
Rescue Squad—a play about safety
A Turtle Named Melvin
Family—a comedy about growing up
Where The Wild Things Are
The Hobbit
Something with the army or the military
A TV show
Stories around a campfire
A cabaret with songs and jokes
A play with animal characters
A play about a dentist
A Western
A circus
A kidnapping
Monty Python and the Holy Grail in the 20th century
Running away from home

After we had generated this long, interesting list, we talked about the pros and cons of each idea. For instance, to try to do a stage version of the movie *Ghostbusters* might be difficult because we didn't have the resources for a lot of special effects, but creating some kind of play about ghosts haunting a house was not out of the question.

I try to steer actors away from adapting a movie or TV show into a play because it doesn't leave enough room for their own creativity. They feel as if they must reproduce the characters and situations image for image, line for line instead of improvising on a theme to create something new.

When I feel we have a list which has enough variety to offer us strong dramatic options, we take a preliminary vote to determine which ideas are the most popular. Everyone can vote for whichever ideas they like (i.e., they can vote as many times as they like).

The most popular ideas from the idea list above were a Western, a kidnapping, cops and robbers, and a family story. From this list, a second and a third vote could have been taken to narrow down the group's choices even further until one idea appeared which appealed to a majority.

However, that year, I decided to try something new. I asked for volunteers to "sell" their favorite idea to the group. A different actor offered to champion each idea. One by one they each stood up and told the group all the different reasons why we should vote for their idea. I was very surprised at how eager and articulate each student was. Even the actors with mental retardation were able to get up and tell why they thought their idea would be fun to work on. "Selling" your idea to the group has now become a traditional part of the process, one which everyone looks forward to each fall.

During this round, due to the enthusiastic salesmanship of the speakers, three ideas—a Western, a kidnapping, and cops and robbers—became the clear favorites of the group. A quick vote confirmed this, with a Western getting the most votes. I suggested that we combine all three of the top ideas and create a Western in which there were cops, robbers, and a kidnapping. This suggestion was greeted with a groundswell of cheers and *Guns Ablazing* was born.

A compromise which includes many different, but compatible ideas can get a group past an impasse and keep a majority of actors happy and interested. Our first year no one was willing to give up his own idea for the show. After many weeks of discussion and debate, we finally settled on creating a play about dreams because all of the other ideas: animals, movies, movie stars, feelings, Kids On the Block (the puppets, not the rock group), an acting class, space, food, and daydreaming about boys could all be incorporated into different dreams.

On the other hand, coming to agreement on an idea can happen very quickly if all the actors in a group are on the same wavelength. In September 1991 everyone in Icarus unanimously agreed in our very first session that they wanted to do a play about falling in love and include their favorite love songs.

I guide and advise on choices, pointing out the pros and cons of each idea that haven't been addressed by any of the actors, but I don't make the final decision on what we're going to do. Furthermore, I have taken the position that whatever the group decides on—even if I don't like it—that's what we'll do the play about.

At the beginning of Pegasus's second season, the movie *Back to the Future, Part II* came out and everyone was wild to do a play about time travel. I was very skeptical that they had the skills to take on what I knew would end up being a much more complex project than the dream play they had created the year before. I knew it would be hard to avoid a lot of line memorization and complex sequencing in a script which bounced from one time period to another. I had a very small budget and no technical support. I didn't feel that I had the skills to build a time machine myself. I knew that travel back to several different periods in history would necessitate four or five different costume and set changes. I had visions of chaos and confusion backstage: panicked actors ripping costumes on and off, long pauses on stage as costume changes delayed entrances, George Washington walking into the middle of King Arthur's Court by mistake. I explained all of this to them and begged them to vote for any other idea instead. They unanimously voted for time travel anyway.

I seriously considered stepping in and saying, "No, I've thought about it and you aren't ready to do this," but I just couldn't reconcile that action with my philosophy that you can do anything if you imagine it clearly enough and work on it hard enough. So I went to rehearsal the next week and said, "OK, we're going to do a play about time travel, but it's going to take a lot of work. I'm going to have to push you very hard. Once we have the script, you are going to have to spend a lot of time working on it at home. You must come to rehearsal prepared. You must learn your lines by the deadlines I give you. Are you willing to do whatever it takes to make this idea work?" They all shouted, "YES!"

Improvising *Just In Time* was a lot of fun, but rehearsing it was—just as I had predicted—a struggle. It was a lot of very hard work for all of us. There was one rehearsal early on where everyone was fooling around, no one had memorized their lines, and I had to throw a "director's temper tantrum." In the end, however, we met the challenge and the whole group moved up to a new level of theatrical ability. I truly believe that the reason the Pegasus actors were able to succeed was because they had taken on the responsibility for the decision to do the play themselves . . . and because I didn't let them forget it!

DEVELOPING THE IDEA

Once the idea has been chosen, it needs to be developed. The first development step I take with my troupes is to hold another brainstorming session. I ask the actors to think of all the different scenes and characters which might be involved in a play about that idea. For *Just In Time* I asked the actors to think of all the famous people in history they would like to go back and meet if they had the chance. For *Some Enchanted Evening* we started by making a list of all the qualities they would want in "The Perfect Someone to Fall in Love With."

For *Guns Ablazing,* our scene list looked like this:

Posse	Campfire
Bank Robbery	General Store
Kidnapping	Stage Coach
Train Robbery	Barroom Brawl
Country School	Wagon Train
Gun Fight/Shootout/Showdown	Hoedown
Court Room Scene	Bonfire
Horse Race	

Characters who might be involved in a Western included:

Gunfighter harassing a town	Saloon Owner/Dance Hall
Cowboys	Girls/Bartender
Indians	Bank Teller
Gamblers	Judge
School Teacher	Stage Coach Driver
Sheriff and Deputies	Pony Express Rider
Robbers/Cattle Rustlers/	
Gun Runners/Desperados	

With our list of characters and scenes complete we began improvising different situations, giving actors the choice to play different kinds of roles. Almost immediately a gang of desperados named the Wild Rascals were born. They made plans to rob the town bank in one scene, then did so, shooting everyone in sight. We replayed the scene with different actors in the roles and instead of shooting everyone, incorporated a kidnapping into the scene.

Following this we improvised a number of scenes in which the sheriff and his deputies investigated the scene of the crime and interviewed the witnesses for clues to the robbers' whereabouts. The actors who had been playing the robbers got tired of waiting around and suddenly showed up at the Sheriff's office with their hostage to discuss the terms of her release.

The next week we continued with the basic situation we had created and tried out a number of scenarios for rescuing the kidnap victim. The robbers were finally captured—very unwillingly—and put on trial.

One week we improvised a series of shoot-outs. Everyone was very anxious to challenge someone else to a quick draw contest. I am not big on using violence as a solution to conflict in plays or in life, but I am not averse to spending time in rehearsal exploring *why* it's not a good option. I made sure that anyone who had expressed the slightest interest in a shootout got the chance to experience one so everyone could get it out of their systems. Everyone wanted to shoot at each other, but no one wanted to die. It became very apparent after the first few go-rounds that a shoot-out was a rather short, limited, and boring situation. After about six replays, the group begged to move on to something more interesting. No one was disappointed when a shoot-out did not appear in the final version of the play.

Guns Ablazing: *The Wild Rascals plot their bank robbery. (Photo by Allison Walker)*

We also developed the wagon train idea, played cards in a saloon, told tall tales around a campfire, invented Indian legends, and explored what school would be like in a one-room schoolhouse on the prairie.

As scenes are improvised, notes should be taken on the dramatic choices, character names, and exciting lines of dialogue which are created. A more thorough way to save dialogue and ideas is to record improvisations. The tape can be transcribed later and will serve as a rich source of dramatic material. This is time-consuming work, but the time spent is worth it. A transcript of improvised dialogue preserves the way each actor naturally expresses himself—his word choice, sentence structure, thought processes, and grammar. This can be an invaluable aid when devising lines for each actor in the written version of the script. It is much easier to memorize lines which are your own creations or which are expressed in your own style of thought and speech than it is to memorize lines in someone else's style.

Sometimes whole sections of improvised scenes can be used in the final script of a play. A lot of the dialogue for *Guns Ablazing* was adapted directly from the transcripts. The following is an unedited transcription of the scene in which the Wild Rascals planned their bank heist:

SCENE: The town saloon. The gang is sitting around the table playing poker. The music is playing really loudly so the gang can talk and no one can overhear them.

BILLY BOB JOE: So, Julia, what do you have?

JULIA: I have fifty aces.

BILLY BOB JOE: I call. What do you have, Suzanna?

SUZANNA: I have a hundred aces.

JULIA (to BILLY BOB JOE): I think you lose.

BILLY BOB JOE: Now, now . . .

INJUN JOE: I got fifty-five hundred aces.

JULIA: I got four men.

INJUN JOE: I got fifty-five hundred men.

PHILEMINA: I got five queens.

JULIA: I've got five kings.

BILLY BOB JOE (to each player in turn): You cheat. You cheat. You cheat. And you cheat.

PHILEMINA: No, I don't!

JULIA (to BILLY BOB JOE): Look at that card on your leg!

EVERYBODY ELSE: Yeah! Look!

BILLY BOB JOE: Naw, naw. One-eyed Billy Bob Joe does *not* cheat! Hey, wait a minute! I've got an idea.

JULIA: What?

BILLY BOB JOE: Why don't we go rip off that bank over there?

PHILEMINA: Oh, yeah! Yeah! That would be real neat!

BILLY BOB JOE: First National Bank.

PHILEMINA: Let's do that. Wanna do that?

INJUN JOE: Yeah, Boss.

JULIA: Yeah! Let's do that!

BILLY BOB JOE: OK, now, Robert?

ROBERT: Yeah?

BILLY BOB JOE: What can you do to help us break into the bank? Can you break the locks?

ROBERT: Locks! OK! Alright! Locks!

INJUN JOE: Yeah!

BILLY BOB JOE (to JULIA): Now you—you have to distract all the people around us so no one notices, OK?

JULIA: OK.

BILLY BOB JOE: You, too, Suzanna. OK? You pretend to steal Julia's purse and the police will be so busy dealing with you that they won't notice the rest of us!

SUZANNA: OK.

BILLY BOB JOE: We gotta keep everyone away and be lookouts.

PHILEMINA: Yeah!

BILLY BOB JOE: Injun Joe, you can break into that vault, can't you?

INJUN JOE: Yeah, I can break into that.

JULIA: Will we dynamite it?

BILLY BOB JOE: Yeah, we gonna use dynamite.

ROBERT: YEAH!!

(INJUN JOE makes the sound of an explosion.)

PHILEMINA: And I'll get the money.

BILLY BOB JOE: No, that's my job and I'll split it up with everyone else.

JULIA: She can put it in the bags.

BILLY BOB JOE: OK. OK! Sounds pretty good. We should all wear black. OK, Injun Joe, what do you need to break into that vault?

INJUN JOE: Let's see . . . a couple fire hydrants . . .

BILLY BOB JOE: Fire hydrants?

INJUN JOE: Yeah!

BILLY BOB JOE: I didn't think they existed yet.

INJUN JOE: Ear muffs. For dynamite.

BILLY BOB JOE: Oh, yeah, it's really loud.

(INJUN JOE and ROBERT make sounds of an explosion.)

INJUN JOE: I could break it to pieces!

BILLY BOB JOE: You gonna use your bare hands to break open that vault? OK.

INJUN JOE: No, I won't! I want dynamite!

BILLY BOB JOE: OK, some dynamite.
(To ROBERT) What do you need to break into those locks? You just need some picks, right?

ROBERT: Right!

BILLY BOB JOE: You're not going to use your gun, are you?

ROBERT: Yeah! My gun! POW! POW!

BILLY BOB JOE: Now, you two, you gonna want some supplies or what?

JULIA: Just our dresses and the purse.

PHILEMINA: What about disguises? You have any ideas, Suzanna?

BILLY BOB JOE: What do you need to look like? What kind of disguise?

JULIA: Let's wear dresses and hats and we need our purses so I can steal it from her.

BILLY BOB JOE: And we need some potato sacks for the cash.

PHILEMINA: Our pictures are up all over the place. Maybe we should use something to cover up our faces.

JULIA: What about big hats?

BILLY BOB JOE: I think I'll just wear a mask.

PHILEMINA: How about a handkerchief on your face?

BILLY BOB JOE: OK.

INJUN JOE: What about me?

BILLY BOB JOE: Oh, nobody can tell one Indian from another. You don't need anything.

INJUN JOE: How about a wig?

SUZANNA: And disguise yourself as a woman?

INJUN JOE: Yeah!

PHILEMINA: No, that would look too suspicious.

INJUN JOE: Whatever you say, Toots!

PHILEMINA: Don't call me Toots!

BILLY BOB JOE: OK . . . Maybe we should rob a train while we're at it. When we have to leave the stage, how about we take the train and pick up a few extra bucks?

EVERYBODY: YEAH!!

JULIA: Don't we need horses to get to the train?

BILLY BOB JOE: How about it we sneak out the back way? They'll think we burned up when the building blew.

END OF SCENE

Here is the scene as it appeared in the play:

SCENE:Molly's Saloon in Tumbleweed, Montana. It is the Spring of 1848. May 8th to be exact. MOLLY is tending bar. SAM is helping her. At the bar sits MOLLY's daughter MELLY, SHERIFF CALAMITY KATE, ANNIE FINN, the bank teller, and EMILY SINGLETON, an attorney at law. At the table up left sits DEPUTY SLIM MCGILLICUTY, DEPUTY CHARLIE JONES, JUDGE CLINT HAWTHORNE, and BAILIFF VIRGINIA TURNER.

BILLY BOB JOE WARREN enters with his brother COLT and their cousin ROBERT. They are followed by INJUN JOE, a renegade Indian. Together they are the infamous WILD RASCALS. They all wear black hats.

BILLY BOB JOE: There's an empty table.

COLT: Great. Let's go sit there. (They sit at the center table.)

BILLY BOB JOE: Hey, Bartender! We need some drinks!

INJUN JOE: Yeah!

ROBERT: Yeah!

MOLLY: Just a minute! I'll be right there.

COLT: Now, behave yourselves. No fighting tonight.

INJUN JOE: Awwww! How come?

BILLY BOB JOE: Because we don't want anyone to notice us.

COLT: Yeah, we don't want to attract any attention so nobody gets suspicious.

MOLLY: What do you want?

INJUN JOE: Whiskey!

COLT: Beer!

BILLY BOB JOE: Sasparilly.

ROBERT: Yeah!!

MOLLY: Coming right up.

BILLY BOB JOE: OK, I say we knock off the First National Bank tomorrow morning. What do you say? Colt?

COLT: Let's do it!

ROBERT: Yeah!

BILLY BOB JOE: Injun Joe?

INJUN JOE: OK, Boss.

BILLY BOB JOE: Colt, you be lookout.

COLT: Why do I always have to be lookout?

BILLY BOB JOE: You've got the best eyes. You have to stand lookout. And Robert?

ROBERT: Yeah?

BILLY BOB JOE: You can hold the money bag.

ROBERT: OK.

BILLY BOB JOE: Now, Injun Joe, you can break into that vault, can't you?

INJUN JOE: Yeah, I can break into it. I can break into anything!

BILLY BOB JOE: What do you need for this one?

INJUN JOE: I'll break it to pieces!

COLT: You gonna use your bare hands?

INJUN JOE: No! I'll need dynamite. And ear muffs.

COLT: Sounds like it'll be really loud.

INJUN JOE: YEAH!!

ROBERT: YEAH!!

BILLY BOB JOE: YEAH!!

(MOLLY arrives with drinks on a tray.)

MOLLY: You're making too much noise over here. This is a quiet neighborhood!

BILLY BOB JOE: Oh, ah, we're members of a bluegrass band. Sometimes we get a little rowdy.

MOLLY: You're musicians? My daughter Melly is a singer. Would you like to hear her sing a little later?

BILLY BOB JOE: Oh, yeah, sure. Thanks for the drinks.

MOLLY: You're welcome. But be quiet!

(MOLLY goes back to the bar.)

BILLY BOB JOE: Whew! That was a close shave!

INJUN JOE: Yeah!

COLT: Better keep your voices down.

BILLY BOB JOE: Now, what about disguises? Does everybody have their neckerchiefs and masks?

INJUN JOE, COLT, and ROBERT: Yeah!

BILLY BOB JOE: And guns?

INJUN JOE, COLT, and ROBERT: YEAH!!

BILLY BOB JOE: Great.

(Musical interlude in which MELLY sings a song.)

BILLY BOB JOE: She's one pretty little nightingale.

INJUN JOE: I'd sure like her to sing me to sleep at night, haw, haw.

BILLY BOB JOE: Yeah, you would, Injun Joe.

COLT: I've been thinkin'. Don't we need some horses for the get-away?

INJUN JOE: I'll rustle up some horses tonight. Want to help me, Robert?

ROBERT: Oh, yeah!

INJUN JOE: OK! Let's go!

BILLY BOB JOE: And I'm going to get some shut-eye so's I'm fresh in the morning.

COLT: Good idea. Let's go.

(The WILD RASCALS exit.)

Sometimes the most amazing and unpredictable things will happen during an improvisation which provide exciting, unexpected material for the play. While a wagon train was not included in *Guns Ablazing*, one event did occur during our series of wagon train improvisations which contributed enormously to the plot of the play.

I set up the wagon train situation by explaining to the actors that in the 1800s when a family left the East to move West, they sold their house and most of their belongings, keeping only the barest necessities. Everything had to fit into a tiny covered wagon. Once people moved West, they usually never returned East and often never saw the friends and family members they left behind again.

There were three four-foot by eight-foot tables in the room. Positioned end to end they became three wagons in the train. The first belonged to the Wagon Master, the second to the family going West, and the last to the Wagon Scout. First, the family sorted through their belongings, deciding what to pack and what to leave behind. Then they said goodbye to their friends and got into the wagons to leave. They stopped to cook a meal and forded a dangerous river.

When they arrived at the edge of Indian territory, they stopped. The Wagon Scout went ahead to investigate. He was denied access by a tribe of angry Indians who did not want any white people to cross their lands. The Scout returned to tell the wagon train the bad news. At this point I offered them three options. They could go forward and be massacred by the Indians for trespassing, they could take the Southern route, which would take an additional three months and seriously endanger their food supplies, or they could turn around and go home. I knew they didn't want to die (we'd already done the shoot-out session), so I knew they wouldn't choose to be massacred. I figured they'd choose the second or third solution. But that's not what happened.

Amelia, an actor with learning disabilities who was playing the mother of the family, came up with a brilliant alternative. She decided to negotiate with the Indians herself. When she made this announcement, all the characters in the wagon train were horrified and begged her not to go because she would surely be killed. But they couldn't dissuade her. She was determined to save her family and get them to their new home. She set out alone and was met by an Indian scout. He brought her to the village and the chief assembled a council of all the wisest women in the village.

I wish my tape recorder had not been broken that day because the scene which followed was so incredibly poetic and emotionally truthful that anyone who was not there to see it and hear it would not believe that teenaged actors—five who had cognitive disabilities and two who didn't—could create such a strong, powerful dramatic scene. Amelia asked the Council of Wise Women for permission for the wagon train to pass through Indian territory. The Wise Women on the council were unimpressed with her request. They listed all the havoc which white people had wrecked on their land in the past. White people killed the buffalo and the beaver, they cut down trees, they hurt little children, they poisoned the water, they destroyed the crops. Amelia insisted that she was different. She wouldn't do those things. The Council asked why she needed to go across their land. She explained that she had sold her home and didn't have any place for her family to live. She needed to travel across their land to get her family to a new home where they could be safe. The Council carefully weighed her reasons and decided that a mother's love for her children was very important and everyone needed a home. They decided to allow the wagon train to cross their land, but the white people must kill nothing and take nothing on their way through. Amelia agreed to this and went back to the wagon train to announce her success. At that point class was over for the day and we didn't continue the improv the next week.

In the script which developed, Amelia became Molly, the owner of the Town Saloon and mother of the kidnap victim. She went with the Sheriff and her Deputies to the Wild Rascal's hideout to arrange for the ransom of her daughter. They took a shortcut to the hideout, forgetting that it necessitated crossing Indian territory. The Sheriff wanted to turn back, but Molly insisted on meeting with the Indian Council and negotiating passage through their land.

Rehearsal surprises like this can add depth and dimension to a script if you allow them to happen instead of cutting them off before they can develop. If I had insisted that the group adhere to the three choices I had given them while I was side-coaching the scene, we would never had discovered a more creative way to solve the dramatic situation.

If improvisations get stuck in a rut or go off track, step in and side-coach to get the actors focused back on the dramatic conflict of the scene. If actors are not listening to the other actors and responding to what is being said, stop working on the play for a session and review basic improvisation skills. Set up situations with very simple, clear conflicts which the characters must resolve through discussion. For instance, a mother could be talking to her daughter about cleaning up her room or a teacher could be talking to a student about the need to study for a test. Both actors in the scene must listen and respond directly to what the other actor has just said. See the section in Chapter Six which deals with improvisational acting for more tips on how to teach actors the improvisational skills they need.

If actors have trouble structuring and developing a situation in which they have little actual experience, cast yourself or your assistant in role in the scene to keep things on track. While improvising the courtroom scene when the Wild Rascals were put on trial for kidnapping and bank robbery in *Guns Ablazing,* my assistant played the prosecuting attorney and I played the defense attorney because we knew the actors had little understanding of how a court trial proceeded. We were able to guide the development of the scene along an appropriate progression with some sense of court decorum. They responded to our questions as we examined and cross examined the witnesses and a lot of new material was generated that was used in the scene which ended up in the play.

We had to use this technique again this past fall while developing *Death By Grammar*. The group had decided that the murdered character would be an overbearing college grammar professor named Phil A. Buster, who constantly corrected everything everyone else said and wrote. The problem was that when we started improvising scenes in which the professor insulted and corrected the other characters, *no one* in the cast had a strong enough grasp of English grammar terms and rules to know when someone else had made a mistake. Our musical director, Carol Gulley, had to take over the role of Professor Buster during improvisations.

Art Work. Art work is another good avenue for collecting and developing ideas. It opens up actors' imaginative thinking in visual, spatial, and kinesthetic ways, providing a concrete approach for exploring an idea. Before taking off on any time travel journeys while we were working on *Just In Time*, I asked the Pegasus actors to design their own time machines. They set to work with paper, markers, and crayons and devised the most amazing array of scientific-looking contraptions I have ever seen. I let each one present his design to the group and explain how it worked and the kind of sound it made. The journeys we took in rehearsal seemed all the more real because they had each conceptualized how they were getting there in a concrete manner.

Double Crossed Bones, a rollicking pirate adventure, developed almost entirely out of a series of treasure maps the actors drew. Each map had an island and a path past many monsters and obstacles to the buried treasure. Each actor presented his map to the group and described how to get to the treasure. Then over the course of the next four weeks we improvised a number of treasure hunting expeditions following the maps.

I recorded the actors' descriptions of their maps as they presented them. Here are a few transcriptions to give you an idea of the complications and conflicts they created for themselves to overcome in the course of their improvisations. Adam and Amelia have learning disabilities; Lisa, Henry, and Jack have Down syndrome; Darryl and Dean are regular education students who have been best friends for years.

ADAM'S MAP

This place is called Adam's Island. Right in the center of here is where the treasure is buried. To get there you have to start at Zebra Point and then you go to Monkey City, Chimpanzee Way, Giraffe City, Duck Avenue, Lion Court, Kitten Boulevard, Flamingo Drive, Swan Alley, Fish Terrace, Bird Park, and this is a lake called Spooky Lake. There are spirits in there. Then there's the buried treasure. It's stolen jewels. No people live on this island. It's been deserted forever. Only animals live here. You have to get past the animals to get to the treasure. But if you get caught by one, they will eat you up.

LISA'S MAP

Here's the buried treasure. And here's the mountain. You have to go past Wendy to steal the treasure. The treasure is on the mountain and Wendy guards it. Wendy stole the treasure and brought it here.

AMELIA'S MAP

This is Amelia Island. There's a purple monster. And if you get to the purple monster, he will shoot you. But if you pass him, you'll come to a sea monster. And here's blood on the ground. And here's a sea castle coming out of the ocean. My treasure is money—gold and silver. If you find it, I'll kill you.

HENRY'S MAP

That's the island. There's the treasure. The treasure is money. That's the ocean.

JACK'S MAP

This is my club house. This is grass. This is a field. This is the treasure—rings, necklace, pearls, everything. I live on my island. No animals or people, just me. No visitors. If someone came, I would just talk to them.

DARRYL and DEAN'S MAP

We start in our hometown of Xanth. Xanth is all magic. Every person in Xanth has magic of some sort.

This is Morag, a treacherous creature in the ocean. And this is Mudah, a monster fish. And this is the Hydra—it has three heads. And they all attack you. So they're very bad and they live in the ocean. Look out for them. They'll attack your boat. They're like termites—they can eat away at your boat.

And then you follow the red dots to Hermit's Land and Demon's Dip which is near Tie-Dyed Island. You go past the Pit of Hell, around Devil's Turn and come down the Strait of Death. And that's guarded by Medusa at Medusa's Manor. And you come out and here is the Lost Forest. It's lost so you have to look very carefully to find it. And once you do, you get lost *in* it. And you come to an X which marks the spot on the map, but in reality there's a big tree shaped like a Y (so Y really marks the spot).

Other sights in our beautiful isle are Patrick's Hippieland, Troll's Town, Goblin's Glen, the Cliffs of Mortality, Dragon's Den, and Spelunker's Hollow.

The Dragons, Goblins, and the Trolls guard the treasure. We leave that to your skillful knowledge and intelligence. The treasure is a huge box of golden toothbrushes. Hollow chocolate. You have to peel off the tin foil.

There's a big commune, a utopian society on Tie-Dyed Island. Patrick's Hippieland is uncharted territory. The Spelunker's Cave is uncharted as well. There are numerous treasures hidden in there as well—among them the toothpaste that goes with the toothbrushes and mouthwash as well. And in the mouthwash bottle lives the genie, Lysterine.

And there really is a great cast-iron compass floating in the water on both of our maps.

The final version of *Double Crossed Bones* had two crews of pirates who were each trying to get to the Island of Lost Causes so they could find the treasure of the Sultan of Xanth. They had to stop off at Tie-Dyed Island and get help from The Old Man of the Sea, the oldest pirate of them all, who lived all alone on the island (and wore tie-dyed clothes). One crew had to face the Three-Headed Hydra in the Sea of Blood and the other had to get past the Mermaids in the Mermaid Sea. Once on the island they had to work together to find the treasure in the Lost Forest and defeat the evil dragon Morag who guarded the treasure. Does any of this sound vaguely familiar?

MUSIC AND DANCE

Music and dance can add variety and depth to an improvisational show, as well as alternative avenues of expression for the actors. Songs can be incorporated into the fabric of the show to move the plot along at the same time they offer the actors a chance to express themselves by singing a solo or a group number. You don't need to sing all the verses in a song. If one verse gets the point across, and two would be too much to memorize, sing one verse.

In *Guns Ablazing,* Casey, a blind actress who loves to sing, played Melly, the Saloon Singer. During the bank robbery, Melly was kidnapped by the Wild Rascals. Normally they never took hostages, but they had heard her singing in the Saloon and wanted her to sing them to sleep at night. This led to a scene in the hideout where all the Rascals joined in on a rowdy version of "Swing Low, Sweet Chariot" unwittingly providing cover for the good guys to sneak up from behind to capture them.

The Wild Rascals' version of "Swing Low, Sweet Chariot" turned out to be a real crowd pleaser and motivated my normally reticent teenagers to willingly turn *Double Crossed Bones,* next season's show, into a full-fledged musical filled with sea chanteys and a pirate dance contest. The sea chanteys were excellent devices for climaxing an exciting scene, covering scene transitions, and bringing everyone together on stage at the end of the play. Written for hard-boiled sailors, these songs were easy to sing. They did not require a large vocal range, they had a strong, clear rhythm, and they didn't *have* to be sung perfectly to be effective.

Even students who don't sing "well" often enjoy singing. As Carol Gulley, our musical director, says, "Music is fundamental." It speaks to the human heart and soul in a direct, immediate, and emotional way. Therefore, the experience of music and participation in it is more important for students than musical accuracy. Accuracy will come with time and practice.

Incorporate dance and music into your shows!
A pirate conga line from Double Crossed Bones.
(Photo by Allison Walker)

Carol approaches teaching music to the performing troupes by exploring the mood and emotions evoked by the songs. We will sing through a song and then Carol asks the actors to share what they think the lyrics mean. She also asks them for "feeling" words to describe the sound of the music and the story that the lyrics tell. After singing through "Greensleeves," Carol might ask, "How does the person who is singing this song feel? Who is he speaking to? What has happened between them? What does he want to happen?" If the lyrics suggest a story, students might try acting them out while Carol plays the music. She might suggest that they explore the song further by improvising a dance to it before sitting back down to sing it again. After the actors can identify and express the feelings while singing the song, the musicality of the song naturally begins to develop as the group continues to learn and rehearse the song.

We have found that the Pegasus and Icarus actors tend to do better with songs which have simple lyrics and a straight-forward, steady beat to serve as an anchor. Slow ballads and rock 'n' roll tunes seem to be their personal favorites for those exact reasons. They find songs which have a familiar repetitious pattern in lyrics and/or melody easy to remember and enjoyable to sing. They tend to have difficulty with songs that have complicated wording or a syncopated beat.

CHOOSING CHARACTERS

Before I sit down to pull together all the improvised ideas that the actors have invented and create a plot structure for the play, I always ask each actor exactly what kind of a role he or she would like to play. During improvisation sessions, they have had the opportunity to try out as many different kinds of roles as possible. Usually by the time I ask them, they have an idea of what kind of part they would like to have in the final play. In addition to type of role, I always ask if they have suggestions for their character's name and for a title for the play. I try to get a first and second choice, to give me flexibility in casting and in case several people are interested in exactly the same role.

In *Guns Ablazing* the lines were clearly drawn between those who wanted to be good guys and those who wanted to be bad guys. Brian had insisted from Day One that he was a renegade Indian named Injun Joe. Darryl and Dean wanted to be Billy Bob Joe and Colt Warren, twin brother bank robbers. They had clearly taken Henry, who wanted to be a bank robber named Robert, under their wing, so he became a Wild Rascal, too. Patrick and Jack, who were best friends, wanted to be the sheriff's deputies, Slim McGillicuty and Charlie Jones. After her experience in the wagon train, Amelia was very clear about wanting to be someone's mother and she wanted her name to be Molly. Casey wanted to be the Saloon Singer so she could sing a song. She didn't have an idea for a name, so Amelia suggested she call herself Melly, and the act of providing Casey with a name, gave me the idea to make Molly Melly's mother. Aaron wanted to be the judge. I had several actors who said, "I'll play anything. Put me where you need me. I know you'll give me a good part." With their flexibility, I was able to fill out the cast.

Double Crossed Bones was a little harder to cast. Everyone wanted to be a pirate, with the exceptions of Betsy, who wanted to be a mermaid, Lisa, who wanted to be a pirate *and* a dragon, and Carolyn, who said she would play any part I needed her to play. So I collected information on the type of pirate each wanted to be (Captain, First Mate, Cook, Lookout, Deck Hand, etc.) and pirate name (Erg, Arg, Meriwether, Swerdfager, Dennis, Seagull, etc.) and went from there.

Sometimes actors cast each other in roles. Charlie came up with an idea for the opening of *Some Enchanted Evening* that sent shivers down our spines. He thought that it would be very dramatic if Ellie, who uses a wheelchair, would mournfully wheel herself out onto an empty stage and say, "I'm sad and lonely. Nobody loves me." Then she could sing "Where Is Love?" which is all about looking for someone special to love. Then, he continued, the Spirits of the Night could appear and offer to help her. Needless to say, everyone thought that was a dynamic beginning. Because the entrance and the dramatic situation was so strong, Ellie became the main character in the play. The rest of the play followed her experiences as she tried to find the perfect someone to love her.

Of course, sometimes actors don't end up in the role they want. In *Death By Grammar* several actors wanted to be characters who were in improvisations, but who didn't end up in the written script. Several other actors asked for one role and got another. After we read through the script, no one ended up feeling disappointed because everyone loved the play and each one ended up playing an interesting character with lots of fun dialogue and stage business. For years Patrick has wanted to play a fireman. He thought he was finally going to have his chance in this play. Instead he ended up as Heywood Jakissime, a Don Johnson-type Hollywood movie star. He tells me now that this is his favorite role ever. Or as he says, "Wow! I really love this part!"

If an actor had been upset about how he had been cast, I would have taken him aside and told him how much I needed him in that particular role, that I had conceived and written the role especially for him, and that nobody else could do the role as well as I knew he could. And because it's an original script, developed *by* the actors and written *for* them, what I said would be absolutely true.

STRUCTURING A WRITTEN SCRIPT

Most well-written plays, whatever their length, usually follow a similar dramatic structure.* Each has a beginning, a middle, and an end. Most plays begin with *exposition* which sets up the characters, their present situation, and the previous action which has lead them to this situation. Exposition can take a page, a scene, or an act to be fully revealed, or it can unfold slowly during the course of the whole play.

A skillful playwright builds exposition into the unfolding of the *present action* or *dramatic conflict,* which can be set in motion almost as soon as the play begins. Sometimes the dramatic conflict can have begun before the curtain even opens! An unskillful playwright wastes a lot of time in the begin-

---

* Plays can be one, two, three, four, five, or more acts in length, depending on how much dramatic material the playwright has to cover.

ning of the play allowing the characters to talk about the past and their relationships without really getting the play off the ground.

The middle (and bulk) of the play follows the unfolding of the plot or *dramatic conflict,* which is developed through a series of causally related incidents called *complications.* As the characters face each complication, they must make choices which may solve the complication or make it worse, but which, in any case, create new situations and complications which must be dealt with in turn.

The dramatic conflict culminates in a *crisis* or turning point, the major, most important incident in the play. This leads to the *climax* of the play where the crisis is resolved—to the satisfaction of the characters and the audience alike.

After the climax, the loose ends of the play are pulled together in the *denouement* or ending. Unanswered questions are answered, mysteries are solved, fences are mended, and the audience can leave with a sense of completion about the events they have witnessed.*

Playwriting professor Eugene McKinney describes the progression in a well-structured play with the acronym PASTO: Preparation (exposition), Attack (beginning of the present action), Struggle (dramatic conflict developing through conflicts), Turning Point (the moment when it all comes to a head: the crisis/climax), Outcome (denouement—which he feels should be suggested rather than spelled out).

When you begin putting together the script from the characters and improvisational scenes which your actors have created, you will need to think in terms of fitting their work into the structure of a well-made play. Exactly how that play will develop will be different every time because each play presents unique dramatic problems.

Sometimes when I sit down to create a written script from the improvisations that a group has done, I have a very clear idea of characters, conflict, and plot. *Guns Ablazing* fell together within two days. I was able to follow

---

* I don't have a playwriting text to recommend. I have had a number of wonderful playwriting teachers who were all professional playwrights: Frank Gagliano, Eugene McKinney, and Glenn Allen Smith. None of them ever used a playwriting text. They all taught playwriting by having students write scenes or plays and then read them out loud. None of them felt playwriting could be taught through a book, only through the experience of doing it.

the basic structure of the improvisations we had done and could use much of the dialogue from the tape transcriptions.

Just In Time, on the other hand, was a very difficult play to structure. We had improvised about ten different scenes from history in rehearsal and everyone had had a say about who their favorite characters to play would be. I chose four scenes from the past that seemed to offer the most potential for dramatic staging: the time of the dinosaurs, a scene from King Solomon's Court, King Arthur and his Knights creating the Round Table, and Columbus asking Queen Isabella and King Ferdinand for money to sail to the New World.

However, I realized as I sat down to weave the four scenes together that we had done very little work on who the Time Traveler was or why he or she needed to go back in time. This character would be crucial to the play as the connecting thread between the different time periods. Without a clear dramatic problem to solve, the time traveler's journey would become an aimless, meandering travelogue and would ultimately be unsatisfying and boring to an audience.

I wasted many hours in dead ends and false starts as I tried to solve the problem on my own. Maybe the Time Traveler was going back to each of the different time periods to get an object which was needed in his time in order to save the world. Maybe the Time Traveler had to ask questions of certain people in history to solve a puzzle that was threatening humanity. Maybe the Time Traveler was chasing another time traveler who was trying to make trouble back in history. These ideas were all good ones, but if I had used any of them, I would have had to create a plot structure and resulting character dialogue that would have been too complex for the memorization and sequencing abilities of my actors.

In frustration I started looking back over the list we'd made when we were brainstorming ideas for the play. I ran across the words "Small Wonder," the name of a TV situation-comedy. All fall Brian, who has Down syndrome, had been talking about "Small Wonder" and how he wanted to play Vicky, the robot girl on the show. At first I was puzzled. Why did he want to play a girl? Then I realized that what he liked about Vicky was the fact that she was a robot. She was smart. She knew how to do everything right. He, on the other hand, was going through a stage where he felt very awkward. He kept getting into trouble. He felt like he always did everything wrong.

My solution to the time travel problem was to create Wushin, the Time Machine Robot, and cast Brian in the part. While on display in a science museum, Wushin is accidentally turned on by a blind girl (played by Casey) who touches him while her school group is taking a tour. As the group moves on to the next room, two of the students, who are lingering behind, discover Wushin is functioning. They ask him to take them back in time to meet their favorite characters from history. Since he is a robot, and, therefore, programmed to follow directions given to him by humans, Wushin follows their orders and the three of them set off into the fourth dimension. Within a day of creating the character of Wushin, the structure of the whole script and the dialogue fell into place.

The lesson to learn from this story is: always listen to your students. Their ideas can solve your dramatic problems much better than you can! In addition, their solutions will tend be on the skill level they can handle, while your solutions will tend to be on your skill level. When in doubt, it is always better to go with their skill level than yours.

DEALING WITH SPEECH AND MEMORY DIFFICULTIES

Since I know the strengths and weaknesses of the different actors in the company, whenever I cast actors in roles and structure a play, I team up different combinations of characters who can look out for each other during the course of the performance. In *Guns Ablazing* two of the Wild Rascals had cognitive disabilities and two did not. The Sheriff, too, had normal cognitive functioning, while her deputies had mental retardation. In each of these teams of bad guys and good guys there were actors who could handle the bulk of the memorized lines. They could ask questions or give orders which would motivate the other actors' actions and responses.

Be careful how you structure dialogue of characters who are prompting lines and reactions from characters played by actors who have cognitive disabilities. As discussed in Chapter Six, many people have trouble processing negative commands into positive action. One actor saying, "Don't touch me," as a reminder to another actor who is supposed to touch him, can backfire. The second actor may hear the command and follow it, instead of disobeying it as he is supposed to do. Try to phrase reminders in a positive manner. Instead of "Don't touch me," the character might say, "If you touch me, I'll scream," or "I'm afraid this bandit is going to touch me!"

In *Guns Ablazing*, several actors had speech that was difficult to understand and/or memorization and sequencing difficulties. In the scene where Molly convinced the tribal council to allow the good guys to cross Indian territory, I created a character who served as translator from English to Sioux and back again to provide enough repetition of lines so the audience could understand what was being said. The scene's dialogue was based almost entirely on the improvisation which came out of the confrontation between the mother of the Wagon Train and the Council of Wise Women.

RED FEATHER (to RUNNING BULL): What does the white woman want?
RUNNING BULL: What white woman want?
MOLLY: Please, my friends and I need to go across your land.
RUNNING BULL: She wants to cross our land.
RED FEATHER: No! She cannot cross our land!
RUNNING BULL: No cross.
MOLLY: Please! It's a matter of life and death!
RUNNING BULL: She says it's a matter of life and death.
RED FEATHER: I'll ask the Council. Council, what do you say? Should we let this white woman and her friends cross our land? I say, No. The white man does not know how to respect our land. What do you say?
BROWN BEAR: I say, "No." The white man kills the buffalo and the beaver. Soon there will be no wildlife left.
CORN MAIDEN: I say, "No." The white man pollutes the land. Soon nothing will be able to grow.
RED FEATHER (to RUNNING BULL): Tell the white woman, "No. Go away."
RUNNING BULL: No. Go away.
MOLLY: But you must help! My daughter is being held captive by some bad men and they will kill her if we can't rescue her! We can only get to her by crossing your land! Please tell him that.
RUNNING BULL: OK. Some bad men have her daughter and they are going to kill her. She needs to cross our land to rescue her daughter.
CORN MAIDEN: Ahh! This makes a difference.
BROWN BEAR: Yes, it does.
CORN MAIDEN: I say, "Yes." A mother must help her daughter when in need.
BROWN BEAR: I agree.

RED FEATHER: If you say yes, I will say yes, too.
(To RUNNING BULL) Tell her she can cross our land, but touch nothing and kill nothing!
RUNNING BULL: You can cross, but touch nothing and kill nothing. Now go!
MOLLY: Oh, thank you! Thank you!

Even though a lot of the actors' speech was hard to understand, with the repetition, the physical actions, and the tone of voice used by the actors, the dramatic action of the scene was clear to the audience.

The only mistake I made was in my casting of specific actors in the roles. Initially, I cast Roberta, who has mental retardation, as Running Bull, the translator, because I knew that her memorization ability and her speech was limited. I thought the role of the translator would be perfect for her because she wouldn't have to memorize—only repeat the lines said to her. I also thought she would sound like someone speaking English as a foreign language because in real life she speaks in a halting manner.

Unfortunately, my brilliant idea didn't work. Roberta was not able to listen to a sentence and then immediately echo it. She became very confused and frustrated. And so did I. I wanted to scream, "It's so easy! It's the easiest part in the play! All you have to do is repeat what Molly and Red Feather say to you! Just get it together!" But I didn't scream. Instead I sat down, thought it through, and realized that her brain was not able to take in and process information in the way I had assumed it could. I had thought I was doing her a favor and instead I was asking her to do something that was very, very difficult.

Once I had established the problem, my next step was to figure out how to resolve the situation so everyone felt comfortable. I asked Roberta if it would be OK to switch roles in the scene with Towanda who played Brown Bear. She was immediately agreeable to the solution, as was Towanda. So Roberta played Brown Bear and Towanda played Running Bull. Roberta was very relieved to be off the hook and Towanda felt like she'd been promoted to a very important part with many more lines.

The moral of this story is that there are many more kinds of information-processing difficulties than you might at first suspect. Make sure you know what your actors' specific strengths and weaknesses are! You might be doing them a disservice rather than a favor.

DEALING WITH PHYSICAL LIMITATIONS

I also take actors' physical limitations into consideration as I structure the responsibilities in the play. During the rehearsal period for *Guns Ablazing* Aaron was recovering from a major operation on his legs. His energy was limited and so was his movement ability. As the judge, he was able to spend his time on stage sitting in his wheelchair, listening sagely to the court case, and banging his gavel for order.

Casey, who is blind, was led around as the kidnap victim, freeing her from worrying how to get gracefully from here to there on a stage where the scenery was constantly changing.

WORKING WITH NON-MAINSTREAMED GROUPS

One of the reasons Pegasus can do such advanced work at this point is because there are actors in the troupe with normal cognitive functioning who can lend support to the others. What can you do when the majority of your actors have difficulty remembering lines and plot sequences? When you don't have anyone who has enough stage experience to keep the play moving forward if others get lost? The more inexperienced your actors, the more tightly you must structure the play.

Narrators. By the standards of good playwriting, a narrator is a weak structural device. However, for the purpose of keeping actors on track, a narrator is one of the most reliable and useful devices at your disposal. Structure the play so that the teacher, an assistant, or a really strong reader in the cast can serve as an omniscient narrator who moves the play from scene to scene. Just like the narrator of a creative drama story, the narrator of the play can remind actors of entrances, lines of dialogue, or bits of business. The narration can be written out, but the narrator should also be able to jump in and improvise when things go wrong.

Teachers "In Role." The teacher or an assistant can take on a character in the play whose role is that of an authority figure or helper. In this way, they serve the same function as a narrator, but they do it from inside the structure of the play.

One spring my improvisational acting class for teens with special needs decided to put on *The Wizard of Oz* for their end of the semester project. The script did not need to be written down because everyone knew the story and what the characters should say in each scene by heart. However, most of my actors had never performed before and I was very nervous about how they would react when they got in front of a live audience. To give them a little extra support, I cast my assistant as Glinda, the Good Witch of the North, and had Glinda serve as the guide for Dorothy's entire journey through Oz.

The afternoon of the performance, I was so glad I had had the foresight to include an adult "in role" in the play. The curtains opened. We heard the winds of the cyclone blowing. Dorothy Gale blew on stage. She took one look at the audience, and blew off again. She was scared to death.

I thought, "The show's over. There's no way we'll get her back on!"

Just then Glinda floated on and called out, "Are you a good witch or a bad witch?"

Immediately, Dorothy ran back on stage and responded, "I'm Dorothy Gale. From Kansas." Having another character to relate to took her focus off her nervousness and the audience. She was fine from then on.

Throughout the performance, Glinda was able to ask pertinent questions, gently remind characters that it was time to move on, or motivate actions through subtle suggestions like "Maybe the Wizard could help him, too."

Music. Music can be very helpful in providing transition cues to actors. Just like in a classical melodrama, every time a character enters and leaves the scene he or she can have signature music. Since I wanted to avoid reproducing the MGM movie version, each character in *The Wizard of Oz* had an appropriate signature tune recorded by the actor's favorite rock artist. For example, the actor who played the Wizard loved MC Hammer, so his theme song became "U Can't Touch This." The actress who played the Wicked Witch of the West loved Michael Jackson, so her theme song was "I'm Bad." Every time they heard their music, they knew it was time to come on or go off.

Sections of a piece might be danced or mimed to music. Many students who have difficulty remembering lines of dialogue can remember movement patterns. If they have difficulty sequencing exact patterns, they can usually follow the beat of the music and rhythmically pantomime their character's actions.

The teacher, an assistant, or a student volunteer can run the tape recorder when music is not created live.

Dialogue on Tape. Another way to introduce or narrate sections of a play which keeps the actors involved is to record the narration or dialogue in their own voices and have them pantomime to it for the show. *Dreams, Nightmares, and Fantasies* used this technique to good effect. Each dream was introduced on tape by an actor's voice:

PATRICK
Dream Number One—The Circus Dream. I had a dream about me being a clown.

Sometimes the narration was followed by music, sometimes by songs, sometimes by an improvised scene or more recorded narration.

The script for Dream Number Seven looked like this:

MANDY (on tape)
Dream Number Seven—The Haunted House!

(Wolves howl and there are scary noises on the tape during the following set change:)

(AMELIA brings the wheelchair across to stage left. AARON gets into it. ESTHER will push the wheelchair. Everyone else sits or stands on the boxes and holds hands. MANDY [the assistant director] comes out from backstage and joins them. ESTHER pushes AARON's chair across the stage and around the box while the following recording plays:)

AARON (on tape): I was driving in a big truck down the highway.
(ESTHER stops the wheelchair on the left side of the box.)

AARON (on tape): I parked the truck outside this big old house.
(ESTHER helps AARON get out of the chair and he walks up to the door of the house.)

AARON (on tape): I walked up to the house and onto the porch. I opened the front door and someone said, "Come in."
EVERYONE (live): COME IN!!!!
(AARON pantomimes opening a door and stepping inside.)

AARON (on tape): I walked in and the door shut behind me. [sound of a door slamming shut]
(AARON turns and grabs onto the doorknob, trying to open the door.)

AARON (on tape): It locked! Everything grew dark and scary! [evil laughter on the tape.]
(EVERYONE, bending very low, is led around by MANDY until they are in front of AARON in a semi-circle.)

AARON (on tape): A trap door underneath me opened [sound effect] and I fell into the basement!

(EVERYONE stands up and raises their arms on the word "basement" to create the effect of AARON falling down the trap door. Then the group splits in the middle in front and lets AARON out to look around.)

AARON (on tape): There were some silver and gold pieces on the floor. I was in a treasure house and this was the robbers' gold!

(EVERYONE turns into monsters and starts making scary noises.)

AARON (on tape): Just then I turned around and saw some monsters. They were coming after me!

(EVERYONE chases AARON around the boxes stage right and across the stage to the box stage left. AARON sits on the box, out of breath. The MONSTERS surround him.)

AARON (on tape): I ran into a corner! I was trapped! I couldn't get away! They got closer and closer and then . . . [alarm clock rings]

MOTHER (on tape): Aaron! Time to get up! It's morning!

AARON (live): Saved by the alarm clock!

The actors were free to improvise dialogue as they felt appropriate, but the structure of the play was preserved for them on tape.

Length of Script. Keep your script short. Twenty to thirty minutes is a good length for a one-act play.

There are no reliable formulas for computing how a given number of pages of script will equal a certain amount of stage time. This is because there are several different styles of formatting a script and different ones put different amounts of material onto a page. In addition, a page that has long lines on it will take more time to perform than a page with short lines. Also, a stage description of blocking may take much more time to do than it takes to read. The only reliable way to gauge how long a script will take to perform is to read it out loud (with good readers), pantomiming any extended physical actions as you go, and time how long it takes.

When deciding on the length a script should be, first consider the basic needs of the story you are trying to tell. What is the essential action that must happen in order for the story to make sense? The audience must understand what is going on.

Second, consider the needs of your actors. Don't overburden them with too much material to memorize, whether it be words, songs, or movement.

Take into consideration the actors' ages, attention spans, sequencing and memorization abilities, verbalization abilities, and dramatic skill level.

Third (and most important), keep in mind how much time you have to rehearse the piece. It is much better to do a short play which is well rehearsed and shows off the actors to their best advantage than to bite off more than you can chew and arrive at opening night unprepared.

Keep the Script Improvisational in Nature. Allow the play to remain basically improvisational in nature as the actors rehearse and perform it.

If your play has been developed through improvisation, it is the creation of the actors in the company. There is no reason to require that each word in the written script be adhered to religiously. After all, the actors are the creators. It's their script! If they want to change something as they go along, they have every right to do so, so long as their changes make sense and make the play better.

An improvisational approach to the lines in a play allows the actors to adjust what they are saying to what they are capable of comfortably remembering. Usually lines taken directly from the actual words spoken by an actor or expressed in his speaking style are easier to remember. However, this is not always the case. Even though it is based on what was once spoken, the written dialogue can turn out to be too difficult for the actor to memorize. The lines might be too long or too complex to commit to memory. If so, they can be simplified in rehearsal.

I have come to view the memorization period of rehearsal as the process by which the extra fat I've put into the script is rendered out as the actors pare the play down to the essential meat and bones of the creature we've created together. If I've done a good job of capturing their voices, very little will change. If I've only done a good job of capturing my own voice, a lot will be modified as we go.

When the script is approached as a tool to create structure for the improvisationally created play, the actors are free to devise strategies for helping each other if someone forgets what to say or do. I always tell the actors that if they listen to what the other characters are saying to them, they can probably figure out an appropriate way to respond. I also suggest that if an actor looks lost, someone else who knows what's supposed to happen next can add a line or change a line or ask a question which can provide the lost actor with the missing information and move the scene forward. In this way the actors are all on stage looking out for each other, putting the good of the play first, instead of only paying attention to their own interests. This creates strong ensemble work and develops problem-solving abilities.

This approach also eases fears actors have about missing lines or making a mistake. They know they aren't up there alone. They feel lots of support from their fellow cast members. When a mistake *is* made (as they inevitably are, even in the best of professional productions), the actors do not start pointing the finger of blame at each other, they jump in to solve the problem and cover up the mistake before the audience realizes anything went wrong.

All of this is *not* to say that the actors shouldn't work very hard to memorize their lines. The lines hold the sequence of actions or events which happen in each scene. They provide a lot of important information which the audience has to know if they are to follow the story. The word choice and syntax of specific lines also serve as characterization devices—certain types of characters tend to speak in certain ways. For example, a very proper, straight-laced character will talk differently than a very relaxed, informal character.

THE REHEARSAL PROCESS

SCHEDULING REHEARSALS

How much rehearsal does a particular script need? Generally, an hour of rehearsal time is necessary to properly prepare for each minute of performance time in a show. I don't know who originally invented this formula, but it seems to work.

I have prepared a twenty-five to thirty-minute play in as little as twenty hours of rehearsal, but I have felt *very* pressured and desperately wished for more time. It is always better to overestimate the amount of rehearsal you will need because things will inevitably happen that put you behind schedule. Blocking often takes longer than expected. Cast members get sick and miss rehearsals. Sometimes actors don't memorize their lines on time. There's always a fly in the ointment to slow you down!

Work out your rehearsal schedule on paper. The cast will need to start with a Read Through of the play. The next task is to block the play. Then each scene needs to be worked through several times from moment to moment so the actors begin to understand what they are doing and develop an ease to their delivery of lines and actions. Once the play has been carefully rehearsed in small pieces, it is time to put it together and run through the whole play from beginning to end without stopping. This creates a sense of sequencing and flow. The last stage of the rehearsal process are Technical and Dress Rehearsals, which add the final ingredients of costumes, props, makeup, sound, sets, and lights to the acting.

Once you have a basic rehearsal schedule, go back and decide when the actors need to have their lines memorized for each scene. It is usually better to wait until after a scene has been blocked before requiring it to be memorized. Blocking makes the lines more concrete and physical. When an actor can visualize himself in space or actually walk through his actions, it is often easier for him to memorize the lines.

Don't require the entire play to be memorized on the same day. It is easier to memorize small chunks over a long period of time than one large chunk all at once. Spread out the memorization assignments over time. I usually require a scene to be memorized on the day we will be working through it moment to moment. Since we will be starting and stopping anyway, it is OK if the actors are struggling with line recall.

The sooner lines are memorized in the rehearsal process, the better. This gives the actors lots of time to practice remembering them, lots of time for forgetting and making mistakes. Do not under any circumstances let actors slip through the entire rehearsal process without getting off book!* Actors who wait until the last minute to memorize their lines will inevitably forget them the first time they get in front of an audience.

Give the actors a copy of the rehearsal schedule with each scene's line memorization deadline CLEARLY MARKED! If the actors are living at home, make sure parents get a copy of the schedule with a written request to assist their child in learning his lines. Parental support (or roommate/friend support in the case of young adults) on this issue will make all the difference

---

* Off book is the theatre term for having lines memorized. Once lines are memorized, the actor does not have to carry his script (or book) around with him. He is free to use his whole body to express his character.

in the world between success and failure. (See Chapter Eleven for more suggestions for line memorization.)

Be efficient in your use of rehearsal time. Call everybody in the cast on those days you are working on large group scenes.* If there are scenes which have just a few characters in them, schedule those scenes for separate rehearsals and call only the actors needed for those scenes. Actors who sit around at rehearsals with nothing to do will lose interest in the play or will get into trouble while your back is turned.

Think about ways to get the most work done in each rehearsal session. Keep your actors as busy as you can. If you have scenes which involve different groups of actors, assign your assistant director to rehearse one scene while you are working on another. If you don't have an assistant, ask a responsible cast member to work with one group of actors while you work with the other. If you are working on a musical, the musical director can work on songs or the choreographer can work on dances with one group while you work on dramatic scenes with another group. If one or two actors are not on stage for awhile, the assistant director or stage manager can take them aside and help them work on their lines.

As the date of the first performance nears, think of ways to build momentum. If you only rehearse once a week, scheduling two or more rehearsals a week during the last weeks will provide the actors with more frequent repetition and help generate excitement.

Keep the actors clearly focused on what they still need to do and how long they have to do it in. Try to do this in a calm, organized manner without creating a sense of impending doom or panic at the immense amount of work which you, as the director, know needs to be accomplished.

Even though rehearsing a show can become stressful, especially as opening night looms before you, it is crucial to keep the process fun and exciting. The director must build the cast's confidence and enthusiasm at the same time he is pushing them to give the best, most polished and professional performance they can possibly give.

---

* "Call" is a theatre term referring to the date and time an actor is required to be at rehearsal or at the theatre for a performance.

TYPES OF REHEARSALS

The first step in the rehearsal process is the **Read Through**. This is when everyone sits down together and reads through the play from beginning to end. Usually when this is done, the actors read their parts and the stage manager or director reads the stage directions out loud. If you have actors who have reading problems, pair them with actors who are good readers during the Read Through. The good readers can help the poor readers follow along in the script and can help them with the hard words when it is time to read their lines. If no one in the cast can read well, you might want to bring in a few volunteers to help read the script out loud for or with them.

Take time during the Read Through to stop and explain things that don't make sense or to act out physical actions that are only described in the stage directions. It is important that the actors visualize what is going on in the play so they can understand it.

It is important that the script is printed in a typeface that is easy to read. Copies of the script should be clear and clean. Bind the scripts in notebooks or paper folders so the pages don't get lost.

Attach a pencil on a string to the script so the actor has it on hand to write down blocking and notes in his script. This idea, invented by the ingenious mother of one of my Pegasus actors, saves a lot of time. When the actor needs a pencil, he doesn't need to go find one; it is there!

Make sure the actor's name, address, and phone number is on the script so if it is left at rehearsal or if it gets misplaced, it can be returned to its owner. An actor can't learn lines without a script!

Have the actors highlight all of their lines and stage directions in the script, so they know exactly what they do and say and can find all their parts easily.

I usually make an audio recording of the Read Through, edit out the stops and starts, and make copies for each member of the cast. Listening to a tape of the dialogue over and over makes memorization easier for many students. If the first Read Through has too many starts and stops, I schedule a second Read Through and make my cast recording from that. The time spent on the second Read Through is a worthwhile investment if it helps the actors with their line memorization.

If the play has a number of songs in it, I make each cast member a rehearsal tape which has the songs with words and music on one side and just

The first Read Through of a script is an exciting time. (Photo by Keith Jenkins)

the music on the other side. The actors can listen to the songs on Side One in order to learn the words and music and they can practice singing the songs at home between rehearsals using Side Two.

Blocking Rehearsals get the actors on their feet physicalizing the actions in the play. If you are not able to rehearse on the stage you will be performing on, it is important to block the show in a space at least as large as your stage will be. Tape out the edges and walls of the stage on the floor of your rehearsal space so the actors can see and experience the physical limits of the performing area and begin to develop a sense of the relationship of stage to audience. If there are curtains, walls, set pieces, or furniture which you don't have for rehearsals, tape them out on the floor, too. Try to rehearse in the same space each time so the actors don't become confused about the spatial relationships.

Blocking is the theatre term for the movements an actor makes during a play. Blocking includes moving from one part of the stage to another; specific body positions such as sitting, standing, or kneeling; specific hand, arm, or head gestures; actor focus (where an actor is looking); and use of props. During a blocking rehearsal, the director tells the actors where to move on stage and what to do at each moment in the play. As the director gives blocking, the actor should write it in his script next to the appropriate line of dialogue. Actors can suggest blocking, too, but it must be approved by the director.

All blocking should be noted in pencil in case it has to be changed later. Sometimes the director will ask an actor to try out a movement idea, only to find that it doesn't work. Then the blocking needs to be changed.

Blocking rehearsals usually feel long, boring, and frustrating to actors and directors alike. It takes an extra effort to pay attention, but it is important to do so. Most actors find it easier to memorize their lines if they know what their body is doing at the same time that the line is being said. They can imagine themselves in the stage space doing the action, reinforcing the lines with a visual image or they can actually do the actions as they learn the lines, reinforcing the lines with a kinesthetic experience.

It is helpful to stop blocking early enough in a rehearsal session to run through everything that was blocked that day at least once. From a Blocking Run Through the director can see if traffic patterns on stage flow easily or if any part of the action looks confusing. The actors can pinpoint what they forgot to write down or where they are confused.

When possible, block the play in chronological order from beginning to end. This will make more sense to the actors. Sometimes, for reasons of scheduling efficiency, it is necessary to jump from scene to scene. If you do this, try to jump from scene to scene in chronological order so there is some semblance of the play's order for the actors.

Once the play has been completely blocked, it is time to work through the play from moment to moment. **Work Through Rehearsals** are important for clarifying the dramatic action so each actor understands his character's motivations and reactions. Work Throughs mean starting and stopping the action. They mean making mistakes, talking through motivation, struggling with newly memorized lines, practicing lines and movements until they flow naturally, and making any necessary changes.

Usually a play that has been improvisationally developed by the group has been explored thoroughly in the development process before the script was written down. However, sometimes more character development is necessary. Additional acting exercises or improvisational games might be done as part of a Work Through Rehearsal.

At the end of each Work Through, save enough time to run through the scene that you have worked on that session at least once from beginning to end. Often things that don't make sense to an actor when looked at in isolation, will make sense when put together with what comes before and after.

Once you have worked through the entire play moment to moment, it is time to **Run Through** the play. In a Run Through the actors start at the beginning of the play and go all the way through to the end. Run Throughs develop pacing and sequencing in a play.

Normally, the first Run Through is done off book. First Run Throughs tend to be extremely long. The very first time through a Pegasus play (which ends up running about 30 minutes) can last anywhere from one to two hours, depending on how many things go wrong, how many different set changes must be choreographed, and how many actors don't know their lines. This time differential can be very disconcerting to the director.

It's difficult to know exactly how much time will be cut off the running time once the actors have found the correct pace and once all the scene transitions are moving smoothly. If the play seems to be horrendously long and there doesn't seem to be enough time left before opening night to properly rehearse all of it, you may need to start looking for places to make judicious cuts in the script.

First Run Throughs are notorious for being agonizingly painful experiences for the director to watch. Most of the work that the actors have done in the Moment to Moment Work Throughs goes out the window. Don't panic. Don't give up. Don't lose your temper. Don't tear off your clothes and go screaming out into the night. It *will* get better.

Take notes during the Run Through. Afterward have the cast come out and sit down with their scripts and pencils. Go through your notes with them in order from the beginning of the play to the end of the play.

Present your comments in an upbeat and encouraging manner, but point out honestly the areas which still need work. Use humor to make your points, but not sarcasm. Demonstrate blocking changes and other notes rather than just talk about them. Actually get up and work through sections that you want to change or correct with the actors.

Stress the work that needs to be done by each cast member. Be specific. "You've got to work harder" is not specific. "Speak loudly and clearly. Say each word. Memorize those lines in Scene 4" are specific comments. Present your notes in a manner that leads cast members to believe they can accomplish each task before them with a little more commitment and hard work.

It is just as important to tell your actors specifically what they are doing well as it is to tell them what they are doing wrong. They need the encouragement. "Scene One was excellent! Everyone came in at just the right time. Everyone is talking at the right speed. Everyone is listening to each other and looking at whoever is speaking. Good job!"

In addition, knowing what is working, knowing what is up to an appropriate level of pacing and energy, provides your actors with concrete models to compare the good with the not-so-good sections. They know how the scene that is working well feels and they know how the scene that isn't working well feels. It is much easier to make a change when you know how that change will feel when you get it right.

It is helpful for actors to write down the director's comments which apply to them in their scripts so they can review them later. If actors cannot write down their own notes, you can type up your notes after rehearsal and give them out before the next rehearsal to be put into script folders.

After the first Run Through, decide if you need to revise your rehearsal schedule or continue with your original plan. You might need to go back and work through certain scenes or you might feel that more Run Throughs would help pull the show together. The last few rehearsals before the Dress Rehearsal should be Run Throughs.

Some directors like to give notes immediately after a Run Through so that whatever happened in that rehearsal is clearly on the minds of all. Other directors find that giving notes before the Run Through at the next rehearsal refreshes the actors' memories on what they need to work on as they run through the play this time.

One technique which works well is to ask each actor before a Run Through starts to think of one or two things they will concentrate on improving during that rehearsal. Allowing the actor to decide which of his notes to focus on helps him to think critically and objectively about his performance.

It also helps the actor to invest himself actively in the improvement of his performance.

Technical Rehearsals provide the technical crew (the light, sound, prop, costume, and set crews under the direction of the stage manager) with a chance to practice what they will be doing during the show. The show should be as together as possible *before* the Technical Rehearsal so the technical crew can get their sight and sound cues clearly from the actors. Patience is the order of the day. Actors should be prepared to stop and start and to run through certain moments of the show several times. Up until this point the actors have had four to ten weeks to get ready. The Technical Rehearsal is the technicians' only opportunity to rehearse.

Sometimes, if a show is very technically complicated, the Technical Rehearsal may be done as a **Cue-to-Cue Rehearsal.** This means the actors don't run through the entire show from beginning to end; they jump from one technical cue to the other. A Cue-to-Cue Rehearsal can be very confusing to a cast because the continuity that they have become accustomed to is suddenly gone. I advise against Cue-To-Cue Rehearsals with groups with special needs unless there is no other way to work out all the cues in the amount of time allotted for the Technical Rehearsal.

A good alternative to a Cue-To-Cue is a **Dry Tech,** which is a Technical Rehearsal that jumps from cue to cue with no actors, only technicians. One drawback to a Dry Tech is that if a number of cues are visual (based on actions done by the actors in the course of scenes) rather than verbal (based on lines spoken in the script), without the actual actors showing the technicians exactly what they do, the technicians will remain unsure exactly when to enact their cue. Another drawback with improvisational shows is that often the lines change from performance to performance. Technicians often need to rely on the sense of the scene rather than on literal lines written in their script.

More information on planning the design and technical aspects of a show follows the description of Dress Rehearsals.

Dress Rehearsals give the actors and technicians a chance to work with *all* the physical aspects of the show before getting in front of an audience for the first time. Try to run the play from beginning to end without stopping in order to simulate a real performance. If you are brave, invite a few friends or parents to preview the show in order to provide the actors with the experience of having someone out there watching their performance. (I am NOT brave so I rarely have invited Dress Rehearsals.)

In the theatre there are no guarantees. Don't believe the old saw about a bad Dress Rehearsal meaning a good Opening Night or vice versa. I've had good Dress Rehearsals which led to good Opening Nights and bad Dress Rehearsal which scared the cast so much they dug in and pulled together for a good Opening Night. I've also had bad Dress Rehearsals which led to bad, embarrassing, dreadful, painful, mortifying Opening Nights (none of them, thankfully, at the Bethesda Academy).

The only thing that inevitably makes a show come together is hard work and commitment from the very first day of the rehearsal process by everyone involved. The Theatre Elves will *not* show up at the eleventh hour to throw some fairy dust around and fix your show for you, so don't expect their arrival.

TECHNICAL ASPECTS OF A SHOW

Try to **keep your show as technically simple as possible**. Leave as much as you can up to the imagination of the audience. There is great beauty in simplicity. And great theatricality. Ultimately, great theatre happens in the hearts and minds of the audience, not in the trappings on the stage.

Superfluous set dressing, costume changes, and props will not enhance the play if the script and the acting are not good. The extra window dressing will only add more things for the actors to remember (or, as will be more likely the case, to forget).

Mechanical error goes hand in hand with human error. The fewer technical cues or scene changes in a show, the fewer opportunities there will be for technical disasters to occur.

It is crucial to get as many of the props and set pieces into the hands of the actors as soon as possible in the rehearsal process. All actors— but particularly beginning actors and actors who have cognitive disabilities—have difficulty imagining props and set pieces. They need to work with the real thing. If you can't get the item that will actually be used in the show, get a reasonable facsimile to use in rehearsal until the real one is bought or made.

Make props, costumes, and set pieces as sturdy and unbreakable as possible. Choose plastic or wooden props over glass or ceramic ones. One of the immutable laws of the theatre is that if there is a way for an actor to break something during a show, he will. For this reason, always think in terms of safety and worst-case scenario.

When you have quick costume changes in a show or actors who have limited mobility, arrange for costumes to be built with velcro fastenings rather than buttons, laces, or zippers. Avoid costumes that will get caught in actors' wheelchairs or other mechanical devices. Make sure long skirts are not so long that they will easily be tripped over by blind actors or that they will get in the way of actors using walkers, crutches, or canes.

If it is possible to have more than one Technical or Dress Rehearsal, do it. Bring the stage technicians in to see a Run Through before the Technical Rehearsal. If they can't come, videotape a Run Through for them. The more knowledgeable they are about your show, the more prepared they will be and the more support they can offer you and your cast.

Technicians might be other students with or without disabilities who have an interest in being part of the show, they might be teachers or other professionals working for your organization, or they might be parents or other volunteers who want to lend a hand. If they have never done this technical job before, provide them with a sheet which lists their responsibilities, rules for backstage conduct, directions for turning on and using technical equipment, what to do in case of emergency, and rehearsal and performance dates and times. If they will be running complicated equipment for the first time, such as a sound deck, lighting board, or followspot, arrange for a time when you, the stage manager, or the technical director can give them an orientation or training session.

Arrange for plenty of backstage help. It is better to have too many stagehands than too few. Stagehands should be given clear assignments during the running of the show. All assignments should be written out and posted on the walls backstage and/or given to the stage manager and stagehands to carry around with them on a clipboard.

Make sure there is a place where the actors can quietly sit when they are not onstage. Assign a stage manager or stagehand to keep an eye on the actors to make sure they don't wander off. Warn actors five minutes before it is time for them to go on, if possible, and then get them to their place of entrance ahead of time.

If actors need to make a costume change, take care of it in a timely fashion. Don't wait until the last minute. Invariably a zipper will get stuck or a hook will get caught and delay the entrance.

Some actors may need a little reminder by the stage manager or a backstage assistant to send them out on stage at the appropriate moment. They might hesitate because of nerves or get so involved in watching what is going on out on the stage that they forget it is their turn to enter.

Don't ask an actor to try anything new at the last minute—especially anything unusual as far as sets, costumes, and props go. Every actor needs time to rehearse and adjust to changes in a show. It is better to wait and work the change in before the next performance than to throw an actor's performance off by changing an entrance or adding an unexpected responsibility.

THE FIRST PERFORMANCE

Opening night is a time of great anxiety and excitement. How the director handles the cast prior to the opening curtain can determine how successful the cast's performance is.

Stay calm and focused. Actors will mirror the director's mood because the director is the leader. This means the person or persons in charge must be very aware of their verbal and non-verbal emotional messages. If the director gets harried or upset or nervous, the actors will assume that they are supposed to feel the same way and mass hysteria will result. If something goes wrong, minimize the size of the problem to the cast. Calmly and efficiently invent a quick and easy solution. After all, the show must go on.

Opening night nerves—stage fright—is a common problem for actors. I know professional actors who have worked in theatre for thirty years who still get so scared before an opening night performance that they throw up. Sir Laurence Olivier, one of the greatest actors who ever lived, went through a period of stage fright in the middle of his career. While he was playing Shylock in Shakespeare's *The Merchant of Venice* he could barely force himself to go out on stage each night. He was so frightened that he couldn't look any of the other actors on stage in the eyes. Some nights he just focused on the floor.

Stage fright can be dealt with if actors understand what causes it. Whenever a person feels stressed, his adrenal glands, which are located on top of his kidneys, secrete a hormone called adrenalin. Adrenalin is used by the body to create extra energy for two completely different purposes. It can be used for attacking a problem or for running away from it—the proverbial fight or flight mechanism that living organisms have instinctively built into them.

Facing a performance in front of a large audience of family, friends, and strangers is a very stressful situation, so great amounts of adrenalin are released into the blood stream, creating all those strange feelings of panic, those butterflies in the stomach. If an actor allows his flight pattern to kick in, he will forget his lines and freeze up on stage. If he concentrates and channels his energy, he can tap into his fight response and use it to enhance his performance.

The key to channeling adrenalin-based energy is getting enough oxygen. Often when a person feels nervous, he begins to breathe very shallowly. This cuts down on the normal supply of oxygen to the body. When this happens, the muscles in the body tense up because the toxins created by the stress are not being cleaned away by the oxygen in the blood. As less oxygen gets to the brain, thinking becomes confused.

To stay calm and use his energy wisely, an actor needs to continue to breathe slowly and deeply. With his oxygen supply restored, his muscles will relax and he will start thinking clearly. His energy will become focused, his body will become centered and relaxed, his emotions will feel balanced, and his mind will become alert. He then has at his disposal all of his most powerful inner resources. Mind, body, and emotions will be connected together and ready to do his bidding.

I explain as much of this process as a group is able to understand. Since one of the symptoms of stage fright is the inability to focus on what is going on around you, I usually go over the information about it with the cast at Dress Rehearsal *before* they start feeling nervous. Then I go over the information again on opening night in my pre-show speech.

An explanation might be as simple as: If you feel nervous or scared during the show, just take a few slow breaths and let yourself relax. Then you won't feel as scared anymore. Try not to think about being scared. Try to think about what you are doing.

When suggesting to actors that they breathe, caution them against breathing too quickly. If they hyperventilate, they will pass out.

Often a short physical and vocal warm-up consisting of easy stretching, swinging, bouncing, and breathing will relax actors' muscles and calm them down before the show.

If the actors aren't wearing a lot of complicated makeup, call them to arrive at the theatre about thirty minutes before curtain time. This is usually enough time to get everyone ready to go on. Nervous actors waiting around backstage with nothing constructive to focus on will only become more nervous.

About five or ten minutes before curtain time, call all the actors together. This is the time for everyone to collect themselves and make last-minute attitude preparations for the performance. You might choose to run a short warm-up with the cast or give them a motivational speech. Different directors have different rituals which they like to perform with their casts before the opening night of a show.

I try to boil my notes down to three things I want everyone to remember while they are performing. One year I told them to "speak loudly, clearly, and slowly. Don't think about how nervous you are, think about how much fun you are having." Another year I told them to remember the 3 L's:

Listen [to the other actors]
Look [at whoever is talking]
Loud [how to speak]

I remind them to relax and keep breathing. Most importantly, I try to build up their confidence by telling them what a great job they are doing. Actors need to feel that their director thinks the world of them.

Then we follow the Academy's pre-show tradition: we all hold hands and pass a hand squeeze around the circle. Once the squeeze had made it all the way around, we all say in unison, "One for all and all for one! Have a good show!"

EXPECTATIONS

In my theatre training, the highest compliment that could be paid to a student actor was that he or she performed as a professional or at a professional level. I hold my actors to the same standard. I insist that they approach the rehearsal process and performance experience with as professional an attitude as possible. But I insist that they have fun at the same time.

The amazing thing about audiences is that they can tell if the actors are miserable or if they are having a good time. They can tell if the experience has been a positive or negative one. An audience's enjoyment of a performance is ultimately tied to their perception of the actors' enjoyment and engagement with the work.

If the performance is not perfect, that is OK. There is no such thing as a perfect performance. Mistakes happen even in professional theatre situations. What is important are the goals you set for yourself and how you handle yourself as you go about striving for those goals. The distance that is traveled from the beginning of the process to the end of it is what determines the success or failure of a project, not the final product.

One summer when I was working at a summer arts camp, I had a student in my musical comedy class who was so shy and quiet I could barely hear her speak when I was standing next to her. I didn't know her background, so I don't know what caused her lack of self-confidence, but she was so afraid to express herself that in conversation she spoke in a monotone. She rarely gestured or showed any kind of emotion. That session I had the good fortune to be working with an incredible team of co-teachers who really knew how to encourage and train young students in acting, music, and dance. By the time we presented our original musical revue at the end of the session, she had developed enough self-confidence and stage presence that I could hear every single word she said clearly from my seat in the back of the house. She danced, she sang, she had expression in her voice. I was so proud of her for facing her fears and working so hard!

After the performance another counselor who had no connection with the project made a remark to me about how mediocre this camper's performance had been. He was judging her solely on her final product. He didn't know the progress she had made and how incredibly far she had come in four short weeks. But the girl knew how far she had come; so did the other cast members; so did the other staff members involved with the show.

As a result of her experience, this young woman became less timid. Her self-confidence grew. Most important of all, she learned how to take a risk. In truth, she probably learned more and grew more as a performer than anybody else in the cast. Out of all of the students I taught that summer, out of all the performances I coached, *she* is the one I consider my biggest success story for the summer season.

In looking at the success or failure of a performance, your evaluation cannot be of the final product, but of the journey that was taken to get there. What skills were learned along the way? What personal insights were achieved? How many friendships were formed? How much fun did you all have together? These are the signposts of success.

So go out and do your best, and have a great time doing it!

chapter ten

using drama as a teaching tool in the classroom

LEARNING STYLES

Each person has an individual learning style, a unique way of taking in and understanding the world. Learning style depends on sensory learning channel preference, strengths and weaknesses in various areas of intelligence, motivation to learn, emotional orientation toward the specific learning environment (i.e. the teacher, the school, the classroom), and the presence or absence of a cognitive disability, as well as various other health, social, and emotional issues.

A teacher who understands the basic learning style of each of her students will be more successful in communicating with and teaching all of her students. A teacher who understands her own basic learning style knows her personal bias for presenting information to others and can compensate for her natural proclivities by presenting material in other ways in order to be more accessible to students who have different learning styles from her own.

Our current educational system is structured to present most information in a manner which favors individuals who have an auditory learning channel preference. Lectures followed by book assignments or worksheets are the primary teaching strategies used in most classrooms. John Goodlad, the former dean of the School of Education at the University of California, Los Angeles, observed 1,000 classrooms across the United States and interviewed over 27,000 teachers, students, and parents about their experiences in our education system. His 1984 report, "A Study in Schooling," reveals that nearly 70 percent of a typical day in school is devoted to the teacher lecturing or giving directions to the students, while less than one percent of the time is spent in student-centered discussions or opinion sharing. Only seven percent of curricular time each week is devoted to art, two percent to dance, and one percent to drama.

The classroom environment tends to be static, stationary, and regimented. Each student is assigned a chair at a desk in an orderly row for the majority of the school day. That small rectangular work space must suffice for all learning activities that are done during the day. This arrangement can create order and structure for students, helping to organize and focus them, providing enough physical and mental discipline to free them to grapple with the material in the curriculum. But for some students, who need to move and use their bodies in order to learn, this type of classroom structure can be stifling.

Many students—whether they have a cognitive disability or not—will not do well in our current educational system because they do not process information best in the style in which it is presented. Teachers can reach more students if they open up their teaching approach by allowing their academic charges to learn through the students' own unique learning styles and intellectual strengths.

At first glance, this sounds very complex, mysterious, and difficult. Teachers feel intimidated and say that it is hard enough to cover all the material they are required to cover now. To provide a number of additional approaches individualized to students or to add any additional areas for study to the curriculum seems as if it would be an overwhelming burden, an impossible task.

The truth is, however, the more learning channels and intelligences (or abilities) that are addressed in the learning process, the more *all* students will learn and the more they will retain. Curriculum material that is retained does not have to be repeated year after year after year. Students can go on to new and more advanced areas of study and can apply previously acquired knowledge to them.

In practice, teaching to students' learning styles is exciting, challenging, and fun. This approach brings out the creativity and the joy of learning in teacher and student alike. Suddenly, students' educational needs are being addressed. They start to look forward to coming to school. Instead of sitting sullenly and passively, they *want* to participate in their education. They *want* to learn more. They begin to actively seek out knowledge and teach themselves.

This chapter offers a number of suggestions for using drama and the other arts as tools to enhance teaching in regular and special education classrooms. Before focusing on specific exercises or looking at different curriculum areas, it would be helpful to take a closer look at sensory learning channel preferences and Howard Gardner's Theory of Multiple Intelligences. A teacher who can incorporate these two philosophies with the arts when looking at, thinking about, and experiencing their students' learning styles has an eye-opening and unbeatable combination on her side.

SENSORY LEARNING CHANNEL PREFERENCE

We experience the world around us—and, therefore, we learn—first and foremost through our senses.

Since the senses are the only avenues by which any information gets from the outside world into the body and brain, the senses are the primary tools each student has for making contact with the curriculum and for communicating her understanding of it. To fully exploit and enhance the senses for learning purposes, every teacher must understand how these learning tools work.

THE SENSES

There is some discussion among experts about how many senses the human body actually has. The senses that are most obvious are known as "The Five Senses": vision, hearing, smell, taste, and touch. The Five Senses carry information from outside the body to the brain. However, there are a number of "Deep Senses" which make it possible for the human body to evaluate its experience from inside. These include balance, proprioception, deep pressure, hunger, thirst, and sensations of internal pain, internal cold, and internal heat. Each sense—interior or exterior—carries a different kind of information through the nervous system to the brain for interpretation, evaluation, and, usually, some type of appropriate action.

Vision or sight provides information on color, line, shape, depth, movement, and distance of objects from the self in the outside environment. The eye is the organ of sight. Light enters the pupil of the eye and strikes photoreceptor cells (called rods and cones because of their shapes) located on the retina at the back of the eyeball. These cells convert the light into electrical impulses, which are carried by the optic nerve to the visual cortex located in the rear of the brain. There in the brain the impulses are translated into information which we recognize as visual.

Humans consciously rely on their sense of sight more than any other sense. The human eye does provide more information, especially in regard to color and depth perception, than do most animal eyes. This is because humans are the only organisms to have cones which are sensitive to the color wavelengths in light and because the shape of our heads and the placement of the eyes on the face makes stereoptical sight (using both eyes to see the same object at once) possible. The importance of vision to the human being is also indicated by the fact that ten percent of the brain is devoted to the visual cortex, a larger percentage of brain area than that given over to any other sense.

Hearing processes sound waves or vibrations that are in the air, providing information about its presence or absence (sound or silence), tone (sometimes called timbre), volume, pitch, harmony or dissonance, rhythm, distance, and direction of its source.

The ear is one of the most complex sense organs. The outer ear or auricle gathers sound waves and channels them into the ear canal and, ultimately, to the ear drum. Sound waves thus gathered are magnified by the middle ear, which consists of three small bones called the hammer, anvil, and stirrup, respectively. The ear drum vibrates and these vibrations are enlarged and passed on in turn by these small bones, which in turn pass them on to the inner ear or cochlea. The cochlea looks like a snail shell and is filled with fluid. The enhanced vibrations create waves in the cochlea which then vibrate the basilar membrane and the hair cells attached to it. This sets off nerve impulses which are sent by the auditory nerve to the auditory cortex in the center of the brain. These impulses are translated into information which we say we "hear."

The ear itself does not differentiate among all the sound waves coming into it. It just collects and passes along all the vibrations in the vicinity. It is the job of the auditory cortex to sort through all the incoming stimuli and decide which information to pay attention to and which to ignore. At any given moment there may be ten different sounds going on in your area, but you may be aware of only one or two at a time. What you are aware of hearing is called foreground noise. The rest, sounds that your attention chooses to place in the background, are temporarily ignored or blocked from consciousness. With a quick refocusing of attention, however, these background sounds can be brought to awareness.

Smell provides information about chemical substances in the air. Tiny molecules of a substance floating in the air are breathed into the nose and passed over the olfactory bulbs, each about one square inch in size, located on the roof of the nasal passages. Millions of tiny smell receptors there interact with the molecules. Almost in the same way a key fits into only one specific lock, molecules of a specific shape will fit into certain olfactory receptors. When this happens, nerve impulses are sent through the limbic system to the olfactory cortex, where the information is processed and recognized as different odors.

The human brain is capable of detecting as many as 10,000 different odors. This sounds like a lot—and it is—but it does not come close to the number of odors most other mammals and insects are capable of identifying.

Smell is used in detecting approaching danger. The first indication of a fire is usually not the sight of flames or the sound of a fire alarm going off, but the smell of smoke. Animals use smell to mark their territory to other animals and for attracting mates. Humans do this, too, evidenced by the millions of dollars spent each year on perfumes, potpourri, sachet, deodorant, and other scented products which change or enhance the odors on bodies and in rooms.

The most interesting aspect of smell in relation to education is its emotional aspect. Perhaps because the olfactory nerve is relayed through the limbic system—the area of the brain that is involved with processing and storing many of our memories and emotions—smells are deeply laden with emotions and associated with past experiences. Particular smells will bring up strong visual, aural, emotional, and kinesthetic memories of moments in the past. The recall experience is often so vivid that for a few seconds, the smeller actually feels as if she is back in that time and place.

The potential for tapping smell as a tool for learning, particularly for memory recall, has been recognized, but never fully exploited by educators. In a series of experiments, children had better recall when a word list was paired with olfactory cues than when it was memorized without any cues.

The idea of teaching through the sense of smell by pairing odors with information to be remembered could offer interesting enhancements for students in general and alternatives for students whose ability to pair information with visual images or auditory stimuli are weak.

Researchers at Yale University Psychophysiology Center are studying the intermittent use of certain pleasant, invigorating smells to heighten alertness, wake up the metabolism, reduce stress, and enhance positive attitudes. University of Cincinnati experiments have shown that certain fragrances injected into the atmosphere at intervals can increase productivity and efficiency in the work place.

Taste provides information about chemical substances (mostly those in food and drink) which come in contact with the taste buds on the tongue. Each taste bud has about fifty receptor cells. These cells send a different chemical transmitter via the taste nerve to the gustatory cortex in the brain, which detects whether a substance is sweet, bitter, salty, or sour.

Taste and smell are closely linked. The subtle and distinctive flavors of different foods are created when the brain combines the messages that it receives from the olfactory nerves, the taste nerves, and other temperature and pressure receptors that are in the mouth. In fact, the whole sensory experience of eating depends on the interaction of all the senses. Food seems to taste better if it looks good. Auditory experience can enhance dining pleasure. This is why many restaurants pipe in soothing music. Part of the delight of crispy foods is their crunch and texture, just as part of the soothing quality of creamy foods is their silence and smoothness.

Touch provides information about surface texture and temperature of objects which come in contact with the skin, as well as alerting the organism to external pain (indicative of a dangerous situation like a hot stove or a sharp knife). There is some argument from sensory scientists as to whether each type of sensor in the skin should be considered a separate sense (pain, hot, cold, pressure) or if they all should be lumped together in the same system. In any case, various nerve endings just below the surface of the skin pick up stimuli which are sent via electrical and chemical impulses through the nerves, through the spinal cord, through the thalamus, to the somatosensory cortex in the brain, where the information is deciphered and interpreted. Certain areas of the human body are more sensitive than others because they have more sensory nerve endings per square inch. Examples of high density areas of skin are the fingertips, the feet, the lips, and other features of the face.

The sense of **balance** comes from the vestibular system, which is located in the inner ears. Three loops, the semicircular canals, provide the brain with information about the exact position of the head in relation to the rest of the body and the direction in which it is moving. Crystals in the fluid inside the canals respond to gravity, creating nerve impulses which travel along the vestibular nerve to communicate the position of the head in relation to the ground. Tiny hairs attached to the sides of the canals respond to the movement of the fluid. Whenever the hairs bend, impulses are sent along the vestibular nerve fibers to the brain to indicate which direction is up and where the head is in relation to the rest of the body.

Proprioception provides the brain with its understanding of the body's position in space. The muscles, tendons, and joints have kinesthetic receptors which pass on movement commands from the brain and communicate back about current body positions. Proprioception is the sense that lets you know you are sitting up or lying down or standing even if your eyes are closed and you can't see your body position.

Most people are only aware of proprioception when they are in the process of learning a new physical skill, such as riding a bike, driving a car with standard transmission, or typing. Once the movements of the muscles, bones, and joints become familiar, awareness of proprioception goes away and the activity can be performed with a minimum of conscious concentration.

Without proprioception, a person would have no inner connection or control. In fact, individuals who have lost their sense of proprioception say they feel disembodied.* Although they are not paralyzed and can move, they feel no connection with their muscles and are, indeed, missing the necessary interior feedback to unconsciously manipulate various body parts. It takes a great deal of conscious effort and the utilization of their senses of sight and sound to substitute for the missing information contributed to the brain by their proprioceptors.

---

* Oliver Sacks reports on several individuals who lost their sense of proprioception in his book *The Man Who Mistook His Wife for a Hat.*

Deep pressure, internal sensitivities to heat and cold, hunger, thirst, and internal pain (like headaches, toothaches, stomach aches, cramps, etc.) are sometimes considered part of proprioception and sometimes considered to be senses on their own. In any case, all respond to stimuli from the inside of the body rather than from outside of it. Because they are located deep within the body, they are harder to study than the eyes, ears, nose, or tongue. For the most part, they are senses of which most people remain unconscious and unaware.

SENSORY LEARNING CHANNEL PREFERENCE

Typically, humans focus on vision, hearing, tactile, and proprioceptive senses as major learning channels and use smell and taste as very minor channels. Each person—disabled or not—relies primarily on one or two sensory learning channels.

Auditory Learners. A person who understands best through hearing information is an Auditory Learner. The current academic system in the United States is geared toward Auditory Learners. If you give verbal directions to an Auditory Learner, she will be able to follow them easily. If you lecture to an Auditory Learner, she will be able to sit still and listen for long stretches of time and will probably remember most of the information without needing to take a lot of notes. Auditory Learners also tend to express themselves most fluently and easily through spoken language. They have good auditory recall and tend to imagine conversations or sounds rather than images. Auditory Learners usually join the debate team and love to answer questions in class. They will be the first to volunteer for panel discussions and oral presentations because that puts them in the medium they feel most comfortable with—the spoken word.

Visual Learners. A person who understands best through seeing and visualizing information is said to be a Visual Learner. A Visual Learner tends to understand information better if it is presented through a visual form, either through pictures, diagrams, charts, or printed words. Visual Learners also tend to express themselves better through visual media rather than through the spoken word. They would rather draw or diagram or write out their contributions than speak them. Their imaginations are primarily visual and they use words with an emphasis on the images they create rather than on the logic or sound of the words.

I am a Visual Learner. I have discovered that focusing on visual activity is the only way I can capture the invisible words of a speaker. Whenever I am at a lecture or a meeting, I can follow what is going on only by taking constant notes (thereby making the auditory stimuli visual) or by doodling. For me and many other doodlers, doodling is a way of paying attention to what is being said, not blocking it out. If I stop doodling, then I can't pay attention—I begin to daydream.

Haptic or Kinesthetic Learners. A person who understands best by using proprioception, touch, taste, smell, or some combination thereof, is said to be a Haptic or Kinesthetic Learner. Haptic Learners must funnel the learning experience directly through their muscles or tactile senses in order to understand information.

Haptic Learners excel on the playing fields, but can't pass their history tests. They design and sew beautiful clothes in home economics or create exquisite furniture in woodshop, but are lost in math class. They succeed in the subjects where the information is experienced primarily through the body, through physically doing something: manipulating with their hands, touching, tasting, smelling. They are capable of abstract thinking, but not through auditory or visual learning channels. They need to learn through physical, concrete means.

Haptic Learners may be able to memorize lines by writing them out again and again, rather than by saying them out loud or looking at them. They may study for a test best while pacing or dancing or rocking in a rocking chair rather than while sitting at a desk. They may need to act out material in order to retain it where an Auditory Learner could listen to a tape or a Visual Learner could read a book. Many so-called learning disabled students are actually Haptic Learners in an educational system that refuses to teach them through their preferred learning channel.

Rarely is a person *only* an Auditory Learner or *only* a Visual Learner or *only* a Haptic Learner. Usually students are capable of learning through all of their sensory channels, but for a wide variety of reasons everyone tends to respond best through one or two. It could be that one sensory channel is highly sensitized or that another is partially blocked. A student who has a heightened sensitivity to color might become a Visual Learner. Another who has difficulty recognizing visual patterns might be able to hear or sense them through rhythm (Auditory Learner). One channel may appeal more to an individual because of emotional makeup. A student who feels she must test ideas out rather than take them on faith might, by temperament, be a Haptic Learner.

How do people discover what their sensory learning channel preference is? Learning channel preference tests ask a variety of questions which can help pinpoint learning style. Dawna Markova, a psychotherapist and learning specialist, has written a very interesting book on learning channels called *The Way of the Possible: A Compassionate Approach to Understanding the Way People Think, Learn, & Communicate*. Another good book on this subject is *Teaching for the Two-Side Mind: A Guide to Right Brain/Left Brain Education*, by Linda Verlee Williams.

The best way to discover your sensory learning channel preference is to become aware of how you respond to different types of information when it is presented. How do you best take in information, process it, and put it back out? Do you like to listen to lectures and tapes or do you prefer reading a book? Can you understand a concept better through looking at images or do you have to physically make something to really understand it? Some people have very clear visual imaginations. Others have vivid auditory imaginations, but no pictures in their heads. Still others feel an imaginary adventure in their bodies rather than visualize or hear it. Do you like to talk about ideas or would you rather write them down or draw them out or make a model of them?

How do you talk about understanding? A Visual Learner will tend to say things like "Oh, I *see* now," or "I *see* what you mean," or "I get the *picture*." An Auditory Learner might say, "I *hear* you." A Haptic Learner might say "This *feels* right" or "Let me *try* this on for size."

What are the situations in which information just goes over your head? Do you get lost during lectures? If you do, you are probably not an Auditory Learner. Do you get confused by maps and charts? If so, you are probably not a Visual Learner. If you are a complete klutz and hate performing experiments or building something with your own two hands, you are probably not a Haptic Learner.

When faced with a project that must be done how would you like to get your directions? From listening to another person who has done it before talk you through it? From a picture or diagram? From written directions?

From watching someone else do it first? From jumping in and figuring it out yourself?

What are your hobbies and recreational activities? When left to your own devices would you rather read, talk to friends, listen to music, write in a journal, draw pictures, listen to a storyteller, dance, play sports, build something in your workshop?

When you communicate with others do you prefer to talk, write, draw pictures, or act things out to illustrate your points?

I didn't realize that I was a Visual Learner until four years ago, when I took a learning channel preference quiz in a workshop. If I had known that I processed information best through visual means when I was a child, my life in school would have been a lot easier. I would have been able to pay attention in a different way. I felt humiliated quite a few times in elementary school when I didn't process the verbal instructions that were given for an assignment correctly. I can still remember my second grade teacher saying, "That's what you get for sleeping in class!" as she handed me back a paper with a big red zero on it. I was truly shocked! I had been listening carefully in the morning when she told us the directions, but obviously I missed some crucial auditory information.

By chance I developed a number of strategies which helped me succeed in secondary school and college. In sixth grade I learned how to take notes and write things down. I never got confused about the requirements for assignments after that. In high school where teachers started staying at the front of the classroom to lecture, I started doodling. Doodling felt right, so I kept taking notes and doodling all through college and graduate school.

Once you figure out your learning style, it is easier to pinpoint that of others. Again, listen to the way they talk about ideas and experiences. Find out how they spend their free time. Try a guided fantasy with them and listen to their descriptions of the experience. Do they report mostly visual details, sounds, smells, feelings, or actions? When you present material to students, be aware of the kinds of sensory information they pick up on easily and those they don't pick up on as quickly.

The safest and wisest teaching strategy is to present information to all students through as many different sensory learning channels as possible. Instead of relying only on lectures and reading assignments to communicate an idea or teach a skill, explain verbally how to do something *and* demonstrate it *and* show pictures or videos of it *and* have your students get up and pantomime it themselves *and* create experiments or projects for students to explore it through their bodies in as many different ways as possible. The more senses that become involved in the learning process, the more the information will make sense in a meaningful way. Additionally, because the information is coming in through a number of sensory channels, it is grasped in more than one way. There is repetition and rehearsal of information, but it is not received in a boring repetitive fashion. Each reinforcing encounter is perceived by the student as fresh and exciting.

The arts are the most comprehensive sensory teaching tool at any teacher's disposal. This is because the arts involve *all* the senses in a two-way process of communication. For example, a student who looks at Picasso's *Guernica* comes to understand the concept of war and man's inhumanity to man through the visual sense and, if she has a physical reaction to the graphic visual images in the painting, also through the kinesthetic senses. A student who uses the act of painting or drawing to create an expression of her own response to war uses her visual, kinesthetic, and proprioceptive responses to express her ideas and communicate them visually (and, hopefully, viscerally) to another person.

Not only do the arts involve the senses, they integrate them, making cross-sensory connections and really cementing the information into long-term memory through experience and rehearsal. Drawing, painting, and sculpting involve both the visual and haptic learning channels. Music creates auditory experiences through sound and haptic experiences through rhythm. Dance simultaneously engages the auditory and kinesthetic channels. Acting combines auditory, visual, and kinesthetic experience.

TEACHING TO ALL THE INTELLIGENCES

Howard Gardner, a psychologist on the faculty of Harvard University's Graduate School of Education, believes that there is not just one kind of human intelligence, as is generally accepted by popular culture and traditional academicians, but seven. Each type of intelligence relates to different forms of cognitive processing, many of which can be traced to specific areas in the brain.

Linguistic Intelligence deals with the ability to use language.

Logical-Mathematical Intelligence relates to the ability to reason logically, sequentially, and mathematically and to recognize patterns and order.

Musical Intelligence is expressed by a sensitivity to the elements of music (pitch, tone, melody, harmony, and rhythm) and the ability to create music.

A person who has **Bodily-Kinesthetic Intelligence** is able to use her body with skill and grace. Dancers, athletes, surgeons, potters, and carpenters need to have high bodily-kinesthetic intelligence.

Spatial Intelligence allows a person to perceive concepts of space and understand the relationship of objects in space to each other. Architects, sculptors, and surveyors use spatial intelligence to do their jobs.

Interpersonal Intelligence has to do with the ability to understand other people socially and to work well with them, while **Intrapersonal Intelligence** allows each individual to understand the interior emotional life of herself and others.

Gardner's M.I. (Multiple Intelligence) Theory is a more complex and inclusive way of looking at the way the human brain processes information. It acknowledges many more of the unique abilities, skills, and talents that human beings possess than the old traditional view which focuses only on verbal and mathematical abilities. According to Gardner, each individual possesses a combination of strengths and weakness in each of the seven intelligences. Rarely is an individual strong in only one area; it is more common to have a number of strong areas and a few weaker ones.

When taken as an educational philosophy, the M.I. theory offers opportunity for students to exercise and develop *all* the strengths and talents they possess in order to become truly well-rounded human beings. Many students who have failed in conventional educational institutions that stress achievement in only the Linguistic and Logical-Mathematical Intelligences, find that they *can* learn when their areas of intellectual strength are addressed and incorporated into the classroom. Not only can they learn, they can use their intellectual strengths to grasp concepts in areas in which they may be weaker. For example, mathematics is usually taught through abstract reasoning methods, but it can also be taught through word problems (Linguistic Intelligence), physical manipulation of objects (Spatial Intelligence and Bodily-Kinesthetic Intelligence), rhythm and song (a combination of Musical and Bodily-Kinesthetic Intelligences), and dance and games (interweaving Bodily-Kinesthetic and Interpersonal Intelligences).

A good book to read on the subject of learning styles and M.I. theory is Thomas Armstrong's *In Their Own Way: Discovering and Encouraging Your Child's Personal Learning Style*.

The Theory of Multiple Intelligences dovetails very nicely with the concept of sensory learning channels and can lead to assessing very specific personal learning styles for each and every student. A student's sensory learning channel preference is influenced by the area or areas of intelligence which are stronger for her. For example, a student with a strong Bodily-Kinesthetic Intelligence would probably be a Haptic Learner. Someone with strong Musical Intelligence might be an Auditory Learner. A student who excelled in Spatial Intelligence might favor a combination of haptic and visual learning channels.

Just as with the sensory learning channel approach, teaching to the multiple intelligences of students can be accomplished most strongly through the arts. Quite obviously, instruction in music and dance will enhance Musical Intelligence and classes in poetry and creative writing will develop Linguistic Intelligence. However, the arts are much more useful. Just as the arts integrate the senses, they integrate the intelligences.

A social studies project in which students learn about Native American cultures by learning Native American music, dances, and legends and then creating a presentation complete with authentically designed costumes, sets, and props will require the exercise of skills from each intelligence area in order to achieve the final product. The knowledge gained through the process will not be limited to isolated details which have been memorized about another culture. It will incorporate more complex knowledge as the students gain personal, hands-on experience with the social customs, belief systems, and values of the people being studied and come to understand the place of the individual within that society and how that particular social system fits into the greater scheme of the cultures that surround it. Additionally, the more students work together to create something, the more they learn how to interact appropriately with other people—how to compromise and find consensus, when to follow and when to lead, how to share ideas in a way that others can understand.

There is great strength in the accumulation and banding together of many small strengths. A bundle of sticks is harder to break than a single stick alone. Students' abilities to learn can be thought of in the same way. If many different intellectual strengths or abilities of a student are engaged in the learning process, the chances are that more learning and more retention will occur.

USING THE ARTS TO ENHANCE LEARNING

The idea of approaching the curriculum through the arts, through the senses, or through the Theory of Multiple Intelligences can be an intimidating prospect at first. It sounds like lesson planning will take a lot more energy and hours more preparation time. At first this may be true. It *will* take more time to think of interactive, sensory approaches to curriculum material if you've never done it before. However, as with any unaccustomed approach to problem-solving, the more you practice, the easier generating exciting ideas becomes. After a while creating lesson plans which teach through the senses and involve the arts will start to feel natural. In any case, the investment of time in planning and preparing for interactive arts-related projects in the classroom pays off in enhanced learning and motivation to learn on the parts of the students.

The first step is to evaluate the problem that needs to be solved; in this case, begin by taking a look at each area of your curriculum. Some subjects and some materials naturally lend themselves to drama, music, or art. Literature, science, and social studies are easy subjects to open up to students through the arts. Try projects with them first. When you experience success in these areas, you will feel as if you are on firmer ground. Then as you begin to feel more confident, branch out into teaching math, spelling, penmanship, and other more abstract subjects through the arts.

LANGUAGE ARTS

STORYTELLING: THE TEACHER AS STORYTELLER

Storytelling is a dynamic way to involve students in any subject. Instead of talking *about* a story that your class is going to read in reading class, introduce it to them by *telling* it to them. Instead of lecturing *about* science or math or history, *tell* a story about how Alexander Fleming discovered penicillin, how Pythagoras developed his ideas about plane geometry, or how Davy Crockett tamed the wild frontier.

Storytelling is a very different approach to sharing information aurally than lecturing about it. Storytelling makes information personal. It engages the listener on an imaginative level, creating images and feelings in the hearts and minds of the listeners. Children will attend to a story in a different way than they attend to directions or the enumeration of dry facts because they are engaged in the material on a deeper level. A good storyteller appeals to all the senses of her audience, creating visual, aural, olfactory, taste, tactile, kinesthetic, and emotional images in her listeners. Once these images are associated with the information being taught, the factual details can be recalled with the recall of the image.

A different energy is involved in storytelling. A personal, direct, intimate connection is made between the storyteller and the listener that is not present when a lecturer is talking at an audience. The listener feels personally included and willingly gives attention to the teller of the tale.

As part of a unit on self-esteem and getting along with others that I was teaching to a group of special education students at the upper elementary level, I decided to tell the story of "The Little Fir Tree." In this story a Fir Tree is very dissatisfied with how she looks. She hates her green needles and wishes for green leaves so she can look like the other trees in the forest. The West Wind blows by and gives the tree her wish, but the goats in the meadow eat the Little Fir Tree's new green leaves. Then the Little Tree wishes for golden leaves, so she will look pretty and no one will want to eat her leaves. But when the West Wind provides her with gold leaves, thieves come into the meadow and steal them. Then the Fir Tree wishes for glass leaves which will look pretty, but not be edible or valuable to anyone but herself. The West Wind provides her with beautiful leaves of glass, but the North Wind blows roughly through the meadow and breaks them to pieces. Finally, the Fir Tree decides that she wants her needles back and realizes that she can be happy and satisfied with herself just the way she is.

Some of the students in the class had moderate to severe learning disabilities; others had mental retardation. Their classroom teacher warned me that they might not be able to sit still long enough to listen to a story. But the moment I started telling the story, the room became so quiet, you could have heard a pin drop. All eyes were on me from the moment I said, "Once there was a Little Fir Tree and she lived all alone in the middle of a meadow . . ." until 15 or 20 minutes later when I finished with "and she is still standing in the meadow and still very happy being a fir tree with green needles." Then we acted out the story several times with different students playing different roles.

Their teacher was astounded at how long and completely they had concentrated on the story. At the time, I was amazed, too. But since then I have realized that the success of the session was not due solely to my storytelling abilities or to the students' joy at being freed from their regular classroom routine; it was due to the ancient contract that has been wordlessly struck between every storyteller and every story listener since prehistoric times. The process of telling and listening to a story moves all parties into the transitional space between the real and the imaginary where everything is possible, where everything has a high, emotional, relational charge. This is the place where meaning is made.

Johnny Moses, a Native American storyteller, says that in the language of his people there is no word for "myth" or "legend." The word Native Americans use for the tales they tell their children translates into English as "the teachings." Story was the original medium of the teacher—the method primitive societies developed to pass important information on from one generation to the next. The information can be remembered because it is woven into the fabric of a narrative which has personal emotional and sensory connections inside the individual. Recalling the narrative retrieves all the information embedded in it.

By neglecting this ancient and primary teaching tool, modern educators are missing out on the strongest, most powerful tool they have in their arsenal. See Chapter Six for a description of how to tell stories.

STORYTELLING: THE STUDENT AS STORYTELLER

Storytelling can also be used to motivate the development of language and oral communication skills in students. Start off by providing students with simple scenarios to tell to their classmates. Base the scenarios on simple familiar fairy tales or fables or make up simple scenarios of your own. Make sure the characters and the actions in the story are clear and sequenced in an orderly, logical progression so they make sense to the teller.

Another good way to start with storytelling is by telling a joke. Jokes are really very short, humorous stories. To avoid off-color jokes or jokes which are too sophisticated for students' age level and understanding, look for ideas in a book of children's jokes (available in most libraries and book stores).

Let each student get up and tell her tale or her joke.

Talk about the ingredients which make stories interesting: exciting details which create pictures in the listeners' minds, interesting dialogue that fits the characters, speaking in the characters' voices and acting out their actions, pacing, building suspense, making eye contact with the audience, caring about communicating your message to your listeners.

Let students practice their jokes or simple stories and share them again. Are the stories more interesting? Do they create stronger pictures in the listeners' minds? Are the storytellers more expressive? Do they feel more comfortable in front of their audiences? Do they feel a connection between themselves and their listeners?

When your student storytellers begin to feel confident, let them move on to more complex stories. Try taking an incident that happened in their own lives and turning it into a tale. Practice telling the story several times, each time improving it. When students get good enough, they could share their stories with another class or with parents at a Back to School Night.

ACTING GAMES TO IMPROVE VERBAL SKILLS

There are many acting games which can help students improve their ability to give directions or express their ideas clearly with words.

"Clues" is a game that can be used to motivate verbal communication skills in group sessions. One child goes out of the room and everyone remaining agrees on where in the room to hide an object. Then they think of a number of clues to describe where the object is. The student returns to the room and is told the first clue. If she can't figure out where the object is, she is told the second clue, then the third, etc. until the object is found.

A teddy bear might be hidden in the supply closet. Three clues might be:

1. It's dark in here!
2. I'm sitting on a shelf.
3. You must open a door to find me.

"Assemble a Design" is a game of verbal description played with two partners. Cut out various shapes from colored paper. Make duplicates of each colored shape so there are at least two sets of each. On one piece of paper glue an arrangement of shapes. Give this design to one partner. She will be the describer. Give the other partner loose duplicate shapes, a blank piece of paper, and tape or glue. She will be the arranger. The describer tells the arranger how to arrange the shapes on paper so they are identical with her glued down arrangement. The describer is not allowed to point or show the design to the arranger. She must use words.

"Airport" and **"Group Storytelling,"** which are described in Chapter Seven, are also good games to teach verbal description skills to students.

Improvisation with Puppets. Children who have difficulty using language or initiating communication with other people will sometimes willingly talk to or for a puppet. If the child has a tendency to be overwhelmed with aural or visual stimuli, the puppet can serve as a distancing device or intermediary object which may be less threatening and less stimulating than relating to a live human being. The child may also be able to project her emotions and words onto the puppet because it is inanimate and makes no demands upon her.

This past year a young man with cognitive disabilities who functions on a very high verbal and social level joined Icarus, my adult performing company. He quickly proved himself to be a highly creative, sensitive, hardworking, and delightful addition to the group. I was astounded several months later when his mother informed me that until he was ten years old, he was echolalic.* He could not initiate conversations with anyone; he could only repeat what they had just said. Then one day he saw a marionette in a store and started to talk to it. His mother realized that something magical was happening and bought him a number of marionettes and puppets to converse with. Through these inanimate theatrical beings he learned how to speak and relate to live human beings.

Use improvisational sessions with puppets to teach basic communication skills and appropriate ways to respond in different social situations,

---

*   Echolalia is the automatic, usually meaningless, repetition of the words one hears someone else say. Echolalia shows up in some individuals who have mental retardation or autism.

such as how to introduce strangers, how to introduce yourself, when to say please and thank you, or how to ask for help. Practice conversation and language skills by having children talk to a puppet operated by the teacher or by pairing children who each have a puppet to role-play a situation for the class.

Make or buy puppets which can "teach" specific skills or information. For instance, a doctor puppet can teach children about health and hygiene issues, a fireman puppet can teach fire safety or fire drill rules, a dentist puppet can teach oral hygiene, a dog puppet can teach how to take care of pets, a fish puppet can teach about the creatures that live in the ocean. After the puppet (with teacher as puppeteer) presents the information, the students can rehearse it by becoming puppeteers and presenting the information themselves (or by answering questions which the teacher or other students ask the puppet about the material covered in the lesson).

Students can use these puppets to create improvised puppet shows for each other on the material that has been presented. For example, a student puppet could go to the dentist puppet for a check up and the dentist could examine her teeth and tell her what she should do to take care of her teeth. Depending on the abilities of the students, the teacher can either set up the scenario of the puppet play for the students or allow the students to create it from the information they learned in class.

Puppets can often elicit information from children about how they are feeling or why a behavior problem exists when other methods fail. The distancing function of the puppet comes into play, allowing the child to examine his feelings and motives in a way she might not be able to when confronted directly by an authority figure.

ACTING GAMES TO IMPROVE VERBAL EXPRESSIVENESS

Students who are having trouble reading out loud with expression can practice vocal expressiveness through tone of voice games. Take a few innocent sentences:

I am going to the store.
Red is my favorite color.
John is going to be a fireman.

Have each student say the sentence with a different emotional meaning. Try each sentence with anger, sorrow, joy, excitement, confusion, unhappiness. Then have students try each sentence as a statement, a question, and a command. Try to read each sentence as a different character might: as a cowboy, as Dracula, as a robot, as a ghost, as a farmer, as an old man, as a baby, as a teenager, as a mother, as a father, as a minister.

If your students have difficulty reading simple sentences, tone of voice and emotional expressiveness can be taught through sounds. Ask your students to roar like a lion who is happy, sad, hungry, sleepy, angry, embarrassed, sloppy, etc. Repeat the exercise with the sounds made by other animals (ribbet like a frog, moo like a cow, meow like a cat). Allow students to add their bodies to express the emotions their voice is creating. The body and the voice are intimately connected and often if the body can't move, the voice becomes "disembodied" and expressionless.

Open Scenes. Open scenes are short dialogues which can be interpreted in a variety of ways. They are used in acting classes to teach subtext and can be useful and fun for practicing vocal expressiveness.

Here is one open scene:

A: Give me the ball.
B: No, I want it.
A: Give it to me.
B: No, I won't.
A: Yes.
B: No.
A: Yes.
B: No.
A: Yes.

Assign each student a specific character role with an emotional outlook on the situation. Character A could be a bully and Character B could be intimidated by the bully. Character A could be a bully and Character B could refuse to be intimidated. Character A could be a parent wanting the child (Character B) to come in and go to bed. Characters A and B could be three-year-olds who don't know how to play together yet.

You can write your own short dialogues appropriate to your students' interests and reading abilities. After reading through them, let students get up and act them out. You might be surprised at the natural acting abilities you uncover through this game.

Whole scenes can be created through the use of two simple words, such as "yes and no" or "red and blue." Give each student a specific objective. Maybe Student A (using the word "Yes") wants to go to the store and Student B (using the word "No") doesn't want to let her go. Maybe Student A (again using "Yes") wants Student B to go to the store *with* her and Student B (using the word "No") doesn't want to go at all. Maybe Student A (using the word "Red") wants to paint her room red and Student B (using the word "Blue") thinks blue would be a better choice. One student must try to convince the other student to her point of view using only her one word. The scene finally ends when one of the students agrees with the other by saying the other student's word.

Acting Out a Story. Acting out a story before or after reading it gives students the opportunity to verbalize and physicalize the plot, characters, and meaning of the story themselves. Standing in the shoes of one of the characters and looking at the situation through her eyes makes an abstract character from the page of a book feel very real and concrete. If a student has had difficulty understanding the conflict of the story, acting it out can often make the conflict clear because it becomes an immediate, personal situation. Switching roles and playing another character who feels something different, opens a student's eyes to differences of opinion and divergent points of view which all good literature tries to provide to the reader.

POETRY AND OTHER FORMS OF CREATIVE WRITING

There are many ways to generate writing projects which excite instead of intimidate students.

Guided Imagery. Take students on a guided imagery journey to a place where they have an adventure or where they meet a famous person. When they come back from the imaginary trip, have them write about what they saw, heard, smelled, tasted, touched, and felt. See Chapter Seven for more about guided imagery journeys.

Sensory Exploration. Any of the sensory learning games described in Chapter Seven are good jumping off points for writing. Students can describe how it felt to be blindfolded or to smell different smells without seeing them or to identify objects only through touch.

Music Generated Writing. Play different kinds of music that evoke strong emotions or situations and ask students to listen with their imaginations, then write about a scene they saw or a story they made up as they listened to the music.

Art Generated Writing. Have students draw pictures of a special place or a special person and then write a story or a poem about what is in the picture.

Have students draw as they listen to music and then create a story or poem out of their drawing.

Storytelling. Begin telling a simple story to the class. Introduce the characters and their conflict, but stop the story just before the point of resolution. Let the students write about how the characters feel or come up with an ending for the story.

Creative Drama. Physically being involved in a story will engage students on a deeper imaginative and emotional level than storytelling will. Set up a situation for the students to dramatize and instead of acting out the ending, have them write out their version.

Dramatize a familiar story and ask students to write about what they think happened after the end of the story or ask them to invent a new ending.

Radio Plays. A radio play can be an exciting project to motivate reading and writing skills, as well as a way to enhance group interaction skills in your classroom. Radio plays also introduce the concept that the spoken word and the written word are interconnected and related. Whenever I have created radio plays or puppet plays with special education students, I have seen the "light bulbs" go on inside their heads when they suddenly realized that their spoken words were being written down and "saved" on paper so that they could be spoken again later.

Since students live in a television-oriented society, they may have never heard a radio play before. Play a tape of a classic or current radio play to your class to introduce them to the concept of radio drama. Radio dramas communicate everything about the story with sounds and words instead of with actual visual images. Talk about how the play you listened to did this.

Divide students up into groups of three to six and let them choose a familiar story to dramatize (see Chapter Eight for methods of developing a script based on a story). Type up the scripts they create and practice reading them out loud, adding sound effects to enhance the story wherever possible. Record the stories. You have created your own radio plays!

Puppet Plays. Puppet plays can also be great reading and writing motivators. They have the added benefit of involving a physical, visual product which can make the characters and the play created seem much more real to Visual and Haptic Learners. Chapter Eight describes in depth how to create a puppet play.

SCIENCE

Since science is about the physical world around us, it makes sense to teach it in a physical way. Dramatizing concepts, systems, processes, or cycles can be very illuminating for students because their bodies become part of a system that interrelates and connects. What initially might have looked to a student like a random jumble of parts with funny names actually follows cause-and-effect patterns. Once the student can experience the patterns in a personal way, the whole system begins to make sense.

For example, the circulatory system can be set up in a classroom. Students can become the different chambers of a heart and act out the way it beats, sending blood (other students) through the heart's chambers, off to the lungs where it picks up oxygen, back to the heart's remaining chambers, and finally off to the other parts of the body where the oxygen can be delivered to the body's cells. An enactment like this can be very simply staged in the classroom or can become a very elaborate class project complete with student-made costumes and props. In the case of the circulatory system, red "molecules of oxygen" could be picked up in the lungs by the red blood cells and taken to the body cells to be replaced there with blue "molecules of carbon dioxide" which are delivered back to the lungs.

Students can become water molecules and take part in the evaporation cycle. They can act out the different planets in the solar system and revolve around the sun. They could even become the atoms on the periodic chart of the elements and combine in different ways to create simple chemical compounds. Drama and science are natural companions in the classroom.

One of the most exciting teaching experiences I've ever had was a series of ten drama sessions which I led for an upper elementary class of learning disabled students who were studying insects, specifically ants and butterflies. As I read several books on the subject, I found the rigid social organization of ants to be fascinating. I was also intrigued by the differences in sensory perception between human beings and insects. Ants' compound eyes see only light and dark. Living underground most of the time, they don't have a need for eyes that focus on images as we do. They rely primarily on their senses of touch, taste, and smell to understand and function in the world. Butterflies have compound eyes which register movement and color, but don't really focus either. They also rely quite a bit on their senses of taste and touch, located on their feet and antennae, respectively. I decided the best way to approach insects was to begin with exercises which let the children experience the world the way the insects do.

We set up a maze in the room using desks and chairs and the students had to find their way through it blindfolded using their sense of touch, smell, or sound. After everyone had a chance to try it at least once, we sat down and talked about what was easy or hard about using the different senses to get around.

Since anthills are often like mazes with tunnels leading in, out, and around to different underground chambers, we practiced solving mazes on paper and drew a few of our own.

In one session we created two anthills in the room using desks and chairs. Everyone was assigned to one of the ant societies by scent. I fastened one of two different types of incense to each student's shoulder. The cones of incense looked similar, but smelled different. Just as an ant tells whether another ant is part of its anthill by how it smells, each student had to sniff the others to find out who were friends and who were strangers.

Once the ant societies had separated themselves to opposite anthills, their jobs in the society were assigned by taste. I passed out pieces of candy to everyone. If they had a lemon taste in their mouths, they were the queens (since each ant society only has one queen, I had only one lemon candy for each group). The queens had to go to their laying chambers in the center of their anthills and for the duration of the enactment could only "lay eggs" (take styrofoam beads out of a bag one by one and carefully arrange them on the floor).

If they had a strawberry taste, they were nursery workers and were to take eggs one at a time from the laying chamber to the nursery. If I said,

Using Drama to Teach about the Eye
by Mandy Hart, MA, CCC-SLP

Classroom teachers at Ivymount School in Rockville, Maryland, were having difficulty teaching about the eye, its parts, and how they function to a class of twelve nine-year-olds with learning disabilities. They asked me for suggestions on how to make the subject more concrete for their students.

First, each child built a model of the eye using styrofoam. This helped them identify the parts that made up the eye; however, they still had difficulty understanding how all the parts worked together as a whole. At this point I suggested that we build a human eye using the children as the working, moving parts.

We began by looking at the styrofoam models and listing the different parts of the eye: the Eyelid, the Iris, the Pupil, the Lens, the Retina, the Cones, the Rods, the Optic Nerve, and the Brain. Each child chose which part he or she would like to be. We decided that two children would work together to be the eyelid and two children would work together to be the iris. All other parts would be played by individual children.

Once the parts were assigned, each child had to answer the following questions:

1. Who/what are you?
2. What color are you?
3. What shape are you?
4. Where are you? Who/What are you next to?
5. What do you do?

The children were allowed to use their models and notes to help answer these questions. The names of the different parts were written on the board along with the definition provided by the child who played that part.

First, we positioned the Pupil. The Pupil lay down on his back and held his arms, slightly rounded, above his head. His arms would open wider as it became darker and close as it became lighter.

For the Iris, two children sat facing each other on either side of the Pupil's arms. They reached around the Pupil's arms and held each others' hands. One set of hands they held up and one set they held down to create a circle which could be widened or narrowed as it became lighter or darker.

In front of the Iris was the Eyelid, which was also formed with two children. They stood facing each other, holding a stick with a towel rolled around it. The towel was secured to the stick with thumbtacks. When the Eyelid was open, the towel was rolled around the stick. When the Eyelid was closed, the towel was unrolled and hung down.

The Lens sat behind the Pupil facing forward. The Lens stretched his arms toward the Pupil's feet.

Behind the Lens sat the Retina. The Retina faced the Lens's back and held his arms out on either side of the Lens.

Directly behind the Retina sat two children. One represented the Rods and one represented the Cones. They sat facing each other. One of their arms went under the Retina's arm to form a Rod or a Cone and one arm went back to touch the hand of the child behind them who played the Optic Nerve.

The Optic Nerve sat sideways behind the Rod and Cone with both arms outstretched to each side. One arm reached forward to touch the Rod and Cone's arms and the other arm reached backward to touch the Brain.

The last part of the eye was the Brain, who sat facing the front of the eye with both arms outstretched in front of him, hands touching the Optic Nerve.

One child played the part of Light. She turned the lights in the room on and off. When the lights were turned on, the Pupil decreased in size, moving his arms closer together, the Iris grew bigger, and the student playing the Cones went into action. When the lights were turned off, the Pupil increased in size, the Iris grew smaller, and the student playing the Rods went into action.

When the Eyelids opened and closed, all the other parts of the eye had to adjust their activities.

We also practiced the process of seeing an object. We held a picture of a tree in front of the eye. This picture was passed along by all the eye parts to the Retina, which turned it upside down before passing it to the Optic Nerve. When the picture got to the Brain, the Brain turned it right side up again.

After we got the eye working well, we switched parts several times. Each time we recast, the children told each other what to do in their new parts. Each had several opportunities to experience the different parts of the eye and to explain verbally who and what they were to another child. At the end of this exercise, everyone really understood the parts of the eye and we'd had a lot of fun, too.

I have done similar exercises with the Circulatory System and the Digestive System. Each time, the process of the organ being studied became clear once the children had a personal experience with it.

These children had been exposed to drama and were used to acting out different things, so they responded immediately to the idea of acting out an eye. If you are working with children who are not very familiar with acting, you may first want to create a simple machine with them–a clock or a popcorn popper–to introduce the concept. First make individual machines, then create a machine using everyone in the group. This will help the children (and you) feel more comfortable with the idea of using your bodies in this way.

First know your subject matter. Then use your imagination to bring it to life. Be creative and have fun!

"It's getting hot outside," the nursery ants had to move the eggs to a chamber closer to the surface of the anthill. If I said, "It's getting cooler," the nursery ants had to move the eggs to a chamber farther in toward the center of the anthill.

Students who had an orange-tasting candy were worker ants and had to go out of the anthill and gather food (small paper tubes and wooden blocks) and carry it back to the anthill's food storage chambers. Worker ants could not carry more than one piece of food at a time and had to use both hands to do it. Each time they came out of the anthill and went in search of food, they had to follow the same trail.

There were a few more rules for the enactment. No one was allowed to talk. No one was allowed to do anything but his or her assigned job. Each time two ants met outside the anthill, (whether the students remembered each other by sight or not) they had to smell each other to see if they were friend or foe. If they were friends, they could help each other. If they were strangers, they had to quickly move away from each other.

 If ants got hungry, they were allowed to stop and eat. Nursery ants and queens had to get food from a worker ant (but they couldn't ask for food— they had to get the worker ant's attention by tapping her on the head and motioning to their mouths). The anthill had to remain neat and clean at all times.

After about twenty minutes of quiet, industrious activity, we stopped and talked about the experience of being an ant. Everyone had lots of ideas and feelings to share. Someone said it was hard not being able to communicate through talking. Another student agreed and said it was sometimes confusing to only be able to gesture or get someone else's attention by tapping her. So many things seemed to take more time to do. Their teacher and I talked more about life in an anthill and the students began making connections between the facts we shared and the experience they had just had. Everyone agreed that being able to do only one job your whole life was boring and decided unanimously that it was wonderful that as human beings we were able to learn new things and to have variety and change in our lives.

That whole week during recess a new excitement for learning gripped the students. They began watching ants on the sidewalk. Their teacher overheard them having long discussions about what kind of ant this was (herder, food gatherer, queen, or nursery worker), how old it was, if it was a member of the same society as the ants on the other side of the playground. Hours were spent in front of the ant farm in the classroom discussing the fine points of ant etiquette and social structure.

They would have been happy to re-create their ant societies and explore them further the next week, but we moved on to act out the life cycle of the butterfly.

Our last few sessions were devoted to writing and illustrating poems about the insects we had studied. Students who had never willingly put pen to paper joyfully jumped in to express what it had felt like to be a caterpillar or butterfly or ant.

I put the poems and illustrations together into a book and made copies for each student. When the books were completed, we had a poetry reading. Everyone actually *wanted* to stand up in front of the room and read her poems to the rest of the class! But the best part of all was when *everyone* passed their science test. No one had any doubts about the correct answers!

Here are some of the wonderful poems that came out of their firsthand experiences with insects:

ANT

Hi.
I'm an ant.
I will tell you how it
would be
If you were an ant.
If you were an ant,
The queen ant would
never give you a rest.
You have to work till you
die.
You could not see

And it's hard to talk.
It's painful to crawl
And you have to watch for predators.
I have three body parts
And I could smell and touch and taste.

THE QUEEN

I am a queen ant.
I lay eggs.
But when I leave my eggs,
My sitters watch my pretty eggs
While I am in the room where I get dressed.

Today I have a meeting with two worker ants
Because I need my house to get bigger
Because I will soon get more eggs.

RED ANTS

I am a red ant.
Red ants sting
And they bite.
I was walking one day
And I saw a man.
He stepped on me.
But I was still alive.
I was mad!
Because he hurt me.
He broke my antenna.
He leaned down and
tried to pick me up,
But I bit him

And he said, "Ow!"
So he left.
So remember this is what will happen to you
When the powers of the red ant comes for you!

THE SOLDIER ANT

I am black and big.
I am a soldier ant.
I am not a nice ant.
I spray formic acid
If you touch my house.
If you touch my house,
I will spray formic acid on you.
So whatcha gonna do
When I come for you?
That's the way I am.
The soldier ant is back!

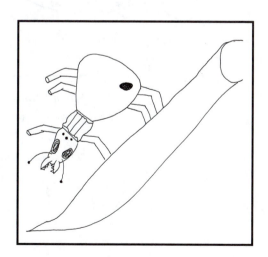

FEELING LIKE A BUTTERFLY

I am a caterpillar.
I shed my skin five times.
Boy, it was hard.
I had to push —
Like having a baby.
Oh my gosh!
I turned into a pupae stage.
I came out on 11/2/1981.
I felt good.
But when I came out,
I fell down on the ground—

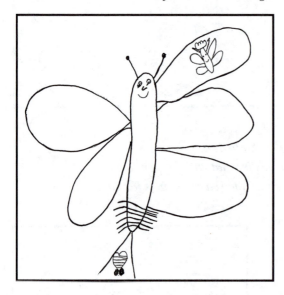

My head first.
I said, "Ouch!"
Then I went walking to a
flower.
It was a rose.
I jumped up.
Then I started to fly.
I met another butterfly.
Her name was Amy.
She became my girlfriend.
An elephant was going to
step on Amy!
I was a super butterfly.
I picked up the elephant
And took him back to Africa.

When I came back,
I asked Amy, "Are you OK?"
She said, "Yes."
Then we kiss with love.

A student creates a medieval coat of arms using stencils and inked sponges. (Photo by Lea Ann Rosen)

SOCIAL STUDIES

History, geography, and the study of human societies across the globe can be greatly enhanced by actively employing the arts as a teaching tool.

Time Machines. Create a "time machine" in your classroom to enable you and your students to travel back in history. Once you have arrived at your destination in the past, students can act out important scenes from the lives of historical characters or everyday life experiences. If you journey back to medieval times, each student could create her own family coat of arms or join a guild and learn how leather was made or shoes were cobbled. If you go back to the 1800s, your class could join a wagon train's westward journey or pan for gold in the California gold rush.

Costumes, Props, and Sets. If involving students through active role playing (as in a Time Machine journey) seems too intimidating at first, involve them passively in roles through the use of costumes, sets, and props during lessons. Dressing up as someone else always appeals to the dramatic sense of children. One of my fondest memories from fourth grade is geography class. Mrs. West, our teacher, always got us physically connected with the place and the people we were studying. I will never forget making a burnoose and wearing it each class period we studied Saudi Arabia. When we learned about Polynesia, we circled our chairs around a "palm tree" in the back of the room and munched on real coconut. I remember virtually nothing about geography class in any subsequent years.

Explore a Culture through its Arts and Crafts, its Food, and its Festivals. Through an experience with folk customs and arts, the people and culture of a society will come alive for your students in an exciting new way. Learn the songs, dances, and games that are integrated into daily life or special holiday traditions. Cook and eat authentic food. Create folk art in the style of the culture. Hold a holiday festival where everyone can share and celebrate their adopted cultural heritage. Facts will no longer be dry meaningless minutiae to memorize, but will become living information.

Bringing Historical Characters to Life. History comes alive when figures from history become real human beings for students. After studying an historical period, have each student choose a famous person in that period who interests her. After students do some research, lead them through a guided fantasy where they meet their historical character at an important moment in her life or where they become this character themselves at a crucial life moment. When the students return from their journey, have them write a short monologue (a first person speech) in which their historical character talks about something important she saw, did, or felt. The monologues could be memorized and performed in costume to create a presentation on this period in history or could be videotaped.

A less formal way to meet historical characters is to invite them to class and interview them in person. Have students choose a character to play and provide time to research the character. During an interview session, run as if your class were a TV talk show, each student in role as her historical character answers questions about her life. The teacher could be the interviewer, one student could be assigned as the TV host, or the whole class could ask questions.

MATHEMATICS

Drama provides a method of grasping abstract concepts through concrete means. Here are a few simple drama games which can be used to teach basic math and geometry.

"Grouping by Number." Students slowly walk around the room until the teacher calls out a number. Students must find the right number of other students to join with in order to create a group made up of that number of students. Left over students should group together in one area. For example, if the teacher calls out "Three!" all students must assemble in groups of three. Once everyone is in a group with the correct number, the round is over and the game starts again.

"Addition." Once students understand how to play "Grouping by Number," a variation of the game can be played which shows students what happens during the process of addition. Just as in "Grouping By Number," students slowly walk around the room until the teacher calls out a number. They assemble in a group of that number of students. Then the teacher adds to that number and students must reform their groups. For example, if the students are in groups of three, the teacher might call out "Add two!" or "Plus two!" Some groups will stay together and other groups will need to break up and add themselves to a group of three. (At first the teacher might want to designate which groups will break up and which will stay the same in order to avoid mass confusion, but after the game is learned, students will be able to do this on their own.) When each group has added two to its number, the teacher asks the students to count and see how many three plus two is. As the game is played, students begin to recognize addition patterns. Every time two is added to three, there are five students in each group.

"Subtraction." This is another variation of "Grouping By Number." In this version, once the students are in a number group, the teacher calls out a number to subtract from each group and the class evaluates the sizes of the groups that are left. For instance, if students are in groups of three, the teacher might call out "Subtract one!" or "Minus one!" One student must leave each group. The original groups will have two students left in them.

"Geometry." The teacher calls out different kinds of lines (straight, zig-zag, curved, long, short, etc.) and different kinds of simple shapes. Students create these lines and shapes with their bodies. Once students understand how to play this game alone, they can learn to play it with other students, creating more complex shapes and lines by using more people. Once students have created shapes and lines with their whole bodies, they will have an easier time drawing different shapes and lines on paper or cutting shapes from paper.

"Story Problems." When introducing story problems in math class, have students actually act the problems out so they have the opportunity to see and actually physicalize the situation instead of just imagining it. A simple story problem like, "If Joan gave Bill three apples and then had four apples left how many apples did she have in the first place?" could be worked through using real or plastic apples.

Working through story problems in this manner not only makes them more concrete and real, but more human. Students with interpersonal intelligences will become more motivated to learn math if they can relate it to actual people and real life situations.

Once students learn to solve story problems through action, have students create their own story problems for the class to solve.

In addition to teaching basic math skills, all of these games teach basic group interaction and problem-solving skills.

DEVELOPING INTERPERSONAL SKILLS

Students with or without disabilities can have difficulty getting along, difficulty respecting the differences or special needs of others, difficulty accepting certain aspects of themselves, or difficulty communicating effectively with each other. Many of the basic drama games described in this book, particularly in Chapter Seven, and improvisational role playing, described in detail in Chapter Six, can help teach skills in all of these areas of interpersonal interaction.

When teaching the unit on self-esteem and getting along with others mentioned earlier in this chapter, I used a combination of drama and social games, art activities, role playing, relaxation techniques, storytelling, and creative dramatics to develop students' abilities to observe others, become aware of their own feelings, and develop positive strategies to work together.

In the first session we played a social game called "Come Along," a variation of musical chairs. Everyone sat in a circle in chairs except for one leader who stood in the center. When I started music, the leader went up to someone sitting in the circle, held out her hand, and said, "Come along." That person grabbed onto the leader's hand and followed her around the circle, moving in time to the music. The second person asked a third person to "Come Along," the third person asked a fourth, and so on until I stopped the music. As soon as the music stopped, everyone ran for a chair. The person left without a seat was the leader for the next round. This is a game which children are excited about playing because it means receiving positive attention by being chosen to come along with someone else. Positive attention is continued throughout the game—everyone who is "coming along" is being watched by the members of the group who are sitting. Even the person who ends up without a chair in the rush for seats at the end of the round isn't a "loser," because she becomes the "leader" (a positive role) for the next round. No one is eliminated or punished for not making it to a chair. Everyone continues to play and have fun together. The group can continue playing the game as long as they want.

After "Come Along," we played an animal pantomime game and The Magic Stick. These games gave the students opportunities to use their bodies, voices, and imaginations expressively and gave me the opportunity to evaluate where they were in terms of expressive, social, and imaginative abilities.

I started the second session by asking each child to draw how she felt that day. I passed out sheets of paper which had outlines of heads with noses and blank eyes on them. The children filled in the rest of the facial features. I asked each child to show the face she had drawn and say how she felt. Everyone drew a happy face, but not everyone said she felt happy. It was obvious they had some confusion with identifying emotions. We talked about why each face looked happy.

Then we listed different kinds of emotions a person might feel. I divided them up into two categories: "comfortable" and "uncomfortable." First I listed all the comfortable emotions they could think of on the blackboard. They thought of happy, excited, surprise, and joy. Then I had them think of uncomfortable emotions and listed them: Angry/mad, sick, sad, grouchy, worried, scared/afraid. We took turns acting out the different emotions we had listed with our faces and bodies. As each person acted out an emotion, I pointed out what parts of the body changed to express it. As we went along, I asked them to help me identify the changes.

Next we moved on to sculpting emotions. I did not think they would be able to sculpt each other because they did not know how to touch each other appropriately, so I sculpted each student into a statue of a different emotion and had the others guess which emotion it represented. They did very well with this.

Then we looked at pictures of people's faces and identified how they were feeling from their facial expressions. There was a little confusion about some expressions, but on the whole the class did well.

To review, we talked about how we could tell how other people are feeling when we look at them: through the expressions on parts of the face (eyes, mouth, cheeks, and eyebrows), through the person's body position, and through the kind of movements that they make. Then we closed the session by breathing together for relaxation. I found that if we slowly raised our arms together as we breathed in and lowered our arms as we breathed out, the students were able to stay together, breathe slowly, and remain serious about what they were doing.

We started the third session by reviewing our list of comfortable and uncomfortable emotions. Then I asked everyone to draw a sad face on the face outlines. We shared the faces that we drew. Some faces looked sad and some didn't. We talked about why they looked sad or why they didn't.

Then we looked at more pictures of people's faces and identified how they were feeling. Students were much better with this exercise the second time around. Each time someone identified a feeling, they had to say what they saw that told them it was that particular feeling.

As soon as interest in the pictures waned, we moved on to play a rousing game of "Making an Entrance," followed by "Come-Go-Stay," and a few simple tone-of-voice exercises. To introduce the concept of tone-of-voice, I said each student's name with different emotions in my voice. They had to identify how I felt about them. This was fun and easy for them. Then I had them practice saying "Hello" to each other with different tones of voice and asked the others what the person who was speaking felt. We ended the session with some breathing relaxation.

The fourth session began the same way as the third had. We listed our comfortable and uncomfortable emotions on the board. Then I asked them each to draw an angry face. Almost everyone was able to do this. We shared our pictures and talked about why they looked angry.

I showed them more pictures of people's faces and asked them to make a sound that that person might make which expressed how she was feeling. Then we role-played a number of situations which they might find themselves in during the day in their classroom. The situations included: someone pushes in front of you in line; someone walks by and takes your pencil off your desk; you feel sick and want to be left alone, but someone keeps talking to you and gets right in your face; a friend has hurt your feelings and comes to apologize to you; the person next to you starts to copy off your paper during a test. In each case we talked about how each character in the scene felt, what the actors did, and what else they could have done. The classroom teacher and I were both quite surprised when the students always opted for positive behavior choices first in every role-play situation. Afterwards she said to me, "This tells me that they really *do* know the appropriate way to behave, even if they don't always make that choice." We ended that session, as we did the others, with breathing slowly together.

The last three sessions I decided to teach positive behavior choices through three different stories which focused on accepting oneself, awareness of others' feelings and needs, and getting along with others. The fifth class we acted out "The Little Fir Tree," the sixth class we acted out "Miss Nelson Is Missing," and the last class we did "The Stone in the Road." We had time to act out each story at least twice, so students could try on different roles and see how they felt. Everyone was on their best behavior and cooperated well together. The classroom teacher said that she observed a positive change in behavior and awareness of feelings in class at other times during the seven weeks we worked together.

DEVELOPING LIFE SKILLS

Some special education classes focus on teaching students life skills, such as how to shop for food at the grocery store, how to travel by public transportation, how to cook, how to go to a restaurant, or how to do laundry at a laundromat. Role-playing real-life situations before actually doing them provides students with the opportunity to rehearse actions and words. Real-life situations don't seem so overwhelming if they have been practiced beforehand.

In addition to practicing what is supposed to happen in a real-life situation, students learn to deal with situations that don't go according to plan. Individuals with special needs can sometimes be taken advantage of by others or they can become confused when something unexpected happens. If they haven't previously developed coping strategies, they can be at a loss. Role-play situations can be set up in which something goes wrong and students must figure out how to solve the problem or correct the situation. For instance, what if you are riding the bus and you fall asleep and miss your stop? What do you do? How do you get home? Or what if you buy something at the store and the store clerk short-changes you? What do you say? How can you prove you did not get the right amount of money back? Students can try several different strategies for dealing with each situation and evaluate which seemed to be most effective for solving the problem.

For more information on how to use role-playing for educational purposes, read *Sociodrama: Who's In Your Shoes?* by Patricia Sternberg and Antonina Garcia.

DEALING WITH TEST ANXIETY

Many times students do poorly in testing situations, not because they don't know the material, but because they are so anxious and worried about failure that they freeze up. Remind your students that the purpose of taking a test is not to prove what they *don't* know, but to provide them with the opportunity to show off how much they *do* know and to let the teacher know what material she has not done a good enough job teaching to the class.

Take time each day to teach and to practice physical relaxation and breathing skills as a part of your regular classroom routine. Some of the basic warm-up activities suggested in Chapter Seven will work quite well to loosen up students' muscles, oxygenate their blood, and clear their minds for concentration. There are also many good suggestions for teaching relaxation and methods of stress reduction in *The Centering Book, The Second Centering Book,* and *Spinning Inward,* all listed in the bibliography at the end of this book.

Positive mental images about learning or taking tests can be suggested in short guided imagery sessions. When creating a guided imagery journey, use positive images which put the student in control. The images could be as literal as having the student imagine herself taking the math test in a relaxed state, effortlessly writing down all the correct answers, and receiving her test paper back with an "A" on it. Images could be symbolic of success. Ask students to imagine they are flying through the air, effortlessly climbing to the top of a mountain and looking around at the surrounding country side, sailing across the surface of the ocean, or jumping hurdles on a horse.

Some students find that spending a few minutes engaged in a right brain activity they enjoy, such as drawing, singing, or dancing, is a good pre-test relaxation technique. This works because by engaging the right brain in activity, the analytic left brain is given a short break. The student comes back to the academic, left brain activity (the test) refreshed and better able to concentrate.

Providing students with a short period of relaxation or guided imagery before each test is very important. It gives them the chance to put their relaxation skills into practice. Teaching relaxation techniques and then not making time in the schedule to use them will undercut your stated message that you want them to do well and not poorly. Actions speak louder than words!

mainstreaming

TO MAINSTREAM OR NOT TO MAINSTREAM

Mainstreaming is a very important issue and can often be an emotionally volatile one. Years ago students with disabilities were separated out of the mainstream and segregated into their own adaptive classrooms or their own special schools. Because in many ways they were hidden away, they became stigmatized. Students in regular education classes rarely met students who had disabilities. They never got to develop friendships with each other and to discover that, disability or no disability, people are all very much the same.

Today the push in education is for the least restrictive environment. Opportunities for mainstreaming are looked for as much as possible. Mainstreaming has become the politically correct thing to do.

I am a firm believer in mainstreaming. I think it works in many situations. However, in order to succeed in a drama classroom, students need to have reached a certain level of appropriate social skills and artistic confidence. Drama involves interactive, cooperative, symbolic play. Students who are still in solitary, parallel, or associative play stages are not developmentally ready to join in with group activities. They will go off by themselves, suffer painful shyness, or get into conflicts with other students. A student who is not socially and emotionally prepared to mainstream in a drama class will not have a successful experience. He can ruin the class for himself and for the other students in it. Faced with yet another situation of failure, he will turn off to the arts.

In order to determine if a student is ready to be mainstreamed, evaluate his group interaction abilities, play style, listening skills, and attention skills. This is easy if you have taught him in a special needs class, for you have been there to see his progress during the semester. If you have not had a previous experience with the student, invite him in for a special session, where you can play a few drama games, such as The Magic Stick, Transformations, or Animal Pantomimes and can act out a short story together. You will be able to ascertain quite quickly if he can follow directions and how long his attention span lasts. You will also be able to tell if he is able to interact with you as he plays or if he prefers to play alone.

After you play a few games, explain what a drama class is like. Ask him if he likes pretending to be other people or animals and if he enjoys acting out stories. Ask if he'd like to take a drama class where he can do those things with other children. It is important to discover whether or not the child *wants* to take a drama class. No matter how highly developed his social or emotional skills are, if he doesn't want to be in a drama class, he is not going to cooperate with the teacher or with the other students.

If you have the opportunity, you can gather a great deal of information from a student's school. Observe the student in his school environment. Speak with his teacher about the child's strengths and weaknesses. Knowing a child's abilities is particularly important because they can be used to provide opportunities for him to shine in drama class. Ask what the academic teacher is working on with the student at this point. He might need to develop some skills, such as learning to listen, following directions, or initiating action, which you can work on through your class.

Talk with the student's parents. Ask them if he does dramatic play at home. Does he play with puppets or dolls? Does he act out animals or characters he sees on TV or from stories which his parents read him? Ask about other drama experiences he might have had at school, at camp, or at day care. Find out if he has had other mainstreamed experiences. Find out what the parents feel his weaknesses and strengths are and why they think a drama class would be good for him. Find out if they've explained to him what drama class is all about and if they have asked him how he feels about taking one.

Avoid relying on a parent's assessment of a child's ability alone without also meeting the child. I have made this mistake more times than I like to admit and it has created problems for the Academy teaching staff. Some parents underestimate their child's abilities and others overestimate them.

Julia was one student who could have been mainstreamed from the outset. She had learning disabilities and went to a private special education school, so her mother assumed that her daughter would need a segregated learning experience in the arts and signed her up for my special needs creative drama class. After a few sessions I realized that Julia had excellent group skills, wonderful balance and coordination, and, although English was not her first language, expressed herself well verbally. If I had known in time, I could have mainstreamed her that first semester, but by the time I discovered her many strengths, classes were already underway. The next semester she joined a dance class and fit in extremely well with the other students, making friends who she invited home to play.

A few parents will try to minimize some aspect of their child's disability, perhaps because it embarrasses them or because they fear you will not accept their child into your program or simply because they have no idea that it has any bearing on their child's success in a drama class. One mother told me over the phone that her son's major involvement was a language delay. This, I assured her, was something we could deal with easily. She neglected to tell me about his distractibility or his spinning behaviors because she didn't realize they would cause a problem!

If a student who has disabilities is not able to function on a social-emotional level close to that of the nondisabled students in his age range, a mainstreamed experience will not have a good chance of succeeding. There are different issues to consider at different ages.

Nondisabled students in the five to nine age bracket are often very accepting of others who are different from them. They will be very curious at first, but if the "differentness" is openly and immediately addressed, they usually forget about it. However, children in this age range are *also* in the process of learning very basic group skills. While they may be at a higher developmental level than their disabled peers, they are still in the beginning stages of learning how to relate appropriately to others. These young students haven't always developed the social skills or the emotional maturity to be able to help and encourage another student who is struggling to function successfully in the group.

By the time they reach their pre-teen and adolescent years, nondisabled students usually have developed better group skills, but they may have become judgmental and unaccepting of others who are "different." One of the major social-emotional themes of adolescence is finding a way to fit in— and the best way to do this is to be as "like" everyone else as it is possible to be! Teenagers often feel insecure and, once they make up their minds about how they feel about someone, can be very stubborn and cruel.

With all age groups, the accepting behavior modeled by the teacher is crucial. His initial efforts to break the ice and get everyone acquainted can make the difference between success and failure in mainstreamed students being accepted as a member of the class.

AGE- AND INTEREST-APPROPRIATE MAINSTREAMING

Whenever possible, mainstream a student into a drama class with students who are the same chronological age. Academic skills which may keep age peers apart in school are usually not at issue in a drama classroom. If reading or another skill that is problematic for the student is needed for a particular exercise, the teacher can address these needs adaptively.

I usually recommend mainstreaming a child with younger students only if his social-emotional development *and* interest levels are more appropriate to that group than to his age peers. Crucial questions to ask yourself are: Where will the student have the most success? Where will he have the most fun? Where will he find most acceptance from the other students?

Miranda was ten, but physically small for her age. At school she was in a special education class. After school she was mainstreamed in a day care center. Her self-confidence was very low and her interests were primarily fantasy and fairy tales. An acting class of her age peers would have focused on a combination of improvisational skills and scene study and would have been intimidating and uninteresting to her. Because of this, I suggested she start out in Creative Drama for Grades 2-3. (At the Academy, Creative Drama is only offered to students through the third grade.) Her fine motor skills and concentration abilities were on the same level as our second and third grade art students, so she took Art Explorations for Grades 2-3. In both classes she was very happy, developed a great many skills, improved her self-confidence, and was able to perform on the same level as the other students in the class. She fit in. She felt wanted. She experienced success. Next year she wants to take a class every day of the week and if we can match her with an appropriate class every day, she can!

In the nine to twelve age bracket, mainstreaming a child whose interests are at odds with the other students in the class is the primary difficulty that can arise. Like Miranda, he may still be deeply into fairy tales and fantasy while his nondisabled peers are more focused on contemporary media images and pre-teen concerns.

My Saturday's Rainbow Classes, which are for elementary-aged children who have orthopedic disabilities, are a case in point. The younger group (ages six to nine) are interested in very simple, highly structured fairy tales which require limited dialogue development. I use material with them that is comparable to what I would use with a regular group of children aged four to seven. The older group (ages nine to twelve) are wildly enthusiastic about more complicated, adventuresome fairy tales. While I could probably entice them into non-fantasy improvisation work, their hearts would not be in it.

Last spring, at the end of two years of working together, they asked me—with great concern—how many fairy tales there were. I replied that there were thousands. A sigh of relief went through the whole group. Then they asked how many of those fairy stories I knew. I said, "I've probably read about two hundred."

Their concern returned. "What if we do all the fairy stories you know?" they asked.

"If we run out of stories I know," I assured them, "I can read some more." That set their minds at ease. I don't know a group of nondisabled twelve-year-olds who would worry if there were enough fairy tales in existence to keep them dramatically occupied.

Usually by the time they are twelve, most students, with or without disabilities, are ready to move into reality-based drama work. However, there are exceptions. I had one adolescent special needs acting class whose members *insisted* on acting out fairy tales. Try as I might, I could not guide them to work on what their parents saw as "age appropriate" material. So we acted out fairy tales all year.

I have two theories about why this particular group felt a need to work on fairy tales. The first deals with play stages. Developmental psychologists have documented that as children grow, they naturally go through a stage of dramatic play. When they were younger, these particular children may never have had the opportunity to act out fairy stories in a drama class or to engage in dramatic play in an informal play setting with other kids from the neighborhood. Perhaps they felt a need to fill this void.

My second theory centers around Bruno Bettelheim's belief that fairy tales express developmental emotional conflicts which all children struggle with in their search for identity and maturity. The class as a whole gravitated to stories which focused on the need for independence and self-reliance, conflict with authority figures, especially parents, and issues around developing sexuality. They asked to act out "Cinderella," "Little Red Riding Hood," "Snow White and the Seven Dwarves," "Jack and the Beanstalk," and "The Wizard of Oz."

"The Wizard of Oz" held particular fascination for them and we worked on that story in different ways both semesters. At the end of the first semester, we videotaped an interview show in which each of the Oz characters were interviewed. The Tin Woodman proposed to Dorothy "on the air," she accepted, and we staged a wedding ceremony for them. The second semester they insisted on acting out the whole story on stage (with the revised ending) for their parents. So we made masks and created a 20-minute production.

Each of the students in the class was drawn to play certain types of roles again and again. Lisa always wanted to be the wicked witch. Rebecca always wanted to be the young heroine. Billy always played the fool. At a younger maturity level than their ages might indicate, they seemed to find their emotional conflicts most symbolically and safely portrayed through their favorite fairy tales.

How to Set Up a Successful Mainstream Experience

When you have determined that a student is ready to be mainstreamed, it is important to match him with the right class and the right teacher. We've talked about finding a class which will interest the student and yet be age appropriate at the same time. It is also important to gauge whether the class is appropriate to his level of drama skills. A student should not be placed into an acting class where the other students are on a more advanced or a less advanced level than he is. He also should not be put into a situation in which his disability puts him at a disadvantage. For example, a TV acting class requires the ability to read cue cards on the spot. This would not be a good situation for a student who has dyslexia.

Before recommending a particular class, make sure it is not overloaded with students. If there are a lot of students signed up already, can you arrange for an assistant for that class? If not, recommend a smaller class.

Check to see if there are any other students with special needs already mainstreamed into the class. Even if he has the help of an assistant, it is not fair to overload a drama teacher, who is not specially trained to work with disability, with too many students who have special needs.

If there are other students mainstreamed into the class, what are their special needs? Two or three students who have Down syndrome might work perfectly well together and with other class members. Two or three students with ADHD, all wandering off in different directions, could easily destroy the class experience for everyone.

ASSISTANTS AND COMPANIONS

If the child being mainstreamed has concentration problems or is easily distracted, an assistant can help keep him (and the other students he begins to distract) on track. If the child has fine motor skill problems and the class will be doing a lot of art work, an assistant can offer an extra hand so that the teacher can keep circulating among all the students. If the child has gross motor skill problems and the class will be doing a lot of movement work, the assistant can help him keep up with the rest of the students so he doesn't feel left behind.

Providing a companion for a student who requires a lot of assistance is an alternative or an additional option to hiring a class assistant. Companions can offer more one-on-one continuous attention than an assistant who must be shared with the whole class. If the companion is close to the age of the student—maybe a young person in high school or college who is interested in working in the area of special needs—he can then become a "buddy" as well as an assistant to the student and help him through stressful or confusing situations. A companion might receive a specific stipend amount for the whole course or be paid wages comparable to class assistants. Sometimes the cost of the companion is covered by the parents and sometimes by the organization. The Academy has used companions with great success in our summer camps, which are day-long programs.

TEACHER SUPPORT

Success in mainstreaming depends a great deal on the leadership of the teacher. Students take their cue on how to relate to each other from the adult in charge. If a teacher feels uncomfortable about working with a student who has a disability, the other students will intuitively sense it and feel uncomfortable, too. They will model their interactions and emotional reactions on his. On the other hand, if a teacher takes an active lead in including everyone and accepting the differences and needs of all students in the classroom, students will follow his lead and do the same.

One way to ensure teachers' comfort is to provide training and support for them. If you are in charge of making decisions about mainstreaming, but not the teacher of the class the child will be in, make sure you prepare the teacher in advance. Give him written information on the child's disability and explain how it may affect his classroom. If he knows ahead of time what kind of adaptations he may have to make, he will be prepared.

If you are the teacher, take it upon yourself to seek out information. Appendix II lists organizations that can provide information on different kinds of disability. Call them or write to them and ask for help. Go to your local library. Some library systems even have special needs divisions. Talk to the child's parents about how best to work with him. Ask them if they have any reading materials they can share or suggest.

One of the major issues that teachers have the most fear about is discipline: what do I do if a student won't do what I ask him to? What if he misbehaves? What are my options? Offer teachers a workshop in behavior management. This will provide teachers with skills they can use with disabled and nondisabled students alike. Let's face it—every student has bad days!

Information on learning styles can also be helpful to teachers. As discussed in Chapter Ten, people generally fall into one of three learning styles: auditory, visual, or haptic. Knowing a student's preferred learning style can be helpful when presenting information; however, knowing each individual's learning style is not necessary. In every class there will be a mixture of learning styles. A teacher who understands the concept of teaching to students' learning styles will provide instruction through all three channels.

There are many disability awareness exercises which simulate different disabilities. A "put-yourself-in-the-other-person's-shoes" type of experience can do more to enlighten a teacher about the challenges and frustrations facing a student than any intellectual presentation on the subject. Even something as simple as trying to write your name while looking at your hand in a mirror provides enough physical and cognitive disorientation to make a non-disabled teacher or student really appreciate what a person with a cognitive or motor disability must deal with on a daily basis.

CLASSROOM ADAPTATIONS

Most of the adaptations mentioned in Chapters Three through Seven can be used in a regular drama classroom as well as in a special needs drama classroom and will only serve to make a teacher's lesson plans and class structure stronger. Everyone—hearing and deaf—speechreads and needs to have good lighting in order to see and, therefore, hear the teacher well. Everyone—blind and sighted—can be confused and distracted by background noise. Everyone—regardless of cognitive processing abilities—can benefit from a clearly presented, carefully sequenced lesson.

Avoid using exercises in your lesson plan which a mainstreamed student will not be able to participate in. Use your common sense. A game of leapfrog would not be appropriate if one of your students uses a wheelchair. However, don't automatically throw out an exercise until you have thought it through creatively for ways to change and adapt it. For example, to adapt a circle game for wheelchair users, everyone could move to a different X on the floor rather than exchange chairs. Pictures can be substituted for words on flash cards used for acting games if you have non-readers mainstreamed in your class.

Be aware of sensitivities students may have. For instance, many children with auditory processing problems, emotional involvements, or certain kinds of hearing impairments may have a sensitivity to loud noises. Usually the only way to find out about this is by asking parents. Students will sometimes, but not always, let you know about it in advance.

Adapt teaching pace to the processing abilities of the students. Students with language or auditory processing difficulties may need a slower pace of delivery and more time to respond. It is possible to slow down the pace of a class by talking just a little bit slower and/or spending just a little more time on each activity in order to allow the mainstreamed child the time he needs to "get it" while simultaneously keeping the other students interested. The key is to focus students on developing concentration skills, seriousness of intent, and intensity of purpose. You will know as soon as boredom sets in; your students will become restless and distracted. If this happens, simply switch to a new activity or add a level of complexity to the exercise for students who are ready for it.

Class pace may need to be speeded up a bit to keep students with attention deficits or impulsive behavior engaged. If the rest of the students have normal to above average cognitive processing, the pace of the class can probably be accelerated just a bit without anyone suffering. Provide a wider variety of exercises in each lesson plan. Instead of staying with one exercise for fifteen minutes, spend ten minutes on it, then move on to the next. Review and repeat the exercises or do variations of them from week to week. In this way, over the course of the semester, certain skills may be more solidly developed because of the repetition and rehearsal students have had with them.

INTERACTIONS BETWEEN STUDENTS

If a mainstreamed student's disability is an obvious one, such as cerebral palsy, deafness, Down syndrome, or an orthopedic disability, be open and honest with all class members about it from the beginning. The other students will see the disability and be curious about it. If the disability and their curiosity are not acknowledged and processed at the outset, they will continue seeing only the disability and never get past it to the person.

The concept of working as an ensemble is an important one in the theatre. It is important to introduce it early to young actors. Stress that everyone is here to help each other and to have a good time together. Actors must learn to work together, to respect each other, and to support each other in order to excel individually and as a group. In an introductory session, let each person share how the others can help him do his best. Each student (and the teacher) can be given an opportunity to share his own special needs and sensitivities with the class—for each of us has them. Kathryn Chase Bryer and Caleen Sinnette Jennings describe how they did this with their classes later in this chapter.

If the disability is an "invisible" one like a learning disability or an attention deficit and the student does not choose to share it during the introductions, the teacher doesn't need to point it out or make an issue of it. He can quietly make adaptations in the class structure to help the student.

Throughout the semester, but particularly during the first few weeks, make sure students are partnered and grouped in a variety of ways in order to mix everybody up together. This allows everyone to get to know each other and discourages the formation of cliques. It also allows students to see each others' strengths up close.

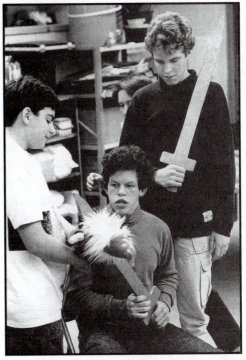

Be ready to stop and confront conflicts between students if they arise. Your class rules should require students to respect others and their ideas. You might be able to nip teasing in the bud with non-verbal cues or verbal reminders. You might need to pull an individual student who is behaving insensitively aside and talk to him. You might need to stop class for a

Improvising together is a great way to discover each others' creativity and strengths. (Photo by John Carter)

group discussion. Maybe some role playing or a few disability awareness exercises would be appropriate to help the nondisabled students understand the disabled student's situation and generate respect. Drama is about resolving conflicts and coming to understand other human beings better by putting yourself for a short time in their shoes. A class which covers less material, but learns something about the human condition and how to relate sensitively to others, has had a more successful semester than a class which produces a slick end-product, but has only generated competition and animosity among the participants.

Use students to support each other. If a student has dysgraphia or an auditory processing problem, another student can help by writing down homework assignments or the director's notes for him. If a written in-class assignment, like a character biography or script analysis, is given, the teacher or assistant could serve as a scribe and take dictation from the mainstreamed student. Another strategy for this situation could be to turn the assignment from an individual project into a partner or group project. A number of students can work together to brainstorm ideas while one writes them all down for the group.

If a student has a reading problem and a script is being read aloud by the class, pair him with a friend in the class who reads well. Both will benefit from the interaction.

When handled correctly, mainstreaming offers as many growth experiences for the nondisabled students as for the mainstreamed student. Experiencing diversity early in life helps children learn to accept and appreciate others for their inner, creative being. It teaches children not to stereotype individuals based on physical appearances or first impressions. It enhances their ability to communicate with many different kinds of people. It encourages them to see people as wonders to be discovered rather than problems to solve.

One mother of a nondisabled student wrote this about her daughter's experience in the Pegasus performing company:

This was a worthwhile experience for Jane, who learned about handicaps and disabilities and how people can still have satisfying and fulfilling lives in spite of them. The Pegasus experience enlarged Jane's world and further sensitized her to people. Furthermore, it enhanced her perspective, which has been, due to limited worldly experiences, somewhat confined. I feel very positive about the Pegasus experience for Jane and feel it might even affect her future choice of career.

CASTING SCENES AND PLAYS

There are a number of ways to approach casting. In educational theatre, a teacher or director needs to balance his personal artistic desires and the need to present a successful overall product to parents with the need for in-

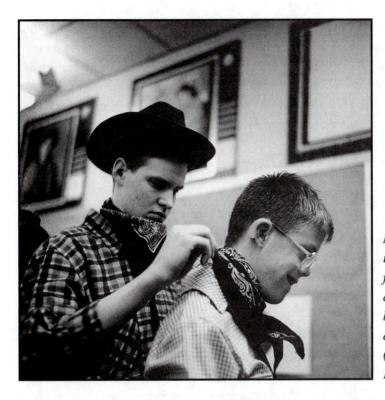

Mainstreaming builds friendships and respect between actors. (Photo by Keith Jenkins)

dividual students to achieve success while they are being challenged and stretched artistically.

Many teachers and directors like to play it safe and stick with typecasting. This approach casts students in roles which are very much like their own personality or physical type. An outgoing student would be cast as a very social, confident character while a shy, quiet student would be cast as the "wallflower" in the play. An athletic-looking young man would always play the jock and a thin, sensitive-looking boy with glasses would always play the nerd.

Applied to students with disability, typecasting means that a student who is deaf could only play a deaf character: Belinda in *Johnny Belinda,* Helen Keller in *The Miracle Worker,* or Sarah Norman in *Children of a Lesser God.* A student who uses a wheelchair might be cast as Brick (whose leg is in a cast) in *Cat on a Hot Tin Roof* or as Franklin Delano Roosevelt (who was a wheelchair user) in *Sunrise at Campobello.*

It is important in the professional theatre to allow actors with disabilities to play disabled roles instead of always casting able-bodied actors in them. Mark Medoff has stipulated that all professional productions of *Children of a Lesser God* must use deaf and hard-of-hearing actors in the deaf and hard-of-hearing roles. This provides obvious employment opportunities for disabled actors. However, to *only* offer disabled roles to actors who have disabilities is limiting.

Teachers and directors who typecast often justify it by saying that typecasting is done in professional theatre, so students should get used to it. While playing a character close to oneself is not necessarily easy, playing only one kind of character again and again does not stretch the physical, emotional, or imaginative range of any acting student. It sends the young person a message of "you can't be . . ." instead of "you can be . . . anything you want to be." This message is easily generalized from the classroom into everyday life.

The opposite of typecasting is casting against type. In this style, students are challenged with roles which are unlike themselves. This can generate growth if the character is not too far away from the student in age and experience and the teacher/director offers plenty of coaching support. However, it will generate only frustration and confusion if the character is too complex or too far away from the student's life experience. Asking a fifth grader to perform King Lear will probably be too big a stretch; asking him to play Demetrius in *A Midsummer Night's Dream* will probably work fine. A teacher/director must be able to judge when a student is ready to be stretched and what kinds of challenges he currently needs.

When casting students with disabilities, I like to use "blind" or nontraditional casting. This type of approach casts the actor in terms of acting ability and emotional rightness for a character rather than physical similarity to it. For example, an actor in a wheelchair who has a strong voice and stage presence might be very appropriately cast as John Proctor in *The Crucible* or as Stanley Kowalski in *A Streetcar Named Desire* regardless of the physical descriptions of the character in the script. Peter Sellars used this nontraditional approach when he cast Howie Seago, a virile actor of great physical presence who is deaf, as the mighty Greek hero Ajax in his production of Aeschylus's *Ajax*.

Casting should also take the actor's strengths and weaknesses into consideration. An actor with a good sense of timing and verbal dexterity can do a lot with a character from a farce by wordmasters like Oscar Wilde or Tom Stoppard. An actor with good physical control and an ability to exaggerate will enjoy the challenge of bringing stock characters from the commedia dell'arte to life.

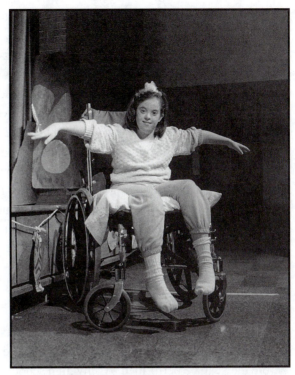

Use your imagination when incorporating assistive devices into shows. A wheelchair can become a moveable throne. (Photo by Allison Walker)

If you know a student has difficulty memorizing lines, you can cast him in roles where most of his lines are motivated by answering the questions of other characters or responding to physical actions done to his character by others. This way the majority of his responses are directly initiated by another character in the play. All he really has to do is to listen and react.

A student who has a poor sense of himself in space can be cast as a member of a group of characters who enter and exit together. He can stick with the other members of his group and take his movement cues from them. If he begins to wander, they can get him back with the group.

Instead of just ignoring them, assistive devices can be creatively incorporated into a play. A wheelchair can become a moveable throne, a boat, or a king's royal carriage, turning it from an image of impairment into an image of strength. A crutch can become a sword. A loop-style hearing aid could be incorporated into a robot's costume or used as an espionage device of a spy.

A brilliant example of creatively employing assistive devices for conscious artistic purposes was used in the Goodman Theatre's production of *She Always Said, Pablo.* The play portrays Gertrude Stein's turbulent relationship with Pablo Picasso by juxtaposing Stein's words with dramatized images from Picasso's paintings. Director Frank Galati cast Susan Nussbaum, an actress who uses a motorized wheelchair, as Gertrude Stein. Nussbaum's wheelchair became part of the design and blocking strategy of the play, integrating Picasso's famous image of Stein in her armchair into every onstage picturization. Nussbaum/Stein in her chair elegantly glided in and out of life-sized Picasso images, weaving the play together with words and movement.

HELPING STUDENTS
WITH SCRIPT MEMORIZATION

Sooner or later in most acting classes, students begin working with scripted material. Monologues and scenes must be committed to memory before they can be performed. As my high school acting teacher used to say, "Acting doesn't really begin until the lines are memorized. You can't act with a script in your hand."

Memorization of lines can cause problems for many students, but particularly for students who have cognitive disabilities. No matter how you slice it, memorization takes time and commitment. Very few individuals have photographic memories or are what theatre people call "quick studies." However, there are ways to make memorization, if not pain-free, at least a little easier.

First, make sure the actors understand what they are saying. If the lines don't make sense, they will be harder to memorize. Memorization is done primarily through a cognitive device called "chunking." Bits of information are associated with other bits and slowly built into easily recognized units or patterns which are stored in the brain. If the information doesn't make sense, it can't be chunked to anything else. Compare the task of memorizing an unrelated list of items—say, a shopping list—with a poem which has a rhythm, images, idea or story, and a rhyme scheme to hold it together. Unless the items on the shopping list are associated with emotional and sensory images, they will be very difficult to bring back to mind. A poem can be remembered for years without rehearsal.

I have found again and again that lines on which students have memory blocks are lines which they don't quite understand. One actor couldn't remember a joke because he didn't understand what was funny. Once I pointed out the play on words—which had been obvious to me, but had escaped him—he was able to remember the joke word for word.

The best method for memorization is different for each person depending on his dominant or preferred learning channel. Most people who have auditory processing strengths will read their lines from the script over and over again out loud. This repetition of saying the lines and listening to them serves to anchor them and their sequence in long-term memory.

Actors who have reading problems, but auditory strengths can tape-record a scene or speech and play the tape over and over again. If they can't read at all, they can just listen while the tape plays. This is how most of us learn popular songs; we hear them forty or fifty times on the radio and suddenly we find we're singing along. If actors can read, following along with the script while listening to the tape can reinforce the lines visually.

If an actor's reading problems are bad enough that he can't read his lines smoothly enough to sound natural on the recording, the teacher or a parent can make the audio tape for him. Whenever Pegasus has their first read through of a script, we tape it and I edit out the mistakes and side comments. Then I make copies and give them to all the cast members. Even some of the nondisabled cast members like to learn their scripts by listening to the tape-recorded version!

Students with kinesthetic strengths sometimes memorize better when repeating their lines out loud while in motion. One of my Pegasus actors always reads through her script while riding in the car. Somehow the motion helps her focus and learn. Other actors pace the room or rock in a rocking chair while they memorize. Some perform their blocking as they say their lines aloud.

Lines and blocking could also be videotaped and sent home to view. I have tried this when teaching sign language to a group of hearing actors and it worked well. It should work as a method of line memorization for a visual learner, too.

Lisa, one of my Pegasus actors who has Down syndrome, found that typing out her lines on the computer and then reading them back to her father helped her learn her lines. Other students find the same benefit from writing out lines over and over again by hand. The kinesthetic and visual repetitions help cement the words into long-term memory.

If a student doesn't know his dominant learning style and if you haven't guessed it from observing which kinds of teaching examples he responds to most quickly, ask him to try several of these methods until he finds one that works well for him.

It is crucial to enlist the help of parents, siblings, and friends in practicing lines. Most lines are in the form of dialogue and each line is a response to what another actor has said. Knowing one's cues is as important as knowing one's lines. Without cues, the actor doesn't know when to come in.

Running lines with another person is one of the best ways to review and maintain lines once the initial memorization is done.

Running lines can become an enjoyable time of positive social interaction between parent and child as they work on the formative stages of a creative project together. Sometimes unexpected bonuses come out of it, too. Lisa's father had this to say about her line-learning experience:

> She was delighted [typing out her lines on the computer and reading them back] and it helped her learn her lines. It also led to a computer letter to her sister describing her role. Eventually she learned her lines very well and could recite the lines of many others as well.

I asked a number of my colleagues at the Bethesda Academy to share a few of their experiences teaching students with special needs who were mainstreamed into their classes. They graciously consented to write the following essays.

Positive Experiences with Mainstreaming

by Caleen Sinnette Jennings

I believe that theatre has the power to heal. I have seen the power of theatre to build self-esteem and confidence and, because of this, I have always prided myself on managing the classroom experience so that each child feels respected and valued. The stakes for me were raised significantly when I learned I would have a student with Tourette syndrome mainstreamed into my acting class. I was, quite frankly, intimidated.

The wonderful thing about teaching is that you are forced to live by your own dictates. Often I tell my students, "When you're feeling scared and nervous, and the stakes are at their highest, that's the greatest opportunity for learning. To risk is everything!" Now it was my time to risk.

The first thing I did was to read several articles on Tourette syndrome, including a chapter from Oliver Sack's book *The Man Who Mistook His Wife for a Hat*, entitled "Wiccy, Ticcy Ray." I was fascinated by this mysterious condition, especially by the fact that it often manifests itself so perniciously in such highly intelligent and creative people.

"Okay," I thought, "it would be terrific if Gerald and I were able to work one-on-one, but I will have at least nineteen other kids in the classroom: kids who are bright, creative, demanding, and somewhat pampered. Now what do I do?" My biggest concern was that either I or one of his classmates would say something to hurt his feelings or, worse, to physically endanger him.

I knew that the only way I could honestly deal with the situation was to confront it outright. I decided to speak with Gerald and ask him openly about his condition, his past experiences in acting, and his concerns about interacting with his classmates. Gerald was a bright, articulate, and compassionate young boy. We spoke briefly and he answered my questions candidly and with unusual maturity.

The first thing I did on the first day of class was to assemble everyone in a big circle. I told them about myself and outlined the way in which we would build the script for our final class presentation together. I told them the importance of working in an ensemble and how they had to trust and respect each other. I then called on them to introduce themselves to the group and tell us what was important to know about them. I made sure that Gerald was towards the middle of the process so that he wasn't immediately put on the spot.

When it came around to him, Gerald talked about himself, briefly mentioning his condition at the end of his introduction. I asked him if he would mind fielding some questions. He said that would be OK. I asked him:

- What is important for us to know about Tourette syndrome?
- How do the symptoms manifest themselves?
- What did he need us to do when he had one of his episodes?

He explained that he knew the sounds he made were strange and disturbing to others and that he did not make them voluntarily. He also knew that many of his classmates would be tempted to imitate the sounds he made. But he told us that this was the worst thing we could do because that would intensify the symptoms. He said that during an episode, he would stay off to the side and asked that the group just ignore him.

I asked the group if they would commit themselves to the ensemble by respecting Gerald's wishes. They agreed unanimously. There were a few more questions from students, then I thanked Gerald heartily for his candor and moved on to the rest of the introductions.

One of my standard first-day exercises has always been mirroring. I have students stand opposite each other and mirror each other's body movements and voices. Clearly this would not do in this situation. So I went back to my acting texts and devised some other ice breakers. Gerald's presence in the class had already forced me to discard some old teaching habits in a positive way.

In the middle of an exercise that day, Gerald had an episode. He made uncontrollable clicking and whooping sounds, tapped with a pencil, and kicked his foot against the chair. The sudden explosion of noise, quite naturally, attracted our attention. But because Gerald had prepared us, we watched only for a few seconds, as if to confirm the information he had told us, and then re-focused on our work.

I wish I could say that the students rallied around him and he instantly became an accepted member of the group. But why should ten-year-olds be any different from adults? Most of the students shied away from him.

However, I only had one instance of a student making fun of him. When I noticed Matt clicking along with Gerald during an episode, I stopped the class. I said in a firm voice, "Matt, do you remember the ensemble commitment we talked about in the first class? Do you remember Gerald's request that we not imitate him?"

"Yes," Matt answered sheepishly.

"Well, I want all of us to stick to those commitments we made. Now let's get back to work."

There were no more incidents.

I paired Gerald with lots of students in different games and exercises throughout the beginning classes. As I got to know the rest of the students, I began to get a sense of who would make good scene partner combinations. I eventually put Gerald in a scene with two other boys and a girl who had shown maturity and compassion throughout the semester. They developed a wonderful rapport working on the scene and this carried through into performance.

As the semester went on, Gerald had many episodes of varying intensity. The astonishing thing was that they never occurred during his scene work. He was an excellent actor. He loved the theatre, could sing any one of a thousand show tunes, and always had his lines memorized before anyone else.

Our show went up and Gerald did a splendid job. I got positive feedback from his parents, but the best feedback was Gerald's smile during the curtain call.

I used some of the same techniques the next year when a young deaf woman joined my summer camp acting class. Leslie was accompanied by an interpreter, a colleague of mine on staff at the Academy.

The first day of class we did similar introductions. I was able to ask Leslie and her interpreter how they worked together and what we could do to ensure good communication. I asked for information that I genuinely wanted to know, in addition to information her classmates might want to know, but be too shy to ask:

- When we talk to you, should we look at you or your interpreter?
- Where do you want us to stand when we are talking to you?
- Will you let me know if I am speaking too quickly?
- Do you prefer to sign without speaking or to speak as you sign?

In this case, my students were fairly mature adolescents and there was less risk of imitation or mockery. My greatest challenges were remembering to speak slowly and not to speak with my back turned away from her. I made it a point that the class learn simple signs to communicate with Leslie.

Leslie's acting was powerful and she soon had the respect of her classmates. Her biggest obstacle, as one might expect, was using her entire body and allowing her voice full volume for maximum expression. I felt that encouraging her to release her voice would free her physically and mentally. Just as with the other students, I gave her acting notes in front of the class. Everyone shared in each other's growth and development. I knew that once Leslie knew we would not be shaken by the sounds she made, she would be freer to commit her body and her mind to the monologue at hand. I wrote her a special monologue entitled, "SHHHHH." The piece dealt with the frustrations of being told to shut up and not talk so loudly. Leslie performed the piece with an anger and intensity that were riveting.

I now teach at the university level and my prior experiences with mainstreaming have been invaluable. I am encountering more and more forms of dyslexia and other learning challenges in performing arts students.

I had a young deaf woman mainstream into one of my improvisational acting classes. Figuring out the logistics for her interpreter during the improvisational scenes took considerable thought and planning, but we created some fabulous improvs! I also taught this same student a semester-long independent study in playwrighting, during which she created a script about her coming of age. We worked without an interpreter in this instance.

I still find what makes me most nervous, but what ensures the greatest success, is to openly acknowledge the special circumstances involved in the interaction and to have each student clearly articulate his/her wishes to me and the group. We can then move forward with awareness and a beginning measure of trust.

It has been helpful to learn from, share resources with, and get support from colleagues who also work with the learning and physically challenged. And, of course, the smiles and hugs I get from my students are the nicest part of the whole experience!

My Experiences with Mainstreamed Students

by Elizabeth Van Den Berg Toperzer

I have been fortunate to have had several students with disabilities mainstreamed into my drama classes. I say "fortunate" because these students have taught me more about teaching than any others and, hopefully, they have helped to make me a better teacher.

My First Experience

I had many concerns the first time I was told I would have a student with special needs in my acting class. My first concern was crucial: would I know how to help this child have a successful experience and not turn her off to theatre and the arts? My second concern was about the other children: how would they react, how would they treat her, would they work with her in the ensemble style of my class? What would I do if there was a problem?

I was given information about Stacy and her disability. Stacy had hydrocephalus which had caused learning disabilities. She also had some difficulties with speech and movement. Even though she had never taken an acting class before, the special needs director had met her and felt she would do very well mainstreamed in an acting class.

At first I thought my worst fears were being realized when the group noticed that Stacy was different and began to ostracize her. I made use of her lateness to class one day to have a talk with them about Stacy's uniqueness. I asked the other students for suggestions on how best to help her and make her part of the class.

As it turned out, Stacy was a wonderful addition to the group. She couldn't remember her blocking, so I enlisted other class members as her helpers. I always paired her with a responsible child who was making her entrance or exit at the same time and who would make sure she got to the right spot on stage.

I helped Stacy draw diagrams of the groundplan [the arrangement of furniture on the set] and trace her blocking pattern. She had trouble with line memorization, so I always gave her mother an extra copy of the script. At home they made a cassette tape of Stacy's portion of the dialogue so she could review her lines through listening to them as well as through looking at them in the script.

Stacy's mom was a dream. She was very open and always in communication with me about how class was going and how Stacy was doing.

Stacy had a successful experience and came back to take many more drama classes at the Academy. It took a lot of give and take, patience, and keeping the lines of communication open with everyone to make it work.

Too Loud!

Peter had auditory processing problems. His mother told me that he had recently gone through the Tomatis ear training method and was now able to make sense of sounds. However, she didn't make it clear to me that because of this, Peter would be extremely sensitive to loud sounds.

I had planned one class around balloons—jumping over, with, and around them, and then becoming a balloon. During the first exercise, one balloon popped. I had prepped the class that this might occur, and they all seemed to feel it was OK, except for Peter, who put his hands over both ears and would not take them away. I recognized the problem and changed my lesson plan immediately so as not to have any more popping balloons. However, the damage was done. It was only after class when he left the room and went into the hallway that Peter finally removed his hands from his ears. His mom then explained his sensitivity. From then on, I avoided loud sounds and we had no more difficulty.

Lines of Communication

To me, the most important issue in mainstreaming students who have disabilities is keeping all lines of communication open. This means being upfront about problems with parents, students, their classmates, and the administration.

Having a special needs director as a liaison has also been invaluable and very important in helping me get the information I need about the disability of each student.

I have learned not to be afraid to ask students what they need in order to learn.

Teaching Mainstreamed Students
by Kathryn Chase Bryer

I feel that having students with special needs mainstreamed in my classes has helped me grow as a teacher and has helped the other children in my classes become better people. I would like to share a few experiences I had last year.

Randy was four years old and had sensory processing difficulties. His mother really wanted him to take a drama class, but did not want him placed in a class for students who have special needs, so she signed him up for my Dramatic Play class on Tuesday afternoon. When the special needs director called to ask about Randy's disability, his mother said his sensory impairment was *very* mild and that his biggest problem was his delayed language development.

As soon as I saw him, I knew mainstreaming Randy in a regular class was going to be a lot of work. Randy was in his own little world. He would talk to himself. He would spin. Frequently he would get up and leave the circle to investigate other things in the room. He had difficulty following directions. His language was at a two-year-old level. I was not sure how much he actually understood of what I was saying and if he even knew what the rest of us were doing.

I asked the special needs director to come in and observe the class. She felt that mentally Randy was following everything that was happening, but that physically his body was not at his command. I asked for some specific techniques to help me make Randy's experience in my class successful.

The class had ten very active students in it. Too much was going on visually and auditorially for him to handle. The first thing we did was to switch him to a smaller class of only six on a different afternoon.

All students were given a different color mat to sit on at the beginning of class, so they would know where to sit. I had never used mats before.

Although we did it for Randy's benefit, I found this technique so useful that I have started using it with all the classes I teach with this age group.

In addition, another mat was placed outside the circle in a corner of the room. This was Randy's "spin mat." When he felt like he needed to start spinning, he could go there and spin until he felt the urge to spin subside. Then he could rejoin us on his mat in the circle. This was not used as punishment, but rather as a safe place where he could go to regain control.

We sat Randy directly across the circle from me so he could focus on what I was doing and saying. My aide sat next to Randy and kept him on task. Instead of cuing him with questions like "Where are you supposed to be looking?" she made simple, direct statements like "Look at Kate," or "Stay on your square."

After the first four weeks of class we invited the parents in and dramatized a short story about rabbits who sneak into a farmer's garden and eat his vegetables. Randy decided he would be a farmer in a story. He was having a hard time keeping it together during our presentation, and I spent much of the time narrating the story with my arms around him. At one point, the farmer is supposed to hear the rabbits outside the garden. I leaned down and asked Randy, "Do you hear that? What could that be out in your garden?" He looked up at me, smiled, and in a very clear voice said, "A weed wacker?" I knew we were on our way.

I saw great improvement in Randy over the year and felt that he was better able to control himself, and thus, really be a part of what we were doing.

Cheryl was another child who did not exactly fit her mother's description. Her mother said that she had cerebral palsy and wore a leg brace, but that she was cognitively normal—very bright and enthusiastic. This was true, but as soon as I saw her, I realized that Cheryl's mother had left a few details out of her description of her child's special needs. In addition to the leg brace, Cheryl also had a speech impediment which made her difficult to understand. She drooled and spat. She constantly wiped the resulting saliva on her hands and clothes.

I could see right away that in a class of this age (Grades Two and Three), where appearance is beginning to be important and working with partners is the norm, Cheryl might quickly become ostracized. So on the second meeting of the class, I sat everyone down and explained that we were all very different and that we were all going to have to work together in this class and that everyone of us had special needs. I asked the class to tell me what a special need was and then I told them we were going to go around in a circle and each person was going to say a special need that she had and how the group could answer this need.

I started the circle by saying that as the teacher, I had a special need that they all listen to me when I was talking, because if they didn't listen, we wouldn't be successful in our class. As we went around the circle, I was amazed by what I heard. One child said that he was very short and he needed people not to make fun of him because of this. Another child said that she got embarrassed easily and needed people not to laugh at her. When we got to Cheryl, she was very upfront and honest, explaining that often others were scared of her or didn't want to be near her because of her leg brace, etc. She asked that everyone just relax around her and treat her normally.

I felt that it was a very successful conversation. It really empowered everyone and made the group feel more together—a great way to start an acting class! I can't say we never had any problems, but I can say that these problems were honestly and directly dealt with and that I feel Cheryl's time in my class was successful.

The most important thing to remember in a mainstreamed situation is that every child in your classroom has special needs to be addressed. The students with disabilities just have the more obvious ones. Try as you might to anticipate every problem, you just can't know what is going to happen. You have to remain flexible and be willing to follow your instincts.

At one point, I was working with a student who had learning disabilities. We were practicing some lines she was going to say on videotape. Try as she might, she couldn't remember them and burst into tears, saying, "I just can't do this." I knew I had to think fast or once again this kid was going to be in a situation in which she had "failed." Instead of giving the part to someone else, I calmed her down and told her that since I was narrating the story, I would just say her lines and she could repeat them. She was very happy with this idea and appeared in the video as planned. Flexibility and instinct.

When I am directing a show, I try to adapt it to fit each child's needs and abilities. When a child with a disability is in the cast, I see what he is capable of and what he wishes to do and then I work around that. If the audience doesn't hear a child who has a speech impediment as clearly as they would like or if the other actors must make room for a wheelchair on stage with them, so be it. The most important thing is that each child has a successful experience. Each individual success enhances the success of the whole group.

Mainstreaming Children with Special Needs
by Tim Reagan

My first experience with a child with disabilities was when I was in high school, working as an assistant swim teacher for the American Red Cross's Learn To Swim Program in Camillus, NY. One energetic eight-year-old had Down syndrome. She had been placed with a group of children two to three years younger and she functioned extremely well in the class. Her love for the water was a positive influence on the other children. They realized that they were all in the same boat—either you learned to swim or you sank to the bottom! I was given no training in terms of special needs, so in my naivete, I made an intuitive choice to treat her like the other kids. I believe that because I set up no psychological barriers through my approach and because she had no physical disabilities which hindered learning to swim, she was accepted by the other children. Her disability did not stop her from meshing with the other children or keep her from "diving" into the lessons.

This experience allowed me to see a child with a disability in a setting where she functioned like other children. So, when I had a child with Down syndrome mainstreamed into my creative drama class, I approached the challenge with enthusiasm, yet with caution.

Brian was ten and had never taken an acting class at the Bethesda Academy, although he had been in plays before at school and at camp. I was briefed on Brian's disability and given some literature on Down syndrome by the Academy's special needs director. Her advice was to treat him like any other child.

There were eight children in the class, including Brian. The other children were very articulate and very imaginative. We acted out stories, played theatre games, and built puppets. I did not have an assistant for the class and hindsight tells me that I should have had one in order to maintain control and re-focus Brian when he became distracted. However, despite the challenges we faced, as a class we did conquer some astounding creative activities.

Brian was genuinely interested in the class. He was well-focused and attentive; however, his attention span was rather short. He would often grow tired of a game or finish an art project before the others. It was sometimes difficult keeping him involved and occupied while the other children were still continuing with an activity. Fortunately, one girl in the class assumed a leadership role with Brian. She often took responsibility for him and assisted him with completing or following through with activities. This young girl seemed to sense that Brian had special needs and she innately was able to respond to them.

The biggest frustration came whenever Brian did not have anything specific to do. When he was watching someone else work or when we were between exercises, he would start making annoying grunting noises. It bothered the children in the class and, at times, myself. I don't think he was making them intentionally; in fact, he may not have even realized it. At first I tried to ignore them, but eventually, I got to the point where I had to ask him to stop. Whenever he would start, I would call his attention to it, just as I would for any other child in a class, and he would stop.

Overall, I don't know if the children in the class ever did become truly comfortable with Brian. I sensed a distance that they placed between themselves and him. Efforts were made by the children to include him, but I think they became frustrated, as I often did, when there was no marked improvement in personal self-management skills from week to week.

In an effort to keep the momentum of the class going and keep all the students challenged, I sometimes felt as if I were leaving Brian behind. On occasion I found I wanted to give him more individual one-on-one help or slow down the pace of the class to give him more time, but I couldn't do so without losing the rest of the class. Sometimes the pace of the class served as an encouraging challenge to him, but sometimes I worried that the "hurdles" I was asking him to jump over were a little too high. Because of this, I felt like I was not meeting his needs, that I was short-changing him. Later, however, I found out that he thoroughly enjoyed himself in the two semesters of creative drama that he had taken from me. I think he really appreciated being treated like a "regular kid."

Now when I run into him in the halls, we exchange brief conversations in a normal way. He seems to enjoy and respect this kind of communication. I do, too!

The Academy conducts an integrated arts program for the Kenwood Park Children's Center, a day care center located in the same building as we are. That is where I met Anita. She had joined KPCC's Kindergarten Complementary Program because she was not having a positive experience with her previous child care provider. I believe this was because Anita had a disability—she was blind in one eye and had partial sight in the other. She wore large, thick glasses and had a tendency to bump into or trip over objects which her peripheral vision did not pick up.

All I was told by the KPCC staff was that Anita was very shy and withdrawn because of her sight problems. Not knowing, at that time, how severe her impairment was, I conducted my creative drama class the way I always do. Anita immediately caught on and began to flourish. The arts seemed to open a door for her. She found something she could do and enjoy as well. Anita became wonderful at using her imagination. She began to use full sentences, express her thoughts and ideas clearly, and communicate very effectively to the other children. After about a semester in the integrated arts program, Anita began taking art and drama classes at the Academy in the afternoon as well.

Later I found out from her mother that drama had been a turning point in Anita's life. Because of her experiences, she generated a strong sense of self-esteem and has come out of her shell.

Vincent is another child who compensates for his lack of mobility and sight with the active use of his imagination. Now eight years old, Vincent had a stroke when he was young. Because of this trauma, he is blind in his right eye and his speech and motor activities are affected.

My first contact with Vincent was in our Summer Camp(us)!, a four-week summer drama day camp, which I direct. At first, the children in

Vincent's group could see that he was different, but it was obvious that they were not quite sure what his "problem" was. Fortunately, the faculty and staff were briefed by the special needs director on Vincent's disability. This enabled them to make the appropriate adaptations and to treat Vincent like any other child. Since his motor skills slowed him down, he was allowed extra time for every activity. The accepting behavior modeled by the faculty and staff seemed to ease the distant behavior of the other children and soon Vincent could be seen playing and socializing with a number of children in his group.

Vincent often visited me in the camp office. He seemed to appreciate and need this one-on-one attention. Conversations in the office were relaxed and often brief, but it appeared that Vincent used this as an opportunity to "re-energize" himself. He developed a wonderful camaraderie with the assistant camp director in these visits as well.

Vincent fully participated in all the creative activities at the camp, which included acting, art, drama, dance, and singing. He did appear a little "lost" in his production of *Magic Theatre,* but I think this was because it was his first time on stage and he took an interest in watching the people watching him! The presence of the audience obviously intrigued him.

Every afternoon at the conclusion of the camp day we have an informal presentation called "Get And Go." Campers can get up and share skits or songs they have developed in class or worked up on their own. Vincent requested that his dad do a "Get And Go" for the camp. His dad is from Ethiopia and plays several instruments native to that country. It was obvious that Vincent was proud of his dad and wanted to share his dad's talents with his friends at camp. It was a very special time for him, and for us. We could see the sense of closeness he had developed from this camp experience.

Mainstreaming a Child Who Is in a Wheelchair

by Jeanie Hayes Hatch

Daniel was a student who had osteogenesis imperfecta, a condition commonly known as brittle bone disease. He was mainstreamed into my Story Theatre class for eight- to twelve-year-olds at a two-week summer drama camp. In each class we played drama games and acted out a story from Greek mythology, fairy tales, or folk tales. The last few classes were focused on creating our own improvised stories.

Daniel was in a wheelchair, but had complete use of his hands, head, and upper body. Accordingly, I chose warm-up exercises at the beginning of each class that could be played sitting down so that Daniel could be involved from the very beginning of class.

One game we played was "Thumper." It involves using your hands to describe your favorite hobby. For example, if a student liked to read, he would put his two hands together, flat out, like a book. After everyone in the circle had pantomimed their hobbies, students would pass them back and forth to each other without speaking.

In another game we passed around a scarf. It was up to each actor to make the scarf into something different from what it actually was. For example, it could be rolled up and worn as a belt or hung around the neck as a necklace or folded up into a sandwich.

After warm-ups we would play a drama game which stressed verbal skills. For example, I might ask each child to describe his favorite play space and show us using the drama space. With the help of an assistant, Daniel was able to describe and show us where he liked to play.

If I used exercises that involved only physical movement, I made Daniel my assistant or the game caller. Here he could be involved and feel important as he monitored the game. At the end of every class we played "On the Bank/In the River." In this game a line of masking tape on the floor creates the "River Bank." When the actors are on one side of the tape, they are "on the bank." When they are on the other side, they are "in the river." A caller tells them to jump "on the bank" or "in the river." When they hear the command, they must immediately hop over the tape to the correct side. Commands are quickly alternated or repeated and if an actor gets confused and lands in the wrong spot, he is "out." Daniel was always the caller and whenever he spoke, the other students jumped. It was one of his favorite games to play.

Next came the story. I chose stories which involved hand movements as opposed to lots of running, jumping, or climbing. For instance, when we acted out the Greek myth "Persephone," I incorporated elaborate gestures and a short game of "Follow the Leader." Daniel was able to participate in all aspects of the story.

The last class was an informal presentation for the parents. We played "Typewriter," an improvisational game in which one actor "writes" the story on the spot and the others have to enact the story as it is being created. Daniel was the Author who "typed up" the story, improvising it as he went along. Daniel was involved in every aspect of the class. He appeared to be having fun and found no obstacles to his participation in any exercises. The other students enjoyed the class as well. They accepted Daniel and responded to his directions with respect when he was serving as the caller for games like "On The Bank/In The River."

The most important factor in the success of the class was Daniel's enthusiasm and intense desire to do drama. He is an excellent actor. Channeling his emotions into drama activities is one of his true delights. I think he could probably never have enough of it. He would be happy doing drama all day long.

Osteogenesis imperfecta is a very frustrating condition for an active and intelligent ten-year-old boy, but Daniel never gives up trying. He is always ready to participate and he always wants to learn more. Because of his creative spirit and his indomitable courage, he has been a teacher to me.

Mainstreaming Deaf Students

by Lisa Agogliati

My background is dance and theatre—in that order. I am a movement person first and foremost. I've been dancing since I was a very small child, but I got my BA in theatre administration so I could make a living! Currently, I serve as the director of the Academy's dance program and I head its financial administration.

My first experience with mainstreaming was life changing. Several years ago I worked as a counselor for the seventh and eighth grade group in the Academy's summer performing arts camp. In my group of 18 students, I had Leslie, a 14-year-old deaf girl. She had always been interested in the arts, but the camp would be her first intensive experience working with dance, acting, and voice classes in addition to performing in a full-scale musical production.

My main concern was communication. I met with Leslie and her mother a month and a half before camp started and learned that Leslie mainstreamed in her school through Cued Speech, a simple speech-based method of communication. Cued Speech is very easy to learn because it involves only eight hand shapes in four positions to represent all the different sounds in the English language. I immediately jumped right in and took a crash course.

Cued Speech combined with fingerspelling worked very successfully. Although sign language was not Leslie's major mode of communicating, we did incorporate sign into several songs in the production, which provided her with a featured role in the production and the entire cast with a new learning experience. That summer proved to be a turning point in both of our lives.

Over the course of the next year both Leslie and I started learning sign language. I became fascinated particularly with sign for the stage, because for me it incorporates the best aspects of theatre and movement, my two life-long loves. When Leslie returned to camp the next summer, I became her interpreter, using mostly Pidgin Signed English and fingerspelling. We hired a deaf actress named Rita Corey to teach a class called "Signing for the Theatre" to all the campers, grades one through twelve, as part of the regular camp day. "Signing for the Theatre" was great movement and improvisation training as it focused on teaching sign language through theatre games. Each production that summer highlighted at least one main production number performed by the cast entirely in sign. These signed performances were extremely well received by the camp community and are now a full part of all of the Academy's summer programs.

The most significant effect of my experience is that I have volunteered to spearhead the development of the Deaf Access component of the Academy's Special Needs Program. This component includes providing sign-interpreted performances for all of the Academy's Young People's Theatre productions, offering outreach classes and workshops at local schools which have deaf students, mainstreaming deaf students into regular Academy classes taught by theatre and dance instructors (deaf and hearing) who sign, integrating sign language into the Academy curriculum, and creating children's theatre programs with the Deaf Access Performing Company. The Deaf Access Company, comprised of deaf and hearing high school students, presents fully signed and voiced productions which also include music, dance, and audience participation. Many of the hearing actors in the company come from deaf families or have a background in sign language, so everyone in the company can communicate with each other. As you can see, my experiences with mainstreaming have given a whole new direction to my career!

Mainstreaming in the Visual Arts Classroom

by Gail Gorlitz

When I first encountered Miranda in my visual arts classroom, I was dismayed. She was small for her age, her skills were low, and she was different. Her voice was unmodulated and, frequently, too loud. She needed information one piece at a time. And she needed full-time attention. The other children were immediately aware of Miranda's differentness. We were all a little intimidated and I knew I needed to take a special approach.

I got an assistant, a high school student named Ellen, for the class. I instructed Ellen to sit next to Miranda and give her all the attention she wanted. Miranda wanted it all! For five sessions, Miranda happily worked with Ellen while I worked with the rest of the class, checking in from time to time. Miranda was in the happily messy stage of art play.

The sixth session Ellen was absent. Miranda expressed regret that Ellen wasn't there, but then she focused on the instructions for the class's assignment and worked mostly on her own for the entire hour. She was intensely involved in the project and her product was incredible—a creative approach to the problem and an orderly solution. It was a breakthrough in independence, skill level, and risk taking.

Her project—a mandala—caught my attention in a new way. Initially, I had focused on Miranda as one of two extremely needy children in a class of thirteen. Now I really looked at the child. As her interest in the project was captured, my interest in her was captured. Over the next six sessions, I spent more time with Miranda and Ellen spent more time with the rest of the class. We were both available to Miranda, but she also felt secure enough to work alone and we encouraged this. Her confidence soared and she became much more outgoing, making friends with some of the other children. I began to appreciate her dry wit and I missed her when she was absent. I showed Miranda my growing affection for her and she returned that affection to the whole class. Since that time, she has taken every class I've offered. Her personal and artistic growth continues.

I think many factors contributed to Miranda's success. Her needs were always met and her wishes were accommodated within reason. She received attention when she needed it. Her abilities and choices were respected. Whenever possible, we said yes to her, as we did to all the students. The classroom was set up so new materials were introduced every week. Their uses and care were explained and then they were made available to the students, placed within reach from that time on. This promoted mastery and free choice. Most important of all was a growing relationship of respect and affection with her teachers and the other children. It all worked together.

Sometimes I look at this child and think about my initial fear and avoidance, a reaction to coping with her differences. I would have missed so much by not getting to know her. She has taught me more and helped me to change more than any student in recent years. I'm grateful.

Lee came into my third grade art class on the first day with a jump through the door, a leap across the table, and a flying tackle that knock-

ed another student backwards. He was very active and his body movements were large. Anyone sitting next to him had their work swept onto
the floor within five minutes.

I offered Lee a whole table to himself. He was delighted. Problem #1
solved.

Twenty minutes later, Lee was on his feet demonstrating karate kicks to
the other children's heads. I asked him to stop and he informed me that
he could not stop because he was "an Indian." OK. I told Lee that he
could go to the carpeted area of the room and do his Indian dance, but
that he was a "NO TOUCHING INDIAN." He could not touch any student or object. This was fine with him. He whirled and flew around for
awhile, then sat down and finished his work.

I immediately saw that his skill level was high, so I presented him with
a challenging project and frequently showed his ingenious solutions to the
class. This helped him focus more on his work and relate more positively
to other students.

During the next several classes he got restless again and become a
"NO TOUCHING INDIAN." Subsequently, he seemed to need to do this
less frequently, but he did want to work in odd places in the room—in the
closet, lying on the rug, sitting in the corner. I allowed this and after
awhile he went quietly to different spaces when he felt the need. Other students began to join him in this creative use of the room.

Lee's skills in visual art were very high and the class benefited from
being around his spontaneity and good humor. He was initially disruptive, but quickly became a strong asset to us all.

epilogue

When Jacob started out in my creative drama class, he didn't have any friends. Why he didn't soon become very clear. He was an instigator. He loved to set up fights between other people and watch them go at it. He was a real master at this. He would sit back and observe the others to see where their emotional weaknesses were that particular day. Then he would start feeding one unsuspecting student ammunition to be used against another, ammunition that was too juicy not to pick up and use.

"Roberto's hair looks stupid today," he'd whisper to Sharon.

"Sharon has a button missing on her blouse," he'd whisper to Roberto.

Soon Roberto and Sharon were busy insulting each other and if I didn't intervene quickly enough, they would come to blows.

Each week when we turned off the lights and lay down to go on our guided fantasy, Jacob would position himself right in the middle of everyone else and kick an arm here, nudge a leg there, bump an elbow, tickle a side, blow on the top of a head.

I'd hear:

"Stop it!"
"Hey, stop it!"
"Don't touch me!"
And it was always caused by Jacob.

Finally one day while we were on an underwater treasure hunt, I couldn't stand it anymore. I silently signaled to my assistant. Marilyn swooped down, picked Jacob up, and bodily carried him out of the center of the group into the hall.

"What's the problem with you?" she asked. "Why do you always pick fights with other people?"

"Because no one is my friend," he replied.

"How can they like you if you pick on them all the time?"

"I don't know. People just don't like me."

"Well, I like you."

Their conversation about making friends and wanting to be liked went on for about twenty minutes. Finally they returned and Jacob was much calmer and more focused.

Slowly, over the course of a year, Jacob stopped being an instigator and became a class leader. He loved acting out animals, particularly large birds. We started having a great time together. In drama class he had found a place where he was accepted for who he was and his creativity was given an appropriate outlet.

With this acceptance came another change. He started to want to have a friend. He picked Willard, another boy about his age, who was also extremely creative and active. They worked together in class and got along well, but since they lived at opposite ends of the metropolitan area, their relationship ended each week when class was over and their mothers took them home.

One day in late November, Jacob decided he wanted to stay after class and play on the swings outside with his new friend —extending his friendship to a new level. Only he couldn't ask. Asking meant facing rejection. His personal history told him nobody ever really wanted to be his friend.

Jacob's mother arrived before Willard's did. Jacob whispered what he wanted to do in his mother's ear.

"Well, ask him," she said.

"I can't," was the reply and he wandered aimlessly around the classroom for awhile.

Back to his mother a few minutes later he whispered in her ear again.

"*You* have to ask him," she said.

"I can't!" He sighed in frustration and wandered away.

It took five whole minutes to summon up the courage to ask, but finally, he did. He went over to Willard and said, "Willard, would you run up the hill with me?"

Willard's face lit up, "Sure!"

And off they went, racing up the hill to the swing set together.

Jacob's mother got tears in her eyes and turned to me. "I can't believe he did that. It's so hard for him to make friends. That was wonderful to see."

Connecting with others is the real reason we are all here. But to connect with another human being means taking a risk. The risk of rejection. The risk of failure.

When I'm afraid of taking a leap into the unknown, I think of Jacob summoning up the courage to say, "Willard, would you run up the hill with me?"

And I know if he could do it, I can do it.

You can, too.

◼ appendix i—bibliography

Books on Drama with People who have Disabilities

Allen, Anne & George, *Everyone Can Win: Opportunities and Programs in the Arts for the Disabled,* McLean, VA: EPM Publications, 1988, 272 pages, softcover.

A look at various programs in the arts which are geared for people who have disabilities. Includes information on the Gallaudet Dance and Drama Departments, the Everyday People Players, Very Special Arts, and more.

Astell-Burt, Caroline, *Puppetry for Mentally Handicapped People,* London: Souvenir Press, 1981, 191 pages, soft cover.

An inspirational how-to puppetry book with excellent construction ideas.

Behr, Marcia Ward, et al., *Drama Integrates Basic Skills: Lesson Plans for the Learning Disabled,* Springfield, IL: Charles C. Thomas, Publisher, 1979, 117 pages, vinyl spiral.

A series of lesson plans using drama, art, and movement to teach basic academic skills and concepts to children who have learning disabilities. Developed at the Lab School of Washington.

Bragg, Bernard and Bergman, Eugene, *Lessons in Laughter: The Autobiography of a Deaf Actor,* Washington, DC: Gallaudet University Press, 1989, 219 pages, hardcover.

The story of Bernard Bragg, a professional actor, mime, playwright, and co-founder of the National Theatre of the Deaf.

Crain, Cynthia D., M.A., *Movement and Rhythmic Activities for the Mentally Retarded,* Springfield, IL: Charles C. Thomas, Publisher, 1981, 126 pages, hardcover.

Ideas for teaching nonverbal communication and enhancing body control and self-image through rhythm and movement. Written for experienced and inexperienced teachers and recreation specialists.

Dunne, T. & Warren, B., *Drama Games,* Ontario, Canada: Captus Press, 1989, 52 pages, softcover.
Drama games for people who have cognitive disabilities. The games in this book could be used with any group.

Eddy, Junius, *The Music Came from Deep Inside: A Story of Artists and Severely Handicapped Children,* Cambridge, MA: Brookline Books, 1989, 203 pages, softcover.
Story of a project which brought artists into several special education schools as an education experiment.

Ludins-Katz, Florence & Katz, Elias, *Art and Disabilities: Establishing the Creative Art Center for People with Disabilities,* Cambridge, MA: Brookline Books, 1990, 197 pages, softcover.
How to set up a visual arts center geared for people who have disabilities.

National Endowment for the Arts, "The Arts and 504: A 504 Handbook for Accessible Arts Programming," Washington, DC: NEA, revised 1989, 97 pages, softcover.
This handbook covers the regulations of Section 504 of the Rehabilitation Act of 1973, which prohibits discrimination against people with disabilities under any program receiving federal financial assistance. It offers many excellent suggestions for making arts organizations physically accessible and barrier-free.

Rickert, William and Bloomquist, Jane, *Resources in Theatre & Disability,* Lanham, MD: University Press of America, 1988, 192 pages, softcover.
Source book published by the Association for Theatre and Disability listing programs, people, and printed resources on theatre and disability.

Shaw, Ann, et al, *Perspectives: A Handbook in Drama and Theatre by, with, and for Handicapped Individuals,* Washington, DC: American Theatre Association, 1981, 247 pages, vinyl spiral.
Collection of articles by different groups who worked with disabled populations in the 70s.

Tomlinson, Richard, *Disability, Theatre and Education,* Bloomington: Indiana University Press, 1982, 186 pages, softcover.
Tomlinson discusses a theatre group for adults with disabilities which he directed in Britain in the 70s.

White, Susan Sternberg, *Social Skills & Self-Esteem Development through Drama Therapy Activities,* Minnetonka, MN: self-published, 1985, 47 pages, vinyl spiral.

A ten-session lesson plan of drama activities which can be used to enhance interpersonal relationships and feelings of self-worth for children and adults. Geared toward individuals with cognitive or emotional disabilities, but could be used with any group.

BOOKS ON DRAMA IN EDUCATION OR RECREATION

Barker, Clive, *Theatre Games: A New Approach to Drama Training,* London: Methuen, 1986, 226 pages, softcover.

How to use theatre games to develop acting skills.

Bett, Lynda and Stockley, Rebecca, *Improvisation through Theatresports: A Curriculum to Teach Basic Acting Skills and Improvisation,* 2nd rev. ed., Seattle: Thespis Productions, 1989, 225 pages, softcover.

Curriculum for teaching improvisational acting through games. Many physical and visually-based activities.

Blatner, Adam and Allee, *The Art of Play: An Adult's Guide to Reclaiming Imagination and Spontaneity,* New York: Human Sciences Press, 1988, 359 pages, softcover.

The Blatners have developed a drama workshop in which adults re-experience the joy of play. The book details the need for play in life, describes an Art of Play workshop, and outlines the educational, therapeutic, and recreation uses of drama and the other arts.

Caruso, Sandra and Clemens, Paul, *The Actor's Book of Improvisation: Dramatic Situations for the Teacher and the Actor,* New York: Penguin Books, 1992, 343 pages, softcover.

Collected source material from plays, films, novels, and real-life situations which can be dramatized by students.

Cullum, Albert, *Push Back the Desks,* New York: Citation Press, 1967, 223 pages, softcover.

How Albert Cullum integrated drama into his elementary classroom.

Delgado, Ramon, *Acting with Both Sides of Your Brain: Perspectives on the Creative Process,* New York: Holt, Rhinehart and Winston, 1986, 303 pages, hardcover.

Acting text which stresses discovery through the senses and using right-brain as well as left-brain processing.

Hodge, Francis, *Play Directing: Analysis, Communication, and Style,* Englewood Cliffs, NJ: Prentice-Hall, 1971, 394 pages, hardcover.
A very thorough step-by-step guide to directing, which takes both technique and inspiration into account.

Johnstone, Keith, *Impro: Improvisation and the Theatre,* New York: Routledge, 1981, 208 pages, softcover.
Improvisation techniques and exercises used by one of England's acting improvisation experts.

Kelly, Elizabeth Y., *The Magic If: Stanislavski for Children,* Baltimore: National Educational Press, 1973, 169 pages, hardcover.
Acting exercises and imagination games for children based on Stanislavski's Acting Method. The student learns how to use his senses and emotional memories to express his character physically and vocally.

King, Nancy, *Giving Form to Feeling,* New York: Drama Book Specialists, 1975, 317 pages, softcover.
An excellent book of warm-ups, acting awareness games, and activities which can be used with all ages.

King, Nancy, *A Movement Approach to Acting,* Englewood Cliffs, NJ: Prentice-Hall, 1981, 240 pages, hardcover.
Acting approach which emphasizes the development of balance, body control, and relaxation.

Lessac, Arthur, *The Use and Training of the Human Voice: A Practical Approach to Speech and Voice Dynamics,* New York: Drama Book Specialists, 1967, 297 pages, hardcover.
The Lessac System of vocal production is based on perceptual awareness of kinesthetic feedback sensations.

Linklater, Kristin, *Freeing the Natural Voice,* New York: Drama Book Publishers, 1976, 210 pages, softcover.
Voice text which focuses on releasing tensions and other blocks that inhibit free vocal expression.

McCaslin, Nellie, *Creative Drama in the Classroom,* 5th edition, New York: Longman, 1990, 448 pages, hardcover.

Excellent creative drama text which includes a chapter on working with children who have special needs.

Spolin, Viola, *Improvisation for the Theatre: A Handbook of Teaching and Directing Techniques,* Evanston: Northwestern University Press, 1963, 395 pages, hardcover.

Classic improvisational game book. The exercises were developed by Spolin, while working with immigrants at Hull House in Chicago. A number of the exercises are too abstract for students who have cognitive disabilities and must be adapted.

Ward, Winifred, *Stories to Dramatize,* Anchorage, KY: The Children's Theatre Press, 1952, 389 pages, hardcover.

A collection of stories and poems which are easy to dramatize. A creative drama classic.

Warren, Bernie, ed., *A Theatre in Your Classroom,* Ontario, Canada: Captus Press, 1990, 252 pages, softcover.

Collection of articles on ways to use drama in the special education and regular classroom.

STORYTELLING, GUIDED IMAGERY, AND GAME RESOURCES

Aycox, Frank, *Games We Should Play in School: A Revealing Analysis of the Social Forces in the Classroom and a Practical Approach to Understanding and Shaping Them, Including over 55 Dynamic and Fun Social Games,* Byron, CA: Front Row, 1985, 103 pages, softcover.

The title tells it all. An excellent resource book.

Barton, Bob, *Tell Me Another,* Markham, Ontario, Canada: Peinbrooke Publishers, 1986, 158 pages, softcover.

How to choose and tell a story. There is a chapter on storytelling in the classroom.

Barton, Bob and Booth, David, *Stories in the Classroom: Storytelling, Reading Aloud and Roleplaying with Children,* Portsmouth, NH: Heinemann, 1990, 194 pages, softcover.

An approach developed by teachers for teachers to integrate storytelling and storymaking by teachers and students into the academic classroom.

Boyd, Neva L., *Handbook of Recreational Games: How to Play More Than 300 Children's Games,* New York: Dover Publications, 1975, 128 pages, softcover.
Collection of social games. Neva Boyd worked at Hull House in Chicago with Viola Spolin.

Danby, Mark and Kemp, David, *Drama through Storytelling: A Practical Approach for the Teacher of Elementary Grades,* Toronto: Simon & Pierre, 1989, 143 pages, softcover.
The authors compare theories of play and drama and explore the connection between storytelling and improvisation. They provide three stories and follow-up activities to model an approach to dramatizing a story in the classroom.

De Mille, Richard, *Put Your Mother on the Ceiling: Children's Imagination Games,* New York: Viking Penguin, 1976, 175 pages, softcover.
Opening up children's creativity through imagination games.

Edwards, Betty, *Drawing On the Right Side of the Brain: A Course in Enhancing Creativity and Artistic Confidence,* rev. ed., Los Angeles: Jeremy P. Tarcher,Inc., 1989, 254 pages, softcover.
An excellent look at how the right brain works with exercises to enhance the visual and kinesthetic thinking skills used in creating art and seeing the world in an open, creative way.

Gawain, Shakti, *Creative Visualization,* New York: Bantam Books, 1985, 127 pages, softcover.
How to use guided imagery and imaginary visualization.

Gersie, Alida and King, Nancy, *Storymaking in Education and Therapy,* London: Jessica Kingsley Publishers, 1990, 407 pages, softcover.
Suggestions for ways teachers and therapists can use myths and fairy tales in education and therapy.

Hendricks, Gay and Wills, Russel, *The Centering Book: Awareness Activities for Children and Adults to Relax the Body and Mind,* Englewood Cliffs, NJ: Prentice Hall Press, 1975, 178 pages, softcover.
Exercises in relaxation, guided imagery, and awareness which can be used in drama classes or as motivational activities for the academic classroom.

Hendricks, Gay and Roberts, Thomas B., *The Second Centering Book: More Awareness Activities for Children, Parents, and Teachers,* Englewood Cliffs, NJ: Prentice Hall Press, 1977, 322 pages, softcover.
More exercises like the ones found in the first book.

Koch, Kenneth, *Wishes, Lies, and Dreams: Teaching Children to Write Poetry,* New York: HarperCollins, 1980, 309 pages, softcover.
Koch's method of teaching children to write poetry and examples of poems written by students at P.S. 61 in New York City. His method can be used to generate material for original scenes and plays.

Murdock, Maureen, *Spinning Inward: Using Guided Imagery with Children for Learning, Creativity, & Relaxation,* Boston: Shambhala, 1987, 158 pages, softcover.
How to use guided imagery techniques to enhance students' emotional growth and academic performance in the classroom. Includes many guided imagery scripts.

Maguire, Jack, *Creative Storytelling: Choosing, Inventing, and Sharing Tales for Children,* New York: McGraw-Hill Book Company, 1985, 189 pages, softcover.
Excellent guide on how to become a good storyteller.

Orlick, Terry, *The Cooperative Sports and Games Book: Challenge without Competition,* New York: Pantheon Books, 1978, 129 pages, softcover.
Good resource on why cooperation is better for developing social skills than competition. Many of the games, however, need more structure if used with children who have cognitive or emotional disabilities.

BOOKS AND PLAYS ON DISABILITY

Armstrong, Thomas, Ph.D., *In Their Own Way: Discovering and Encouraging Your Child's Personal Learning Style,* Los Angeles: Jeremy P. Tarcher, Inc., 1987, 211 pages, hardcover.
How to identify and teach to a child's learning style using Gardner's Theory of Multiple Intelligence.

Barkley, Russell A., *Hyperactive Children: A Handbook for Diagnosis and Treatment,* New York: The Guilford Press, 1981, 458 pages, hardcover.
Very thorough book on Attention Deficit Hyperactivity Disorder which stresses the use of behavior therapy at home and in the classroom.

Batshaw, Mark L. and Perret, Yvonne, *Children with Disabilities: A Medical Primer,* Baltimore: Paul H. Brookes, 1992, 664 pages, softcover.
Provides readable overviews of characteristics of the most common mental and physical disabilities, including mental retardation, vision and hearing impairments, LDs, cerebral palsy, spina bifida, and communication disorders.

Duncan, John; Gish, Calasha; Mulholland, Mary Ellen; and Townsend, Alex, "Environmental Modifications for the Visually Impaired: A Handbook," New York: American Foundation for the Blind, 1977, 14 pages, softcover.
Handbook of standards and suggestions for making facilities barrier-free for the visually impaired.

Gibson, William, *The Miracle Worker,* New York: Samuel French, 1960, 95 pages, softcover.
Three-act play about seven-year-old Helen Keller, who was deaf-blind, and her teacher Annie Sullivan.

Grandin, Temple and Scariano, Margaret M., *Emergence: Labeled Autistic,* Novato, CA: Arena Press, 1986, 184 pages, softcover.
Temple Grandin, a "recovered autistic" adult, tells what it was like to grow up with autism.

Haerle, Tracy, ed., *Children with Tourette Syndrome: A Parents' Guide,* Rockville, MD: Woodbine House, 1992, 340 pages, softcover.
Written by a team of professionals and parents, this book offers up-to-date, concrete information and advice for dealing with Tourette syndrome and related conditions.

Jones, Reginald L., ed., *Reflections On Growing Up Disabled,* Reston, VA: ERIC, Council for Exceptional Children, 1983, 103 pages, softcover.
Excellent collection of articles written by people who have a variety of different disabilities (including deafness, blindness, LD, and orthopedic disabilities) about their experiences dealing with barriers and prejudices in our society.

Jacobs, Leo M., *A Deaf Adult Speaks Out,* 3rd rev. ed., Washington, DC: Gallaudet University Press, 1989, 169 pages, softcover.
Deaf educator Leo Jacobs writes about his experiences growing up in the deaf community.

Keller, Helen Adams, *The Story of My Life,* New York: Bantam Books, 1990, 225 pages, softcover.

Helen Keller's autobiography of growing up deaf and blind and her struggles to learn language and speech.

Kisor, Henry, *What's That Pig Outdoors? A Memoir of Deafness,* New York: Penguin, 1990, 269 pages, softcover.

Deaf journalist Henry Kisor tells what his life has been like growing up in a hearing world.

Lane, Harlan, *The Mask of Benevolence: Disabling the Deaf Community,* New York: Knopf, 1992, 310 pages, hardcover.

A book about current controversies in deaf education and deaf culture.

Medoff, Mark, *Children of a Lesser God,* Clifton, NJ: James T. White & Company, 1980, 91 pages, hardcover.

Tony Award winning play about the clash of cultures in the relationship between a deaf woman and a hearing man.

Moore, Cory, *A Reader's Guide for Parents of Children with Mental, Physical, or Emotional Disabilities,* Rockville, MD: Woodbine House, 1990, 248 pages, softcover.

Annotated descriptions of hundreds of reader-friendly books about specific disabilities and disabilities in general.

Murphy, Robert F., *The Body Silent,* New York: Henry Holt and Company, 1987, 242 pages, hardcover.

This account of the author's struggle with paralysis caused by a tumor of the spinal cord is written from a personal and anthropological perspective, exploring public fears, myths, and misunderstandings of physical disabilities and the barriers individuals who have them face in our society.

Quinn, Patricia O., M.D. and Stern, Judith M., *Putting On the Brakes: A Young People's Guide to Understanding Attention Deficit Hyperactivity Disorder,* New York: Magination Press, 1991, 64 pages, softcover.

Easy-to-read manual for students describing the symptoms and causes of ADHD and offering methods of developing self control, good study habits, and better interpersonal skills.

Sacks, Oliver, *The Man Who Mistook His Wife for a Hat and Other Clinical Tales,* New York: Summit Books, 1985, 233 pages, softcover. Collection of articles on a number of neurological disorders, including Tourette syndrome, mental retardation, and loss of proprioception, and how individuals have coped with them.

Sacks, Oliver, *Seeing Voices: A Journey Into the World of the Deaf,* Berkeley: University of California Press, 1989, 180 pages, hardcover. Three extended essays which explore the history of the deaf and the nature of sign language. Provides a number of suggestions for further reading about the deaf and deaf culture.

Smith, Romayne, ed., *Children with Mental Retardation: A Parents' Guide,* Rockville, MD: Woodbine House, 1993, 450 pages, softcover. Although primarily a parents' guide, useful sections for drama teachers and special educators cover how and why children with mental retardation learn differently than others, as well as teaching and behavior management strategies.

Smith, Sally, L., *No Easy Answers: Teaching the Learning Disabled Child,* Cambridge, MA: Winthrop Publishers, 1979, 250 pages, hardcover. Dr. Smith shares her philosophy of teaching learning disabled students through the arts and describes the program which implements her theories at the Lab School of Washington.

Taylor, John F., *Helping Your Hyperactive Child,* Rocklin, CA: Prima Publishing & Communications, 1990, 483 pages, hardcover. A thorough book written to help parents understand ADHD, its causes and how it effects the entire family. It details a variety of treatment methods, from prescription stimulants to behavior therapy to the Feingold Diet.

Vitale, Barbara M. *Unicorns Are Real: A Right Brained Approach to Learning,* New York: Warner Books, 1986, 176 pages, softcover. Barbara Vitale believes students with learning disabilities are right-brained learners in a left-brained educational system. In this book she presents 65 exercises and lesson plans which help students succeed at learning.

Williams, Linda Verlee, *Teaching for the Two-Sided Mind: A Guide to Right Brain/Left Brain Education,* New York: Simon & Schuster, 1986, 213 pages, softcover.

Specific classroom activities which develop right brain thinking skills (i.e., visual thinking, fantasy, metaphor, and multisensory learning) are presented for the classroom teacher to activate a full range of cognitive and creative activities in students.

BOOKS ON DRAMA THERAPY

Anderson, Walt, ed., *Therapy and the Arts: Tools of Consciousness,* New York: Harper and Row, 1977, 203 pages, softcover.

Collection of articles by artists and therapists making the connections between the arts and therapy and making a case for the arts as an effective therapeutic tool.

Grainger, Roger, *Drama and Healing: The Roots of Drama Therapy,* London: Jessica Kingsley Publishers, 1990, 156 pages, hard cover.

How drama therapy draws on its roots in drama and ritual. Focused on uses with depression, thought disorder, and schizophrenia.

Jennings, Sue, *Dramatherapy: Theory and Practice for Teachers and Clinicians,* Cambridge, MA: Brookline Books, 1987, 279 pages, softcover.

Ideas for professionals using drama with children and adults who have disabilities.

Jennings, Sue, *Dramatherapy with Families, Groups, and Individuals,* London: Jessica Kingsley Publishers, 1990, 155 pages, hardcover.

Presents a working framework for dramatherapists, social workers, family and marital therapists, and others conducting groups using dramatherapy in a non-clinical setting such as family centers, residential children's homes, etc.

Jennings, Sue and Minde, Ase, *Art Therapy and Dramatherapy: Their Relation and Practice,* London: Jessica Kingsley Publishers, 1991, 176 pages, hardcover.

Explores the relationship and differences between art and drama therapy: theories, processes, and practice.

Landy, Robert J., *Drama Therapy: Concepts and Practices,* Springfield, IL: Charles C. Thomas, Publisher, 1987, 248 pages, hardcover.
Drama therapy text which traces the origins, theory, concepts, and practices of drama therapy.

Schattner, Gertrude and Courtney, Richard, ed., *Drama in Therapy, Volume One: Children,* New York: Drama Book Specialists, 1981, hardcover.
Collection of articles about drama used as a therapeutic tool with a variety of child populations.

Schattner, Gertrude and Courtney, Richard, ed., *Drama in Therapy, Volume Two: Adults,* New York: Drama Book Specialists, 1981, 337 pages, hardcover.
Collection of articles about drama used as a therapeutic tool with different adult populations.

Sternberg, Patricia and Garcia, Antonina, *Sociodrama: Who's in Your Shoes?* New York: Praeger, 1989, 201 pages, hardcover.
Guide to the therapeutic and educational uses of role playing and sociodrama. Eminently practical, clearly written description of techniques.

Warren, Bernie, ed., *Using the Creative Arts in Therapy,* Cambridge, MA: Brookline Books, 1984, 169 pages, softcover.
Collection of articles on the therapeutic uses of visual art, music, movement, dance, storytelling, and drama.

OTHER RESOURCES OF INTEREST

Ackerman, Diane, *A Natural History of the Senses,* New York: Random House, 1990, 331 pages, hardcover.
Become more aware of the senses and how they affect our lives.

Bettelheim, Bruno, *The Uses of Enchantment: The Meaning and Importance of Fairy Tales,* New York: Random House, 1977, 328 pages, softcover.
Written from a Freudian perspective, this book provides psychological insight into children's literature.

Csikszentmihalyi, Mihaly, *Flow: The Psychology of Optimal Experience,* New York: Harper & Row, 1990, 303 pages, softcover.
When "Magic" happens in a classroom, you have created a situation of "Flow."

Dewey, John, *Art As Experience,* New York: Putnam Publishing Group, 1959, softcover.
Based on Dewey's Harvard lectures on how life and art interact and inform each other.

Gardner, Howard, *Frames of Mind: The Theory of Multiple Intelligence,* New York: Basic Books, 1985, 464 pages, softcover.
Presents Gardner's theory that we each possess seven different kinds of intelligence.

Hall, Edward T., *Beyond Culture,* Garden City, NY: Anchor Press, 1976, 256 pages, hardcover.
Thought-provoking look at the nonverbal aspects of culture.

Hunt, Morton, *The Universe Within: A New Science Explores the Human Mind,* New York: Simon and Schuster, 1982, 415 pages, hardcover.
Very clearly written book about the brain: how cognition works, how language and thinking skills develop.

Markova, Dawna, Ph.D., *The Art of the Possible: A Compassionate Approach to Understanding the Way People Think, Learn & Communicate,* Emeryville, CA: Conari Press, 1991, 237 pages, softcover.
A method of looking at learning styles and perceptual pathways into the brain. Focused mainly on interpersonal communication styles and learning to recognize and understand your perceptual orientation.

Nachmanovitch, Stephen, *Free Play: Improvisation in Life and Art,* Los Angeles: Jeremy P. Tarcher, Inc., 1990, 208 pages, softcover.
A book on observations of the creative process and the need for playfulness, spontaneity, and flexibility in life.

National Endowment for the Arts, "Toward Civilization: Overview from a Report on Arts Education," Washington, DC: NEA, May 1988, 54 pages, softcover.
A report which identifies that the arts should be taught in school, presents the reasons for studying them, and suggests avenues for improving the currently unsatisfactory state of arts education.

National Endowment for the Arts, "Understanding How the Arts Contribute to Excellent Education," Washington, DC: NEA, Fall 1991, 51 pages, softcover.

Report on a number of schools across the country which have integrated the arts into their curriculums, how it has changed the way their students learn and why.

Ott, John Nash, *Health and Light: The Effects of Natural and Artificial Light on Man and Other Living Things,* Greenwich, CT: Devin-Adair, 1973, 208 pages, softcover.
Ott's studies of the effects of different kinds of light on people and plants.

Ott, John Nash, *Light, Radiation, and You: How to Stay Healthy,* Greenwich, CT: Devin-Adair, 1990, 199 pages, softcover.
Further developments from Ott's studies of lighting and other electronic sources in our technological world.

Pfeiffer, John E., *The Creative Explosion: An Inquiry into the Origins of Art and Religion,* New York: Harper & Row, 1982, 270 pages, hardcover.
Fascinating account of the origins of art based on archaeological evidence.

Restak, Richard M., M.D., *The Brain: The Last Frontier,* New York: Warner Books, 1979, 461 pages, softcover.
Very readable book about the brain and cognition written by a practicing neurologist.

Sarason, Seymour B., *The Challenge of Art to Psychology,* New York: Yale University Press, 1990, 188 pages, hardcover.
Sarason believes all human beings are born creative and that this ability is extinguished through our cultural values and educational system. In one chapter, he describes how Henry Schaefer-Simmern taught visual art to institutionalized mentally retarded adults, unlocking their long-hidden creativity.

Steinem, Gloria, *Revolution from Within: A Book of Self-Esteem,* Boston: Little, Brown, and Company, 1992, 376 pages, hardcover.
An excellent book on the topic of self-esteem.

U.S. Department of Labor, The Secretary's Commission on Achieving Necessary Skills, "What Work Requires of Schools: A SCANS Report for America 2000," Washington, DC: USGPO, June 1991, 31 pages, softcover.

Report concerning the skills which students need to learn in school to be prepared for jobs in the 21st century.

U.S. Department of Labor, SCANS, "Learning a Living: A Blueprint for High Performance: A SCANS Report for America 2000," Washington, DC: USGPO, April 1992, 86 pages, softcover.
A follow-up report detailing the changes which need to be made in schools in order to teach requisite work skills for the 21st century.

Winn, Marie, *The Plug-In Drug: Television, Children, and the Family,* rev. ed., New York: Viking Penguin, 1985, 283 pages, hardcover.
How television is changing the way children process information.

Winnicott, D.W., *Playing and Reality,* London: Routledge, 1986, 169 pages, softcover.
Collected articles which focus on the need for play and imagination in psychoanalysis, emotional healing, and life. He talks about the difference between internal and external reality and how "Magic" happens in the transitional space.

Zigler, Edward F. and Finn-Stevenson, Matia, *Children: Development and Social Issues,* Lexington, MA: D.C. Heath and Company, 1986, 799 pages, hardcover.
Child development textbook which includes information on disabilities and atypical development throughout the childhood and adolescent years.

■ appendix ii

National Organizations with Information on Disability Access

Architectural and Transportation Barriers Compliance Board
1331 F Street, NW, Suite 1000
Washington, DC 20004-1111
Voice: (202) 272-5434
(800) USA-ABLE
TDD: (202) 272-5449
FAX: (202) 272-5447

The Access Board provides technical assistance, and informational and technical manuals regarding architectural and transportation access.

Barrier-Free Environments, Inc.
P.O. Box 30634
Raleigh, NC 27622
Voice/TDD: (919) 782-7823
FAX: (919) 787-1984

A for-profit company which provides design and consultation services to individuals, families, corporations, and institutions on barrier-free architecture and product design.

Disability and Business Technical Assistance Centers
Voice: (800) 949-4232

Answers questions and provides referrals regarding access issues and the requirements of the Americans with Disabilities Act. Your call will be automatically routed to a center located in your region of the U.S.

National Council on Independent Living
2111 Wilson Blvd., Suite 405
Arlington, VA 22201
Voice: (703) 525-3406

Can provide information on affiliated and non-affiliated centers for independent living across the country.

FULL SPECTRUM LIGHTING

Environmental Lighting Concepts, Inc.
3923 Coconut Palm Drive, Suite 101
Tampa, FL 33619
Voice: (800) 842-8848

Pure Health Concepts, Inc.
2430 Herodian Way, Suite 280
Smyrna, GA 30080
Voice: (404) 859-9040
Voice Mail: (404) 264-6179

ADAPTIVE SPORTS, GAMES, AND DANCE

American Dance Therapy Association
2000 Century Plaza, Suite 108
Columbia, MD 21044
Voice: (410) 997-4040
FAX: (410) 997-4048

Non-profit professional association for dance and movement therapists.

National Handicapped Sports
451 Hungerford Drive, Suite 100
Rockville, MD 20850
Voice: (301) 217-0960
TDD: (301) 217-0963
FAX: (301) 217-0968

NHS, which has a network of local chapters across the country, sponsors a variety of sports, recreation, and fitness programs for people with disabilities. They have adaptive aerobic videos for sale.

National Therapeutic Recreation Society
National Recreation and Park Association
2775 South Quincy Street, Suite 300
Arlington, VA 22206-2204

Voice: (703) 578-5548
FAX: (703) 671-6772

NTRS supports and represents therapeutic recreational professionals who work in both clinical and community settings. Therapeutic recreation provides services in three areas: therapy, leisure education, and recreation participation for individuals with disabilities or limiting conditions.

THE ARTS AND DISABILITY

Association for Theatre and Disability
c/o Access Theatre
527 Garden Street
Santa Barbara, CA 93101
Voice/TDD: (805) 564-2063
FAX: (805) 564-0051

Networking organization for educators, professionals, and organizations doing theatre with and by individuals who have disabilities. Annually holds a joint conference in August with The American Alliance for Theatre and Education. Publishes *Resources in Theatre & Disability*.

Deaf Artists of America, Inc.
87 North Clinton Avenue, Suite 408
Rochester, NY 14604
Voice: (716) 325-2403
TDD: (716) 325-2400
FAX: (716) 325-2413

Organization to support and promote deaf and hard of hearing artists.

Disabled Artists' Network
P.O. Box 20781
New York, NY 10025

An information exchange for disabled artists in the visual and sculptural arts. Send a self-addressed, stamped envelope or a cassette when requesting information.

Enabled Artists Unlimited
P.O. Box 178
Dobbins, CA 95935-0178

Voice: (916) 692-1581

Non-profit organization for advocacy and networking assisting the transition of disabled artists into mainstream and public life.

Kids On The Block
9385C Gerwig Lane
Columbia, MD 21046
Voice: (301) 290-9095
(800) 368-KIDS

A touring puppet company which uses puppets with a variety of disabilities to provide disability awareness education for school-aged children. Shows are available in 49 states.

National Association for Drama Therapy
2022 Cutter Drive
League City, TX 77573-6916
Voice: (713) 334-4421

Non-profit professional association for drama therapists.

National Endowment for the Arts
Office for Special Constituencies
1100 Pennsylvania Avenue, NW, Room 605
Washington, DC 20506
Voice: (202) 682-5532
TDD: (202) 682-5496
FAX: (202) 682-5613

Office of the NEA that assists its grantees in making the arts available to older adults, individuals with disabilities, and people in institutions. The office produces a wide variety of technical assistance materials, including "The Arts and 504 Handbook," a handbook for making arts organizations' facilities and programs accessible and barrier-free, and "Profiles in the Arts." These publications are marketed by the Government Printing Office.

Nontraditional Casting Project
Box 4480 Grand Central Station
New York, NY 10163
Voice/TDD: (212) 682-5790

FAX: (212) 922-0553

A not-for-profit organization devoted to increasing the participation of ethnic, female, and disabled artists in theatre, television, and film through advocacy, networking, artist files, seminars, and workshops.

Very Special Arts
John F. Kennedy Center for the Performing Arts
Washington, DC 20566
Voice: (202) 662-8898
TDD: (202) 622-8899

Very Special Arts spearheads VSA Festivals, conferences, and programs. Each state has an office and many localities also have offices.

ATTENTION DEFICIT DISORDERS

C.H.A.D.D. (Children with Attention Deficit Disorder)
499 Northwest 70th Avenue, Suite 308
Plantation, FL 33317
Voice: (305) 587-3700
FAX: (305) 587-4599

C.H.A.D.D. is a non-profit organization that provides information and support to parents who have children with attention deficit disorder. There are many local C.H.A.D.D. support groups.

Feingold Association of the United States
P.O. Box 6550
Alexandria, VA 22306
Voice: (703) 768-FAUS

FAUS is a non-profit association which disseminates information about the Feingold Diet which is used as a treatment for ADD/ADHD.

AUTISM

Autism Society of America
8601 Georgia Avenue, Suite 503
Silver Spring, MD 20901
Voice: (301) 565-0433
FAX: (301) 565-0834

Formerly NSAC, the Autism Society is a national membership organization which serves as an advocate for individuals who have autism. Over 200 local chapters across the country. Conducts an annual conference for parents and professionals as well as regional conferences throughout the year.

BLIND and VISUALLY IMPAIRED

American Council of the Blind
1155 15th Street, NW, Suite 720
Washington, DC 20005
Voice: (202) 467-5081
(800) 424-8666
FAX: (202) 467-5085

ACB is a membership organization with state and local affiliates which provides support services and information about vision impairments.

American Foundation for the Blind
15 West 16th Street
New York, NY 10011
Voice: (212) 620-2000
(800) 232-5463
TDD: (212) 620-2158

AFB is a private, non-profit agency which collects and disseminates information on blindness.

National Federation of the Blind
National Center for the Blind
1800 Johnson Street
Baltimore, MD 21230
Voice: (410) 659-9314
TDD: (410) 625-1287 (answering machine only)
FAX: (410) 685-5653

NFB works for the integration of blind people into society as equal members through advocacy and education.

The Metropolitan Washington Ear, Inc.
35 University Blvd, East
Silver Spring, MD 20901

Voice: (301) 681-6636

The Metropolitan Washington Ear pioneered audio description for the blind and can provide training and information in audio description for theatres, television, film, museums, and exhibits.

CEREBRAL PALSY

United Cerebral Palsy Association
1522 K Street, NW, Suite 1112
Washington, DC 20036
Voice: (202) 842-1266
(800) 872-5UCP
FAX: (202) 842-3519

UCP is a non-profit organization which offers networking and support for individuals who have cerebral palsy and their families.

CYSTIC FIBROSIS

Cystic Fibrosis Foundation
6931 Arlington Road
Bethesda, MD 20814
Voice: (301) 951-6378
(800) 344-4823
FAX: (301) 951-6378

CFF supports basic and clinical research projects and research centers finding a cure for Cystic Fibrosis.

DEAF and HARD OF HEARING

Alexander Graham Bell Association for the Deaf, Inc.
3417 Volta Place, NW
Washington, DC 20007
Voice/TDD: (202) 337-5220
FAX: (202) 337-8317

Collects and shares information on hearing loss.

Deafpride, Inc.
1350 Potomac Avenue, SE
Washington, DC 20003

Voice/TDD: (202) 675-6700
FAX: (202) 547-0547

Advocacy organization for human and civil rights of deaf persons and their families.

National Association of the Deaf

814 Thayer Avenue
Silver Spring, MD 20910
Voice: (301) 587-1788
TDD: (301) 587-1789
FAX: (301) 587-1791

Membership organization for the deaf and hard of hearing. Have a bookstore, deaf awareness programs, public information center, employment programs, publishing, professional leadership, and Sign Instructors Guidance Network.

National Cued Speech Association

P.O. Box 31345
Raleigh, NC 27622
Voice/TDD: (919) 828-1218
FAX: (919) 828-1862

Membership organization that provides advocacy and support for cued speech.

National Information Center on Deafness

800 Florida Avenue, NE
Washington, DC 20002-3695
Voice: (202) 651-5051
TDD: (202) 651-5052
FAX: (202) 651-5054

NICD is a centralized source of information about hearing loss and deafness. NICD collects, develops, and disseminates up-to-date information on deafness, hearing loss, and organizations and services for deaf and hard of hearing people.

Registry of Interpreters for the Deaf, Inc.

8719 Colesville Road, Suite 310
Silver Spring, MD 20910-3919

Voice/TDD: (301) 608-0050
FAX: (301) 608-0508
RID is a professional organization that certifies interpreters and provides information on interpreting to the general public.

Self-Help for Hard of Hearing People
7800 Wisconsin Avenue
Bethesda, MD 20814
Voice: (301) 657-2248
TDD: (301) 657-2248
FAX: (301) 913-9413
Promotes awareness about hearing loss, communication, assistive devices, and alternative communication skills.

DOWN SYNDROME

National Down Syndrome Congress
1605 Chantilly Road
Atlanta, GA 30324
Voice: (800) 232-NDSC
FAX: (708) 823-9528
NDSC provides information and networking support for individuals who have Down syndrome and their families.

National Down Syndrome Society
666 Broadway
New York, NY 10012
Voice: (212) 460-9330; (800) 221-4602
FAX: (212) 979-2873
NDSS provides information on Down syndrome.

FRAGILE X SYNDROME

National Fragile X Foundation
1441 York Street
Suite 215
Denver, CO 80206

Voice: (303) 333-6155; (800) 688-8765

Offers a newsletter and other information about fragile X syndrome; supports research.

LEARNING DISABILITIES

Learning Disability Association of America
4156 Library Road
Pittsburgh, PA 15234
Voice: (412) 341-1515
(412) 341-8077
FAX: (412) 344-0224

Formerly the Association for Children with Learning Disabilities, LDA is a non-profit networking and information association for individuals with learning disabilities. There are more than 800 local chapters across the country. Write for their bibliography of over 500 publications on learning disabilities.

National Center for Learning Disabilities, Inc.
99 Park Avenue, 6th Floor
New York, NY 10016
Voice: (212) 687-7211
FAX: (212) 697-7350

Formerly the Foundation for Children with Learning Disabilities, NCLD promotes public awareness about learning disabilities, neurological disorders, and deficits which can be a barrier to literacy. Provides resources and referrals on a national level.

Orton Dyslexia Society
8600 LaSalle Road, Suite 382
Baltimore, MD 21204-6020
Voice: (410) 296-0232
(800) 222-3123
FAX: (410) 321-5069

A non-profit organization which focuses research on and public awareness about dyslexia. Publishes books, packets, and reprints pertaining to dyslexia.

MENTAL ILLNESS

National Alliance for the Mentally Ill
2101 Wilson Boulevard, Suite 302
Arlington, VA 22201
Voice: (703) 524-7600
FAX: (703) 524-9094

NAMI is a non-profit, self-help organization composed of families and friends of persons who have mental illness. NAMI and its local chapters advocate, support research and treatment, and disseminate information about mental illness.

MENTAL RETARDATION

The ARC: A National Organization on Mental Retardation
500 East Border Street, Suite 300
Arlington, TX 76010
Voice: (817) 261-6003
TDD: (817) 277-0553
FAX: (817) 277-3491

Formerly the Association for Retarded Citizens, The ARC is a national networking organization offering support to individuals who have mental retardation and their families. Involved in advocacy, training, and education. There are local chapters in every state and most counties in the U.S.

MULTIPLE SCLEROSIS

National Multiple Sclerosis Society
733 Third Avenue, 6th Floor
New York, NY 10017
Voice: (212) 986-3240
FAX: (212) 986-7981

NMSS is involved in research, patient services, and education concerning MS.

MUSCULAR DYSTROPHY

Muscular Dystrophy Association, Inc.
3300 East Sunrise Drive
Tuscon, AZ 85718

Voice: (602) 529-2000

FAX: (602) 529-5300

MDA supports research into MD and offers professional and public education programs. There are 170 local chapters.

SPEECH AND LANGUAGE DISORDERS

American Speech-Language-Hearing Association

10801 Rockville Pike

Rockville, MD 20852

Voice: (301) 897-5700

(800) 638-8255

FAX: (301) 571-0457

ASLHA is a non-profit professional association for speech and language pathologists and audiologists. It supports research, provides referrals for professionals, and provides information on communication disorders.

SPINA BIFIDA

Spina Bifida Association of America

4590 MacArthur Blvd., NW, Suite 250

Washington, DC 20007-4226

Voice: (202) 944-3285

(800) 621-3141

FAX: (202) 944-3295

TOURETTE SYNDROME

Tourette Syndrome Association

42-40 Bell Blvd.

Bayside, NY 11361

Voice: (718) 224-2999

(800) 237-0717

A networking, support, and information resource on Tourette syndrome. Assists with local support groups across the country.

GENERAL INFORMATION ON DISABILITY

Beach Center on Families and Disability

c/o Institute for Life Span Studies

3111 Haworth Hall
The University of Kansas
Lawrence, KS 66045
Voice: (913) 864-7600
FAX: (913) 864-5323

The Beach Center is a networking, advocacy, research, and training center for persons with disabilities and their families. The Center stresses the necessity of full citizenship, choices, and integration of persons with disabilities into all aspects of community life. Write for a publication list.

Council for Exceptional Children
1920 Association Drive
Reston, VA 22091-1589
Voice: (703) 620-3660
FAX: (703) 264-9494

CEC is a professional organization dedicated to improving the quality of education for all exceptional children: disabled and gifted alike. They are host organization for several projects, including the ERIC Clearinghouse on Handicapped and Gifted Children, National Clearinghouse for Professions in Special Education, and the Center for Special Education Technology. Write for a catalog of products and services.

National Easter Seal Society
70 East Lake Street
Chicago, IL 60601
Voice: (312) 726-6200
 (800) 211-6827
TDD: (312) 726-4258
FAX: (312) 726-1494

Easter Seals provides treatment and equipment for disabled children and adults, sponsors research into many types of physical and associated disabilities. They distribute literature and sponsor educational programs as well. There are state and local chapters in all 50 states, Puerto Rico, and the District of Columbia.

National Information Center for Children and Youth with Disabilities (NICHCY)
P.O. Box 1492
Washington, DC 20013
Voice: (703) 893-6061
Voice/TDD: (800) 999-5599
TDD: (703) 893-8614
FAX: (703) 893-1741

NICHCY provides free information on specific disabilities, resources, and general disability issues to parents, educators, and others working with children and youth with disabilities.

National Organization for Rare Disorders
P.O. Box 8923
New Fairfield, CT 06812
Voice: (203) 746-6518
(800) 999-6673
FAX: (203) 746-6481

NORD has a networking program and information on over 900 rare disorders.

National Organization on Disability
910 16th Street, NW, Suite 600
Washington, DC 20006
Voice: (202) 293-5960
(800) 248-ABLE
TDD: (202) 293-5968
FAX: (202) 293-7999

NOD is a private, non-profit organization concerned with increasing the acceptance and participation in all aspects of life for all individuals who have disabilities.

Checklist for Building Accessibility

GETTING IN THE FRONT DOOR

1. Outside pathways from parking lot to front door
   - Are they smooth, solid traveling surfaces?
   - Are there any steps or abrupt changes in level (more than one-quarter inch)?
   - Are pathways wide enough for a wheelchair?

2. Handicapped Parking
   - Is the space large enough?
   - Is it close to the accessible entrance?
   - Is it correctly marked?
   - Is the way to the closest accessible entrance marked?

3. Curb-cuts
   - Is there one by the handicapped parking?
   - Are any along the path to the accessible entrance?
   - Is there one at the main accessible entry drop off?

4. Entryway
   - Are there steps?
   - If so, do the steps have handrails?
   - Do you need a ramp or a lift?
   - Is the door wide enough?
   - Is the door revolving?
   - Is the door a double vestibule?
   - If so, does it need to be automated?
   - Is the entry floor slip-resistant? If not, do you need to add mats?

RESTROOMS

1. Doors
   - Are the doors wide enough for a wheelchair?
   - Are the doors too heavy to open easily?
   - Is the door a double vestibule? If so, can the inside door be propped open?

2. Flow of space inside room
- Can wheelchairs manuever around freely?

3. Toilet stalls
- Is the door wide enough for a wheelchair?
- Is the stall wide enough?
- Are there grab bars in the right places?
- Are they hung at the right height?
- Is the toilet paper within reach?
- Is the toilet easily flushable?

4. Sinks
- Is there clearance under the sink for a wheelchair?
- Can the faucets be reached?
- Can the soap dispenser be reached?
- Is it easy to use the faucets and soap dispenser?

5. Other items
- Can the towels be reached?
- Can vending machines be reached?
- Is the mirror low enough?
- Is the floor surface not too slick/not too rough?
- Is there enough lighting?

GETTING AROUND INSIDE THE BUILDING

1. Floor surfaces
- Are they slip-resistant?
- Are they too rough?
- Are they carpeted?
- If so, are the carpet edges tacked down?
- Do you need an alternate surface for wheelchairs to roll on?

2. Stairs vs ramps vs elevators vs lifts
- Are all floors accessible to wheelchair users?
- Which places in the building are not accessible?
- Do all stairs have handrails?
- Do all ramps with more than a six-foot rise have handrails?
- Are buttons in elevators within reach of someone sitting in a wheelchair?

- Are buttons in elevators clearly marked? Are they in braille or raised numbers for low vision patrons?

3. Doorways
   - Are they wide enough for a wheelchair?
   - Do they have raised door sills which might impede movement?
   - Are doors too heavy to open easily?
   - Do they need to be automated?
   - Are the door handles easy to use?

4. Lighting
   - Is it bright enough?
   - Is it even enough?
   - Is it easy on the eyes?
   - Are light switches within reach and easy to operate?
   - Are important places, potentially hazardous areas, and signs highlighted by lighting?

5. Hallways and aisles
   - Are they wide enough?
   - Are they lit well?
   - Is there a good traffic flow?
   - Are there obstacles protruding from the wall which a patron using a cane might run into?

6. Office equipment
   - Do tables and desks have wheelchair clearance?
   - Is there a good movement flow within offices?
   - Can a wheelchair maneuver around in the space?

7. Communications
   - Do you have a TDD?
   - Can you amplify the sound on at least one phone?
   - Do you have an amplified pay phone?
   - Is the pay phone mounted correctly on the wall?
   - Is the pay phone designed with clearance for a wheelchair?
   - Are the phones easy to dial?

8. Signs
   - Are all rooms and areas clearly marked?

- Are all accessible areas and adaptive devices clearly marked?
- Are signs clearly lit?
- Do you use international pictographs and accessibility symbols?
- Are signs easy to read?
- Clear and large lettering?
- Color contrasted?
- Are there raised lettering, shapes, or braille?
- Are signs at eye level?

9. Water Fountains
- Is at least one accessible to wheelchair users?
- If not, do you have paper cup dispensers by at least one?

10. Emergency Devices
- Do you have flashing fire alarms in addition to sound ones?
- Are all fire exits accessible?
- Are the routes to the fire exits clear and accessible?

ACCESSIBILITY IN YOUR THEATRE SPACE

1. The Stage and Backstage Areas
- Can all actors get onto the stage?
- Can all actors get around backstage and through all backstage passageways?
- Are dressing rooms accessible?
- Can wheelchairs get around inside them?
- Do makeup tables have enough clearance for wheelchairs?
- Are costumes accessible?
- Is there a comfortable bench for actors who can't stand on their own to use to change on?
- Is the lighting/sound/stage management booth accessible?

2. The Auditorium
   Aisles
- Are the aisles wide enough for a wheelchair?
- Are the aisle surfaces smooth and without obstacles?
- Are the aisles clearly lighted?
- Are there strips of glowtape on steps and potential hazards for patrons moving around in the dark?

Seating
- Are spaces left for wheelchairs?
- Do they have clear sightlines of the stage?
- Are seats reserved for deaf patrons in a spot with good sightlines of sign interpreters *and* the stage?
- Are seats reserved for blind and low vision patrons where they can see and hear well?
- Do seats have a space for patrons with seeing eye dogs to lie at their owners' feet during the performance? If not, arrange for an empty seat next to the patron so the dog can lie in front of it.

3. Box Office
- Do staff know how to accommodate the needs of different patrons?
- Is there a TDD so deaf patrons can order tickets?
- Is there a writing surface for patrons in wheelchairs?
- Is there a low window for patrons in wheelchairs?
- If not, staff needs to come out of the office to take care of ticket and information transactions.
- Have you posted notice of all accommodations available to disabled patrons?

4. Programs and Brochures
- Have you used appropriate language and correct terms when referring to disabilities and the individuals who have them?
- Do you publicize all accommodations available to disabled patrons where applicable?
- Do you have large print versions of publications for patrons with low vision?
- Do you have versions available on cassette tape, along with tape recorders, for patrons who can't see or read?
- Do you have versions in braille?
- Do you have volunteers who could read material to patrons who can't see or read?

5. Translation and Amplification Systems for Performances
- Do you have an auxiliary listening system for hard of hearing patrons?

- Do you offer audio description of performances for patrons with low vision?
- Do you offer sign interpreted performances for deaf and hard of hearing patrons?
- Do you caption the dialogue in performances for deaf and hard of hearing patrons?
- Do you use another kind of assistive captioning, interpreting service, or interpretive device?

index

about the author

Sally Dorothy Bailey, R.D.T., is an established playwright, director, and drama therapist with an M.F.A. degree in theatre from Trinity University. She has been the director of the Special Needs Program at the Bethesda Academy of Performing Arts (BAPA) in Bethesda, MD, since 1988 when she established the program. Her work at BAPA includes teaching special needs classes, and directing three barrier-free performing companies for individuals with and without disabilities. A registered drama therapist, who has also trained at the Gestalt Therapy Training Center of Washington, DC, Bailey additionally serves as the drama therapist for Second Genesis, Inc., a long-term residential rehabilitation center for recovering alcoholics and drug addicts. *Wings to Fly* is based upon her eighteen years of experience involving students with special needs in drama.